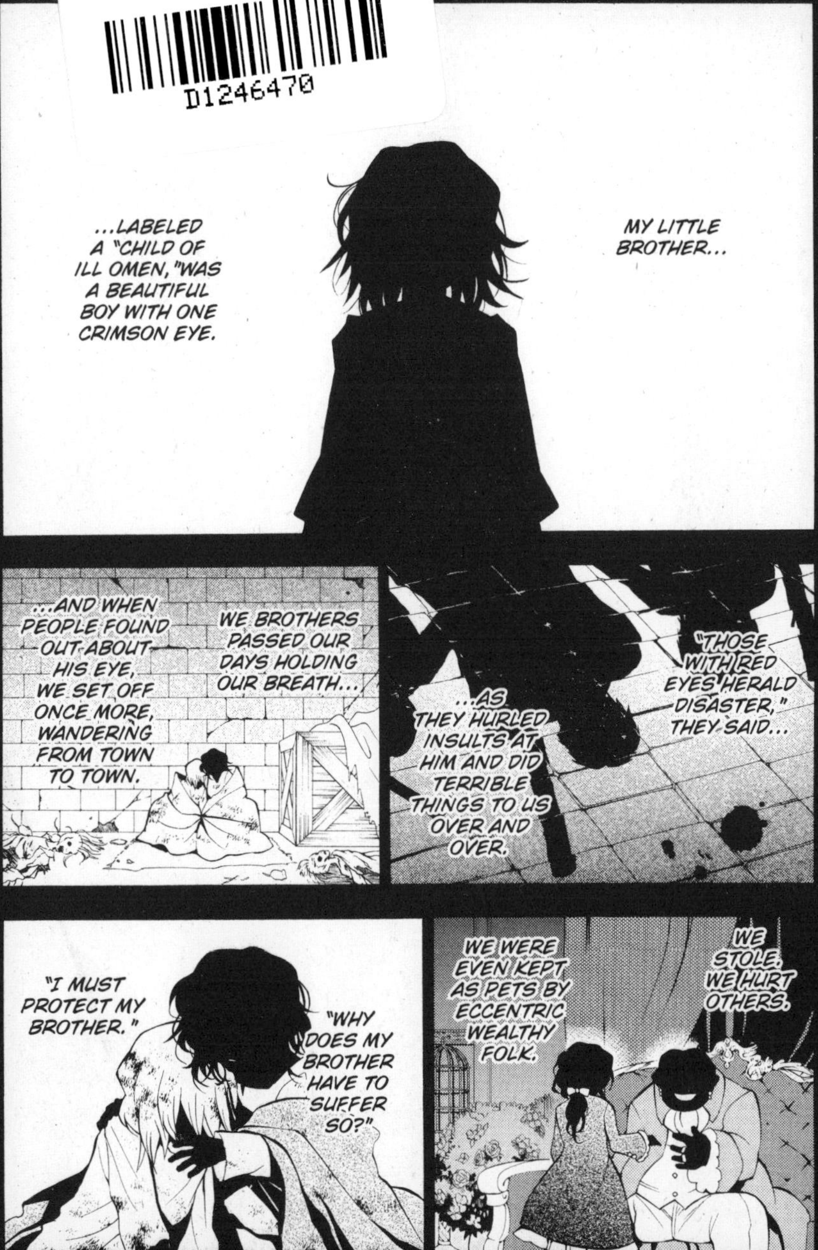
MY LITTLE BROTHER...
...LABELED A "CHILD OF ILL OMEN," WAS A BEAUTIFUL BOY WITH ONE CRIMSON EYE.
"THOSE WITH RED EYES HERALD DISASTER," THEY SAID...
...AS THEY HURLED INSULTS AT HIM AND DID TERRIBLE THINGS TO US OVER AND OVER.
WE BROTHERS PASSED OUR DAYS HOLDING OUR BREATH...
...AND WHEN PEOPLE FOUND OUT ABOUT HIS EYE, WE SET OFF ONCE MORE, WANDERING FROM TOWN TO TOWN.
WE STOLE, WE HURT OTHERS.
WE WERE EVEN KEPT AS PETS BY ECCENTRIC WEALTHY FOLK.
"WHY DOES MY BROTHER HAVE TO SUFFER SO?"
"I MUST PROTECT MY BROTHER."

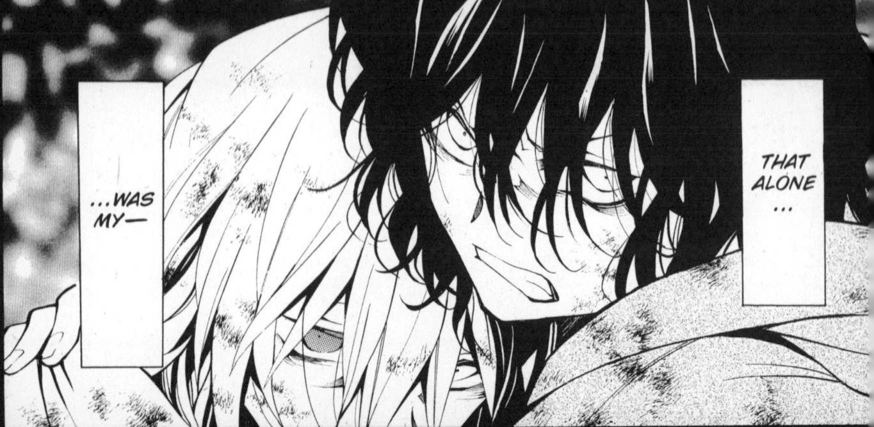
THAT ALONE ...
...WAS MY—

Retrace:XXXVIII Scapegoat

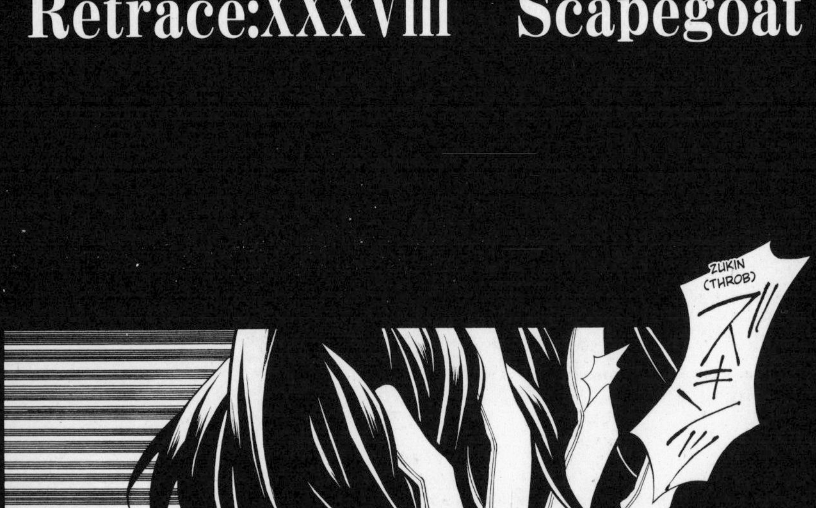
ZUKIN (THROB)

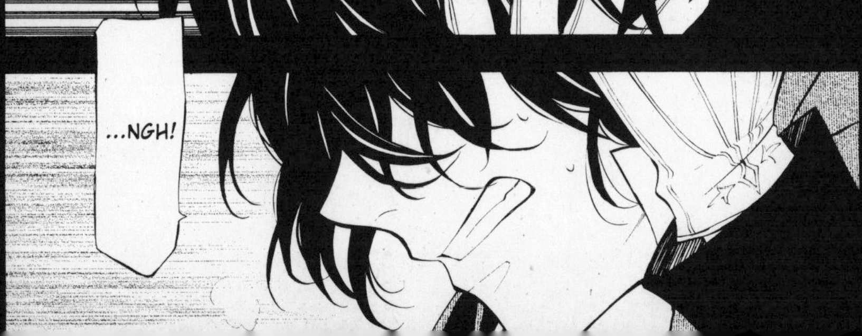
...NGH!

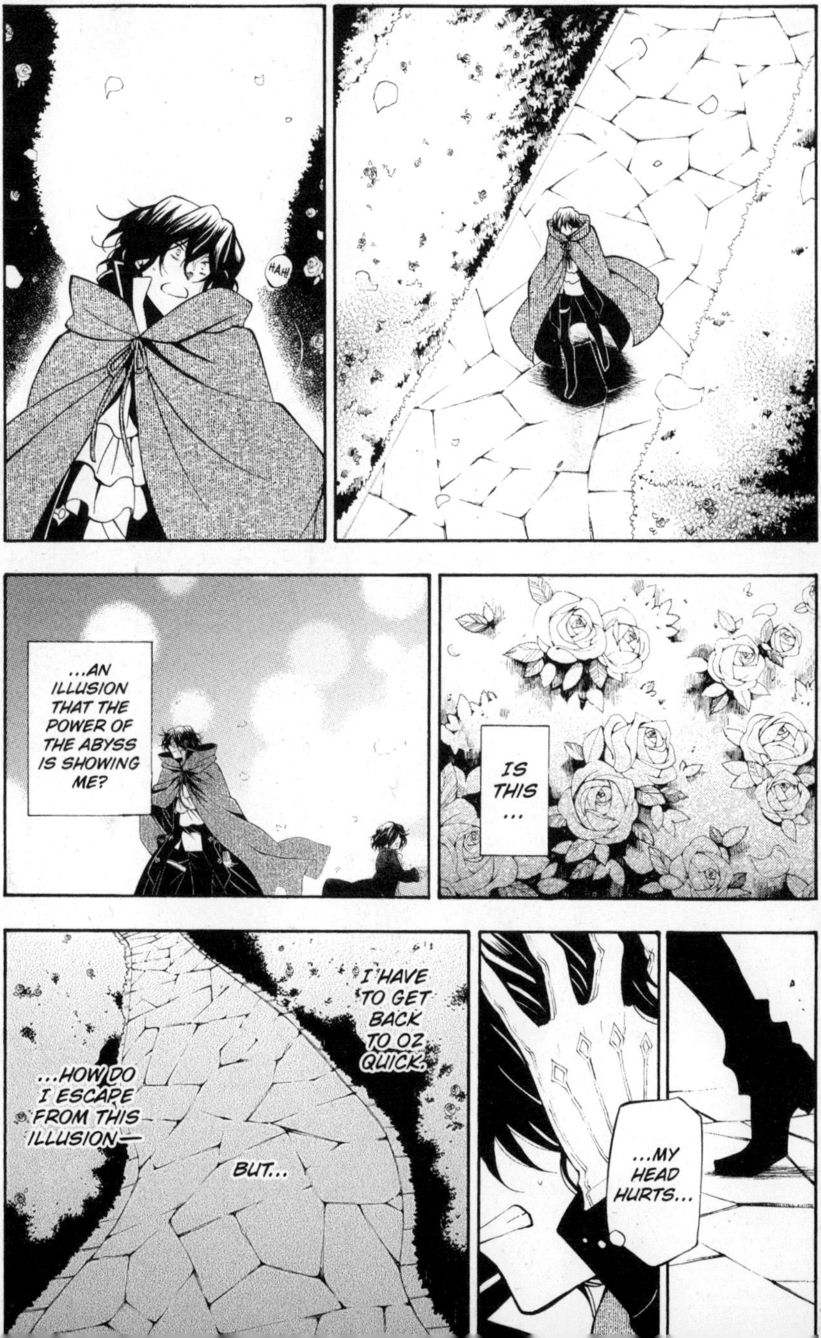
HAH!
IS THIS ...
...AN ILLUSION THAT THE POWER OF THE ABYSS IS SHOWING ME?
...MY HEAD HURTS...
I HAVE TO GET BACK TO OZ QUICK.
...HOW DO I ESCAPE FROM THIS ILLUSION—
BUT...

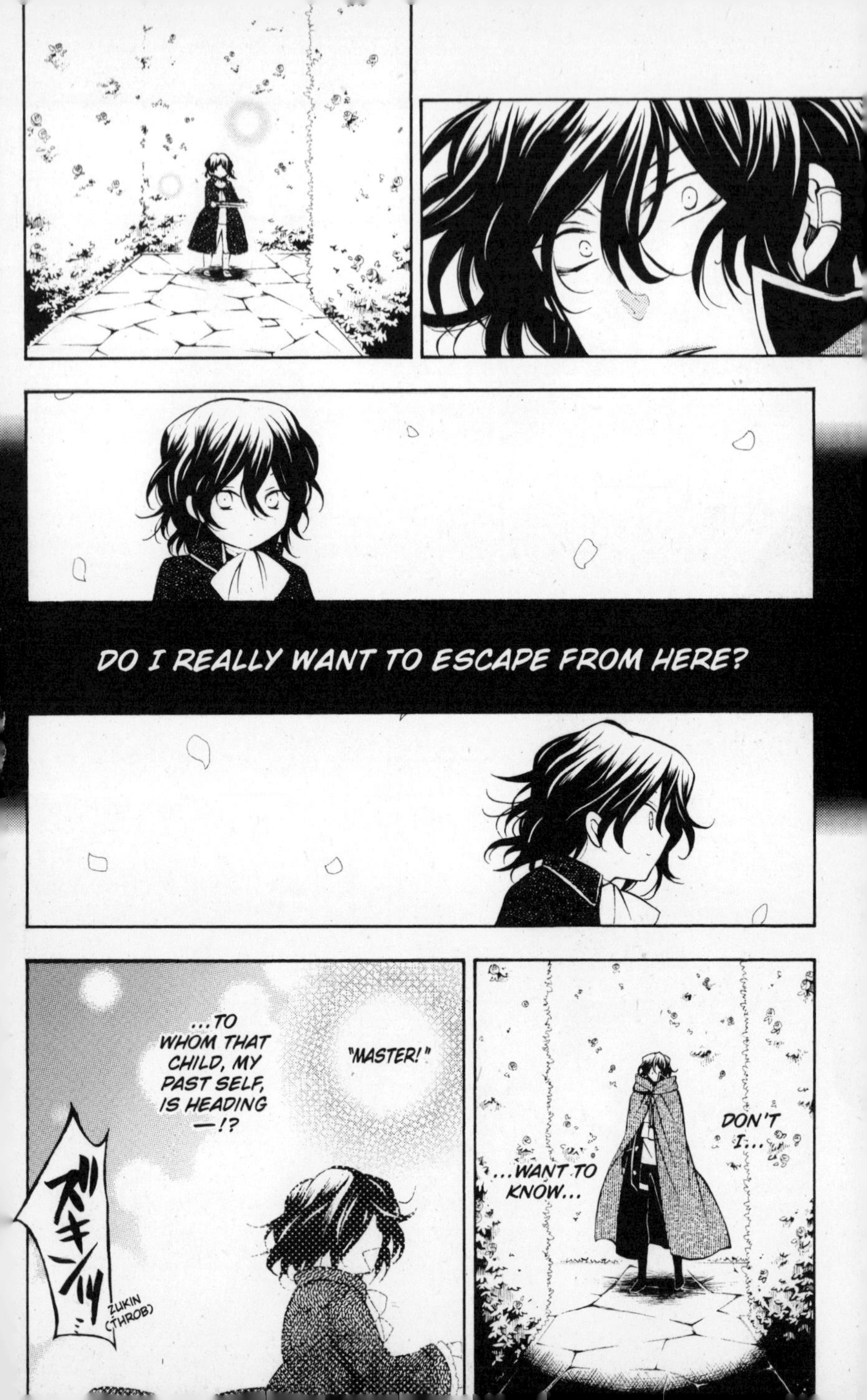
DO I REALLY WANT TO ESCAPE FROM HERE?
DON'T I...
...WANT TO KNOW...
"MASTER!"
...TO WHOM THAT CHILD, MY PAST SELF, IS HEADING—!?
ZUKIN (THROB)

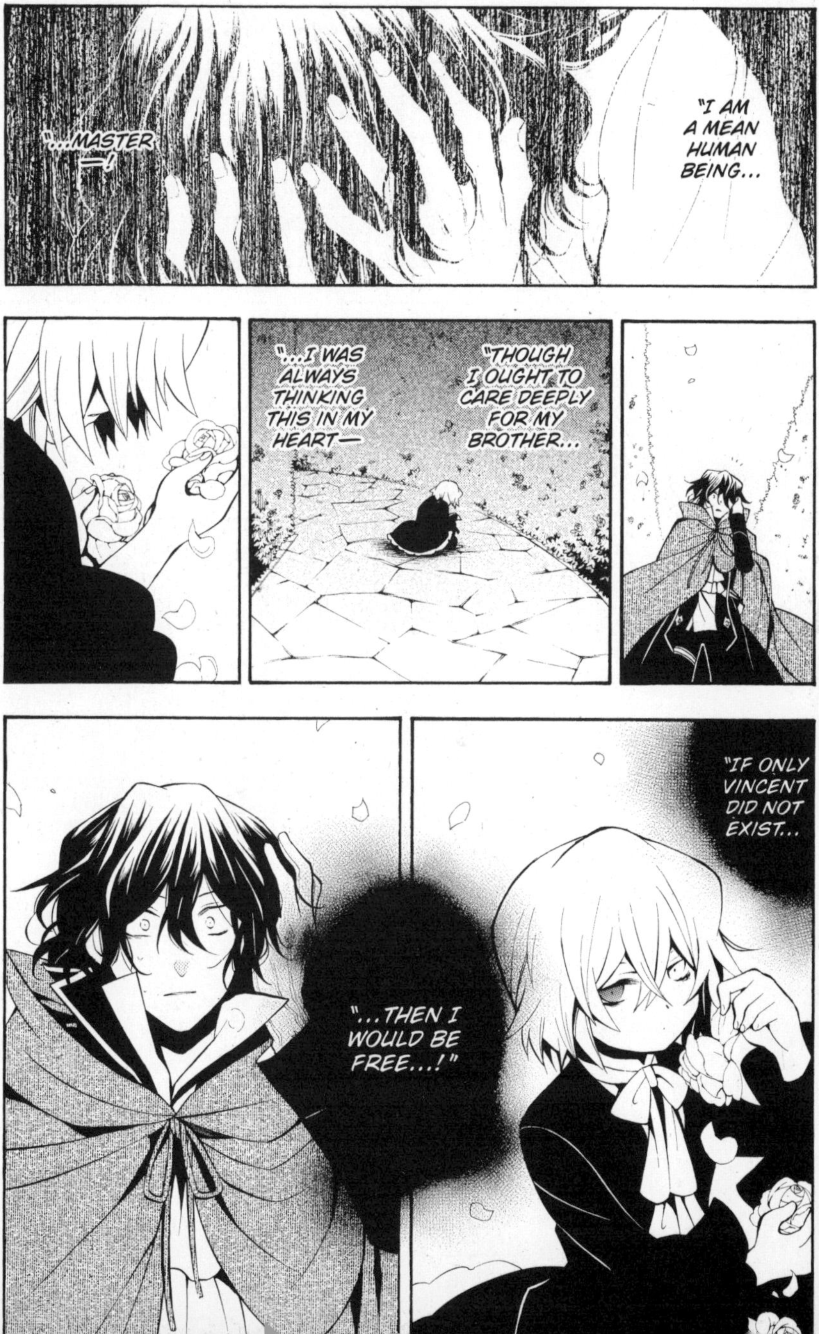
"I AM A MEAN HUMAN BEING...
"...MASTER—!
"THOUGH I OUGHT TO CARE DEEPLY FOR MY BROTHER...
"...I WAS ALWAYS THINKING THIS IN MY HEART—
"IF ONLY VINCENT DID NOT EXIST...
"...THEN I WOULD BE FREE...!"

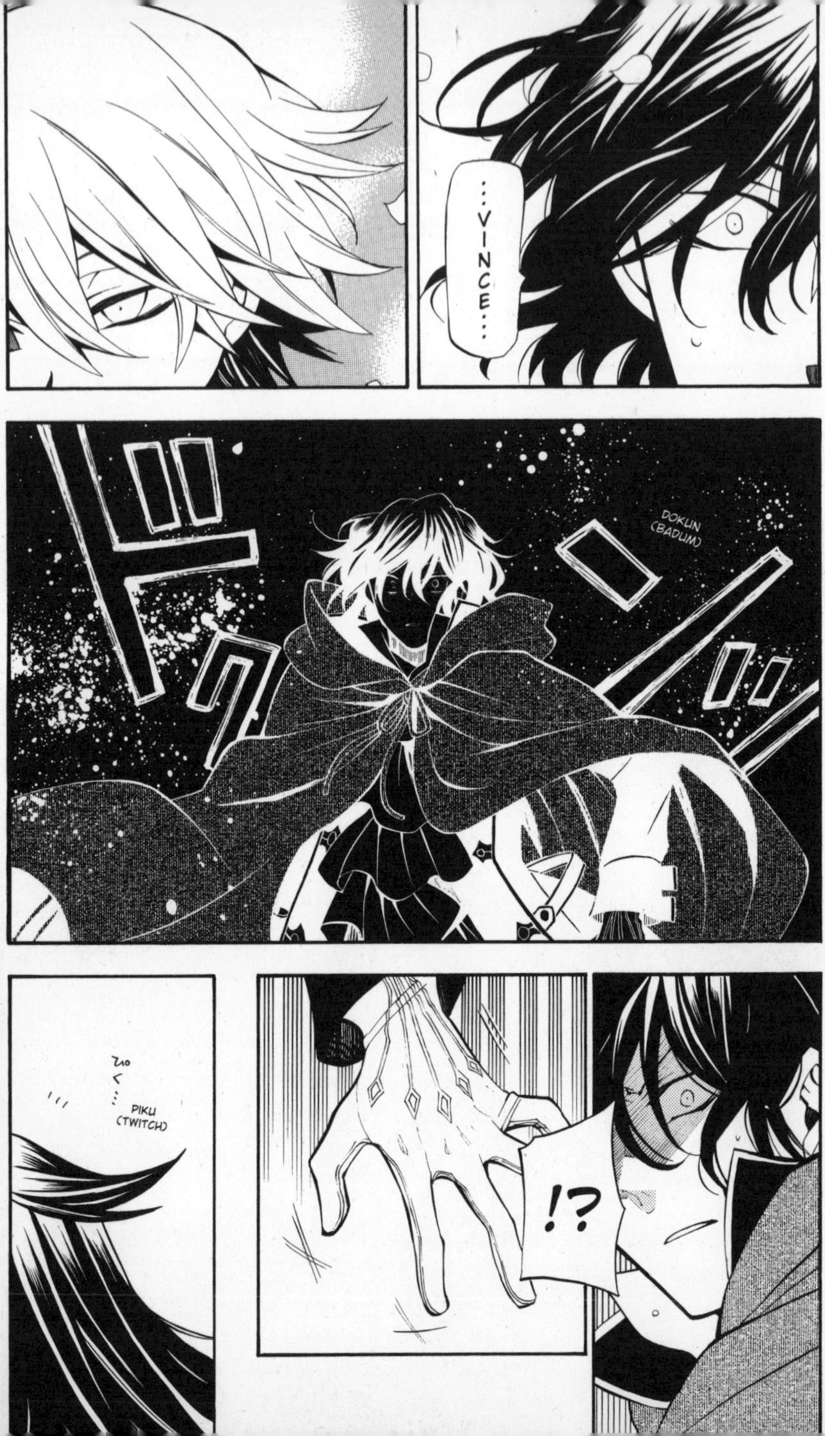
...VINCE...
DOKUN
(BADUM)
!?
PIKU
(TWITCH)

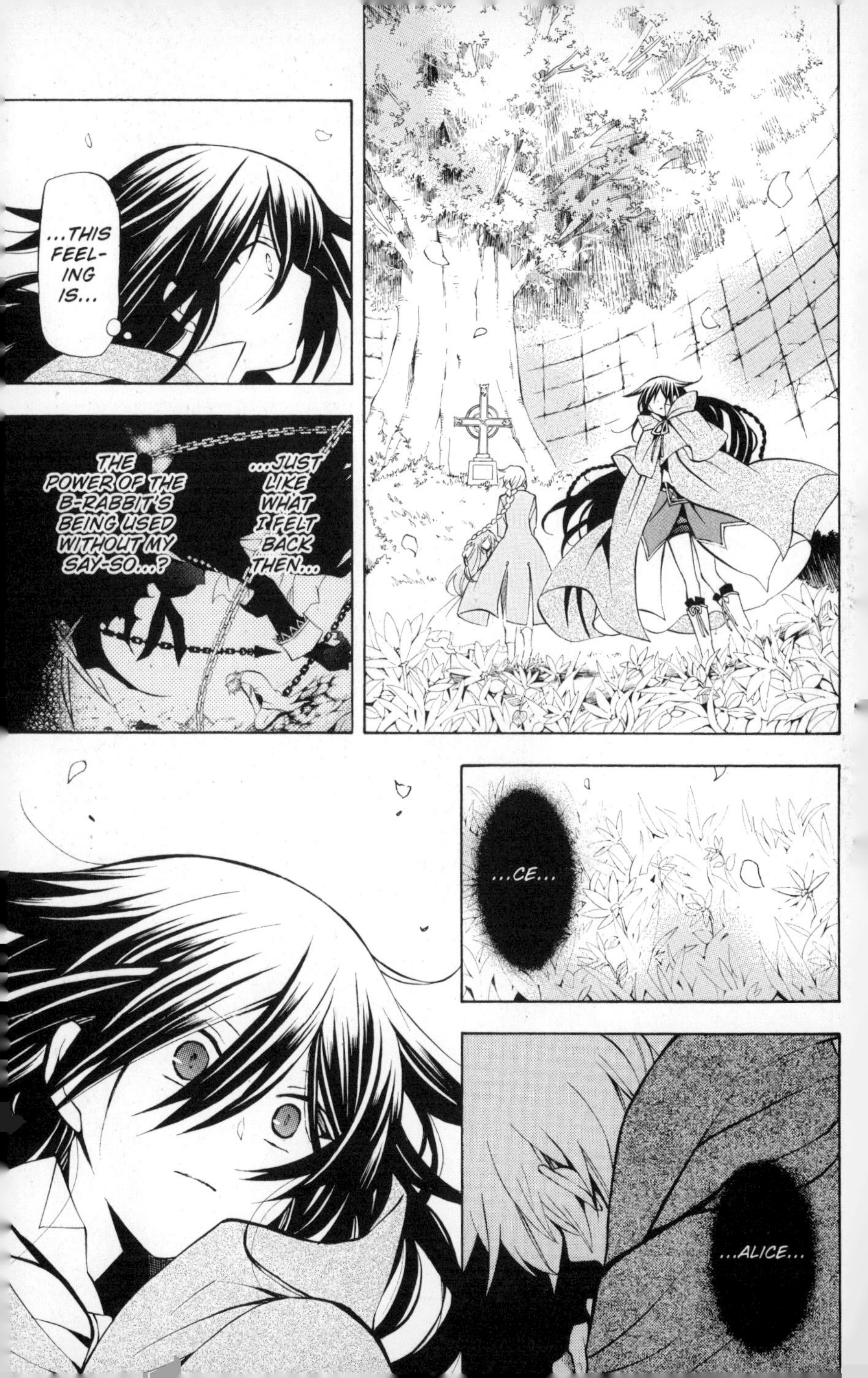
...THIS FEELING IS...
...JUST LIKE WHAT I FELT BACK THEN...
THE POWER OF THE B-RABBIT'S BEING USED WITHOUT MY SAY-SO...?
...CE...
...ALICE...

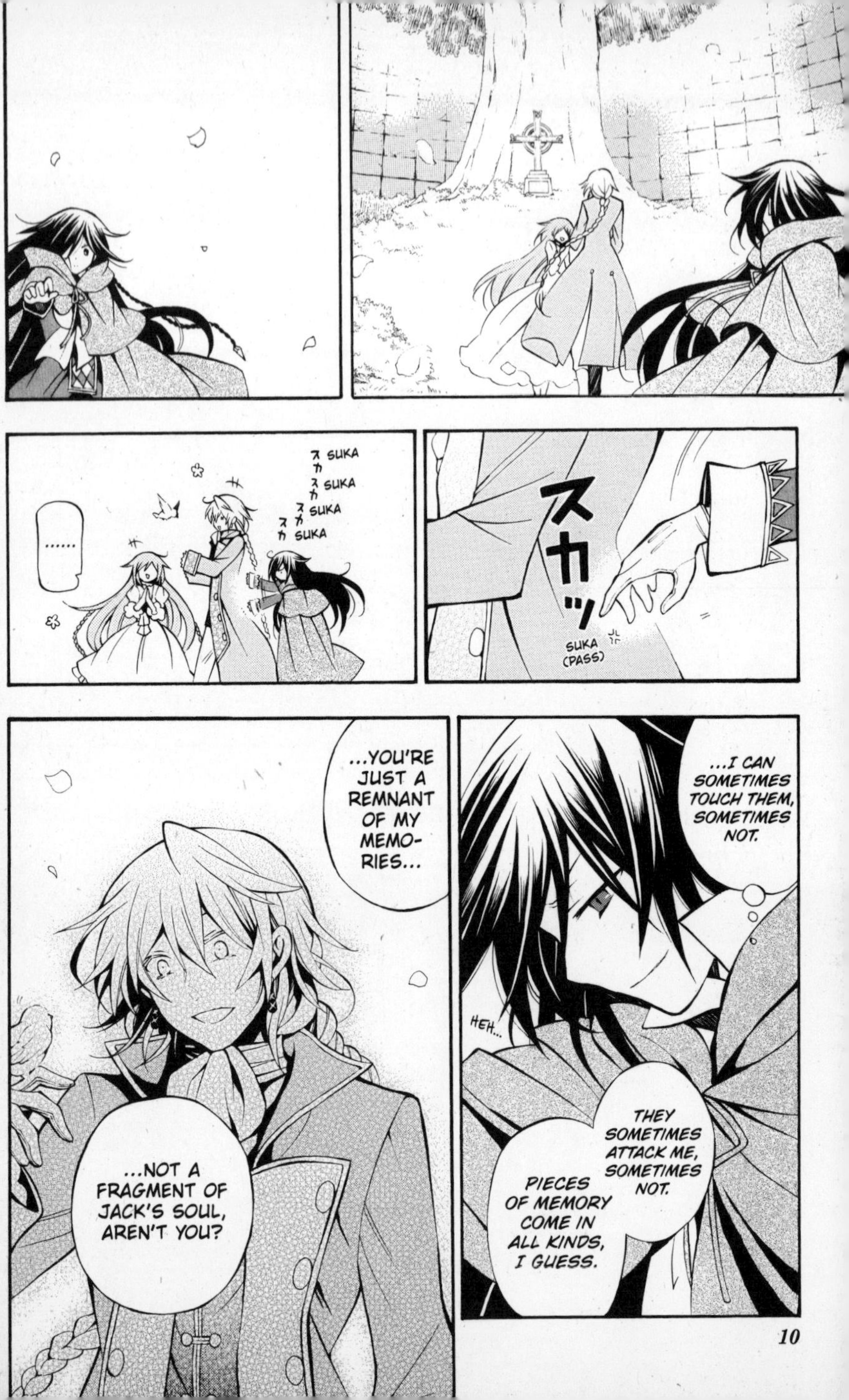
スカッ
SUKA (PASS)
スカ SUKA
スカ SUKA
スカ SUKA
スカ SUKA
......
...I CAN SOMETIMES TOUCH THEM, SOMETIMES NOT.
HEH...
THEY SOMETIMES ATTACK ME, SOMETIMES NOT.
PIECES OF MEMORY COME IN ALL KINDS, I GUESS.
...YOU'RE JUST A REMNANT OF MY MEMO-RIES...
...NOT A FRAGMENT OF JACK'S SOUL, AREN'T YOU?

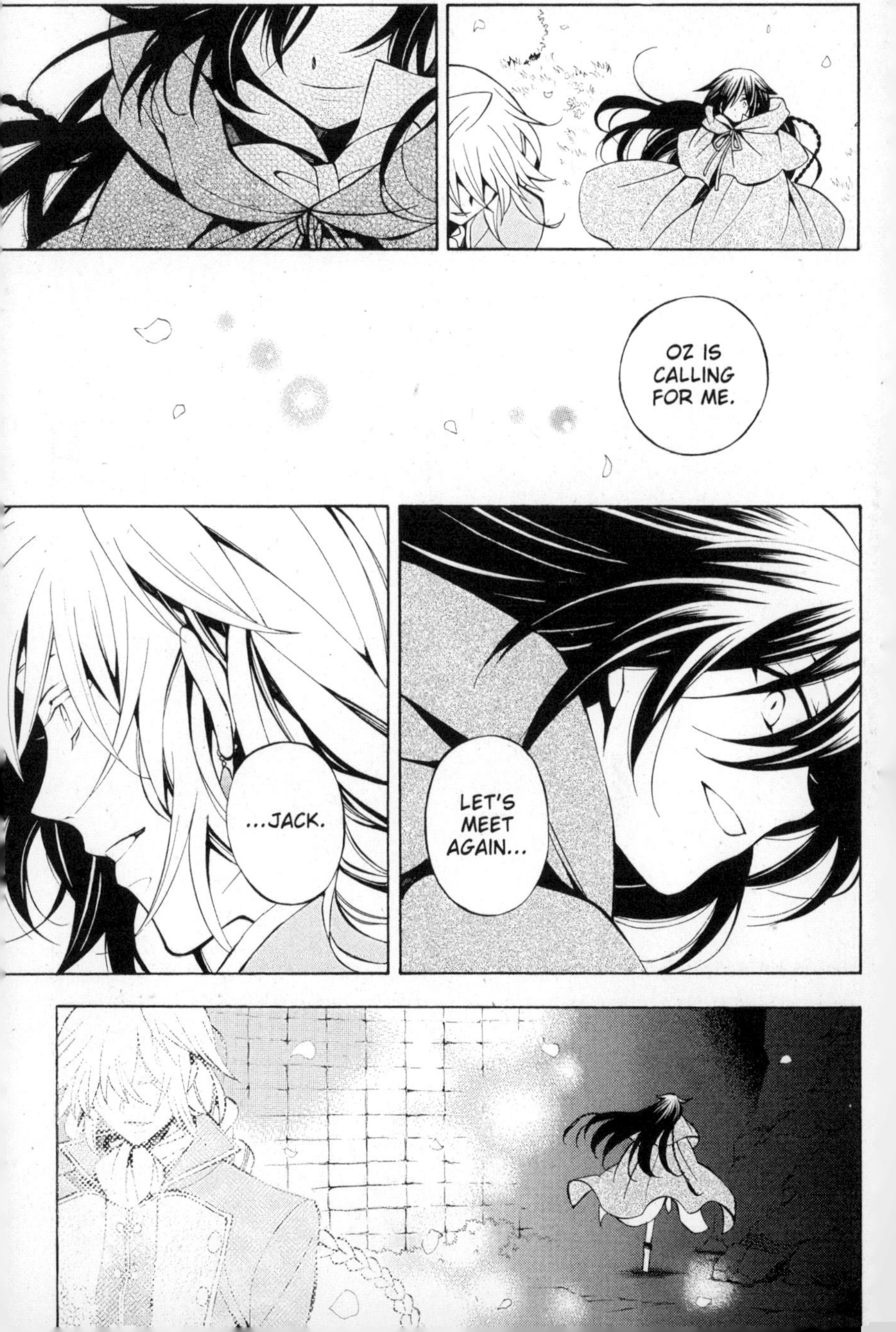
OZ IS CALLING FOR ME.
LET'S MEET AGAIN...
...JACK.

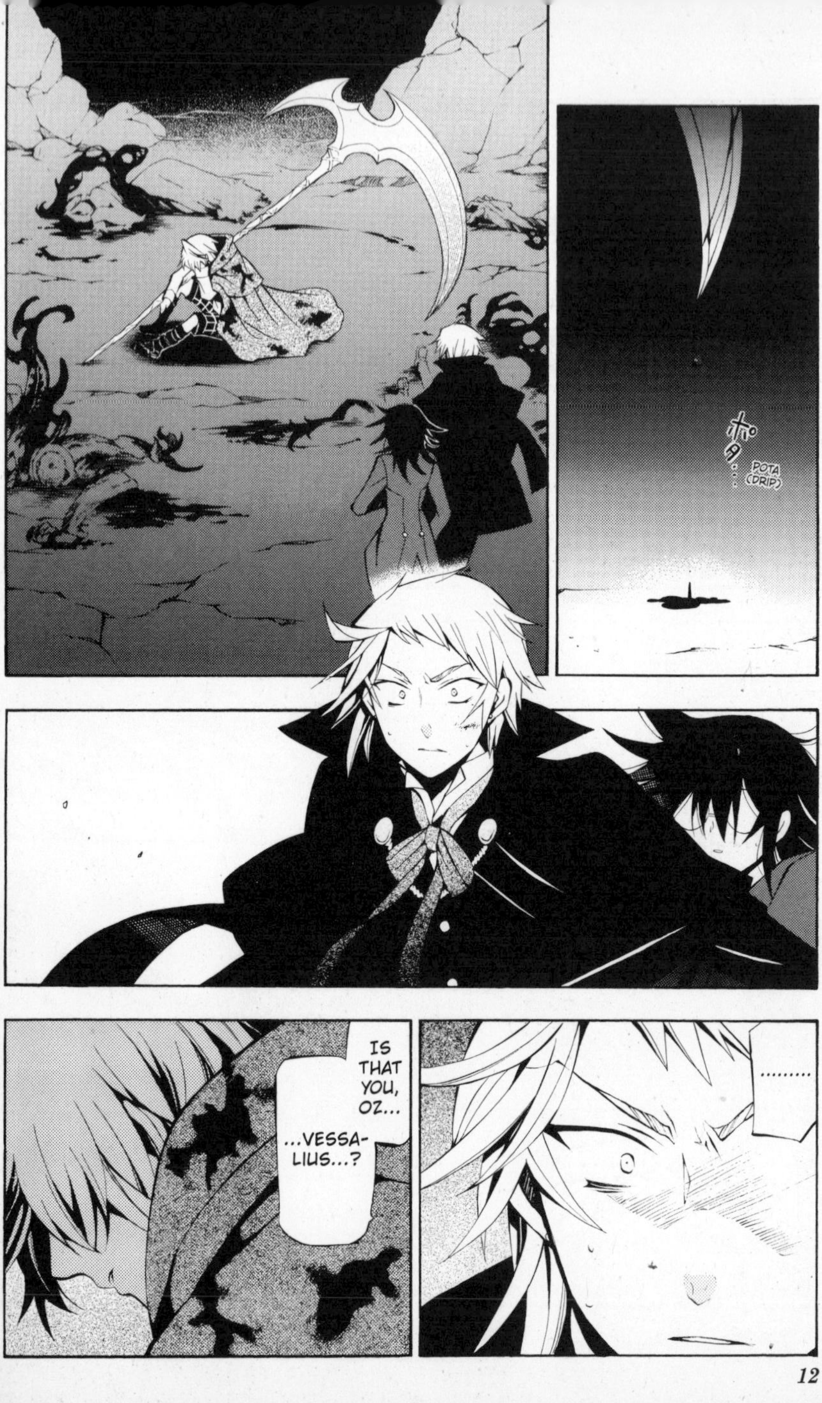

ポタ…
POTA (DRIP)
IS THAT YOU, OZ...
...VESSA-LIUS...?
....

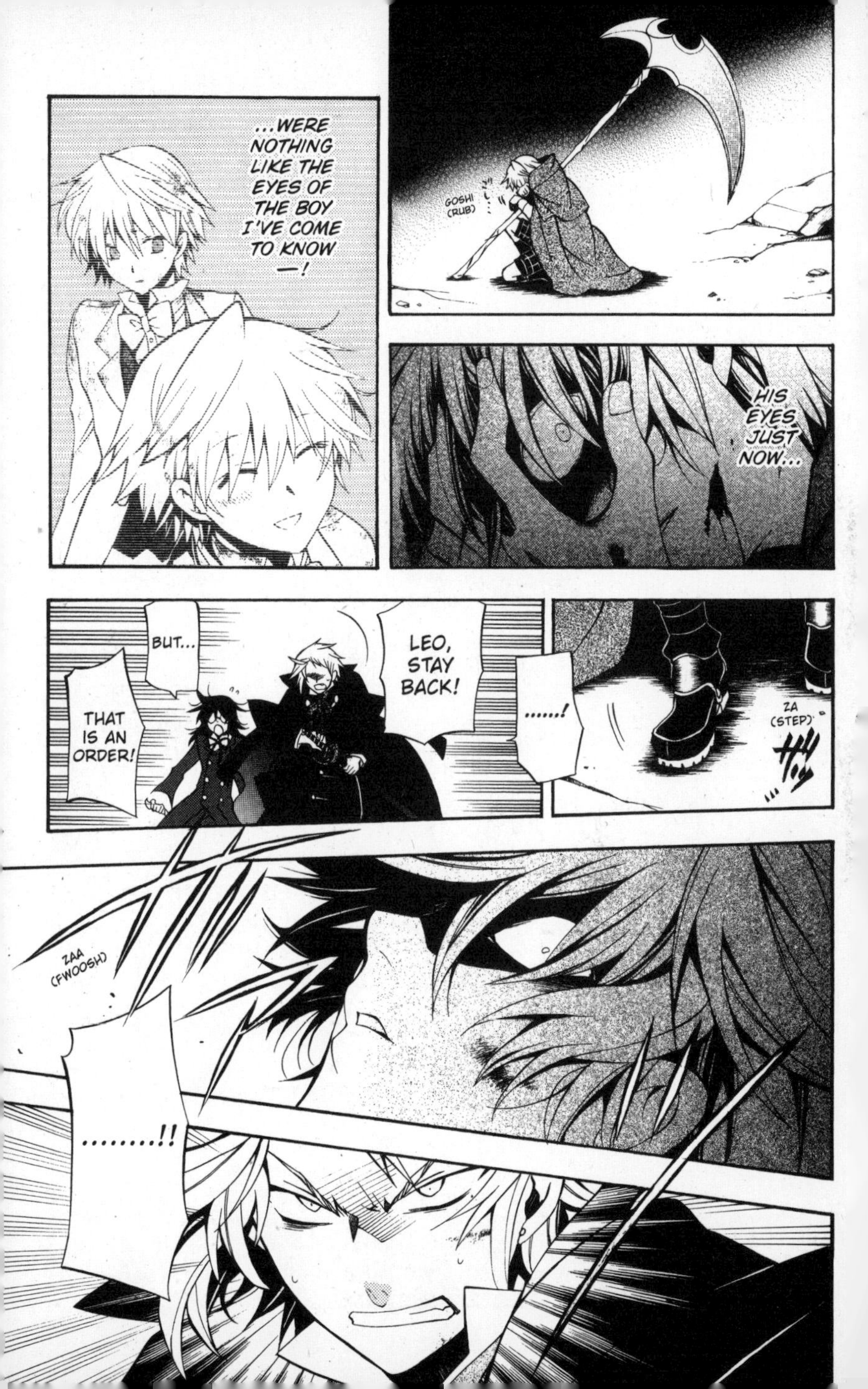

GOSHI (RUB)
HIS EYES JUST NOW...
...WERE NOTHING LIKE THE EYES OF THE BOY I'VE COME TO KNOW—!
ZA (STEP)
......!
LEO, STAY BACK!
BUT...
THAT IS AN ORDER!
ZAA (FWOOSH)
........!!

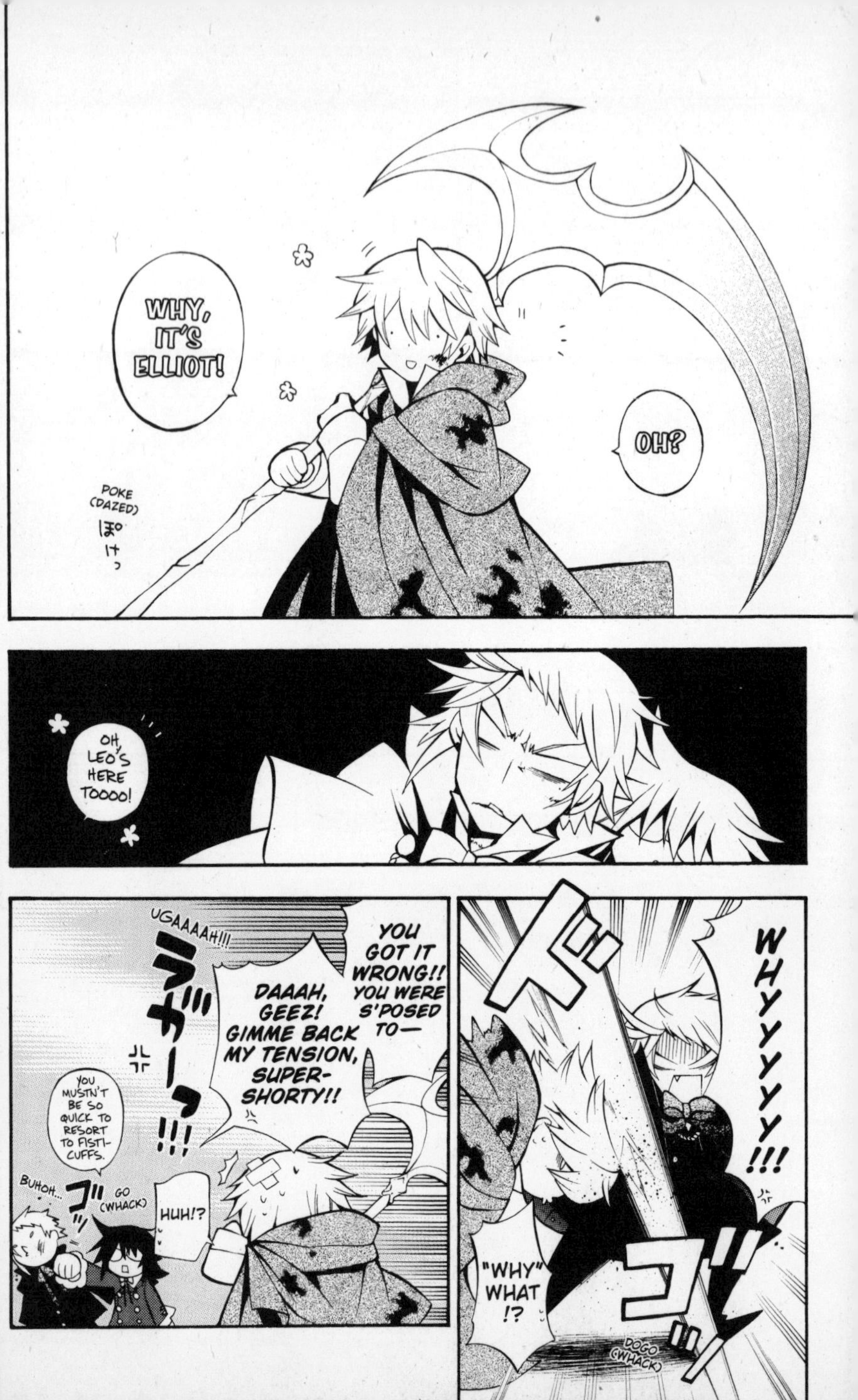
OH?
WHY, IT'S ELLIOT!
POKE (DAZED)
ぽけっ
OH, LEO'S HERE TOOOO!
WHYYYYYY!!!
"WHY" WHAT!?
DOGO (WHACK)
YOU GOT IT WRONG!! YOU WERE S'POSED TO—
DAAAH, GEEZ! GIMME BACK MY TENSION, SUPER-SHORTY!!
UGAAAAH!!!
HUH!?
YOU MUSTN'T BE SO QUICK TO RESORT TO FISTI-CUFFS.
BUHOH...
GO (WHACK)

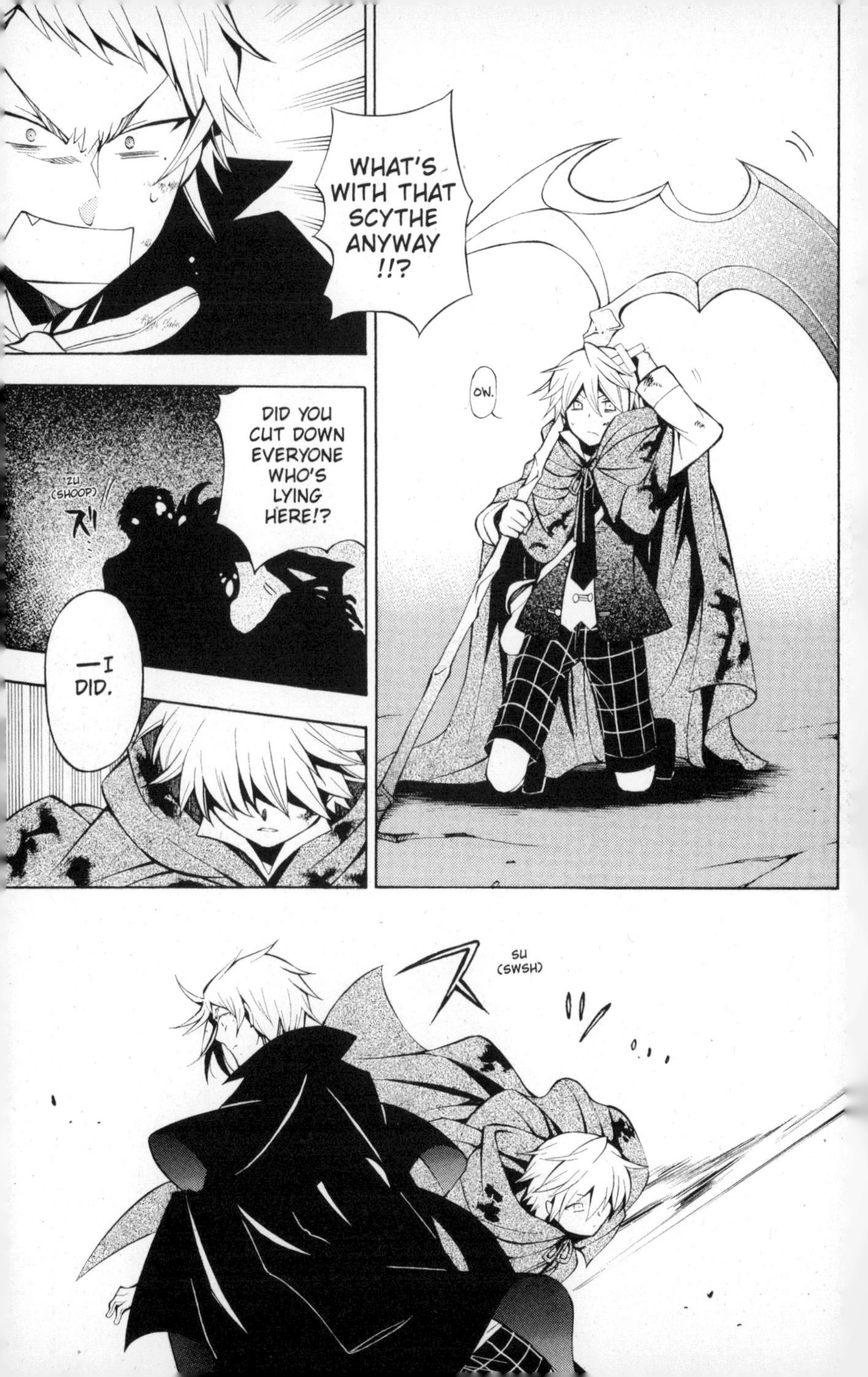
WHAT'S WITH THAT SCYTHE ANYWAY !!?
OW.
DID YOU CUT DOWN EVERYONE WHO'S LYING HERE!?
ZU (SHOOP)
—I DID.
SU (SWSH)

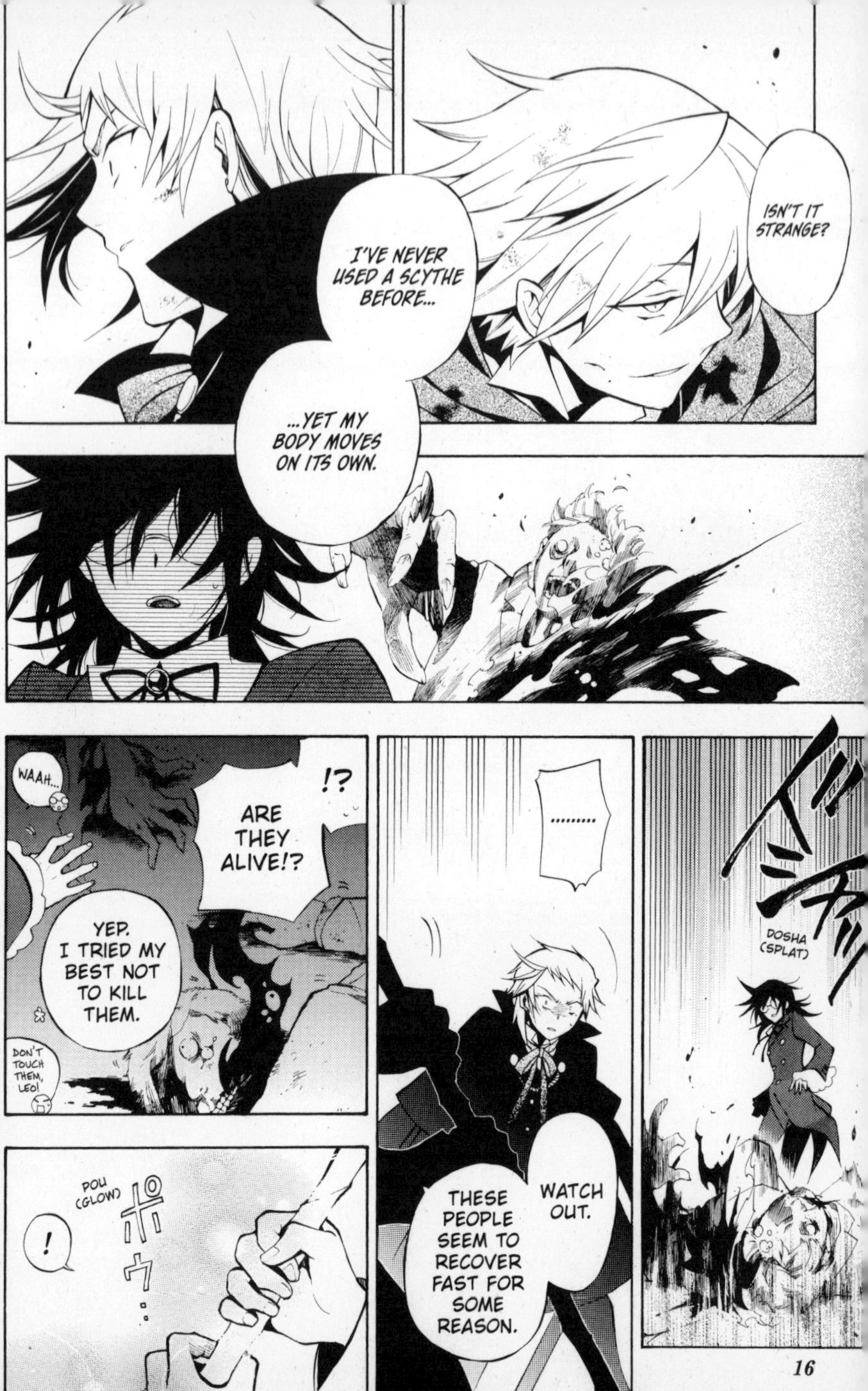
ISN'T IT STRANGE?
I'VE NEVER USED A SCYTHE BEFORE...
...YET MY BODY MOVES ON ITS OWN.
DOSHA (SPLAT)
....
WATCH OUT.
THESE PEOPLE SEEM TO RECOVER FAST FOR SOME REASON.
!?
ARE THEY ALIVE!?
WAAH...
YEP. I TRIED MY BEST NOT TO KILL THEM.
DON'T TOUCH THEM, LEO!
POU (GLOW)
!

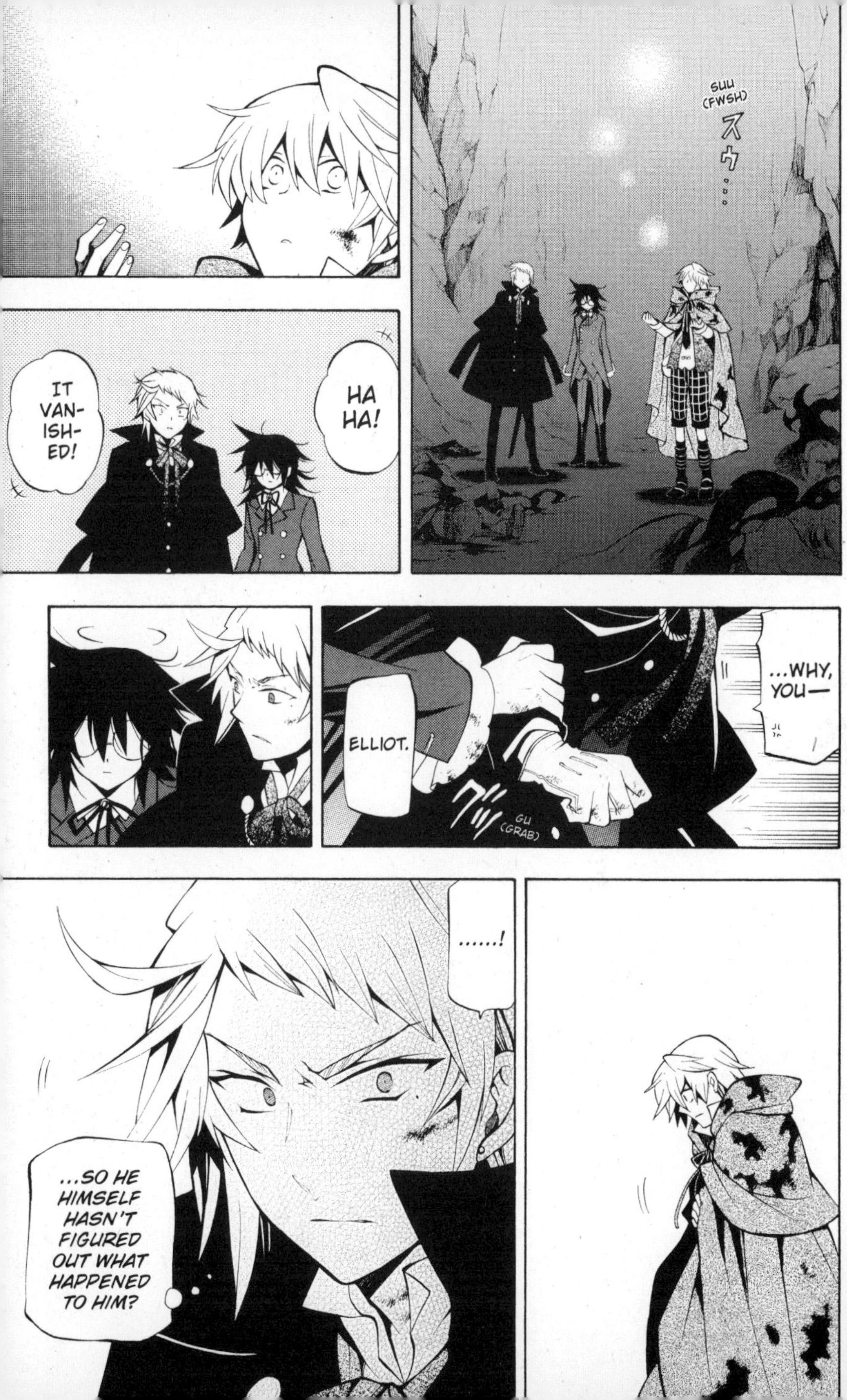
SUU (FWSH)
スゥ...
HA HA!
IT VAN-ISH-ED!
...WHY, YOU—
ELLIOT.
グッ
GU (GRAB)
......!
...SO HE HIMSELF HASN'T FIGURED OUT WHAT HAPPENED TO HIM?

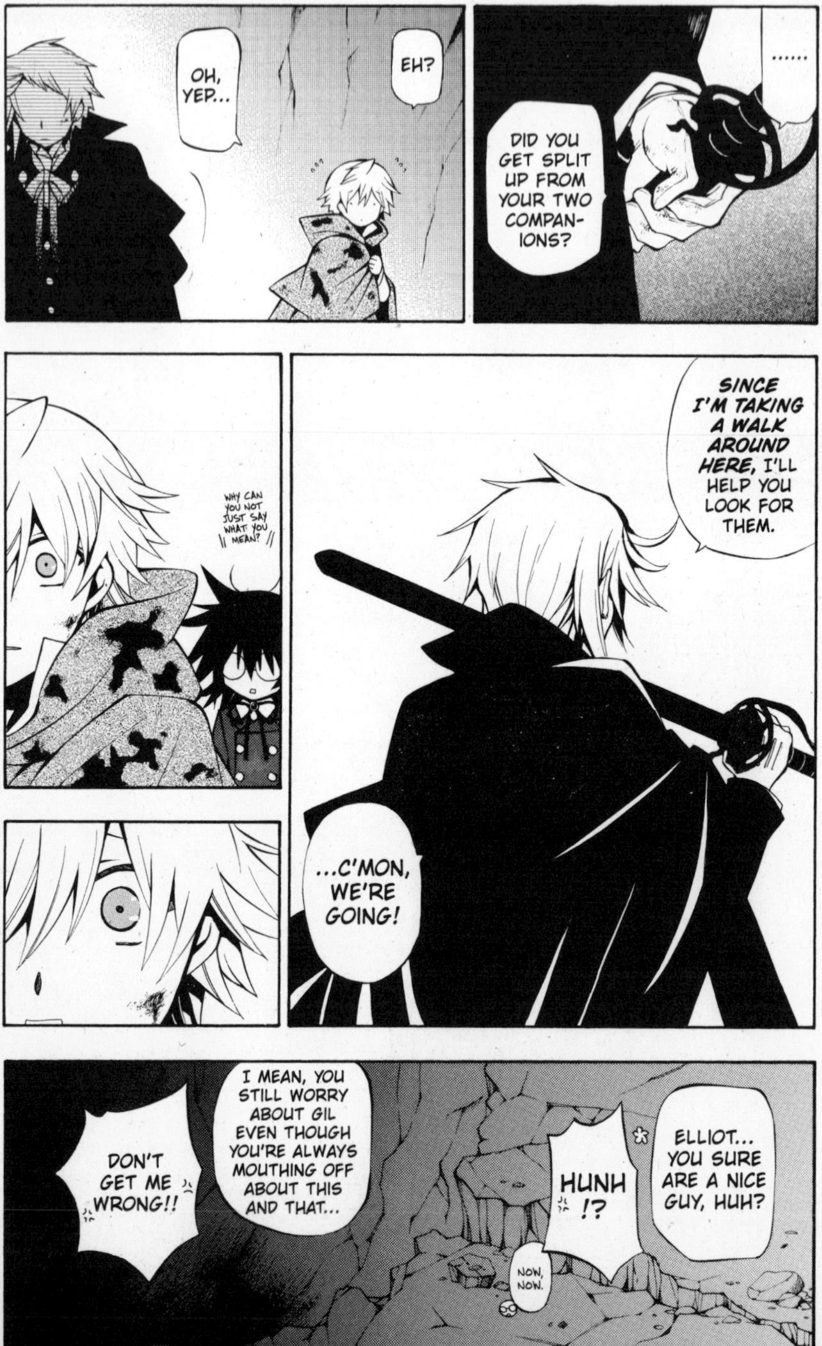
......
DID YOU GET SPLIT UP FROM YOUR TWO COMPANIONS?
EH?
OH, YEP...
SINCE I'M TAKING A WALK AROUND HERE, I'LL HELP YOU LOOK FOR THEM.
...C'MON, WE'RE GOING!
WHY CAN YOU NOT JUST SAY WHAT YOU MEAN?!
ELLIOT... YOU SURE ARE A NICE GUY, HUH?
HUNH !?
NOW, NOW.
I MEAN, YOU STILL WORRY ABOUT GIL EVEN THOUGH YOU'RE ALWAYS MOUTHING OFF ABOUT THIS AND THAT...
DON'T GET ME WRONG!!

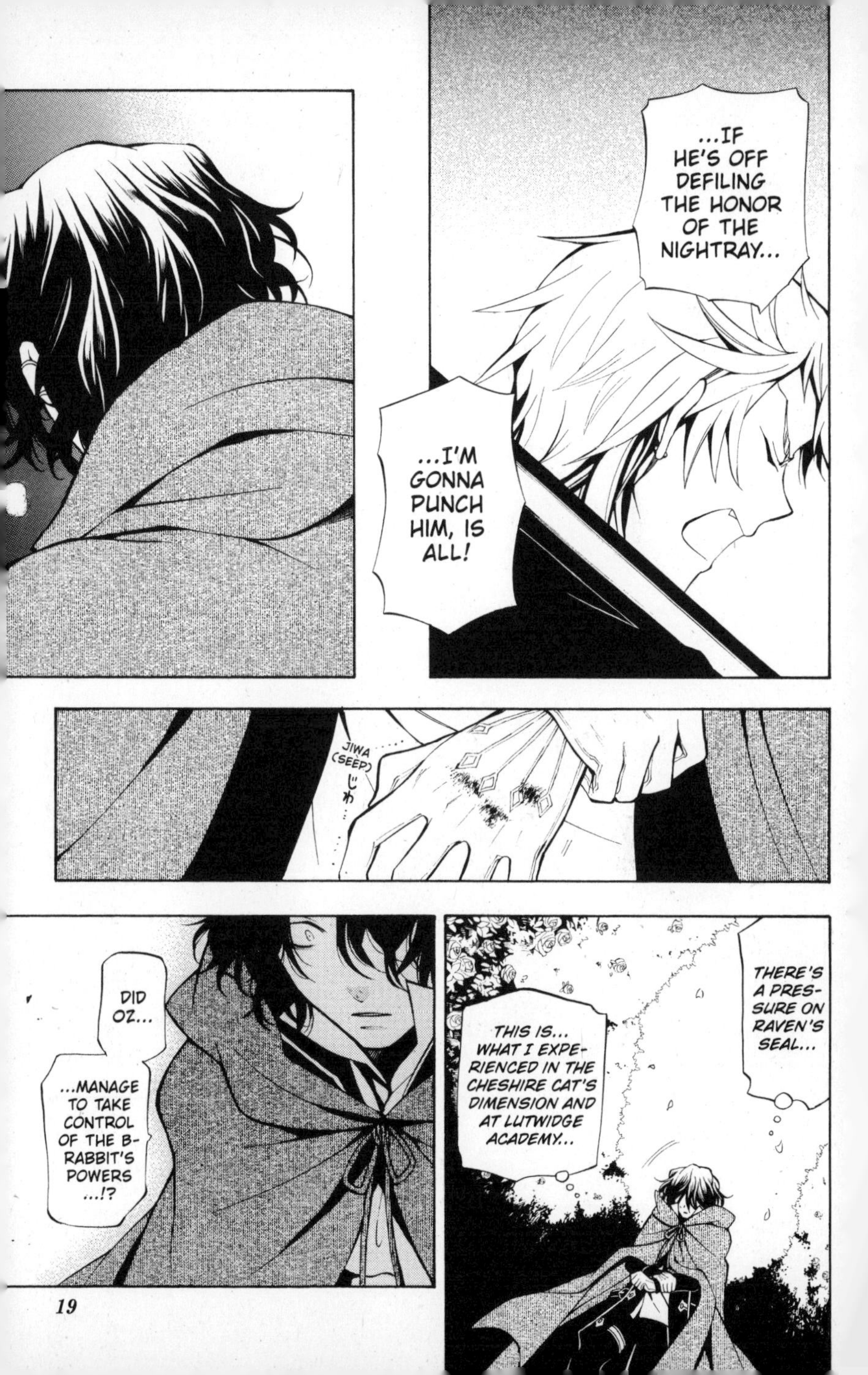
...IF HE'S OFF DEFILING THE HONOR OF THE NIGHTRAY...
...I'M GONNA PUNCH HIM, IS ALL!
JIWA (SEEP)
じわ…
THERE'S A PRES-SURE ON RAVEN'S SEAL...
THIS IS... WHAT I EXPE-RIENCED IN THE CHESHIRE CAT'S DIMENSION AND AT LUTWIDGE ACADEMY...
DID OZ...
...MANAGE TO TAKE CONTROL OF THE B-RABBIT'S POWERS ...!?

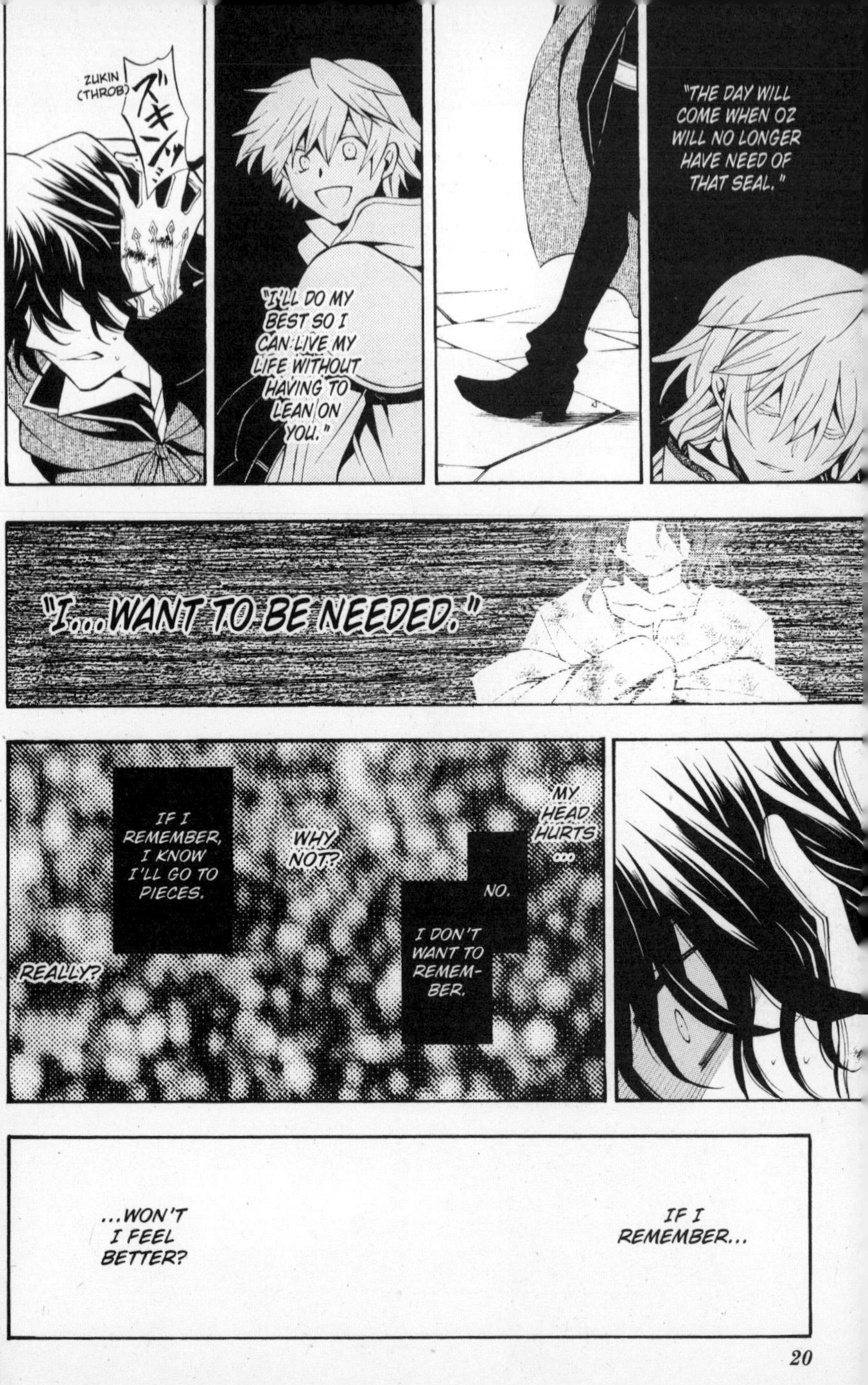
"THE DAY WILL COME WHEN OZ WILL NO LONGER HAVE NEED OF THAT SEAL."
"I'LL DO MY BEST SO I CAN LIVE MY LIFE WITHOUT HAVING TO LEAN ON YOU."
ズキンッ
ZUKIN (THROB)
"I...WANT TO BE NEEDED."
MY HEAD HURTS...
NO.
I DON'T WANT TO REMEMBER.
WHY NOT?
IF I REMEMBER, I KNOW I'LL GO TO PIECES.
REALLY?
IF I REMEMBER...
...WON'T I FEEL BETTER?

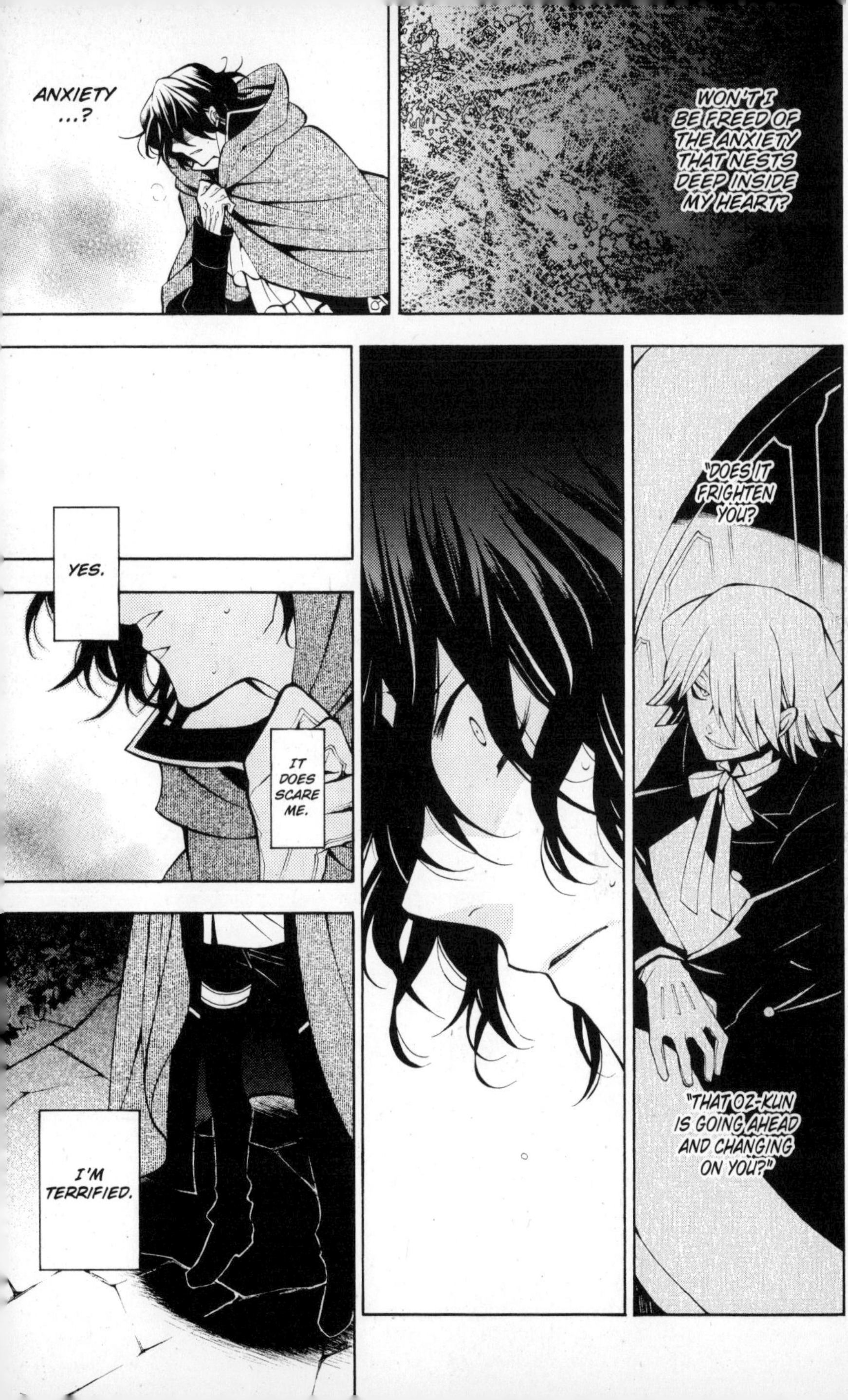
WON'T I BE FREED OF THE ANXIETY THAT NESTS DEEP INSIDE MY HEART?
ANXIETY ...?
"DOES IT FRIGHTEN YOU?
"THAT OZ-KUN IS GOING AHEAD AND CHANGING ON YOU?"
YES.
IT DOES SCARE ME.
I'M TERRIFIED.

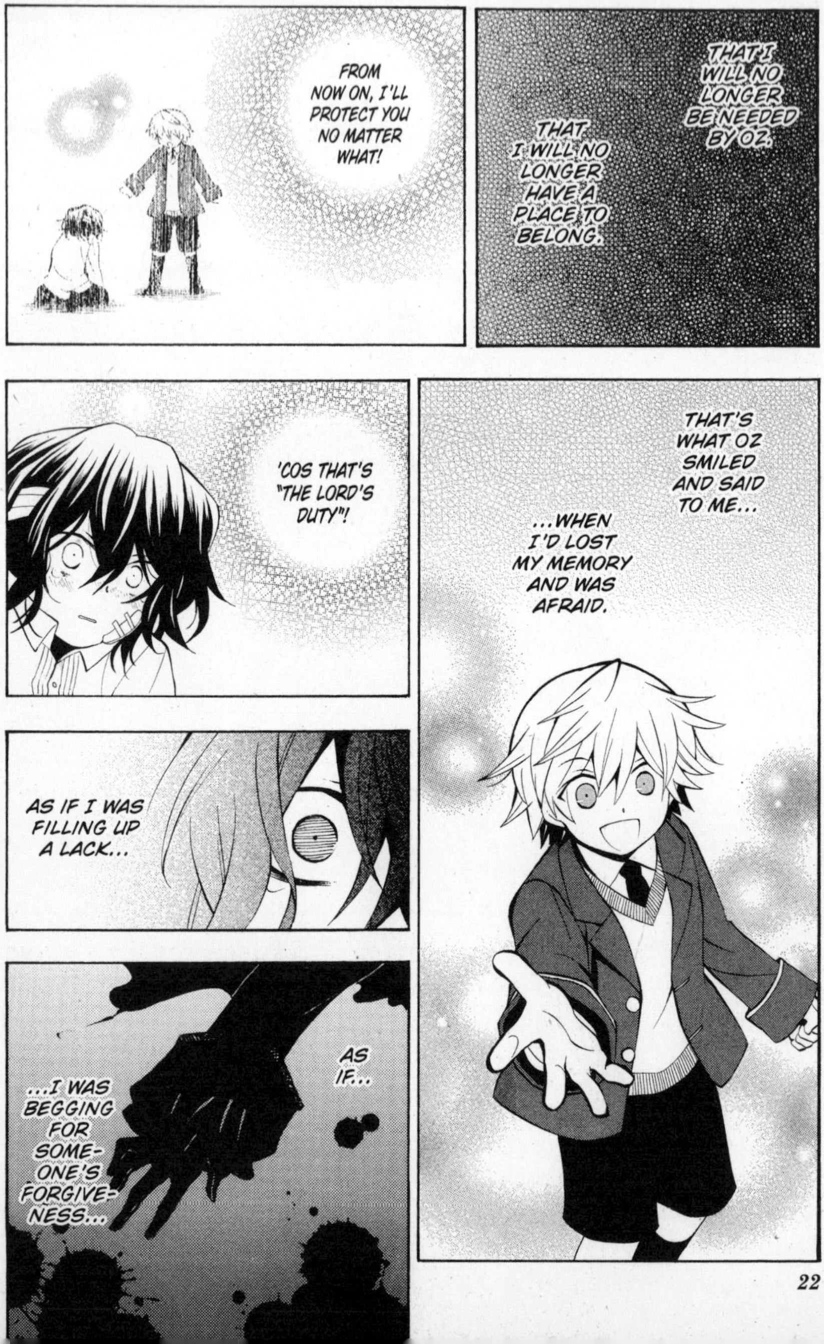
THAT I WILL NO LONGER BE NEEDED BY OZ.
THAT I WILL NO LONGER HAVE A PLACE TO BELONG.
FROM NOW ON, I'LL PROTECT YOU NO MATTER WHAT!
THAT'S WHAT OZ SMILED AND SAID TO ME...
...WHEN I'D LOST MY MEMORY AND WAS AFRAID.
'COS THAT'S "THE LORD'S DUTY"!
AS IF I WAS FILLING UP A LACK...
AS IF...
...I WAS BEGGING FOR SOME-ONE'S FORGIVE-NESS...

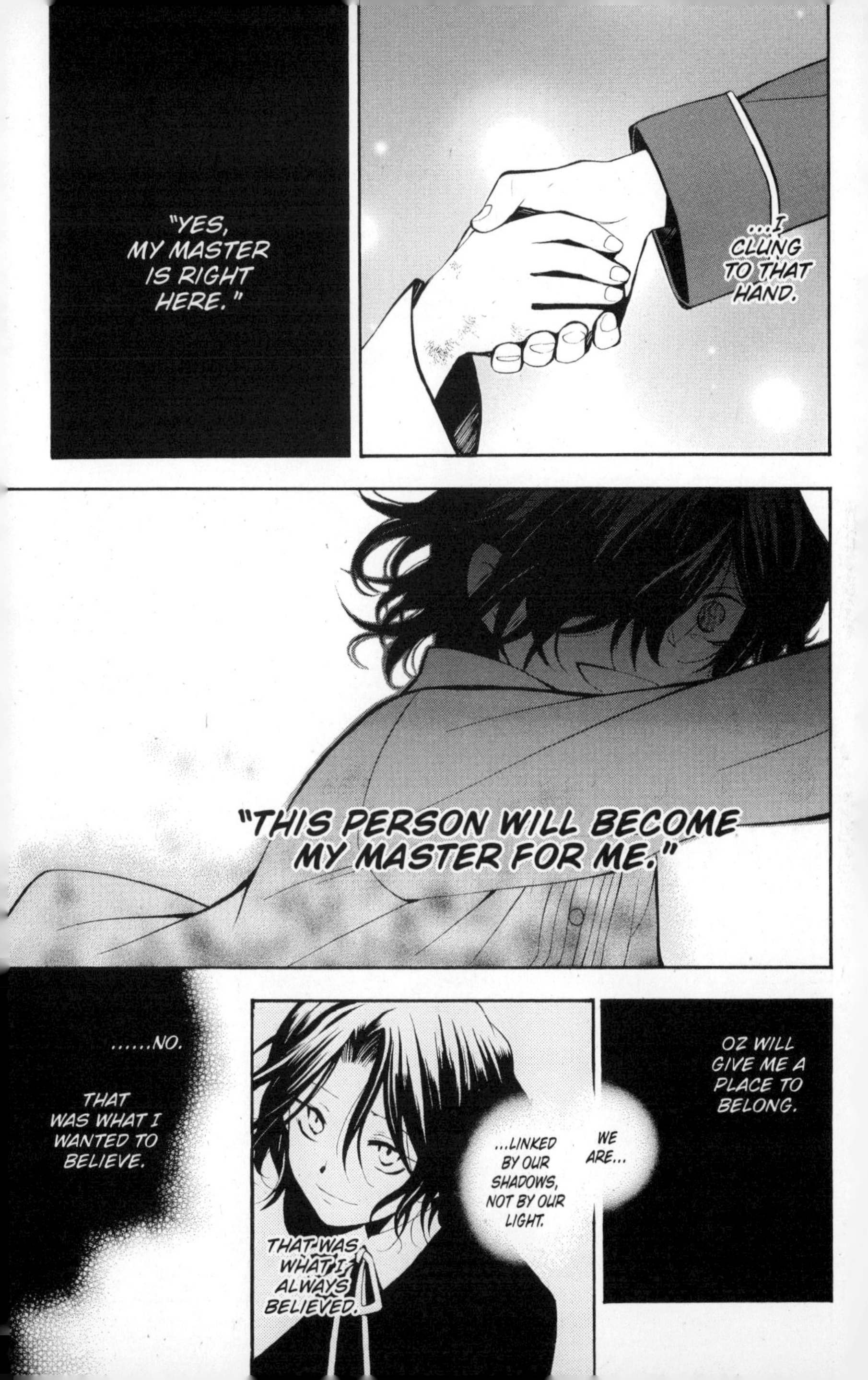
...I CLUNG TO THAT HAND.
"YES, MY MASTER IS RIGHT HERE."
"THIS PERSON WILL BECOME MY MASTER FOR ME."
OZ WILL GIVE ME A PLACE TO BELONG.
WE ARE...
...LINKED BY OUR SHADOWS, NOT BY OUR LIGHT.
THAT WAS WHAT I ALWAYS BELIEVED.
......NO.
THAT WAS WHAT I WANTED TO BELIEVE.

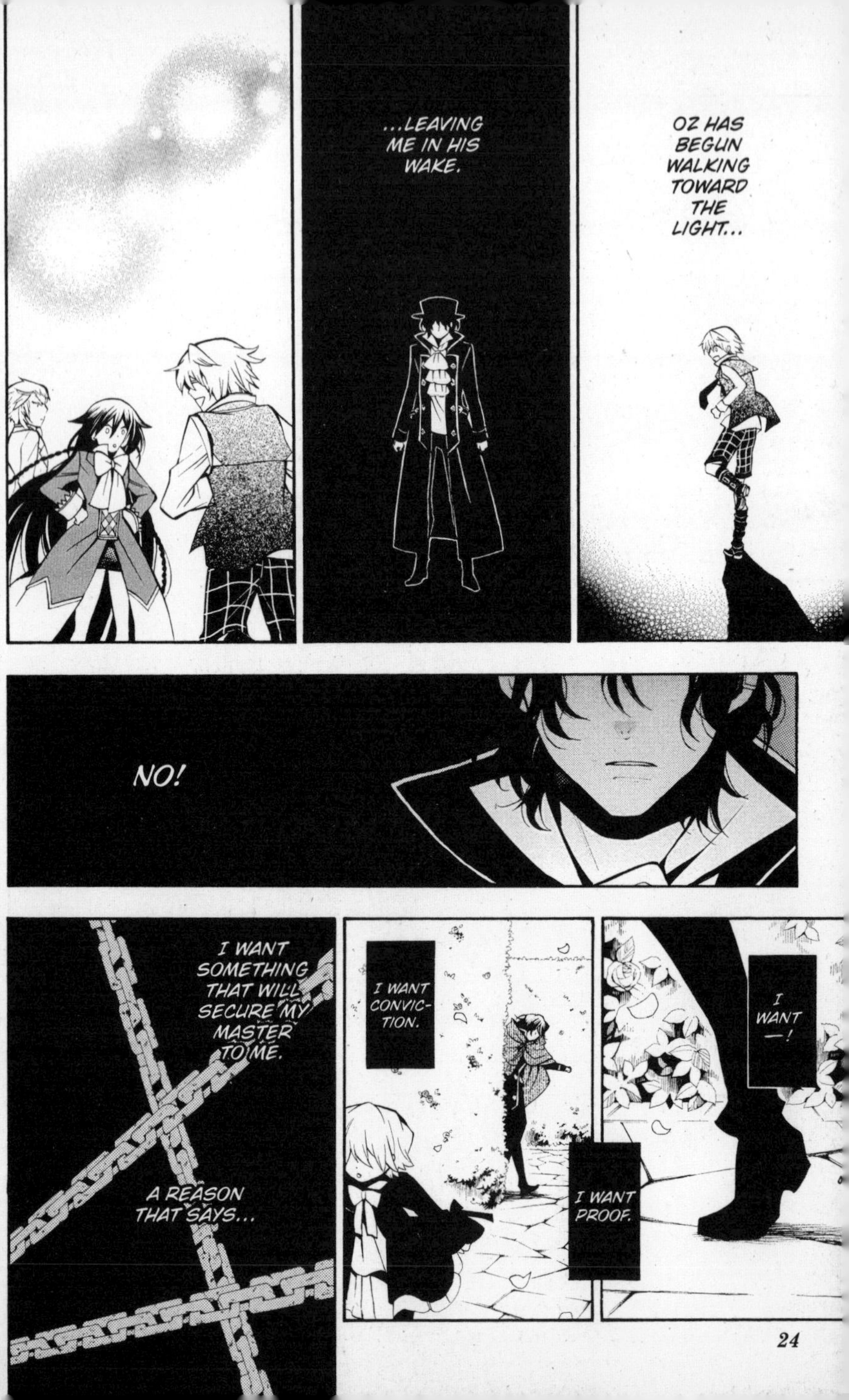
OZ HAS BEGUN WALKING TOWARD THE LIGHT...
...LEAVING ME IN HIS WAKE.
NO!
I WANT —!
I WANT CONVIC-TION.
I WANT PROOF.
I WANT SOMETHING THAT WILL SECURE MY MASTER TO ME.
A REASON THAT SAYS...

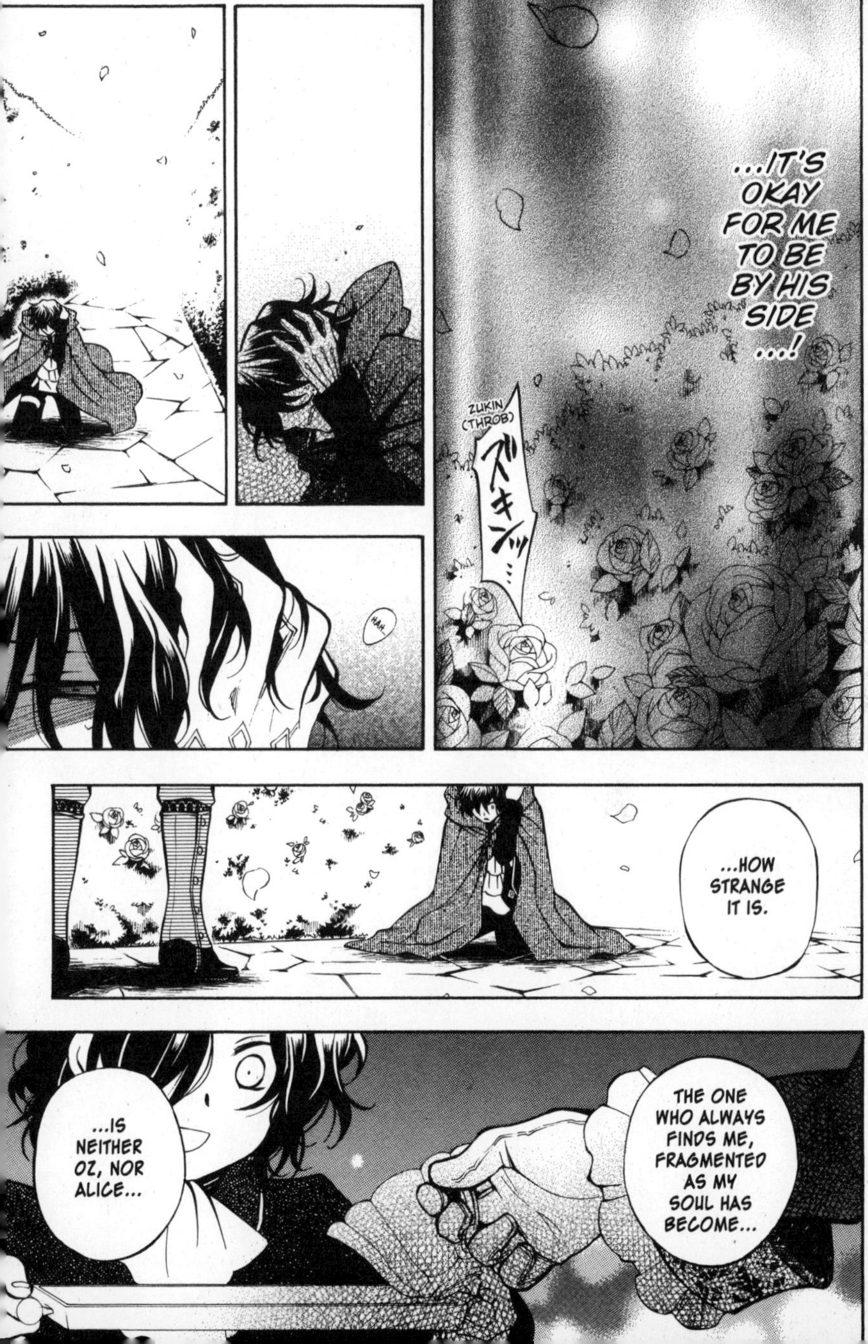
...IT'S OKAY FOR ME TO BE BY HIS SIDE ...!
ZUKIN (THROB)
ズキンッ
HAH...
...HOW STRANGE IT IS.
THE ONE WHO ALWAYS FINDS ME, FRAGMENTED AS MY SOUL HAS BECOME...
...IS NEITHER OZ, NOR ALICE...

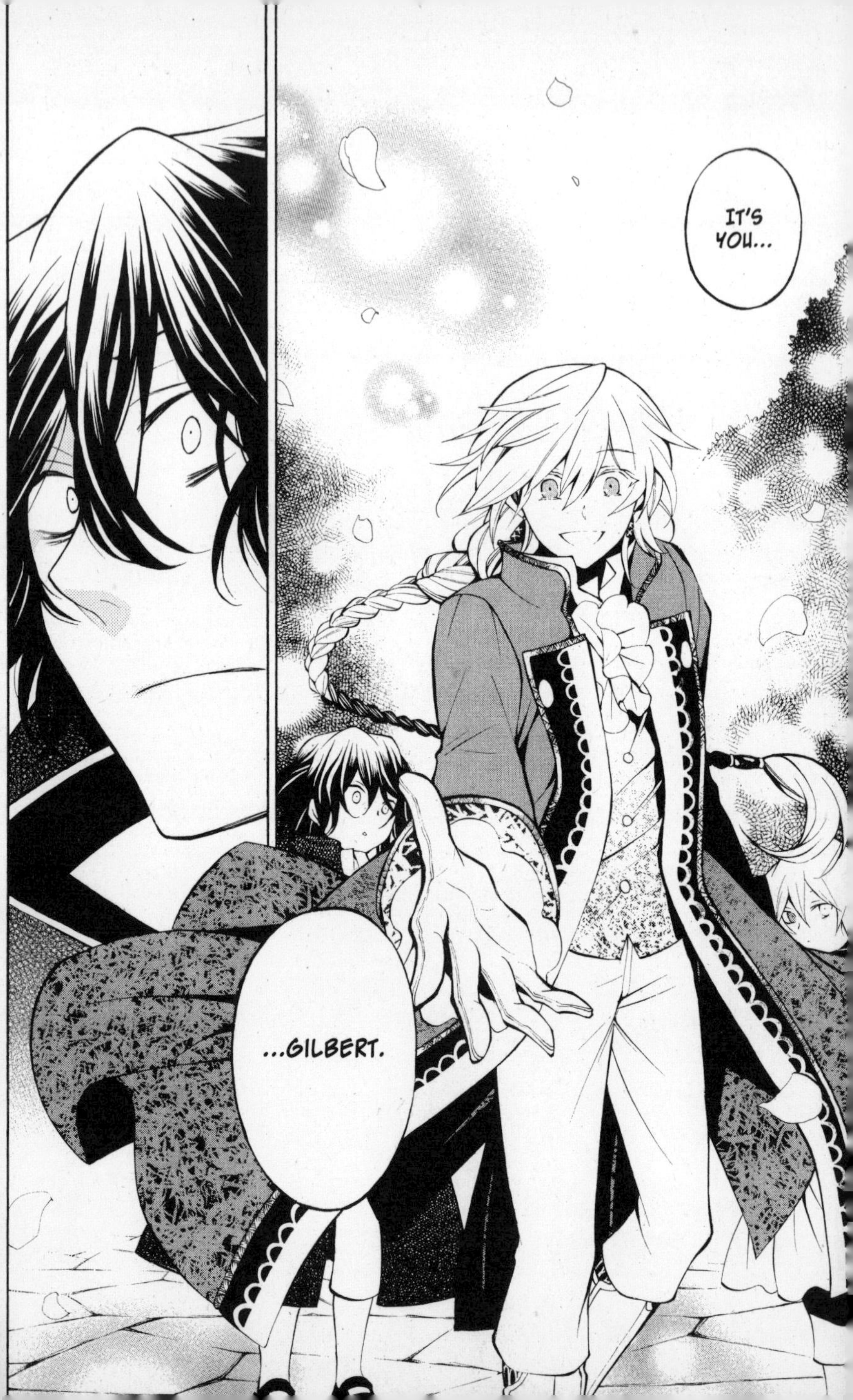
IT'S YOU...
...GILBERT.

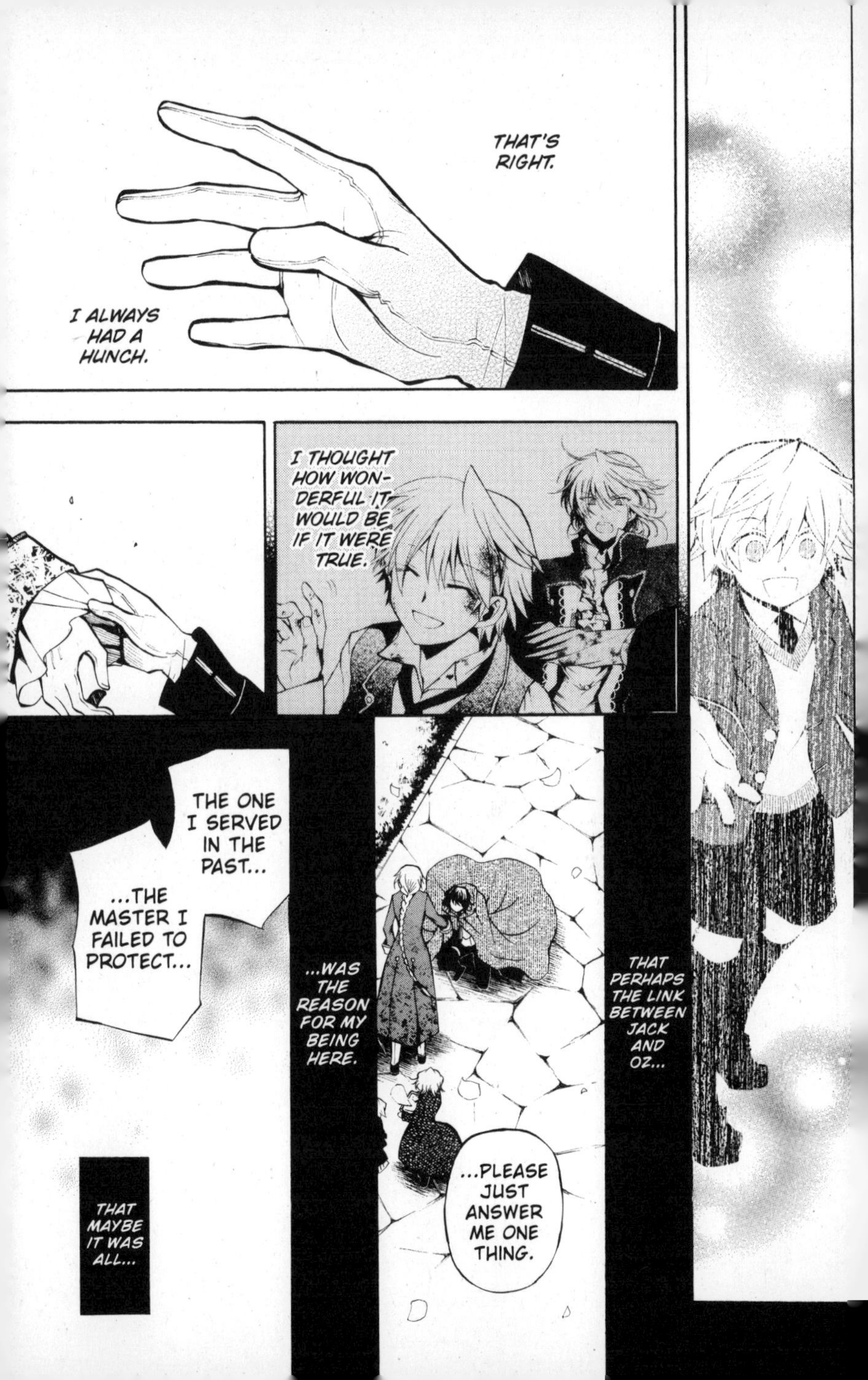
THAT PERHAPS THE LINK BETWEEN JACK AND OZ...
THAT'S RIGHT.
I ALWAYS HAD A HUNCH.
I THOUGHT HOW WONDERFUL IT WOULD BE IF IT WERE TRUE.
...PLEASE JUST ANSWER ME ONE THING.
...WAS THE REASON FOR MY BEING HERE.
THE ONE I SERVED IN THE PAST...
...THE MASTER I FAILED TO PROTECT...
THAT MAYBE IT WAS ALL...

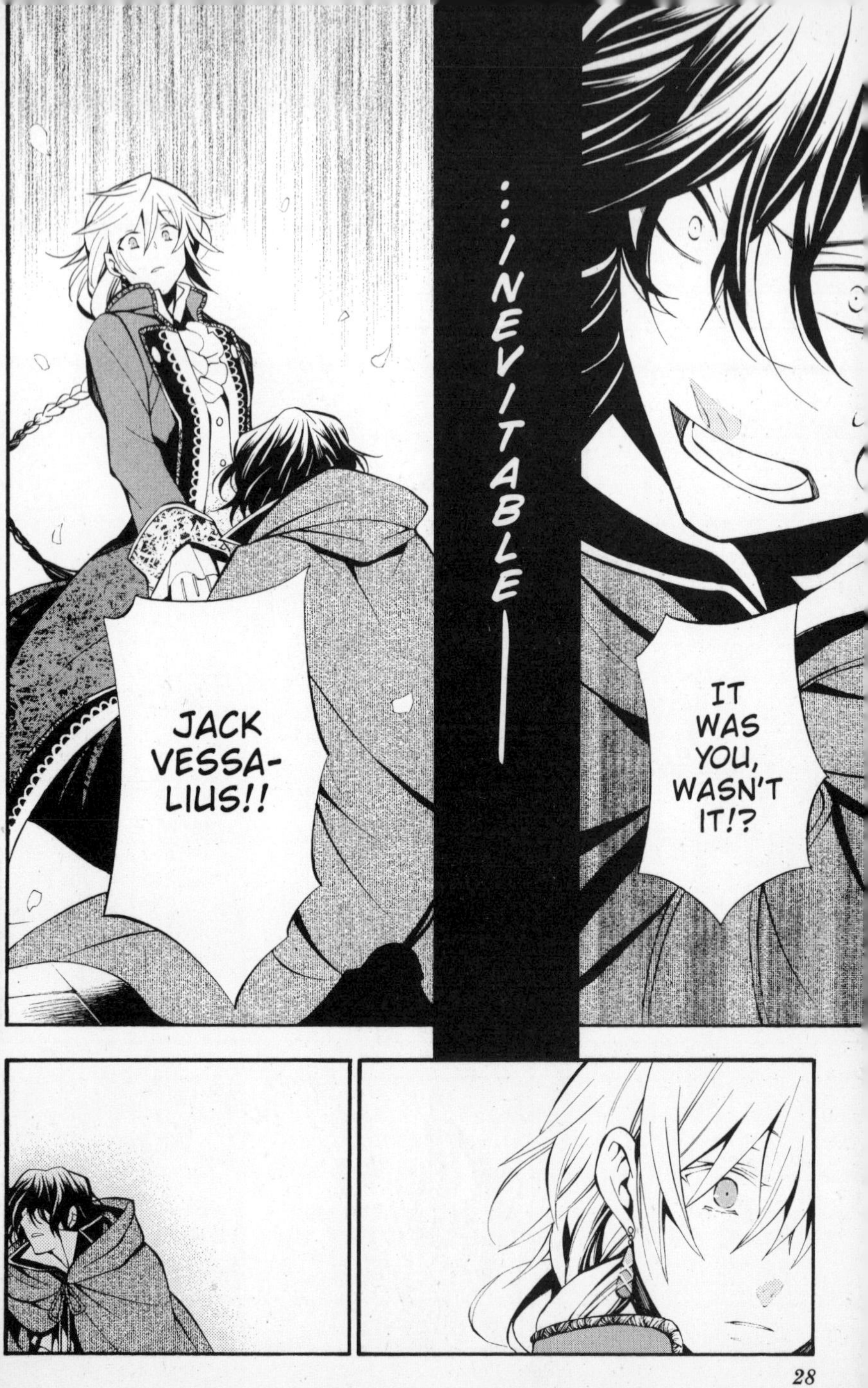
IT WAS YOU, WASN'T IT!?
...INEVITABLE—
JACK VESSALIUS!!

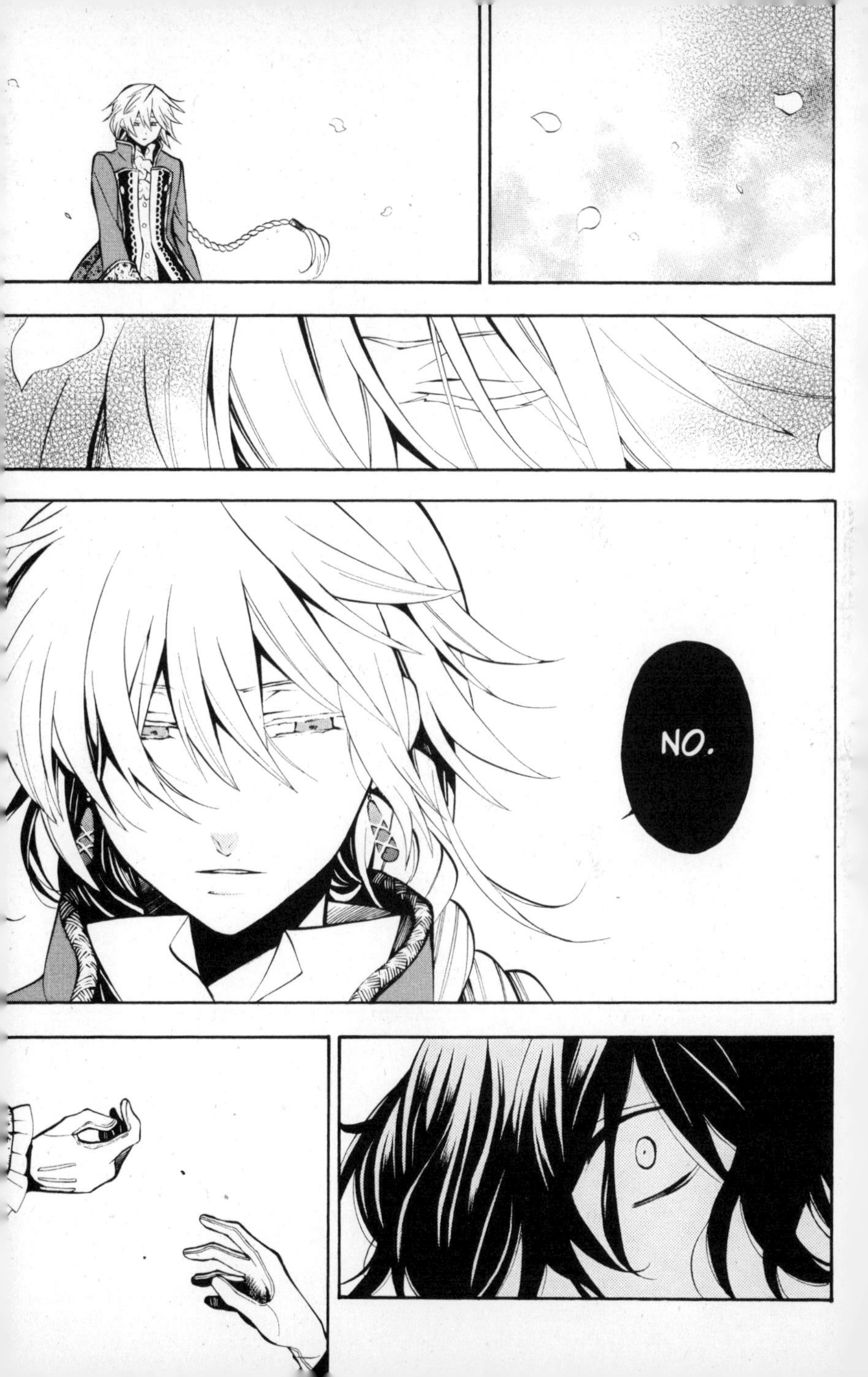
NO.

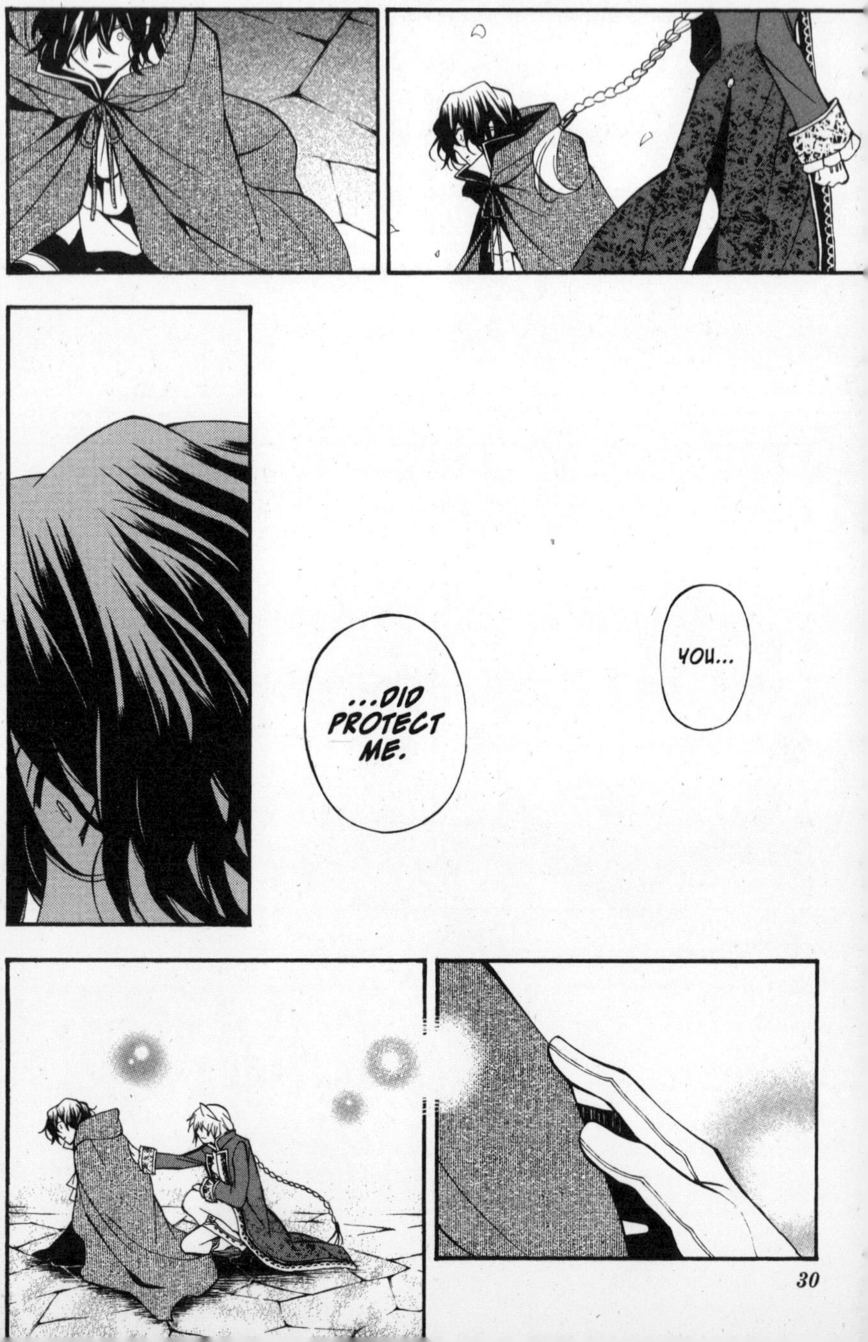
YOU...
...DID PROTECT ME.

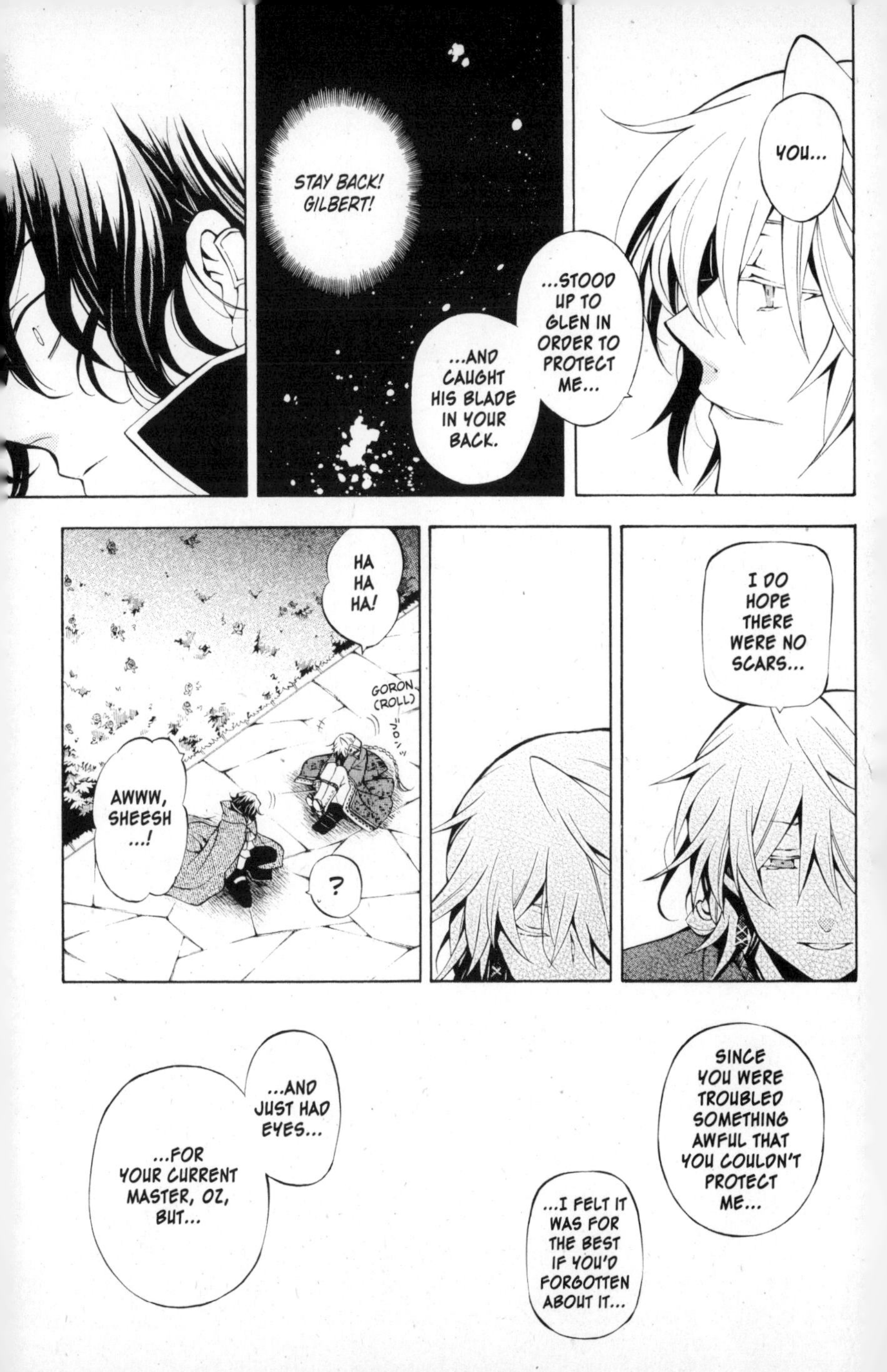
YOU...
...STOOD UP TO GLEN IN ORDER TO PROTECT ME...
...AND CAUGHT HIS BLADE IN YOUR BACK.
STAY BACK! GILBERT!
I DO HOPE THERE WERE NO SCARS...
HA HA HA!
GORON (ROLL)
AWWW, SHEESH ...!
?
SINCE YOU WERE TROUBLED SOMETHING AWFUL THAT YOU COULDN'T PROTECT ME...
...I FELT IT WAS FOR THE BEST IF YOU'D FORGOTTEN ABOUT IT...
...AND JUST HAD EYES...
...FOR YOUR CURRENT MASTER, OZ, BUT...

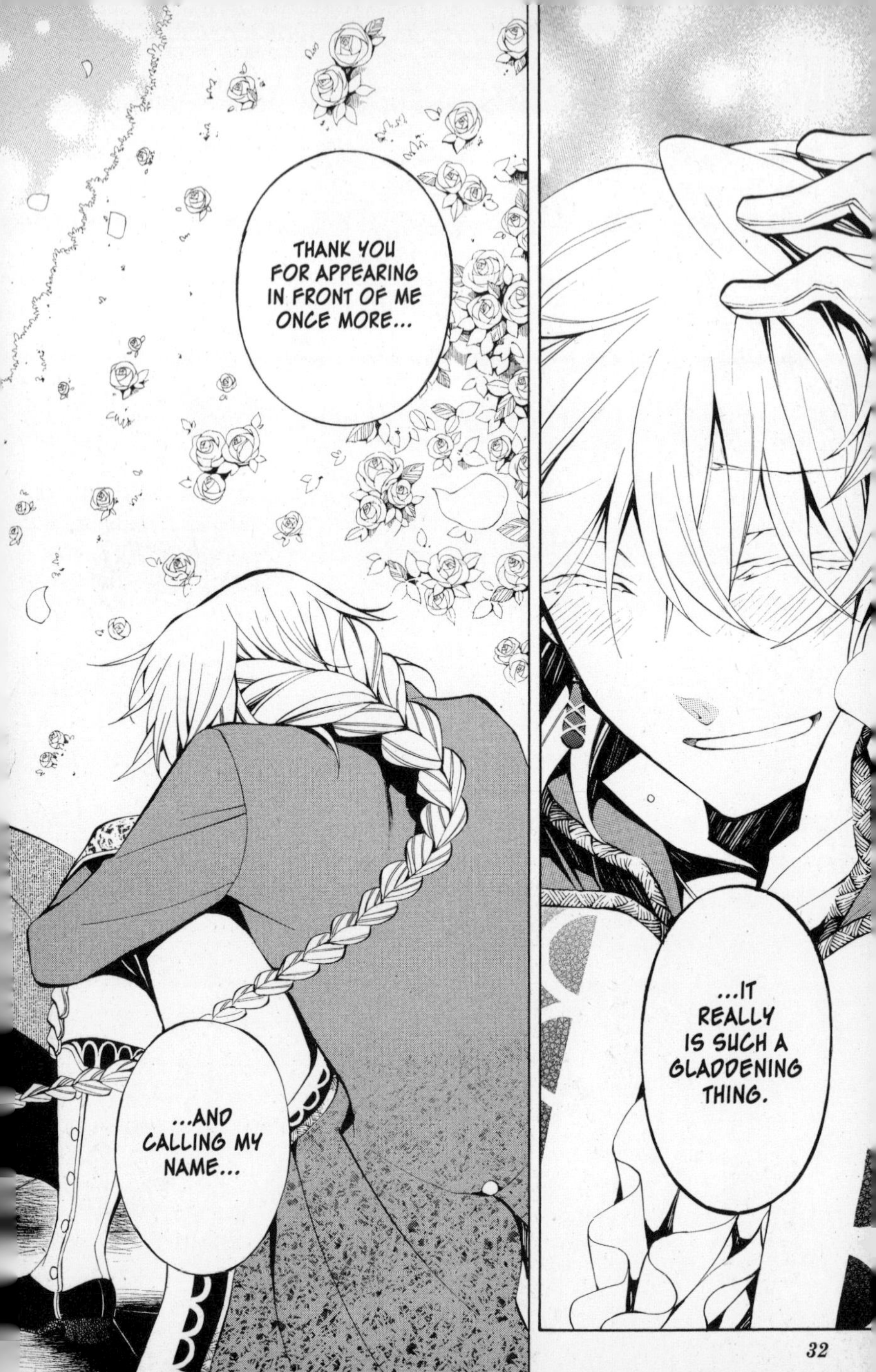
...IT REALLY IS SUCH A GLADDENING THING.
THANK YOU FOR APPEARING IN FRONT OF ME ONCE MORE...
...AND CALLING MY NAME...

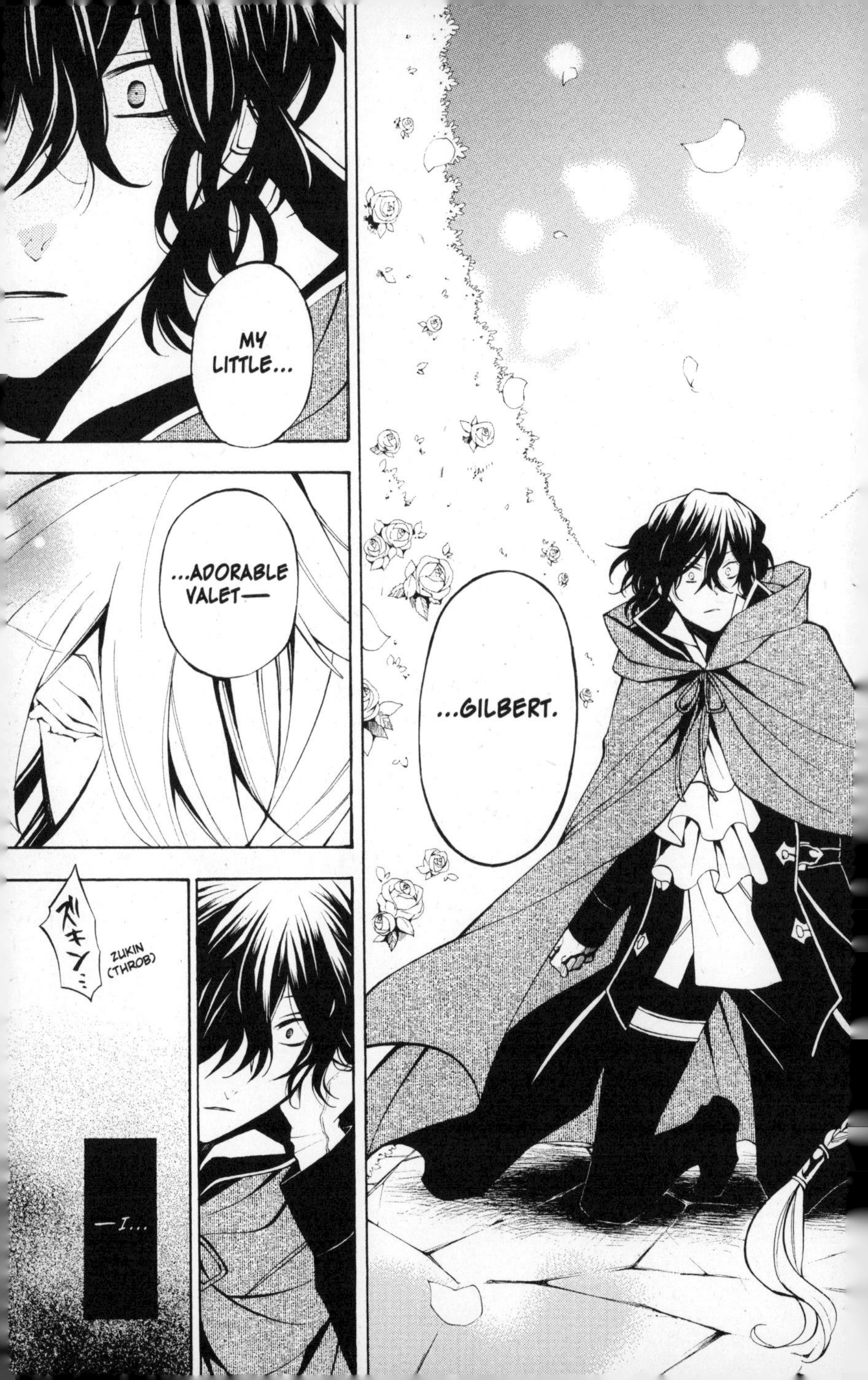
...GILBERT.
MY LITTLE...
...ADORABLE VALET—
ズキン
ZUKIN (THROB)
—I...

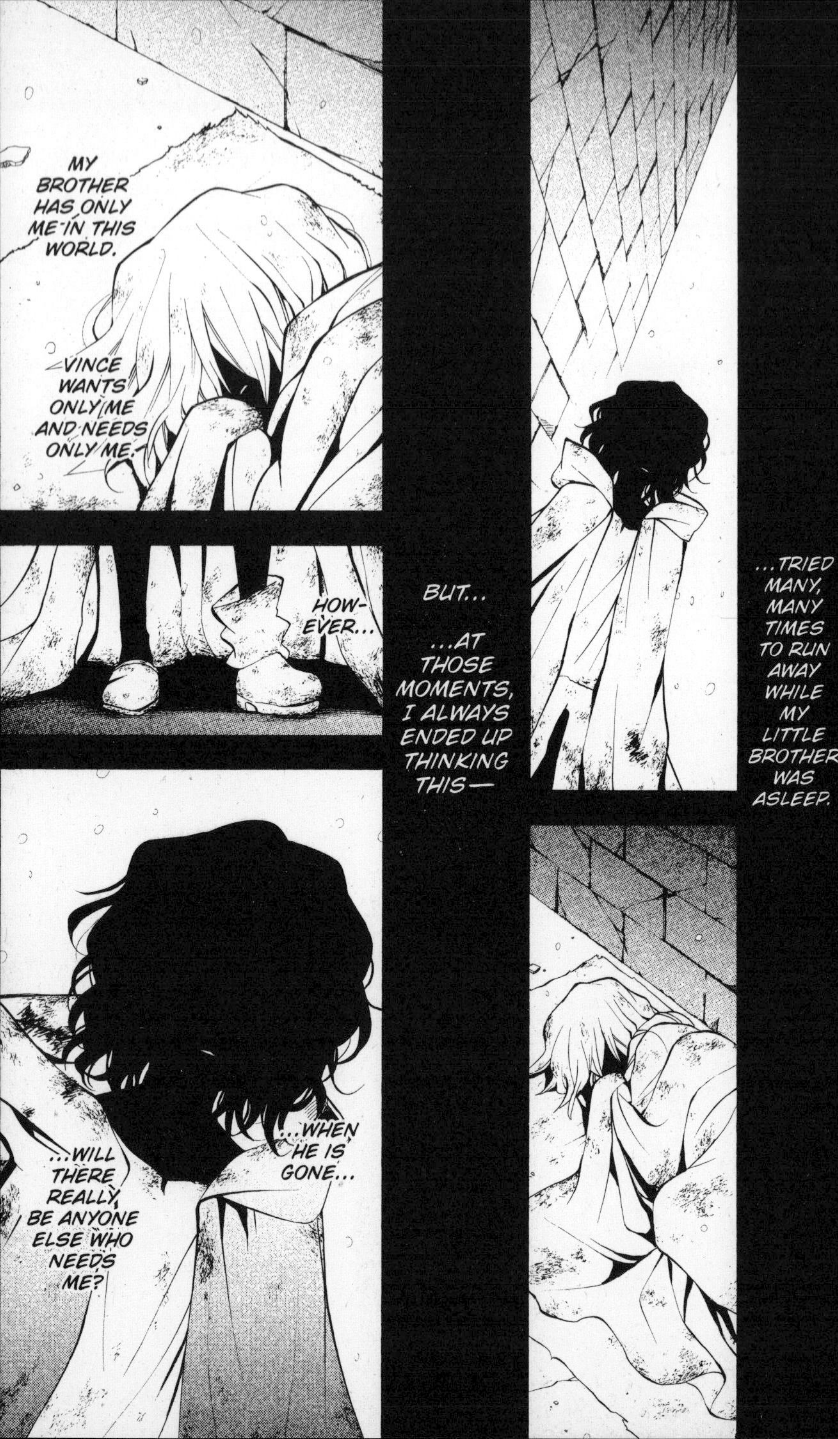

...TRIED MANY, MANY TIMES TO RUN AWAY WHILE MY LITTLE BROTHER WAS ASLEEP.
BUT...
...AT THOSE MOMENTS, I ALWAYS ENDED UP THINKING THIS—
MY BROTHER HAS ONLY ME IN THIS WORLD.
—VINCE WANTS ONLY ME AND NEEDS ONLY ME.
HOW-EVER...
...WHEN HE IS GONE...
...WILL THERE REALLY BE ANYONE ELSE WHO NEEDS ME?

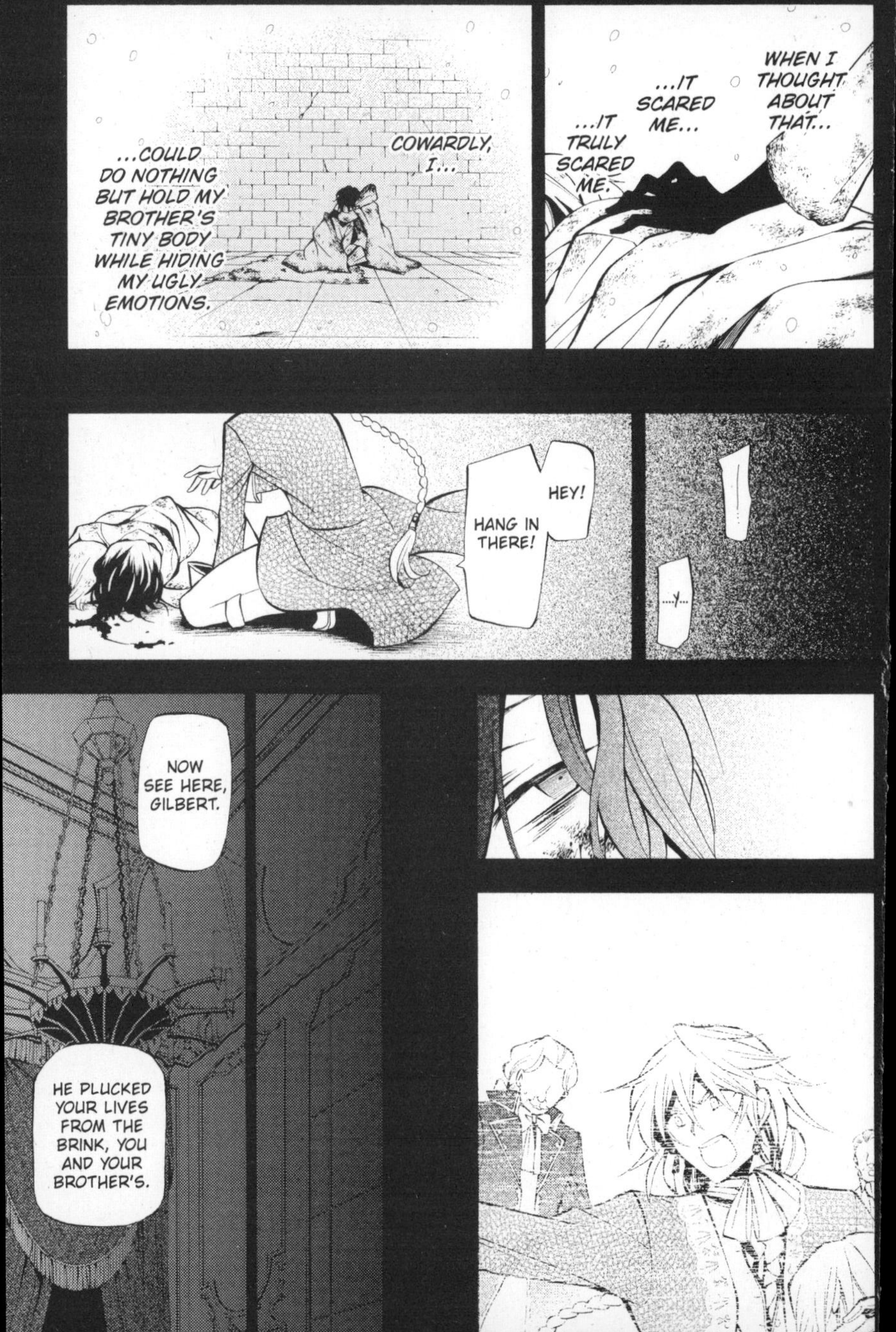
WHEN I THOUGHT ABOUT THAT...
...IT SCARED ME...
...IT TRULY SCARED ME.
COWARDLY, I...
...COULD DO NOTHING BUT HOLD MY BROTHER'S TINY BODY WHILE HIDING MY UGLY EMOTIONS.
!
...y...
HEY!
HANG IN THERE!
NOW SEE HERE, GILBERT.
HE PLUCKED YOUR LIVES FROM THE BRINK, YOU AND YOUR BROTHER'S.

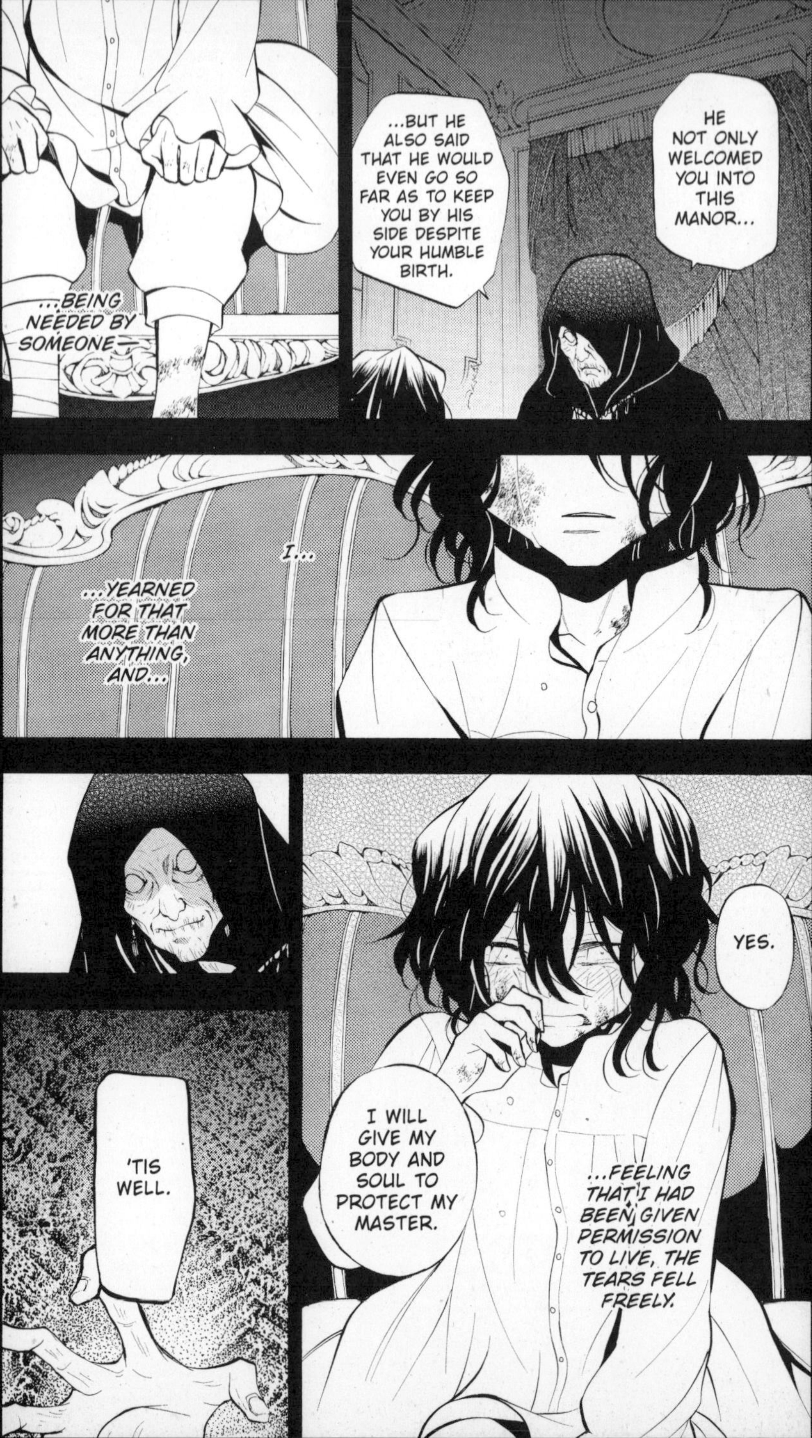
HE NOT ONLY WELCOMED YOU INTO THIS MANOR...
...BUT HE ALSO SAID THAT HE WOULD EVEN GO SO FAR AS TO KEEP YOU BY HIS SIDE DESPITE YOUR HUMBLE BIRTH.
...BEING NEEDED BY SOMEONE—
I...
...YEARNED FOR THAT MORE THAN ANYTHING, AND...
YES.
...FEELING THAT I HAD BEEN GIVEN PERMISSION TO LIVE, THE TEARS FELL FREELY.
I WILL GIVE MY BODY AND SOUL TO PROTECT MY MASTER.
'TIS WELL.

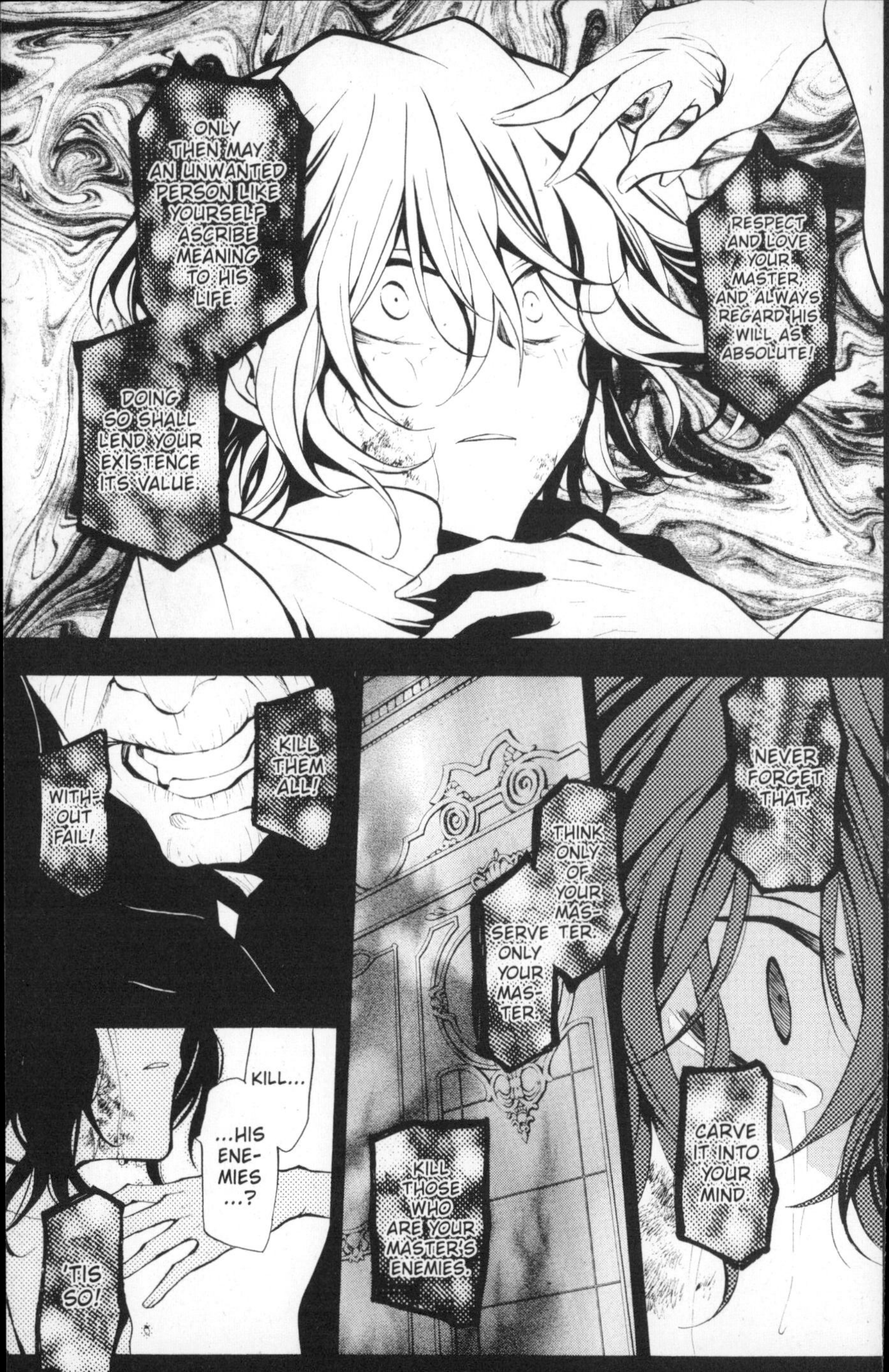
RESPECT AND LOVE YOUR MASTER, AND ALWAYS REGARD HIS WILL AS ABSOLUTE!
ONLY THEN MAY AN UNWANTED PERSON LIKE YOURSELF ASCRIBE MEANING TO HIS LIFE.
DOING SO SHALL LEND YOUR EXISTENCE ITS VALUE.
NEVER FORGET THAT.
THINK ONLY OF YOUR MASTER.
SERVE ONLY YOUR MASTER.
CARVE IT INTO YOUR MIND.
KILL THOSE WHO ARE YOUR MASTER'S ENEMIES.
KILL THEM ALL!
WITHOUT FAIL!
KILL...
...HIS ENEMIES...?
'TIS SO!

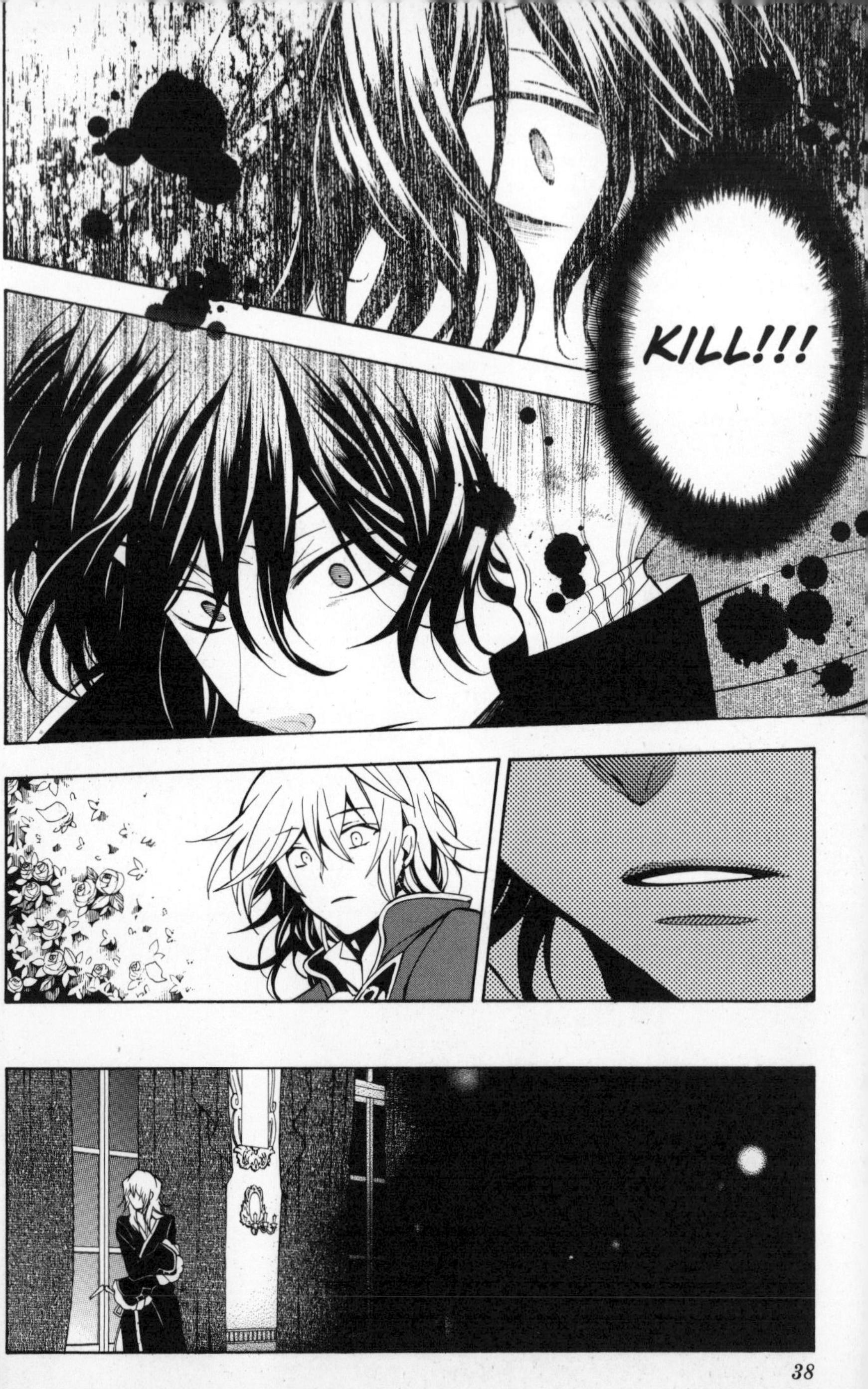
KILL!!!

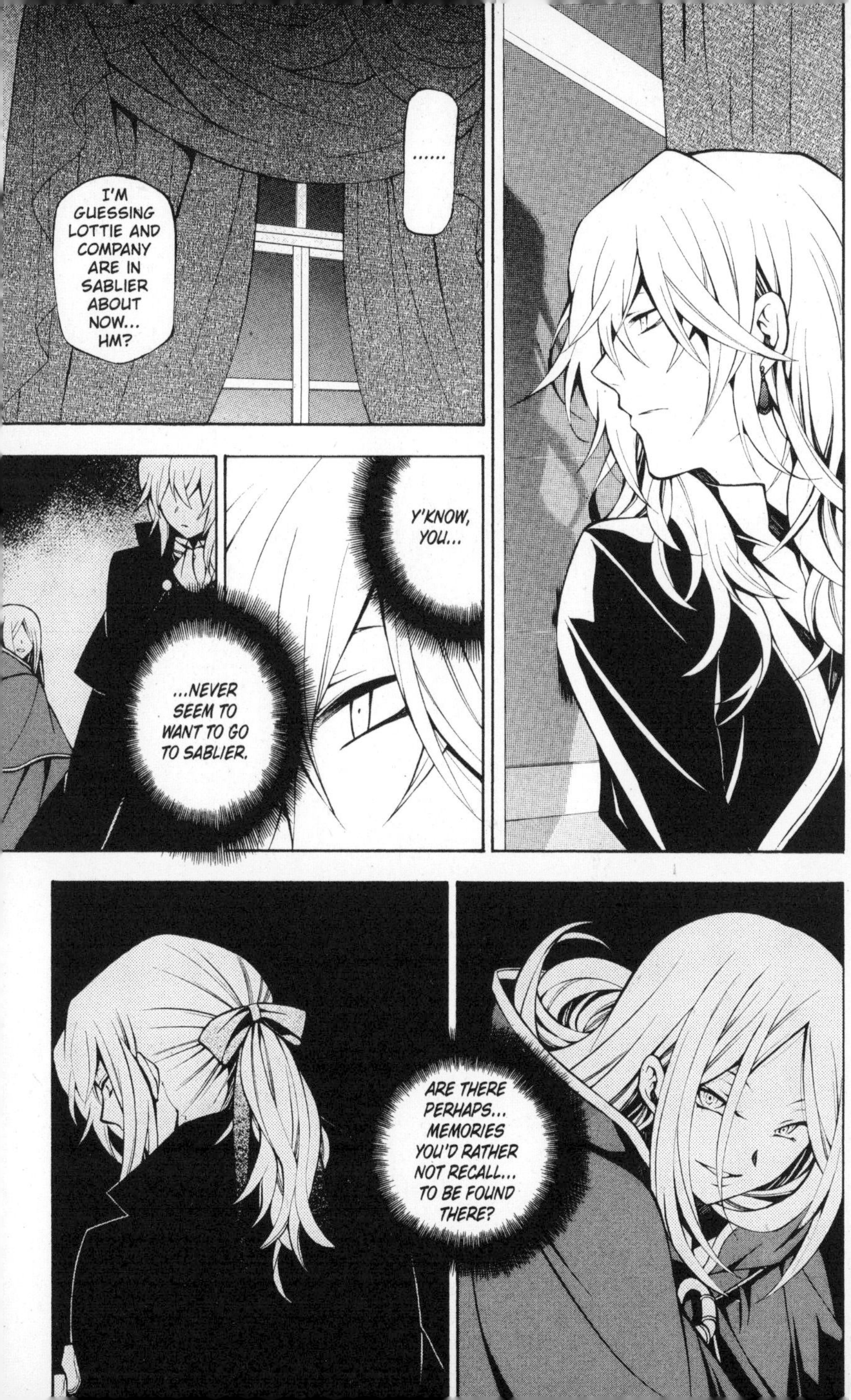
......
I'M GUESSING LOTTIE AND COMPANY ARE IN SABLIER ABOUT NOW... HM?
Y'KNOW, YOU...
...NEVER SEEM TO WANT TO GO TO SABLIER.
ARE THERE PERHAPS... MEMORIES YOU'D RATHER NOT RECALL... TO BE FOUND THERE?

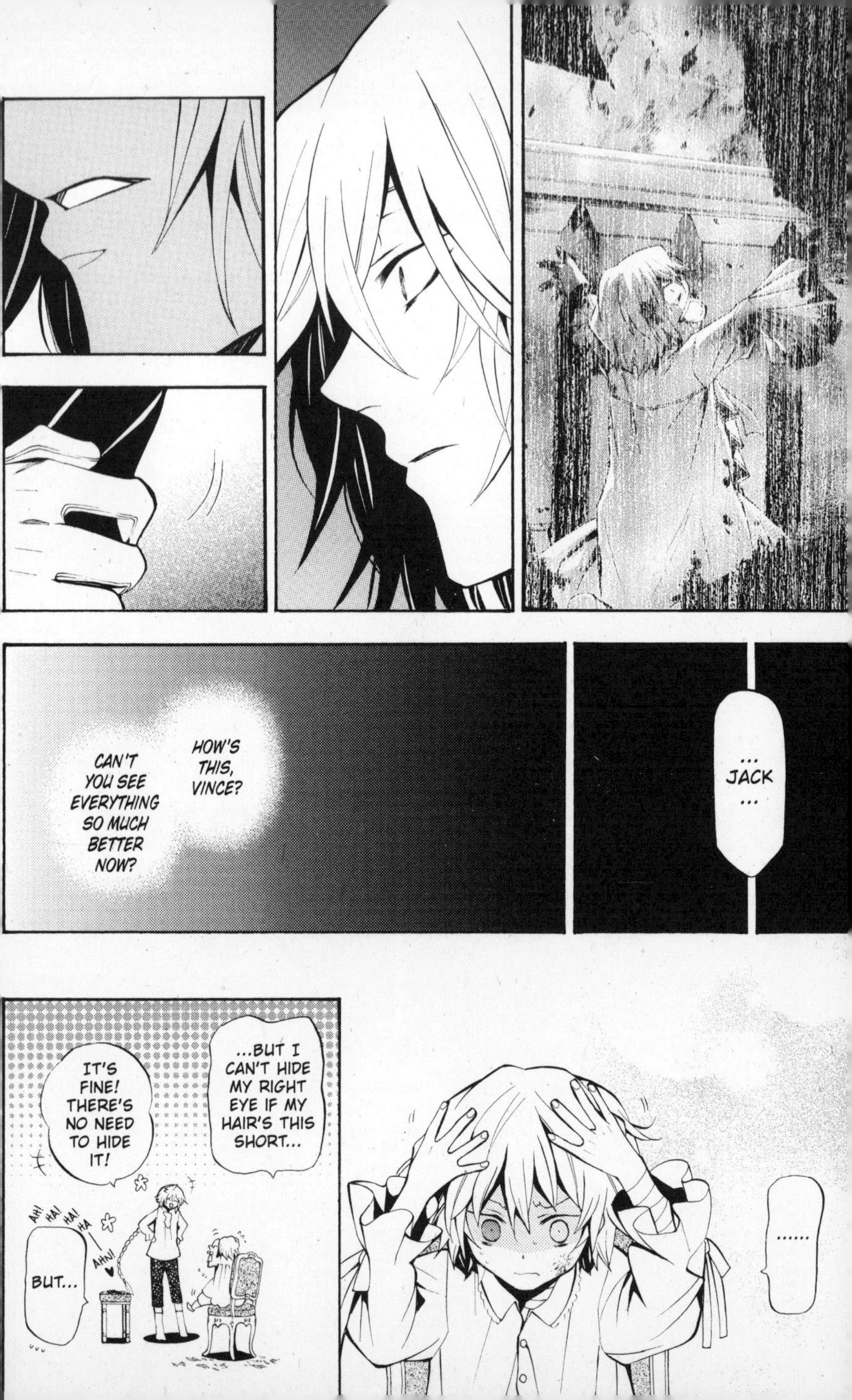
...JACK...
HOW'S THIS, VINCE?
CAN'T YOU SEE EVERYTHING SO MUCH BETTER NOW?
......
...BUT I CAN'T HIDE MY RIGHT EYE IF MY HAIR'S THIS SHORT...
IT'S FINE! THERE'S NO NEED TO HIDE IT!
AH! HA! HA! HA
AHN!
BUT...

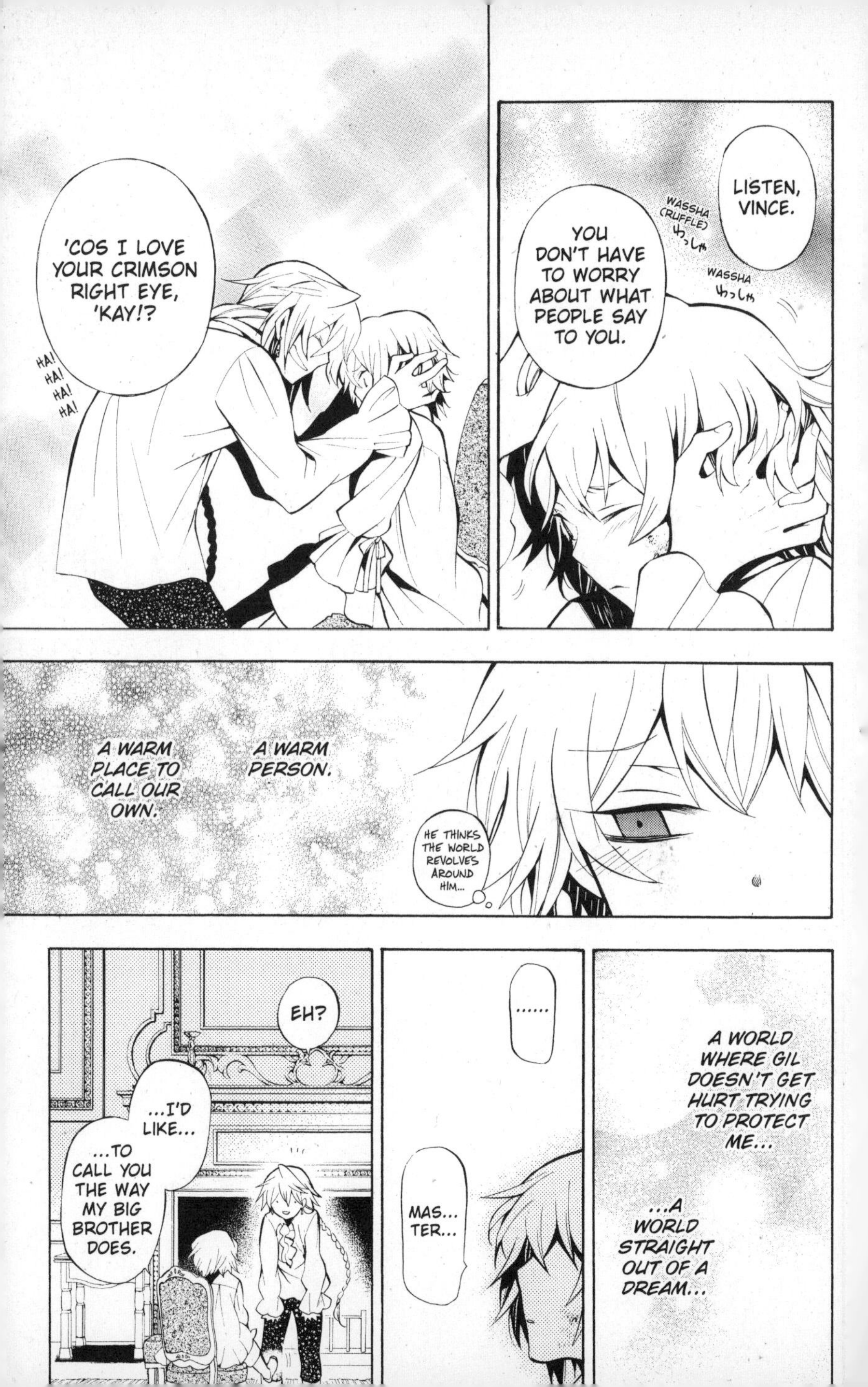
LISTEN, VINCE.
WASSHA (RUFFLE)
WASSHA
YOU DON'T HAVE TO WORRY ABOUT WHAT PEOPLE SAY TO YOU.
'COS I LOVE YOUR CRIMSON RIGHT EYE, 'KAY!?
HA! HA! HA! HA!
HE THINKS THE WORLD REVOLVES AROUND HIM...
A WARM PERSON.
A WARM PLACE TO CALL OUR OWN.
A WORLD WHERE GIL DOESN'T GET HURT TRYING TO PROTECT ME...
...A WORLD STRAIGHT OUT OF A DREAM...
......
MAS... TER...
EH?
...I'D LIKE...
...TO CALL YOU THE WAY MY BIG BROTHER DOES.

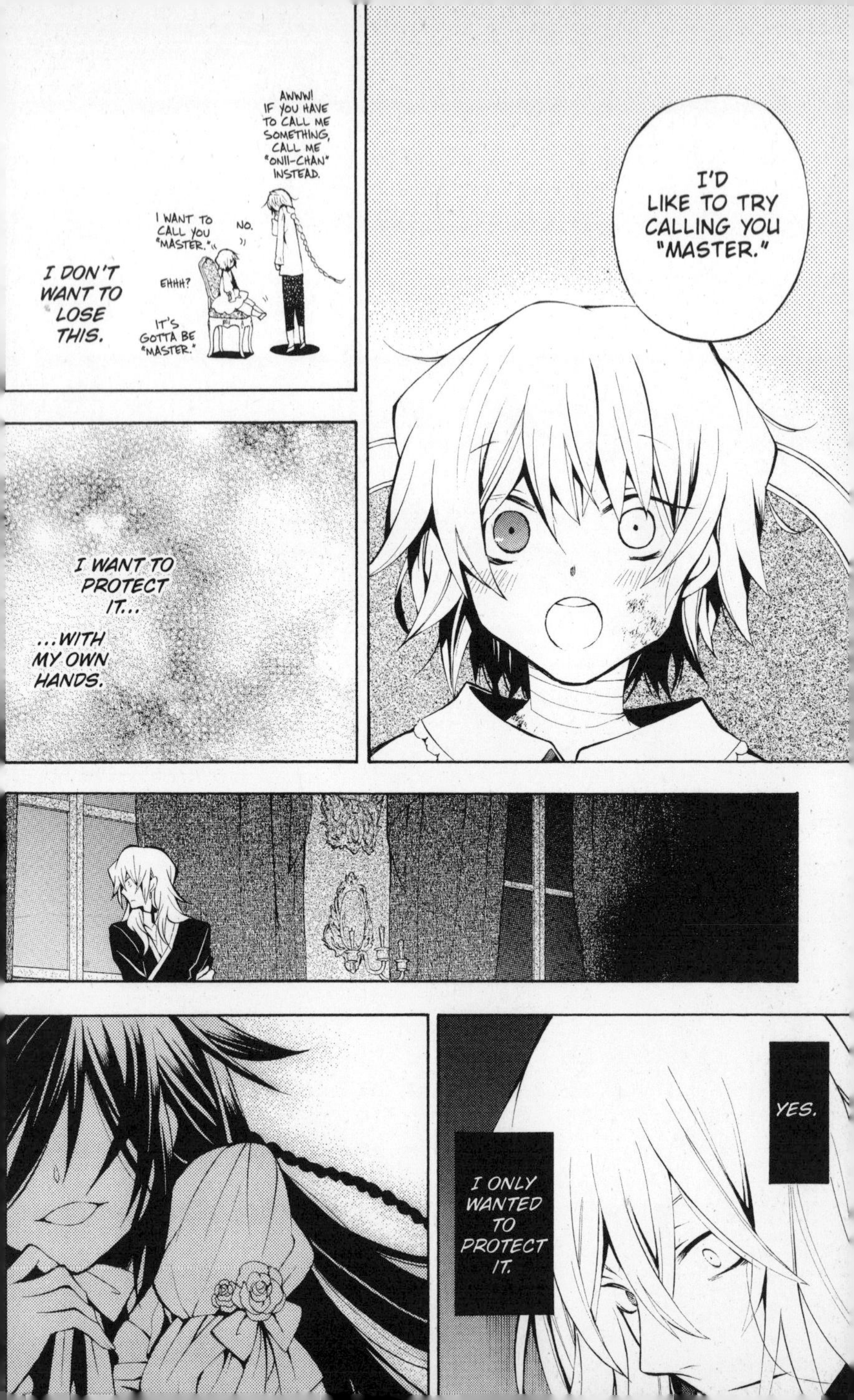
I'D LIKE TO TRY CALLING YOU "MASTER."
AWWW! IF YOU HAVE TO CALL ME SOMETHING, CALL ME "ONII-CHAN" INSTEAD.
NO.
I WANT TO CALL YOU "MASTER."
EHHH?
IT'S GOTTA BE "MASTER."
I DON'T WANT TO LOSE THIS.
I WANT TO PROTECT IT...
...WITH MY OWN HANDS.
YES.
I ONLY WANTED TO PROTECT IT.

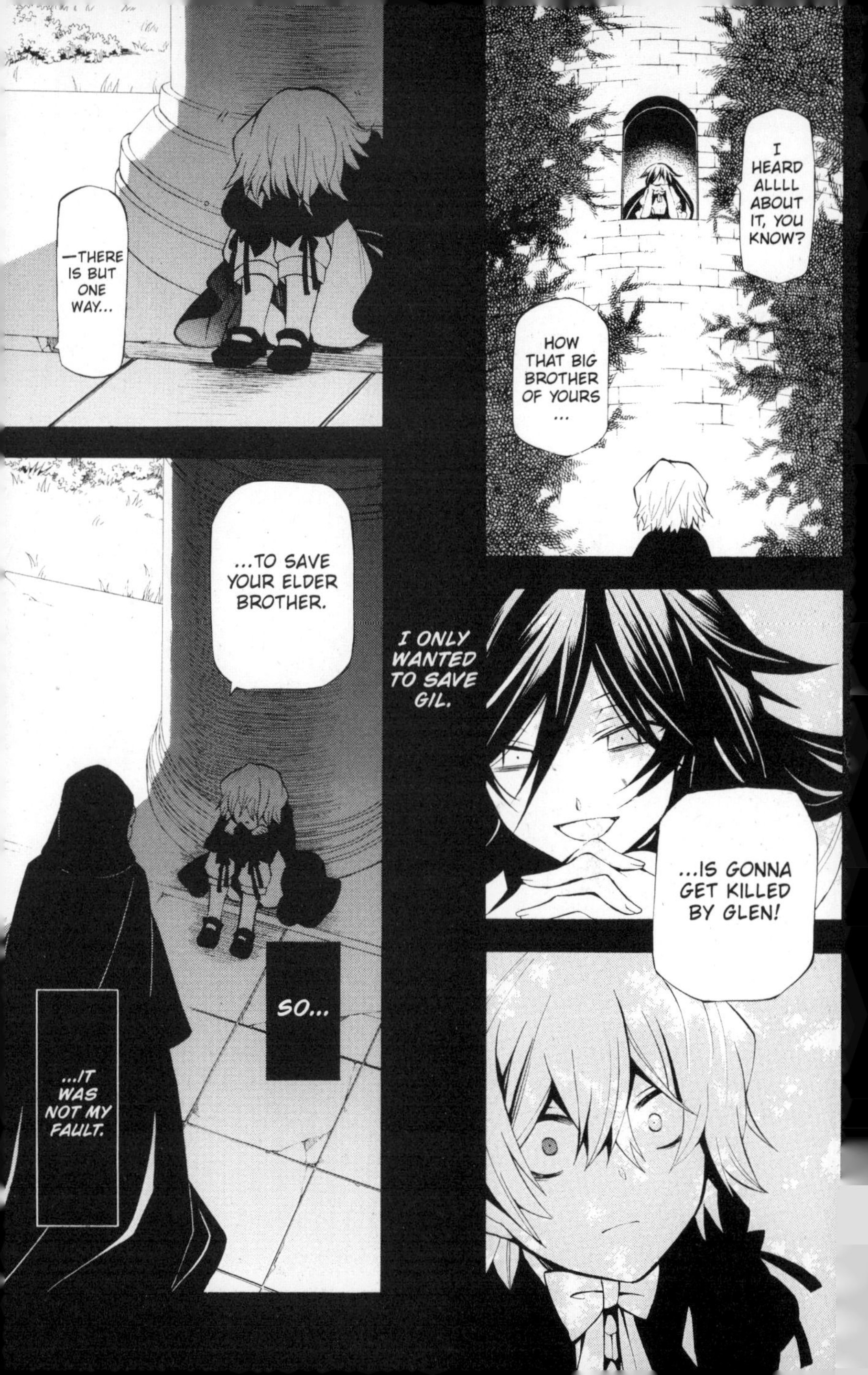
I HEARD ALLLL ABOUT IT, YOU KNOW?
HOW THAT BIG BROTHER OF YOURS ...
—THERE IS BUT ONE WAY...
...IS GONNA GET KILLED BY GLEN!
I ONLY WANTED TO SAVE GIL.
...TO SAVE YOUR ELDER BROTHER.
SO...
...IT WAS NOT MY FAULT.

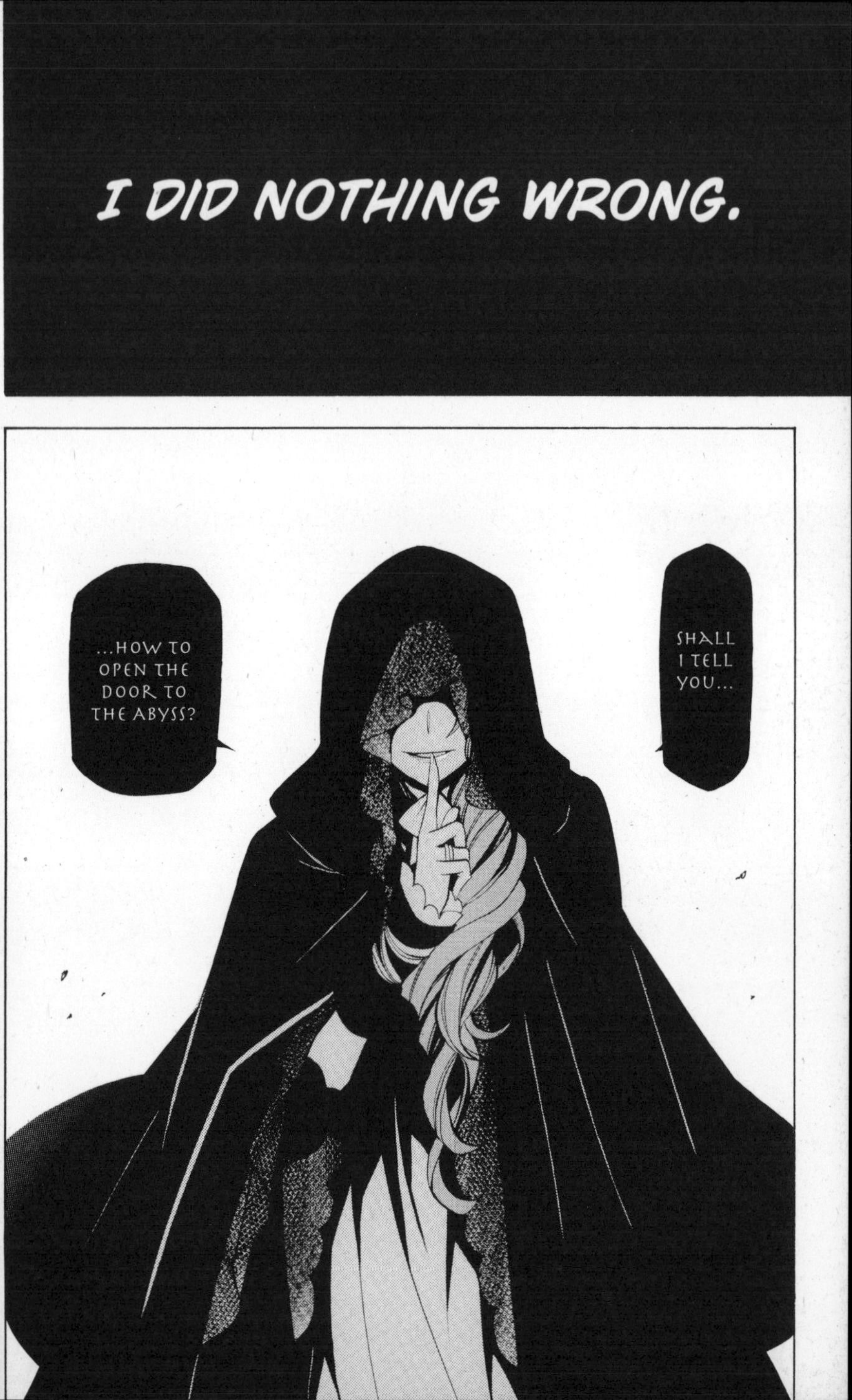
I DID NOTHING WRONG.
SHALL I TELL YOU...
...HOW TO OPEN THE DOOR TO THE ABYSS?

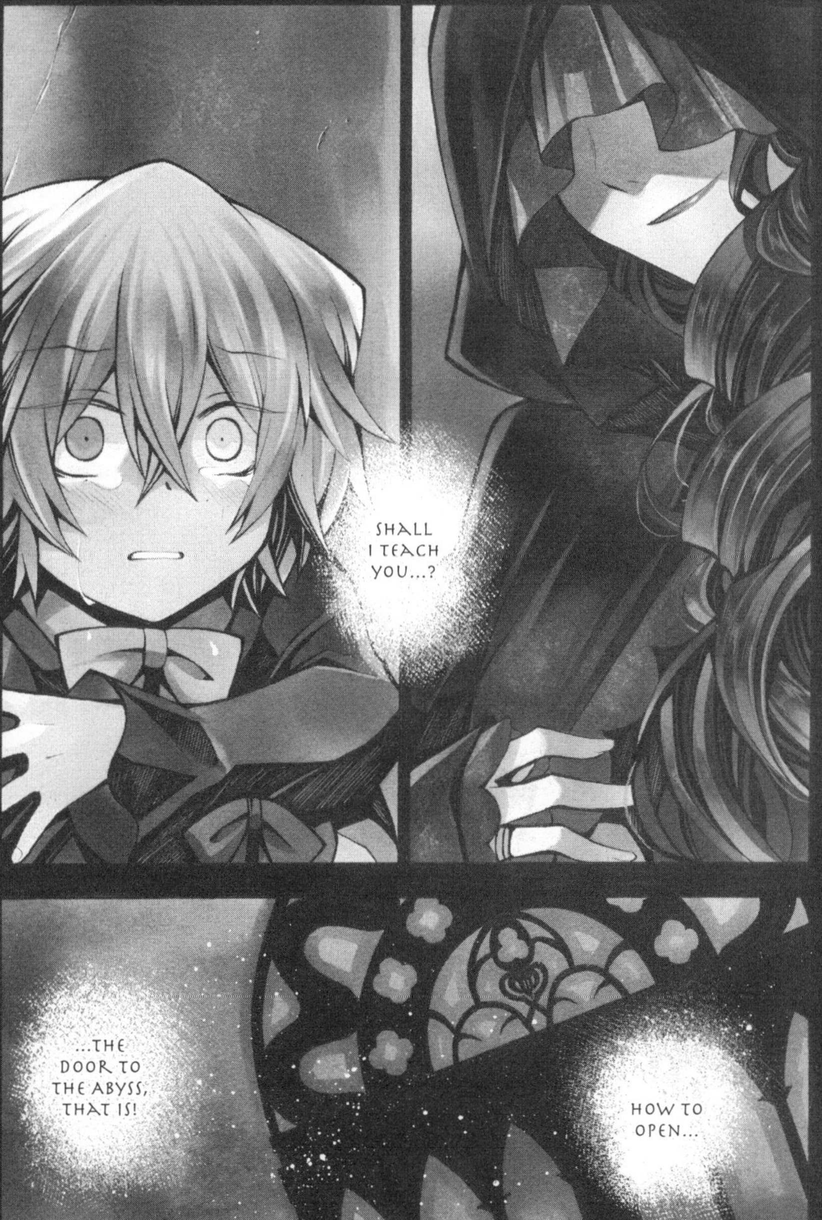
SHALL I TEACH YOU...?
HOW TO OPEN...
...THE DOOR TO THE ABYSS, THAT IS!

Retrace:XXXIX
Gate of Blackness

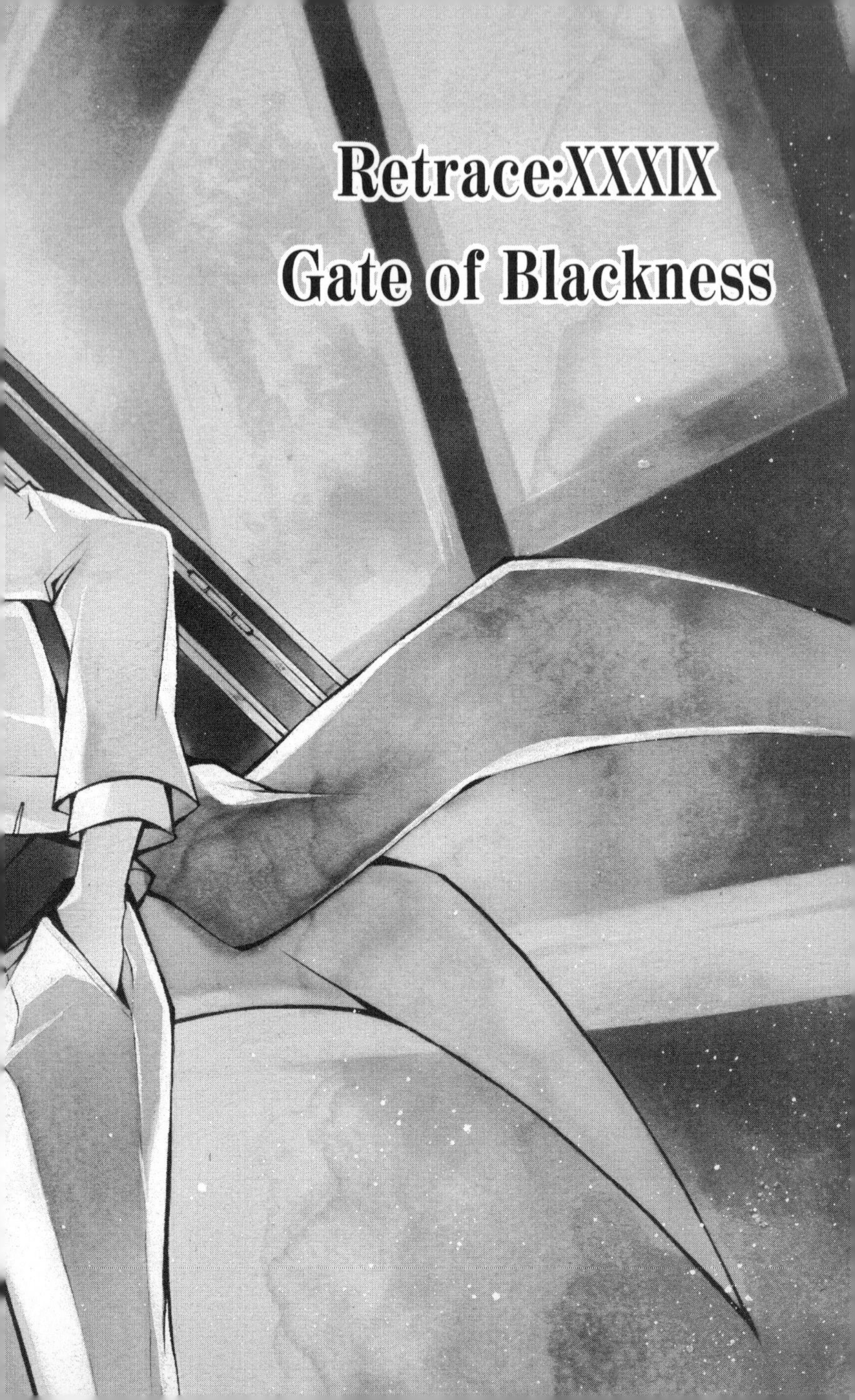

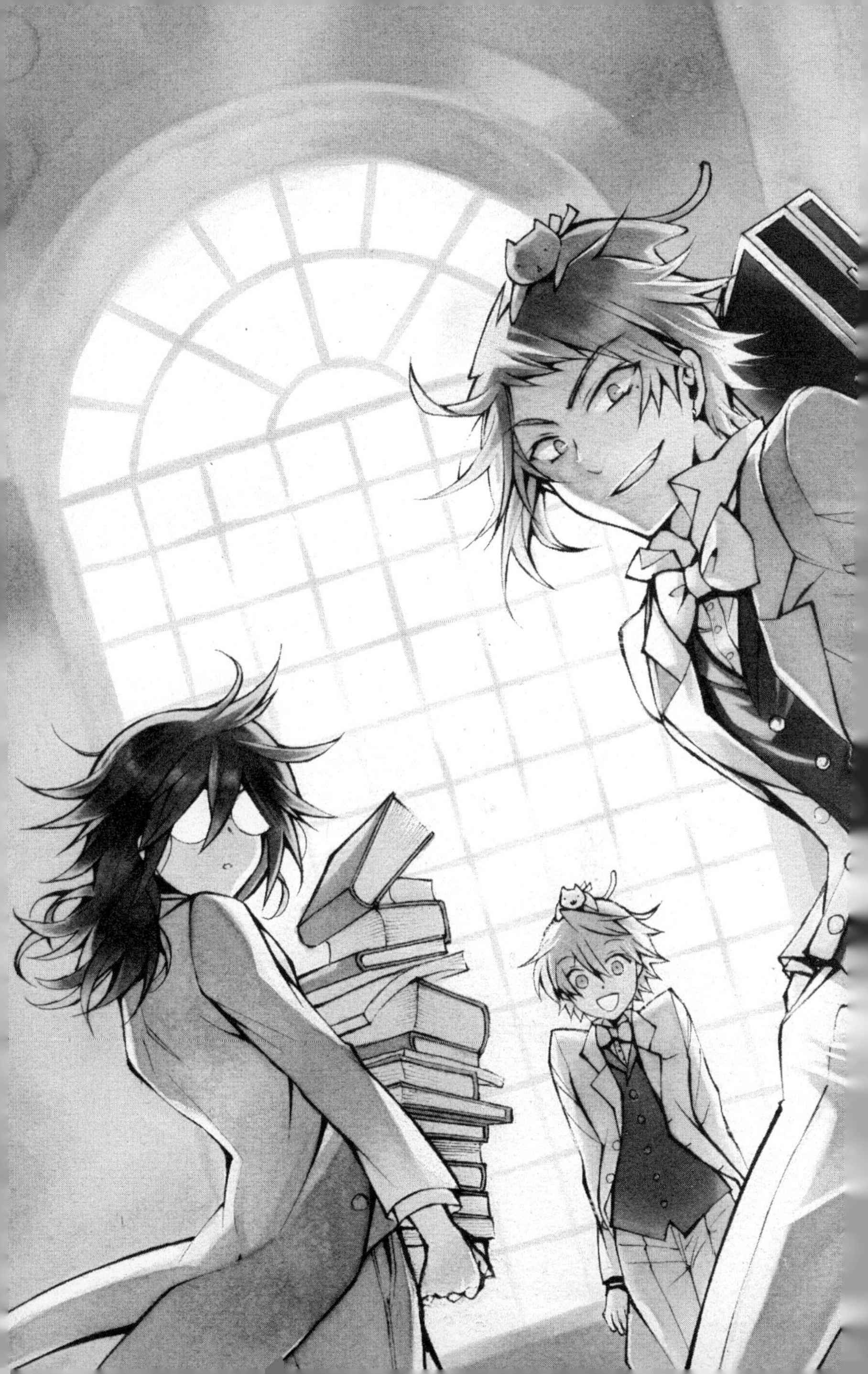

BONUS: MASTER GILBERT'S B-RABBIT OBSERVATION RECORD

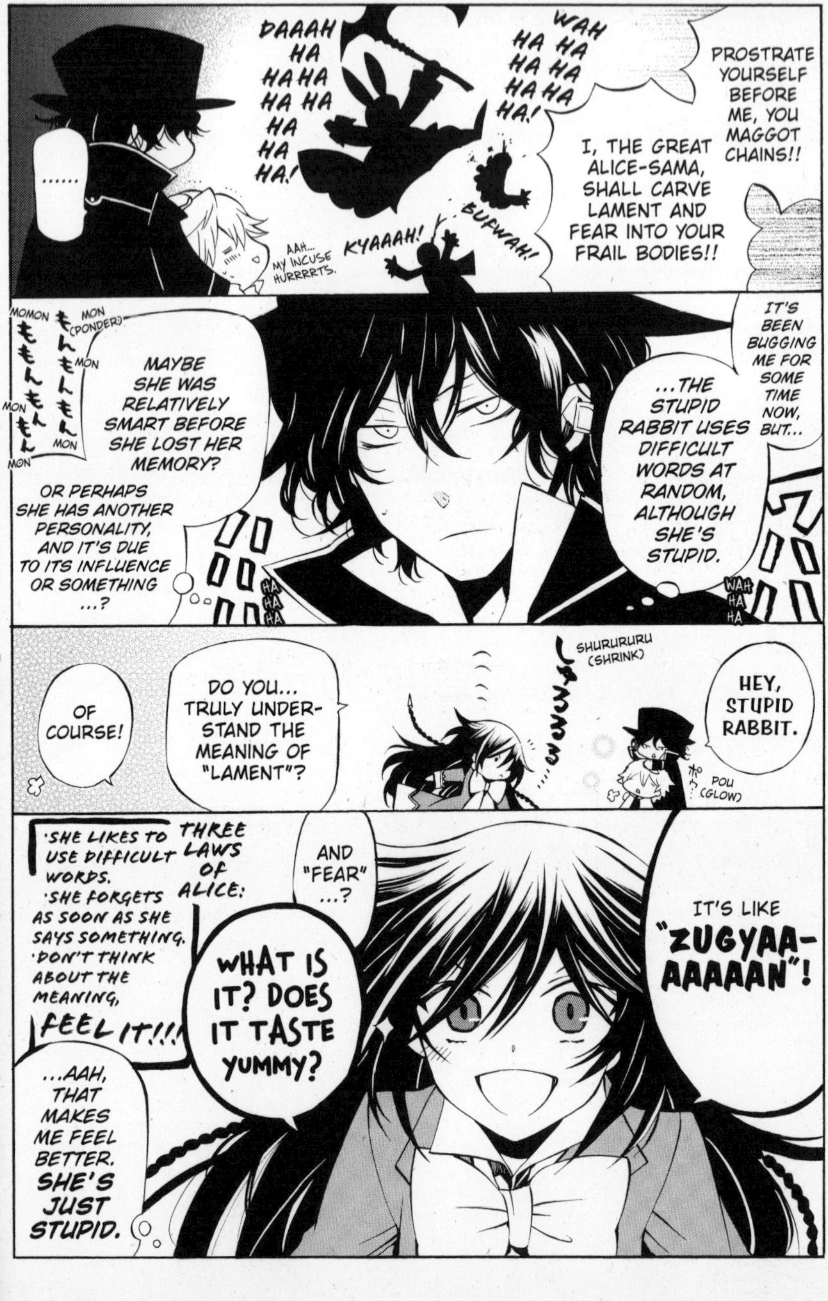
PROSTRATE YOURSELF BEFORE ME, YOU MAGGOT CHAINS!!
I, THE GREAT ALICE-SAMA, SHALL CARVE LAMENT AND FEAR INTO YOUR FRAIL BODIES!!
WAH HA HA HA HA HA HA HA HA HA!
BUFWAH!
DAAAH HA HA HA HA HA HA HA HA!
KYAAAH!
AAH... MY INCUSE HURRRRTS.
......
IT'S BEEN BUGGING ME FOR SOME TIME NOW, BUT...
...THE STUPID RABBIT USES DIFFICULT WORDS AT RANDOM, ALTHOUGH SHE'S STUPID.
WAH HA HA
MAYBE SHE WAS RELATIVELY SMART BEFORE SHE LOST HER MEMORY?
OR PERHAPS SHE HAS ANOTHER PERSONALITY, AND IT'S DUE TO ITS INFLUENCE OR SOMETHING ...?
MOMON MON (PONDER) MON MON MON MON
HA HA HA
HEY, STUPID RABBIT.
POU (GLOW)
SHURURURU (SHRINK)
DO YOU... TRULY UNDER-STAND THE MEANING OF "LAMENT"?
OF COURSE!
IT'S LIKE "ZUGYAA-AAAAAN"!
AND "FEAR" ...?
WHAT IS IT? DOES IT TASTE YUMMY?
THREE LAWS OF ALICE:
·SHE LIKES TO USE DIFFICULT WORDS.
·SHE FORGETS AS SOON AS SHE SAYS SOMETHING.
·DON'T THINK ABOUT THE MEANING, FEEL IT!!!
...AAH, THAT MAKES ME FEEL BETTER. SHE'S JUST STUPID.

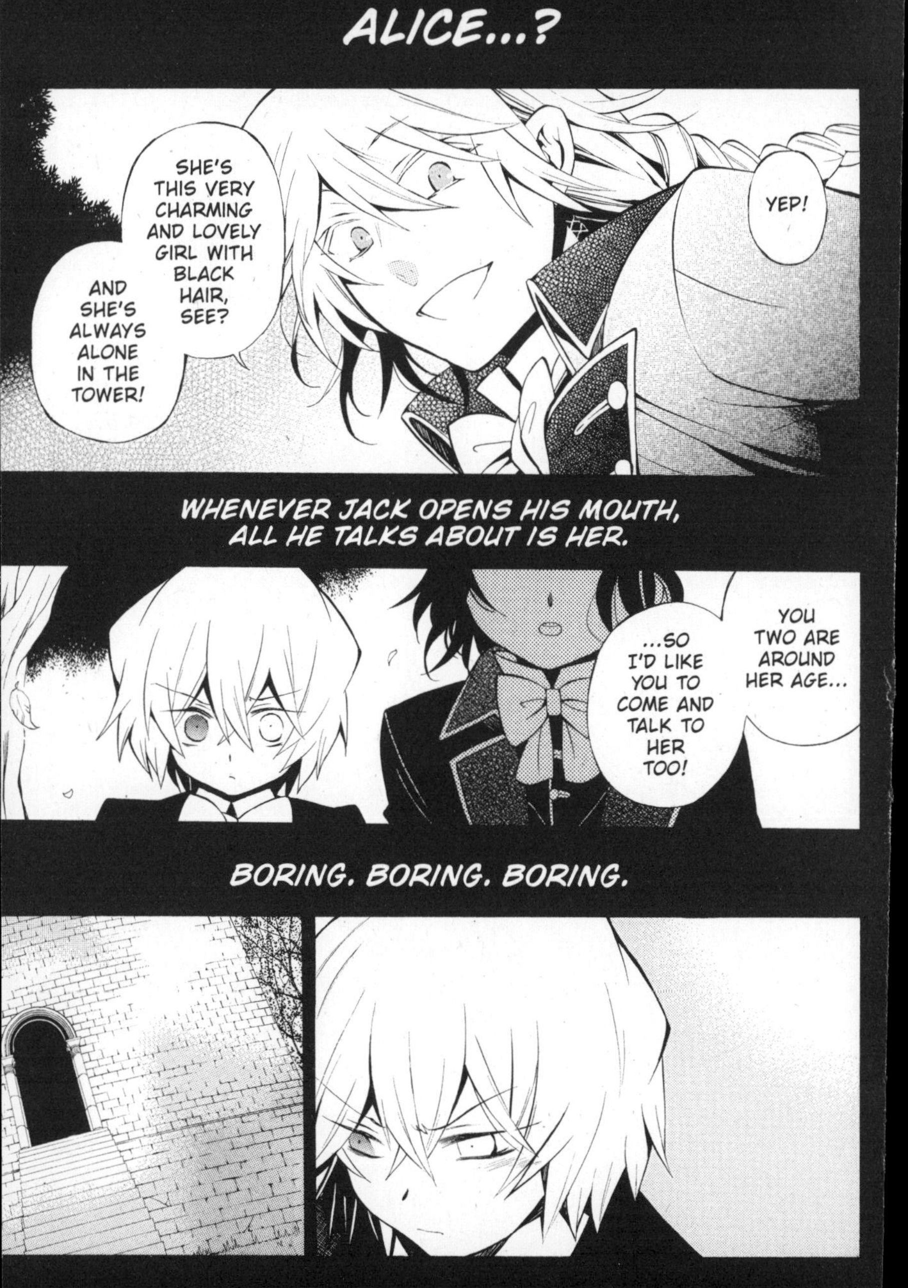
ALICE...?
YEP!
SHE'S THIS VERY CHARMING AND LOVELY GIRL WITH BLACK HAIR, SEE?
AND SHE'S ALWAYS ALONE IN THE TOWER!
WHENEVER JACK OPENS HIS MOUTH, ALL HE TALKS ABOUT IS HER.
YOU TWO ARE AROUND HER AGE...
...SO I'D LIKE YOU TO COME AND TALK TO HER TOO!
BORING. BORING. BORING.

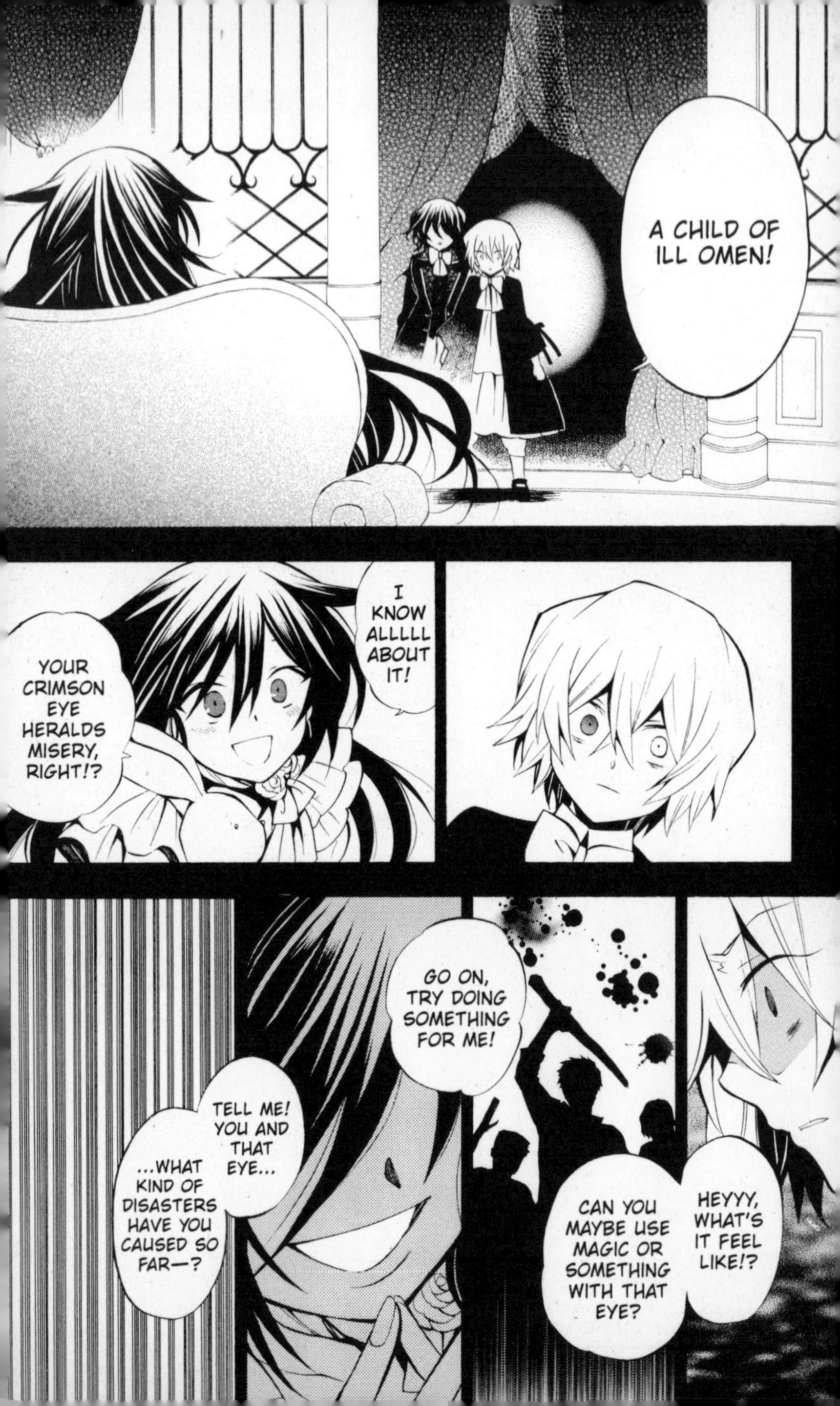
A CHILD OF ILL OMEN!
I KNOW ALLLLL ABOUT IT!
YOUR CRIMSON EYE HERALDS MISERY, RIGHT!?
HEYYY, WHAT'S IT FEEL LIKE!?
CAN YOU MAYBE USE MAGIC OR SOMETHING WITH THAT EYE?
GO ON, TRY DOING SOMETHING FOR ME!
TELL ME! YOU AND THAT EYE...
...WHAT KIND OF DISASTERS HAVE YOU CAUSED SO FAR—?

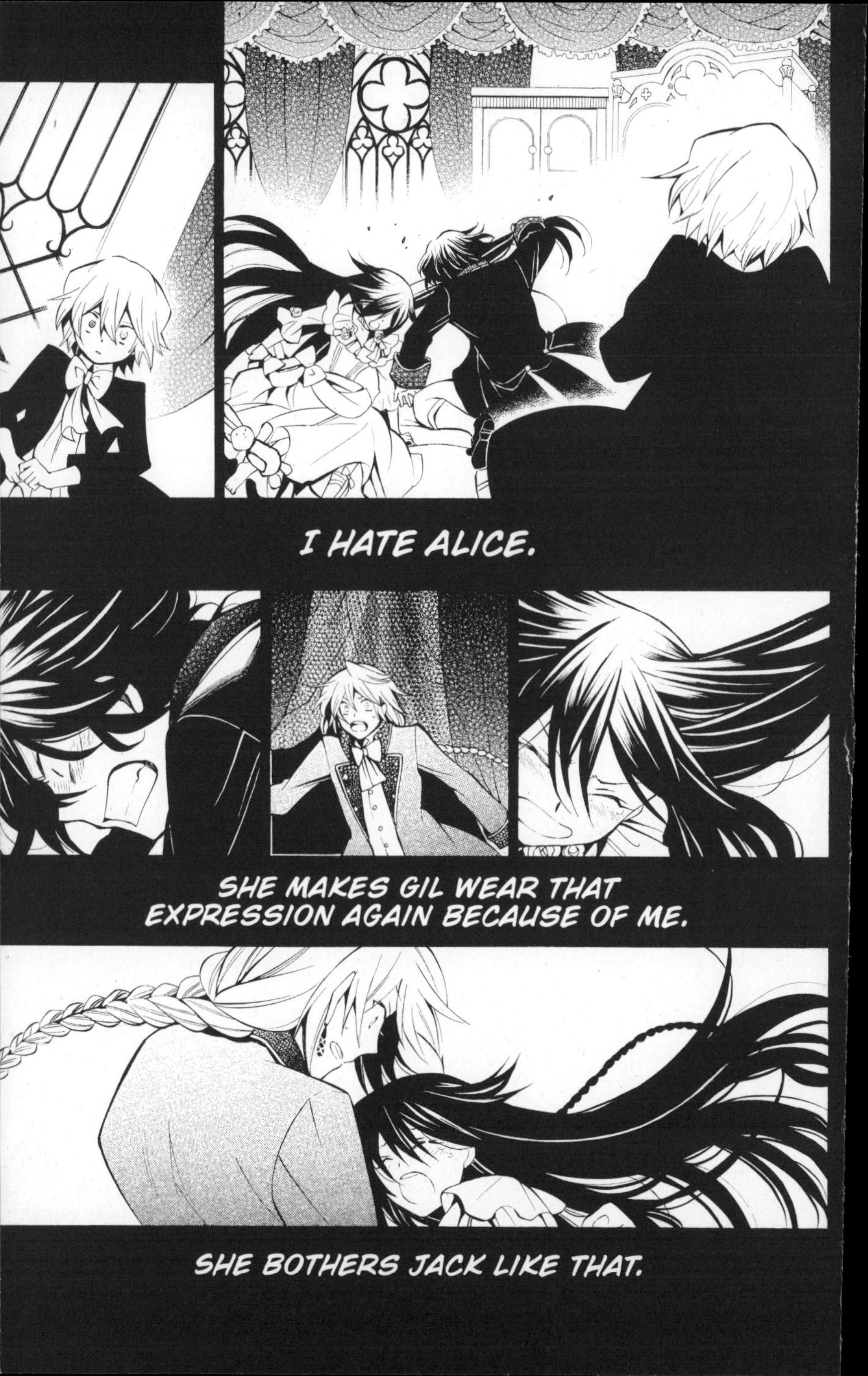
I HATE ALICE.
SHE MAKES GIL WEAR THAT EXPRESSION AGAIN BECAUSE OF ME.
SHE BOTHERS JACK LIKE THAT.

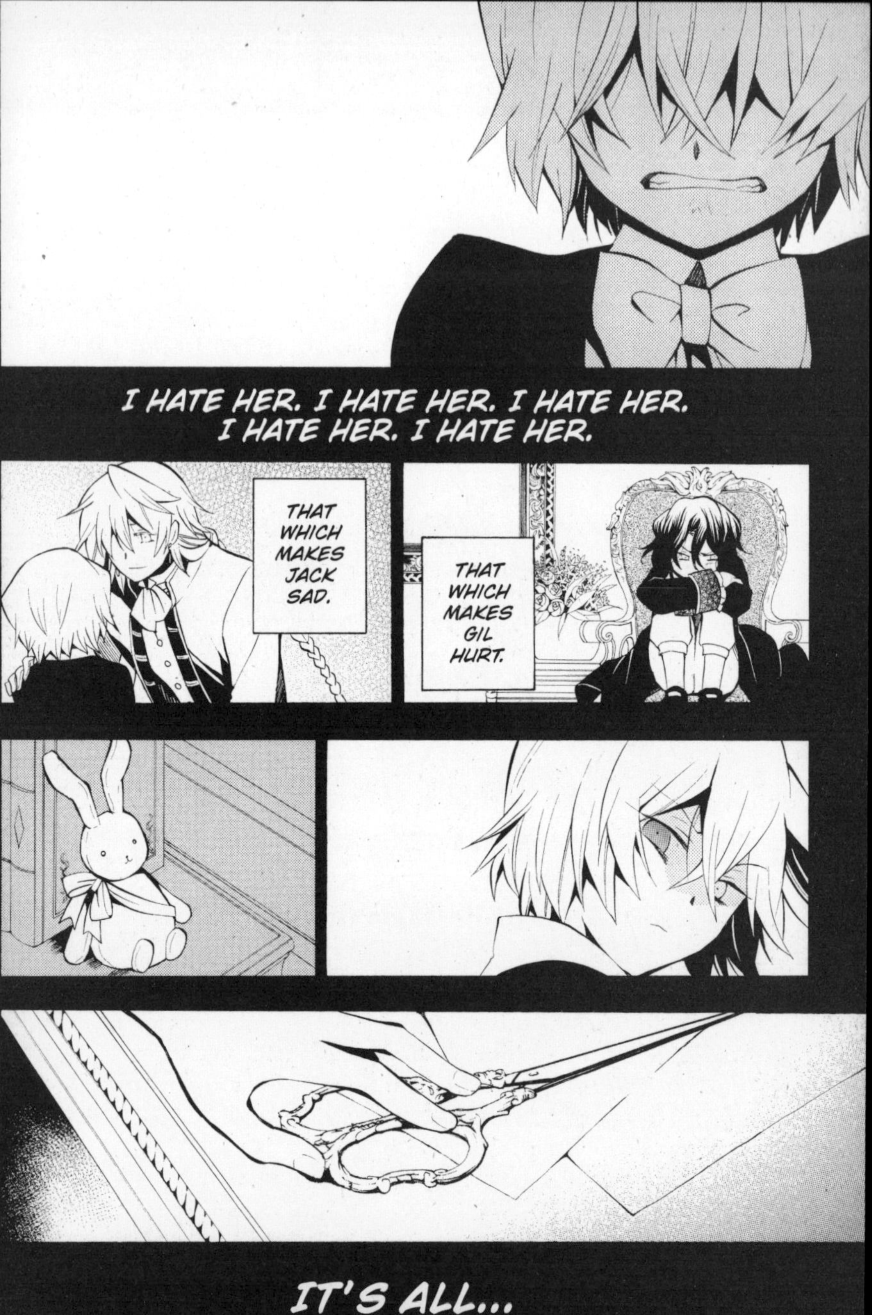
I HATE HER. I HATE HER. I HATE HER. I HATE HER. I HATE HER.
THAT WHICH MAKES GIL HURT.
THAT WHICH MAKES JACK SAD.
IT'S ALL...

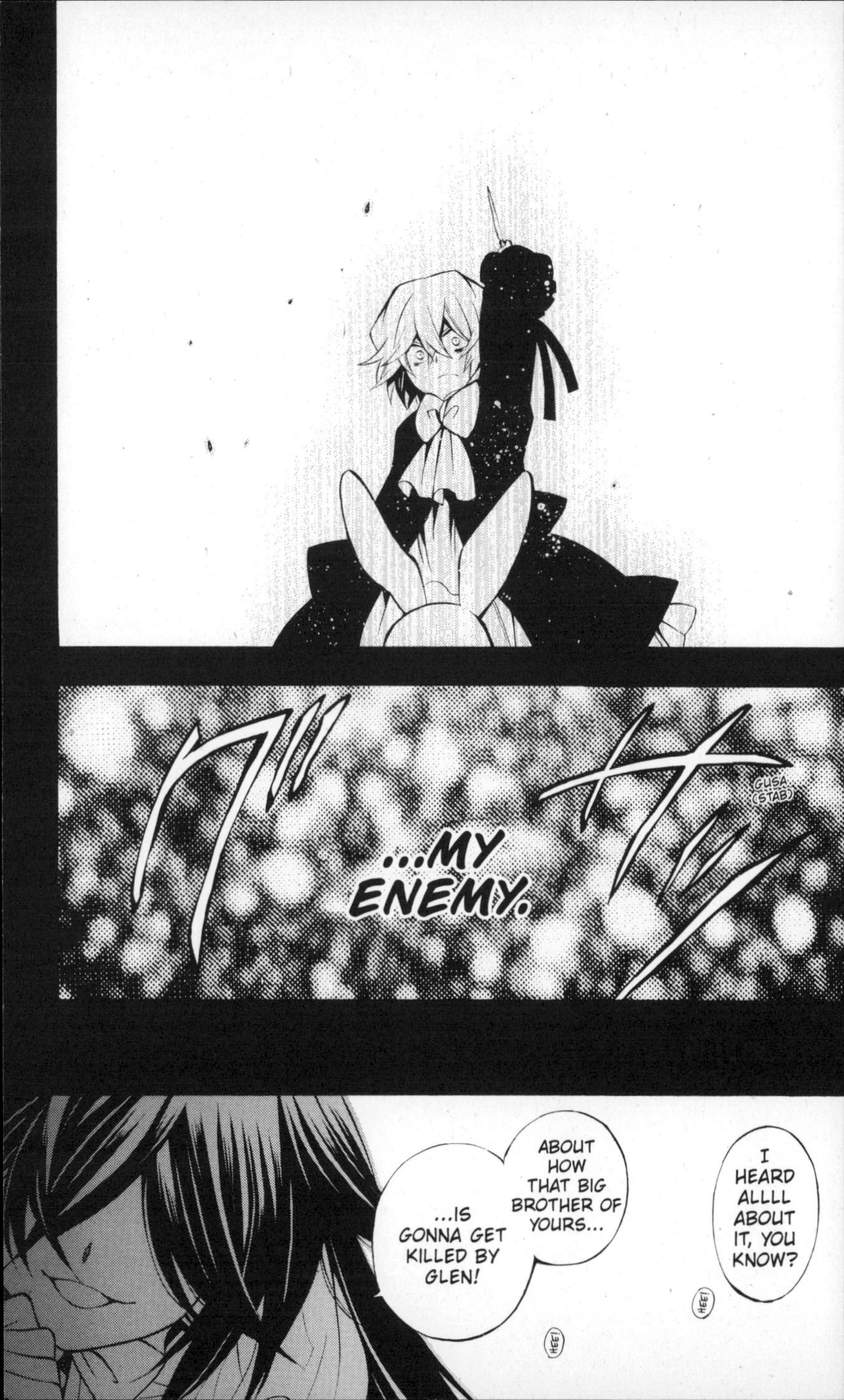
GUSA (STAB)
...MY ENEMY.
I HEARD ALLLL ABOUT IT, YOU KNOW?
HEE!
ABOUT HOW THAT BIG BROTHER OF YOURS...
...IS GONNA GET KILLED BY GLEN!
HEE!

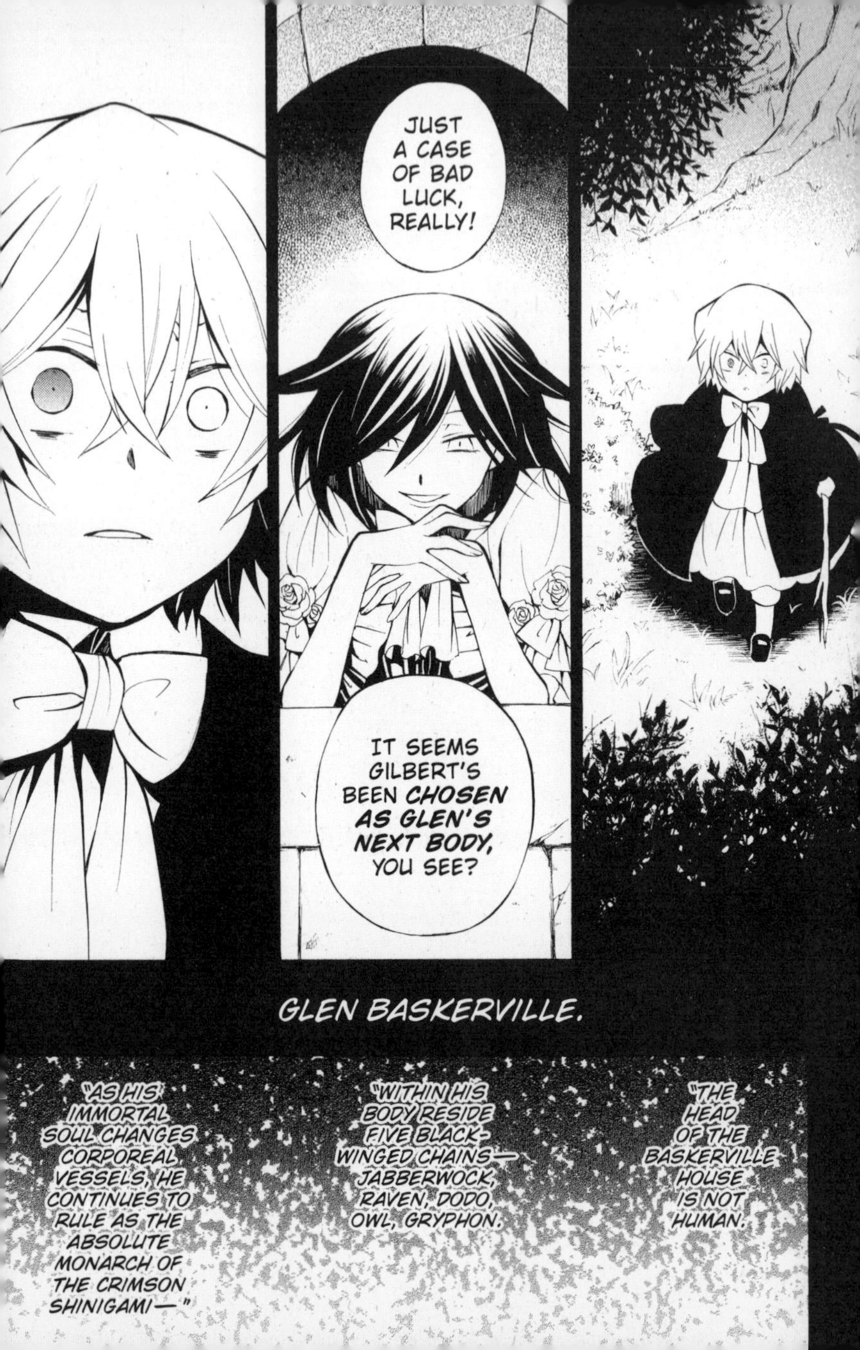
JUST A CASE OF BAD LUCK, REALLY!
IT SEEMS GILBERT'S BEEN ***CHOSEN AS GLEN'S NEXT BODY,*** YOU SEE?
GLEN BASKERVILLE.
"THE HEAD OF THE BASKERVILLE HOUSE IS NOT HUMAN.
"WITHIN HIS BODY RESIDE FIVE BLACK-WINGED CHAINS—JABBERWOCK, RAVEN, DODO, OWL, GRYPHON.
"AS HIS IMMORTAL SOUL CHANGES CORPOREAL VESSELS, HE CONTINUES TO RULE AS THE ABSOLUTE MONARCH OF THE CRIMSON SHINIGAMI—"

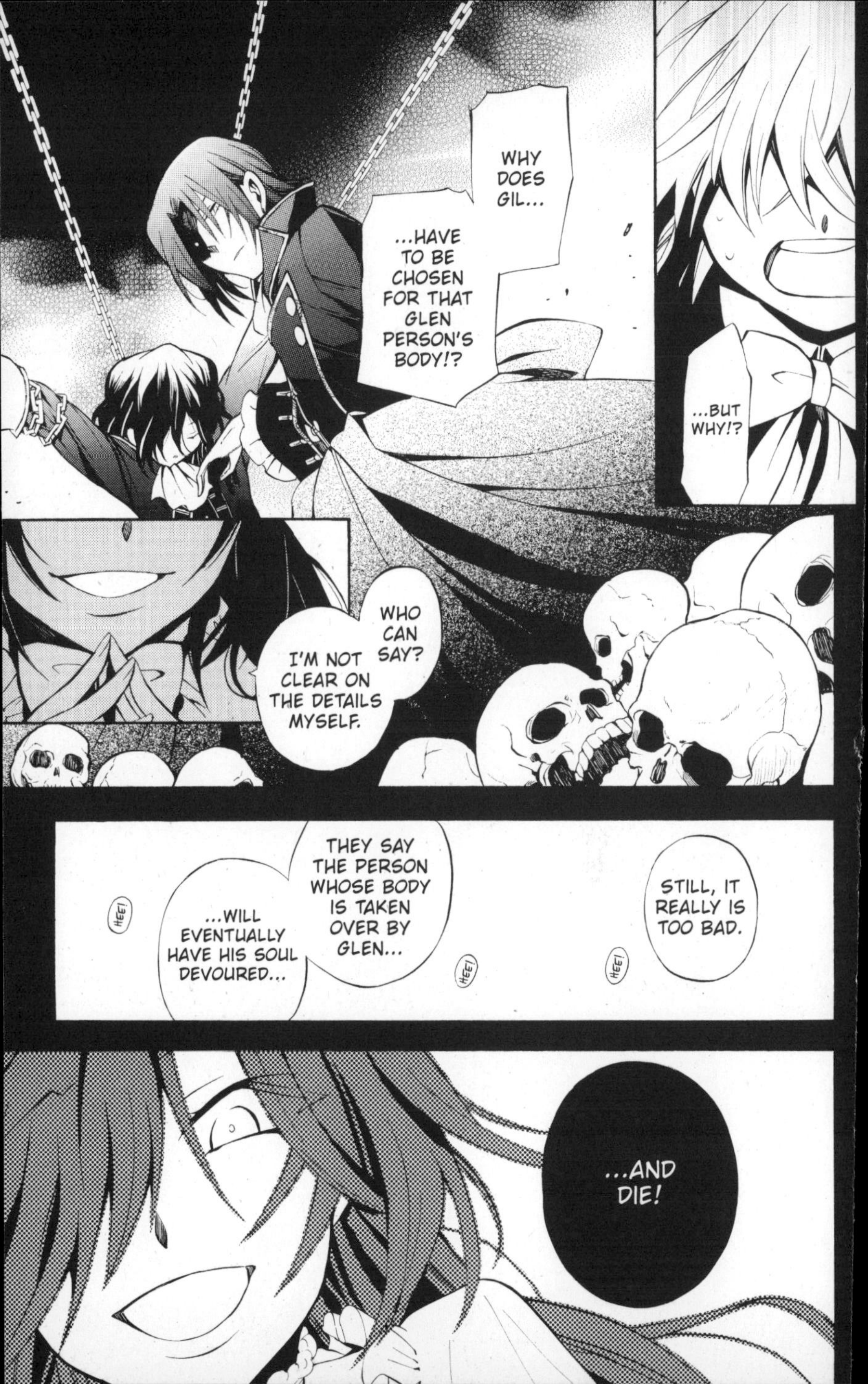
...BUT WHY!?
WHY DOES GIL...
...HAVE TO BE CHOSEN FOR THAT GLEN PERSON'S BODY!?
WHO CAN SAY?
I'M NOT CLEAR ON THE DETAILS MYSELF.
STILL, IT REALLY IS TOO BAD.
HEE!
HEE!
THEY SAY THE PERSON WHOSE BODY IS TAKEN OVER BY GLEN...
...WILL EVENTUALLY HAVE HIS SOUL DEVOURED...
HEE!
...AND DIE!

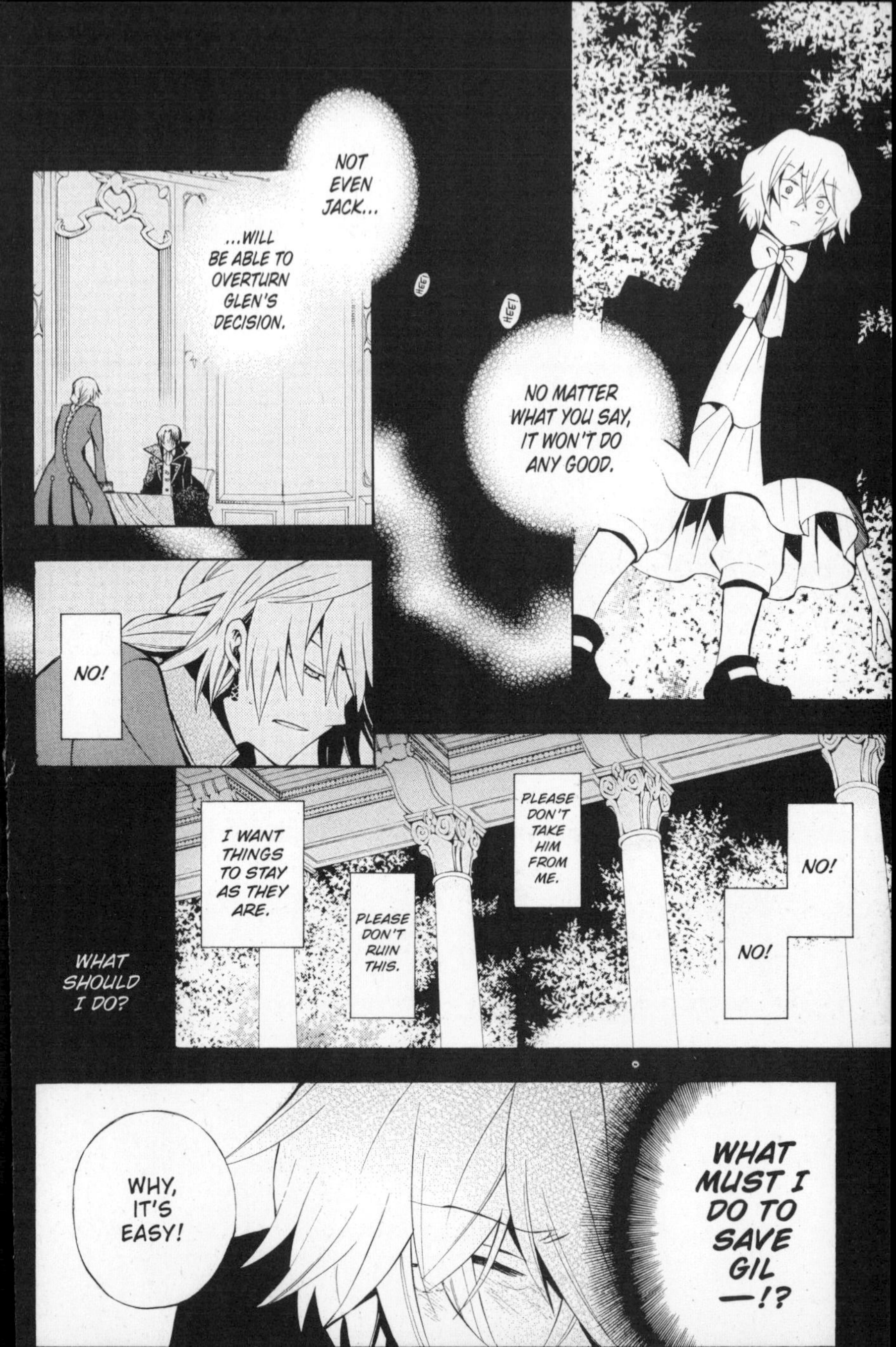
NOT EVEN JACK...
...WILL BE ABLE TO OVERTURN GLEN'S DECISION.
HEE!
HEE!
NO MATTER WHAT YOU SAY, IT WON'T DO ANY GOOD.
NO!
NO!
NO!
PLEASE DON'T TAKE HIM FROM ME.
PLEASE DON'T RUIN THIS.
I WANT THINGS TO STAY AS THEY ARE.
WHAT SHOULD I DO?
WHAT MUST I DO TO SAVE GIL—!?
WHY, IT'S EASY!

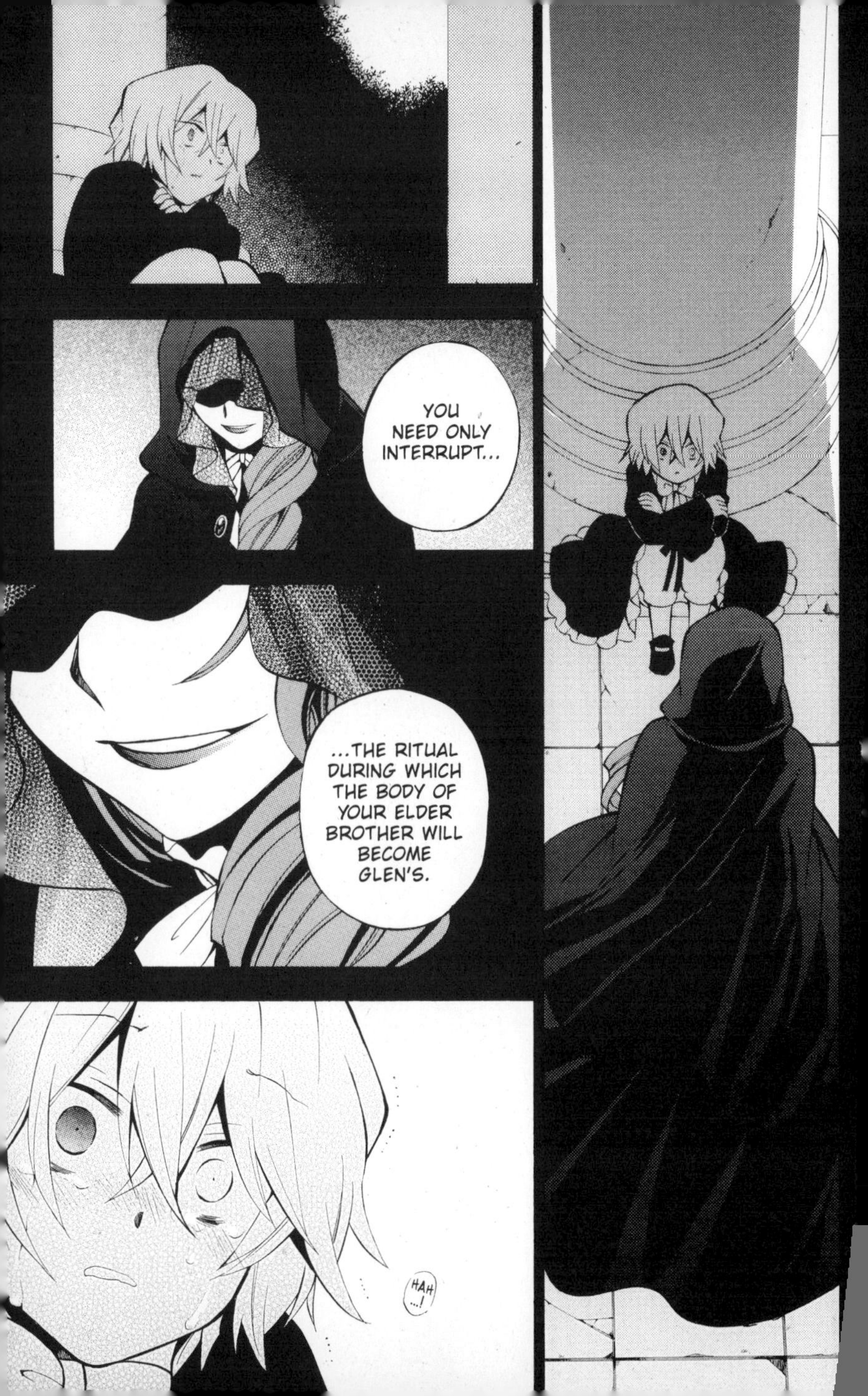
YOU NEED ONLY INTERRUPT...
...THE RITUAL DURING WHICH THE BODY OF YOUR ELDER BROTHER WILL BECOME GLEN'S.
HAH ...!

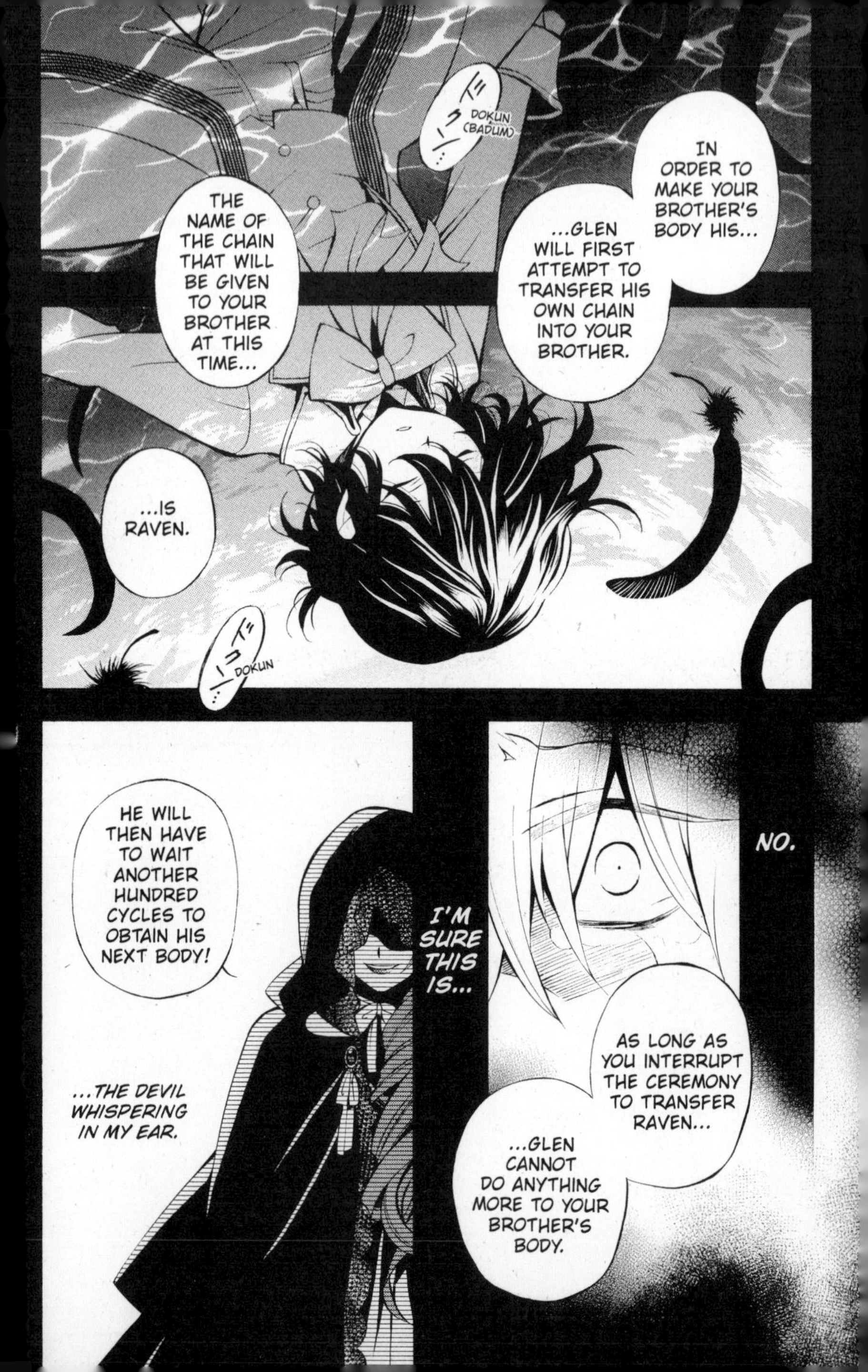
IN ORDER TO MAKE YOUR BROTHER'S BODY HIS...
...GLEN WILL FIRST ATTEMPT TO TRANSFER HIS OWN CHAIN INTO YOUR BROTHER.
DOKUN (BADUM)
THE NAME OF THE CHAIN THAT WILL BE GIVEN TO YOUR BROTHER AT THIS TIME...
...IS RAVEN.
DOKUN
NO.
AS LONG AS YOU INTERRUPT THE CEREMONY TO TRANSFER RAVEN...
...GLEN CANNOT DO ANYTHING MORE TO YOUR BROTHER'S BODY.
HE WILL THEN HAVE TO WAIT ANOTHER HUNDRED CYCLES TO OBTAIN HIS NEXT BODY!
I'M SURE THIS IS...
...THE DEVIL WHISPERING IN MY EAR.

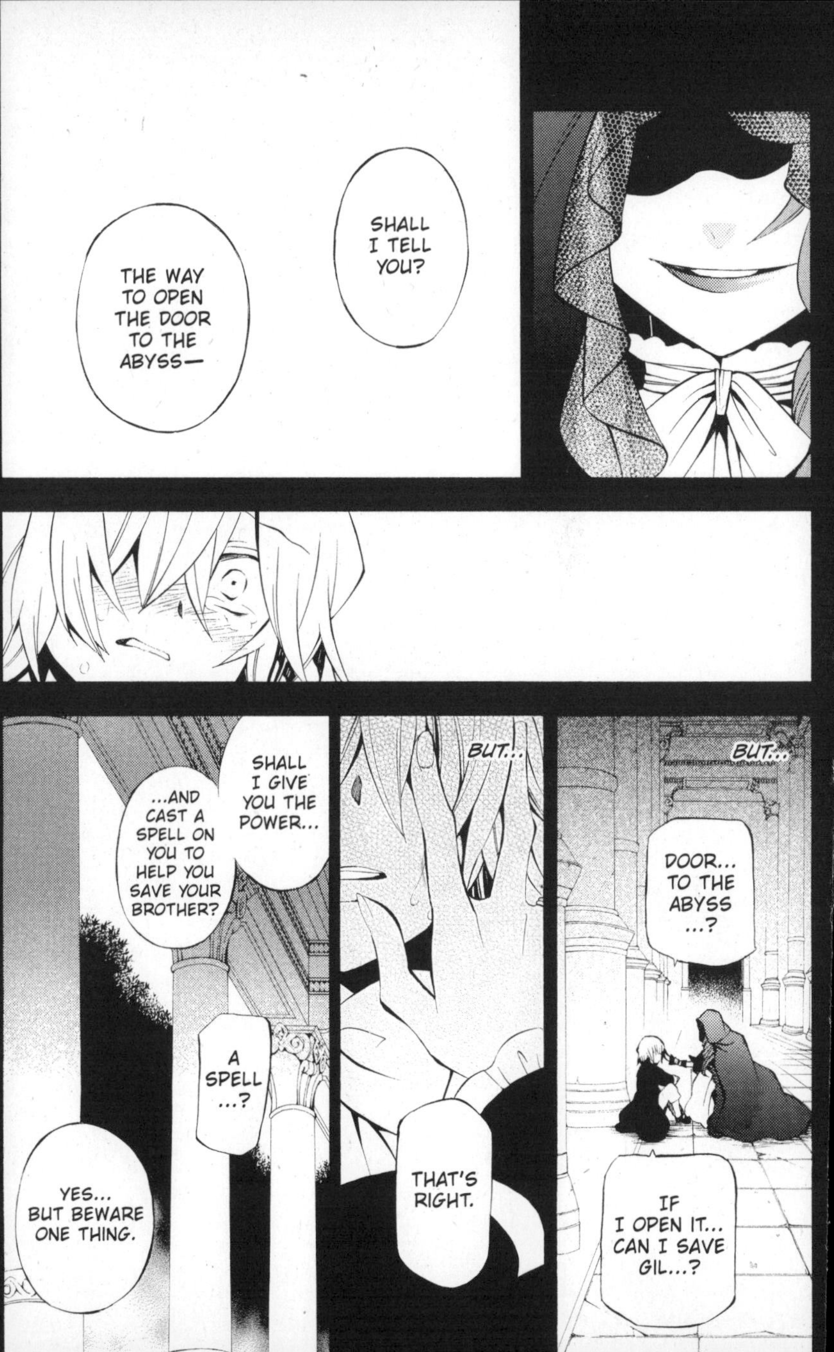
SHALL I TELL YOU?
THE WAY TO OPEN THE DOOR TO THE ABYSS—
BUT...
DOOR... TO THE ABYSS ...?
IF I OPEN IT... CAN I SAVE GIL...?
BUT...
THAT'S RIGHT.
SHALL I GIVE YOU THE POWER...
...AND CAST A SPELL ON YOU TO HELP YOU SAVE YOUR BROTHER?
A SPELL ...?
YES... BUT BEWARE ONE THING.

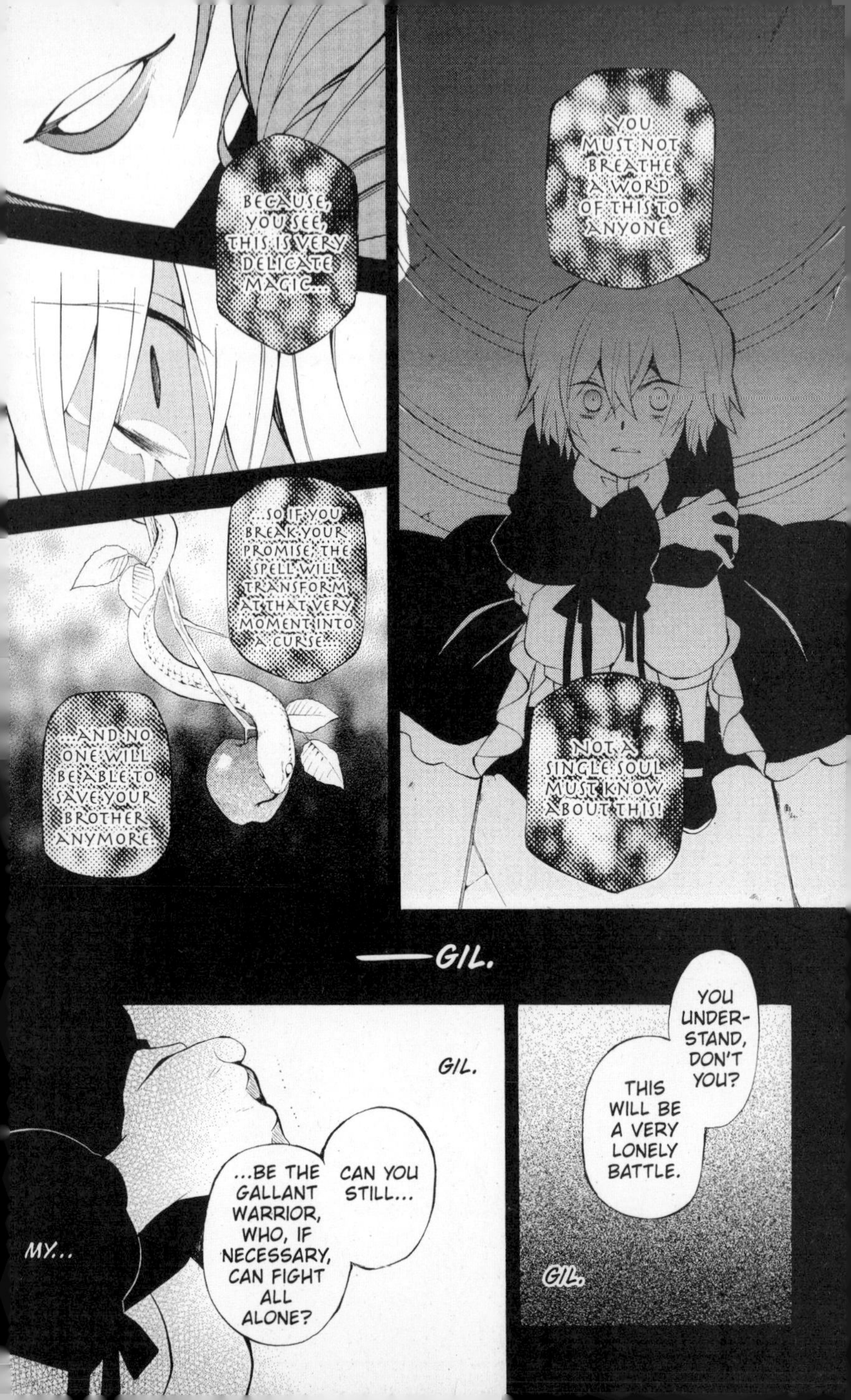
YOU MUST NOT BREATHE A WORD OF THIS TO ANYONE.
NOT A SINGLE SOUL MUST KNOW ABOUT THIS!
BECAUSE, YOU SEE, THIS IS VERY DELICATE MAGIC...
...SO IF YOU BREAK YOUR PROMISE, THE SPELL WILL TRANSFORM AT THAT VERY MOMENT INTO A CURSE...
...AND NO ONE WILL BE ABLE TO SAVE YOUR BROTHER ANYMORE.
—GIL.
YOU UNDERSTAND, DON'T YOU?
THIS WILL BE A VERY LONELY BATTLE.
GIL.
GIL.
CAN YOU STILL...
...BE THE GALLANT WARRIOR, WHO, IF NECESSARY, CAN FIGHT ALL ALONE?
MY...

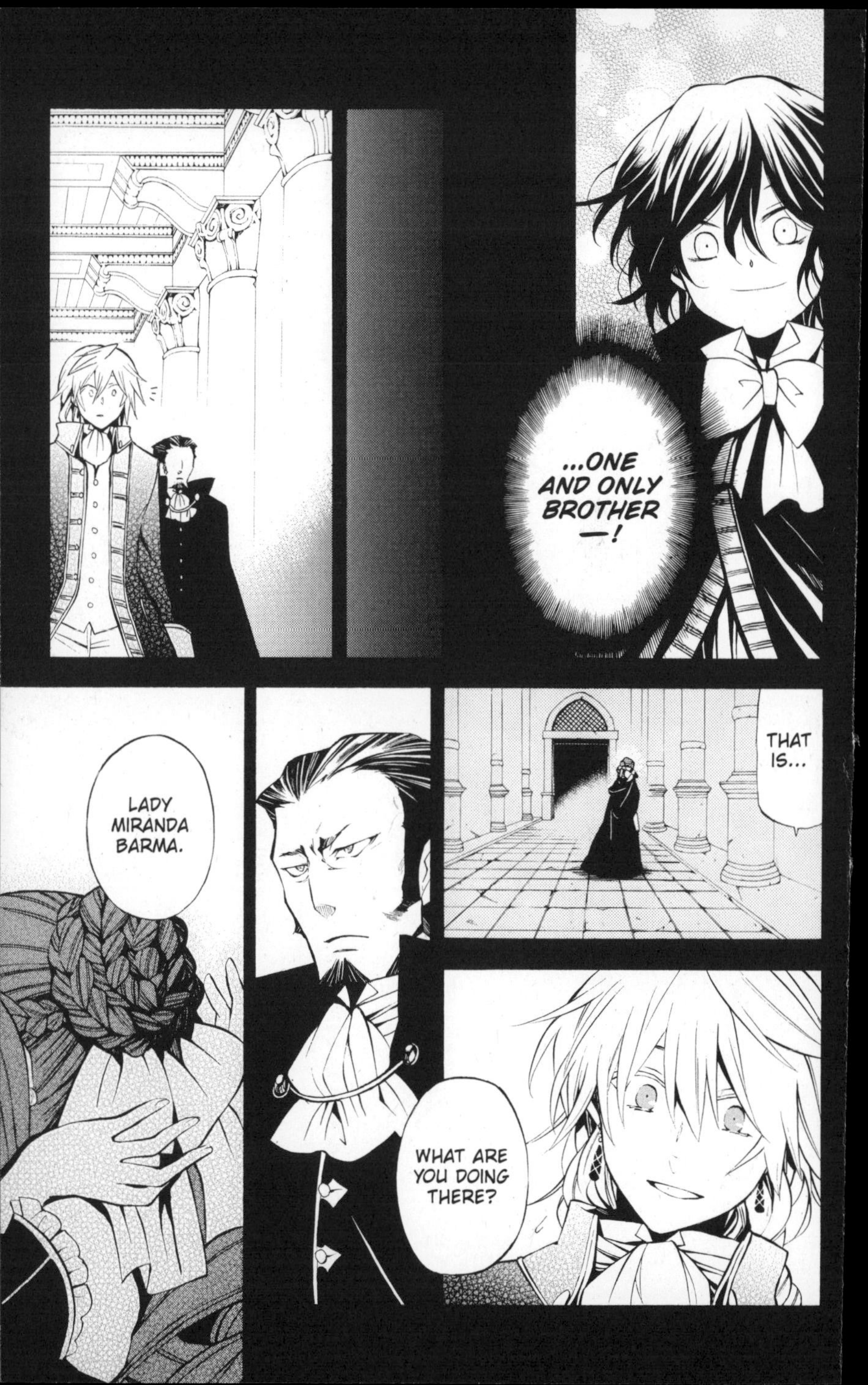
...ONE AND ONLY BROTHER —!
THAT IS...
WHAT ARE YOU DOING THERE?
LADY MIRANDA BARMA.

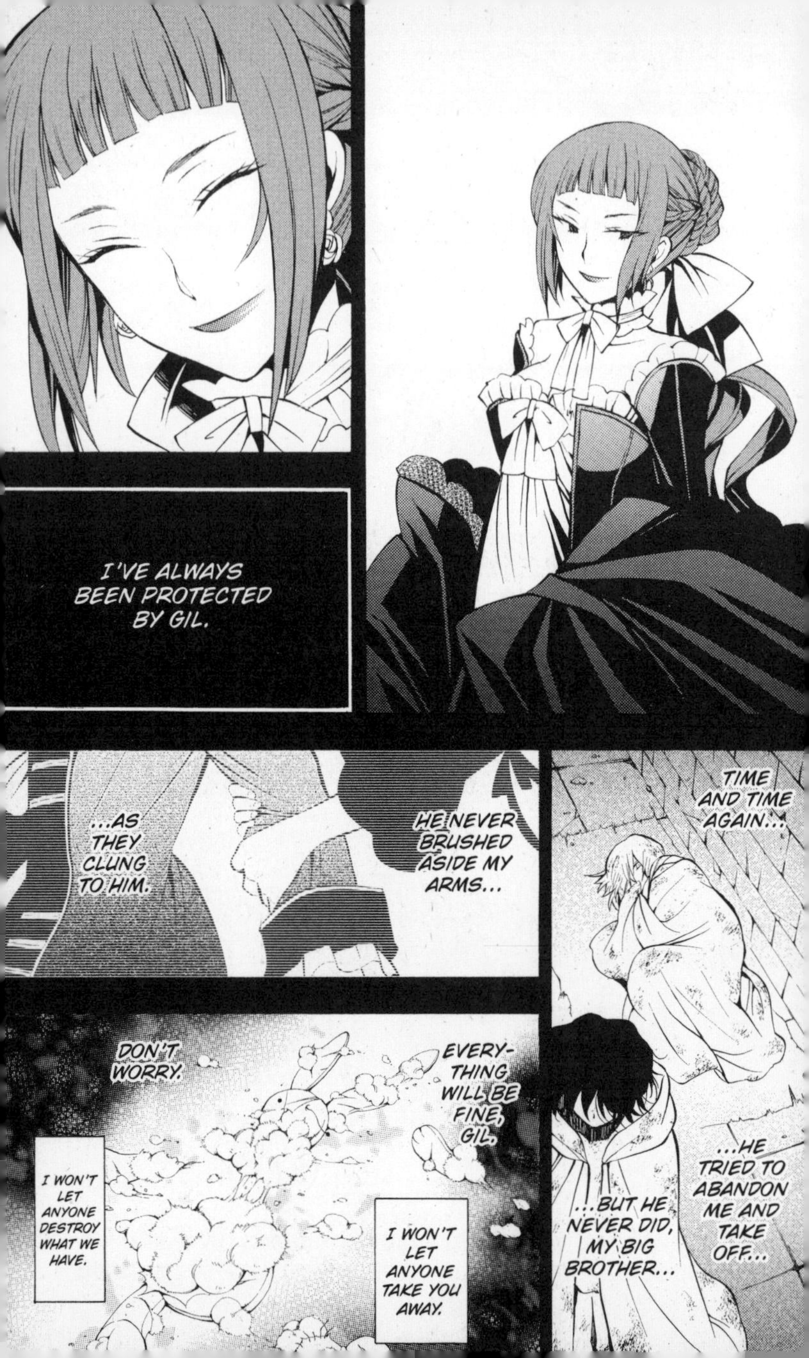
I'VE ALWAYS BEEN PROTECTED BY GIL.
TIME AND TIME AGAIN...
...HE TRIED TO ABANDON ME AND TAKE OFF...
...BUT HE NEVER DID, MY BIG BROTHER...
HE NEVER BRUSHED ASIDE MY ARMS...
...AS THEY CLUNG TO HIM.
EVERY-THING WILL BE FINE, GIL.
DON'T WORRY.
I WON'T LET ANYONE TAKE YOU AWAY.
I WON'T LET ANYONE DESTROY WHAT WE HAVE.

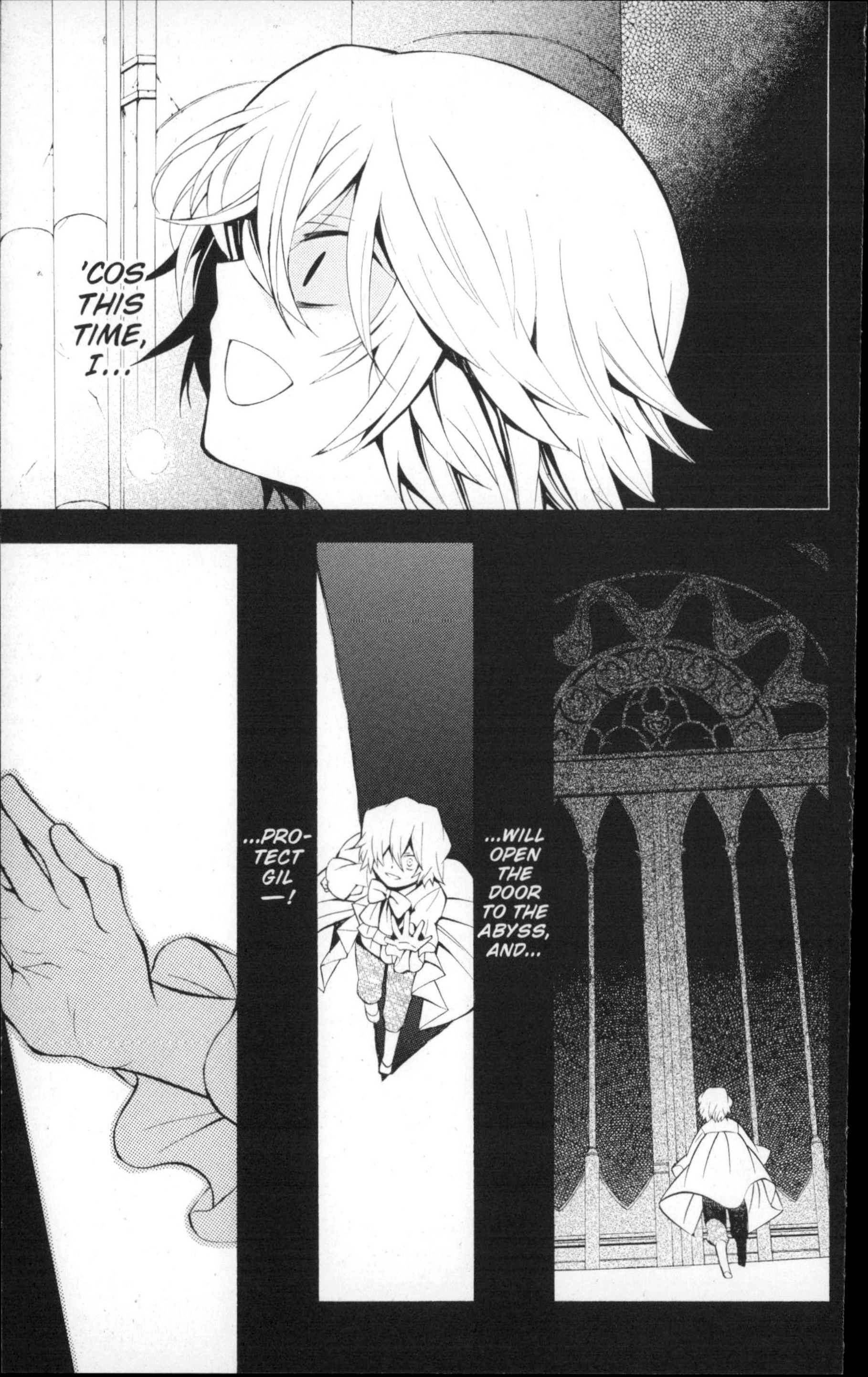
'COS THIS TIME, I...
...WILL OPEN THE DOOR TO THE ABYSS, AND...
...PROTECT GIL—!

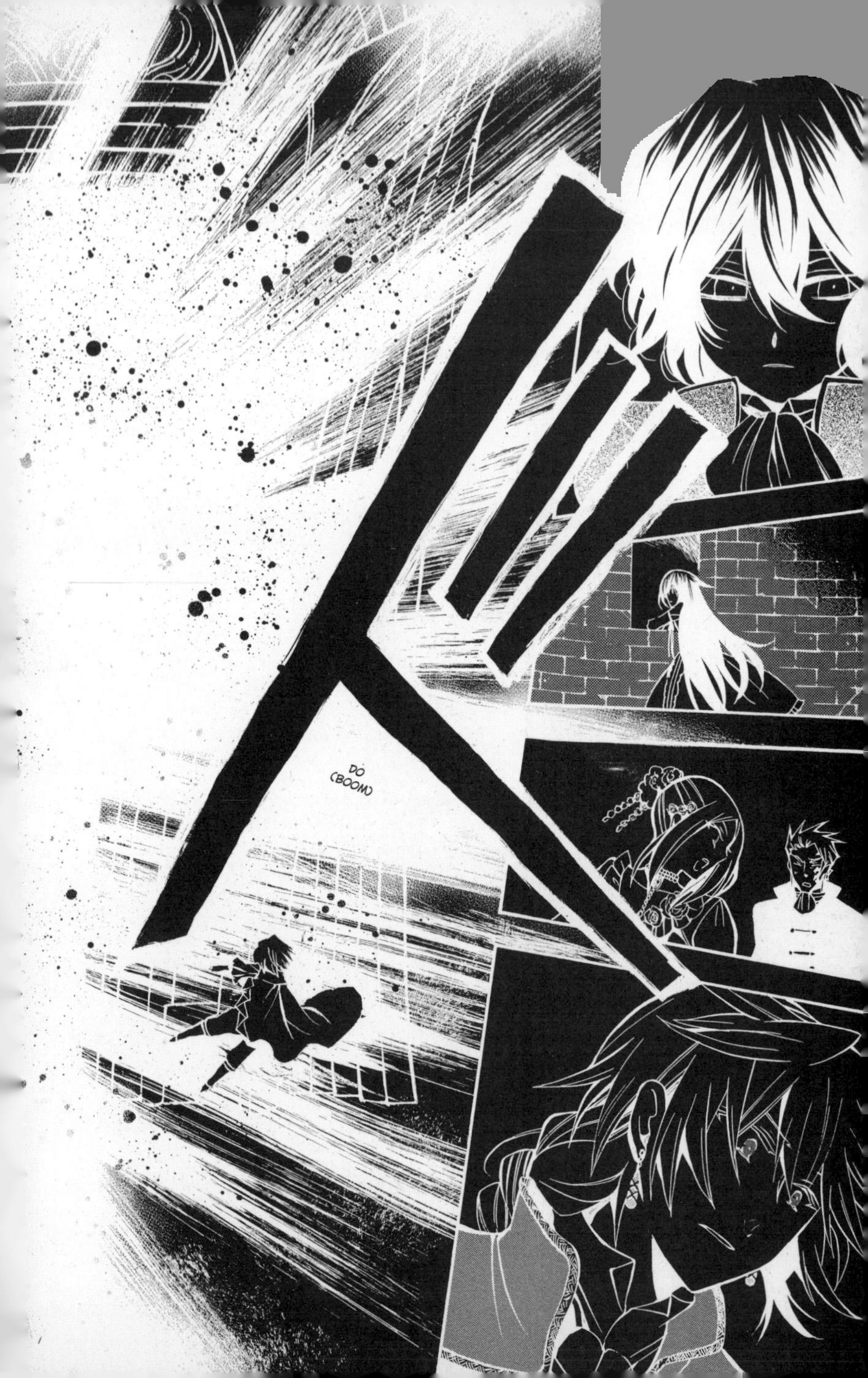
DO
(BOOM)

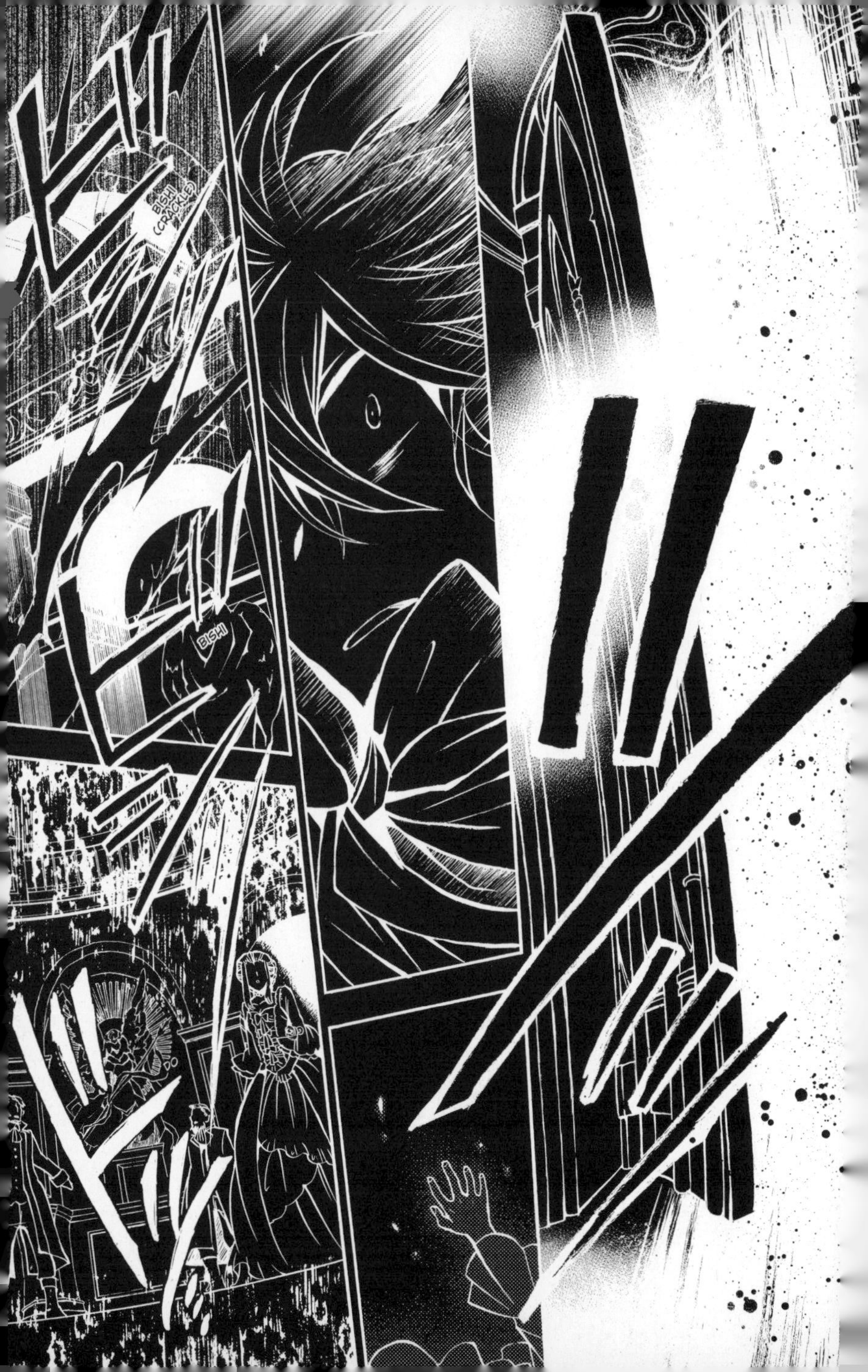
BISHI (CRACKLE)
BISHI
DO

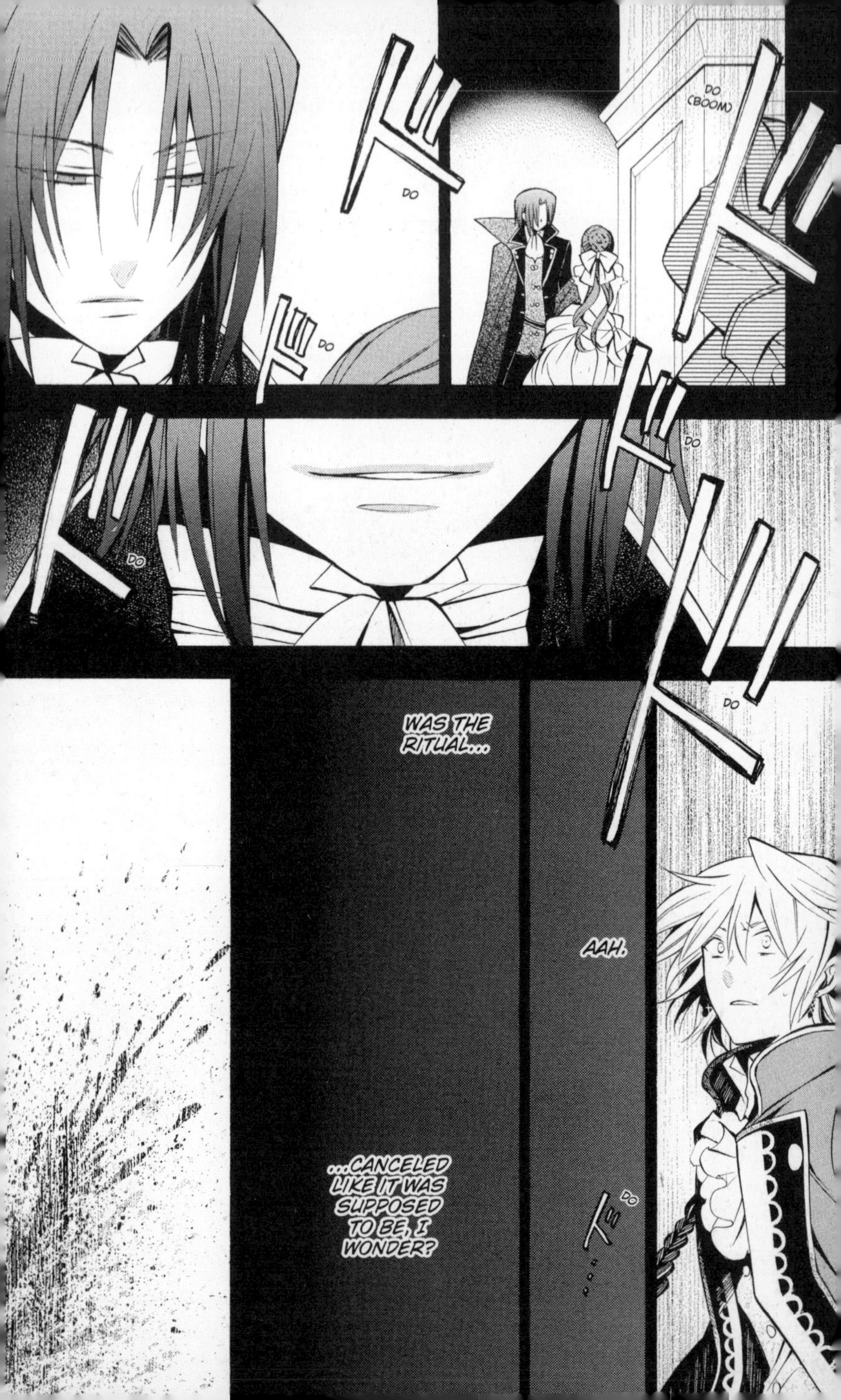
DO
(BOOM)
DO
DO
DO
DO
DO
AAH.
DO
WAS THE RITUAL...
...CANCELED LIKE IT WAS SUPPOSED TO BE, I WONDER?

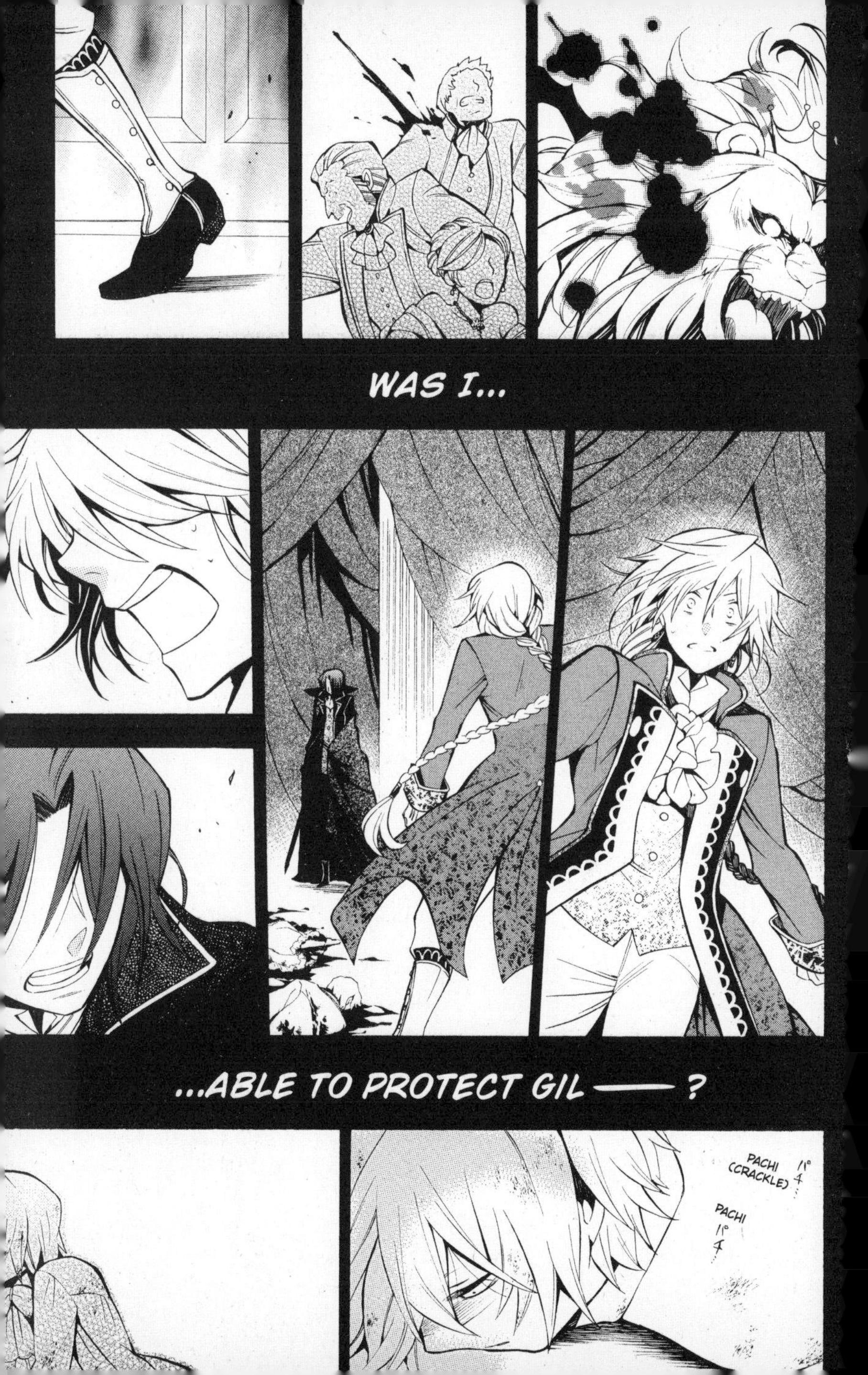
WAS I...
...ABLE TO PROTECT GIL——?
PACHI (CRACKLE)
パチ…
PACHI
パチ

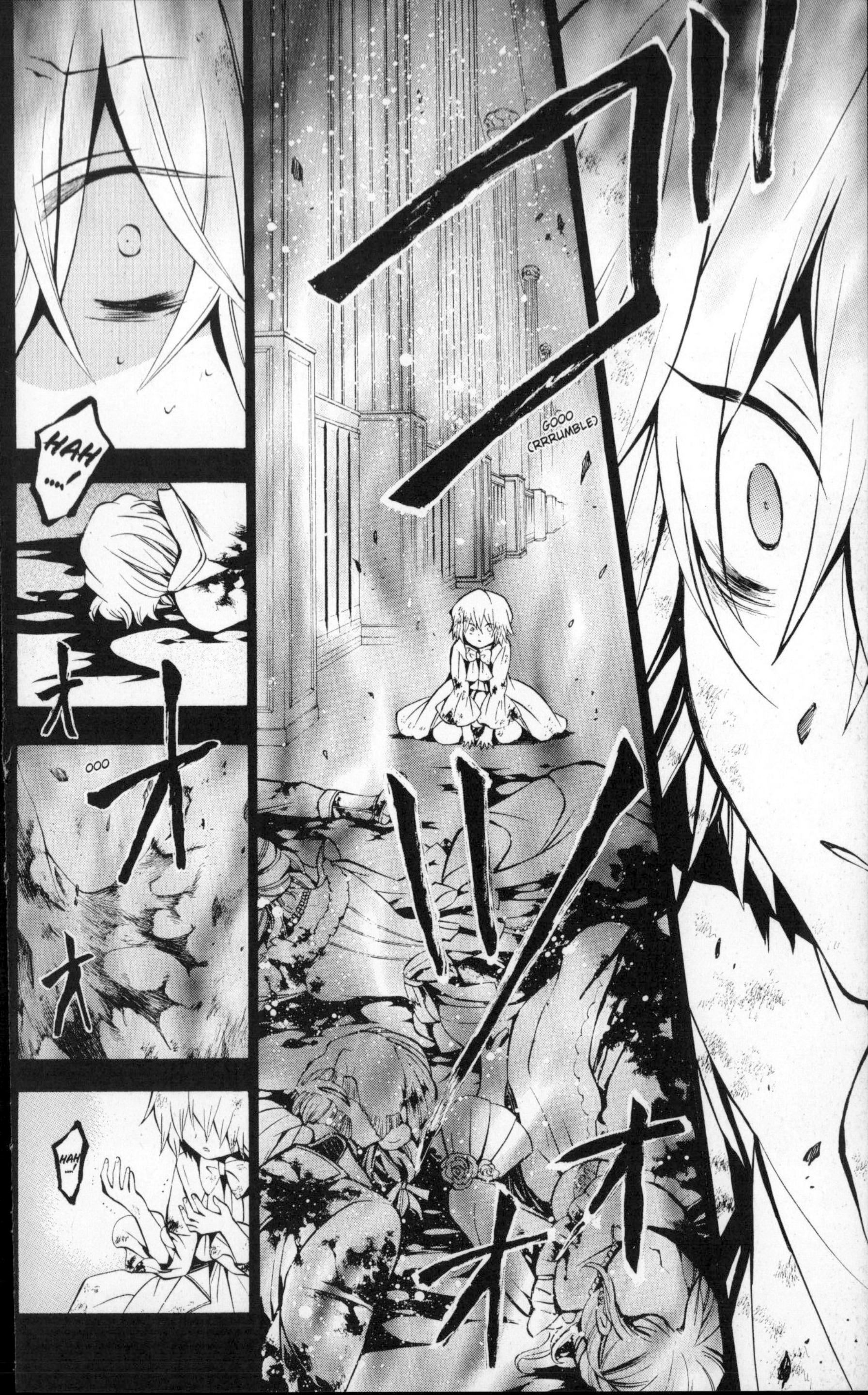
GOOO
(RRRUMBLE)
HAH ...!
ooo
HAH ...!

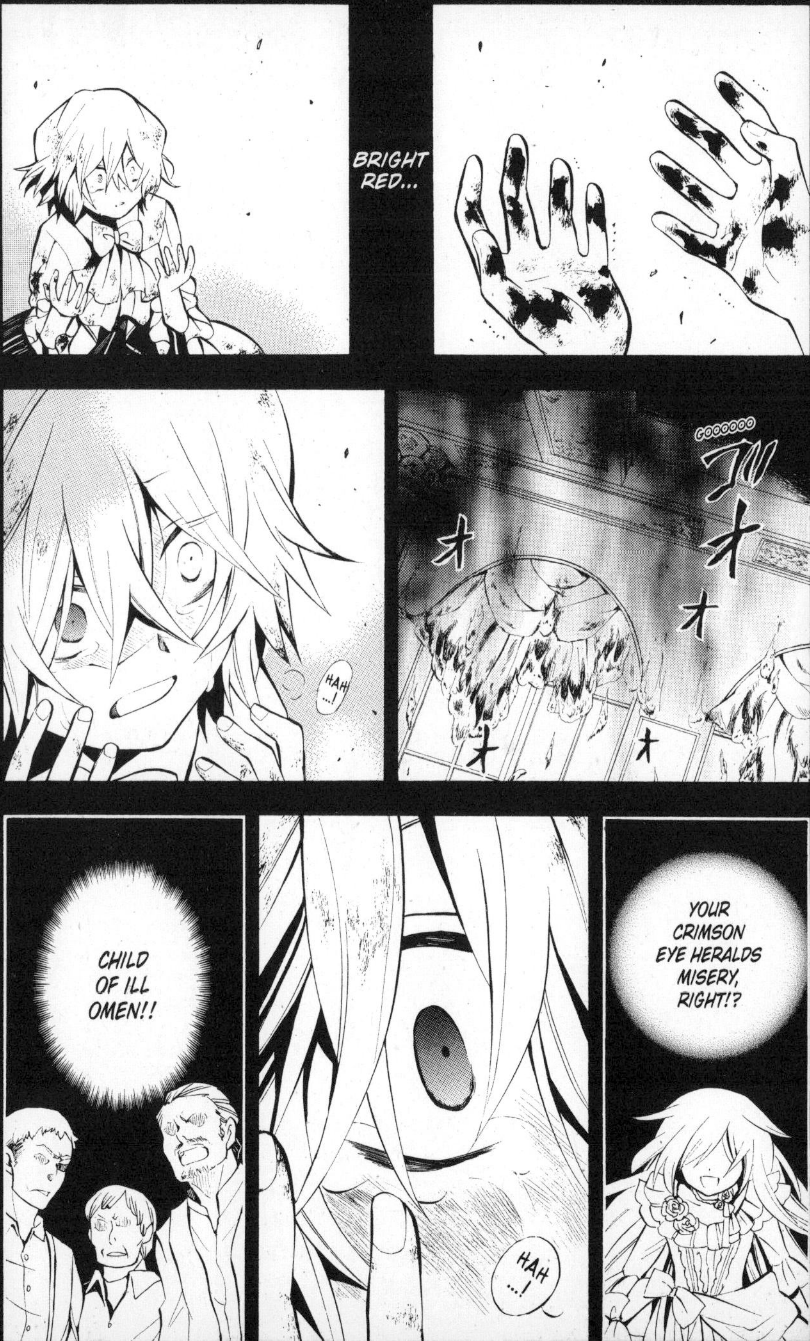
BRIGHT RED...
GOOOOOO
HAH ...!
YOUR CRIMSON EYE HERALDS MISERY, RIGHT!?
HAH ...!
CHILD OF ILL OMEN!!

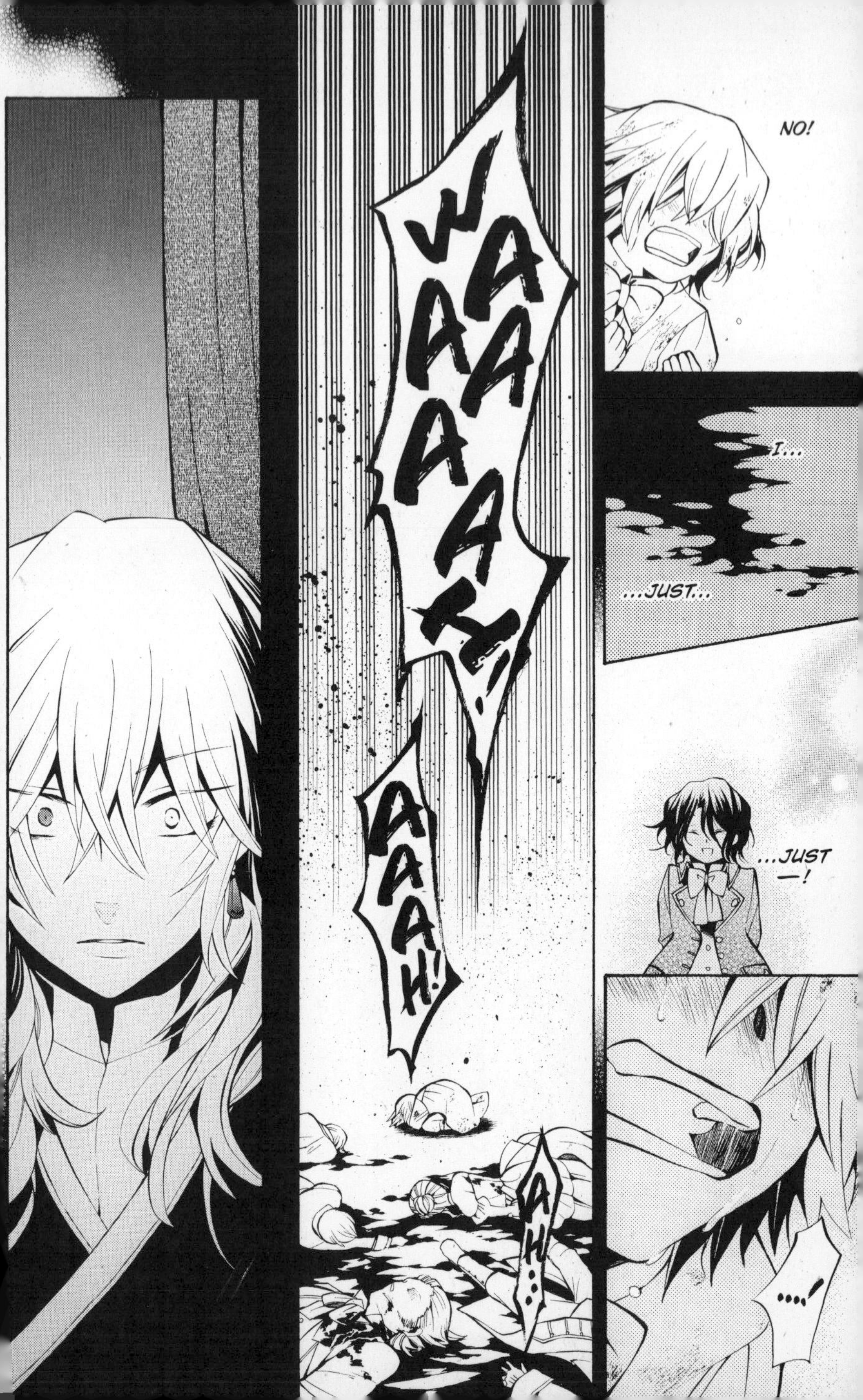
NO!
I...
...JUST...
...JUST —!
....!
WAAAAAAH!
AAAAH!
AH...

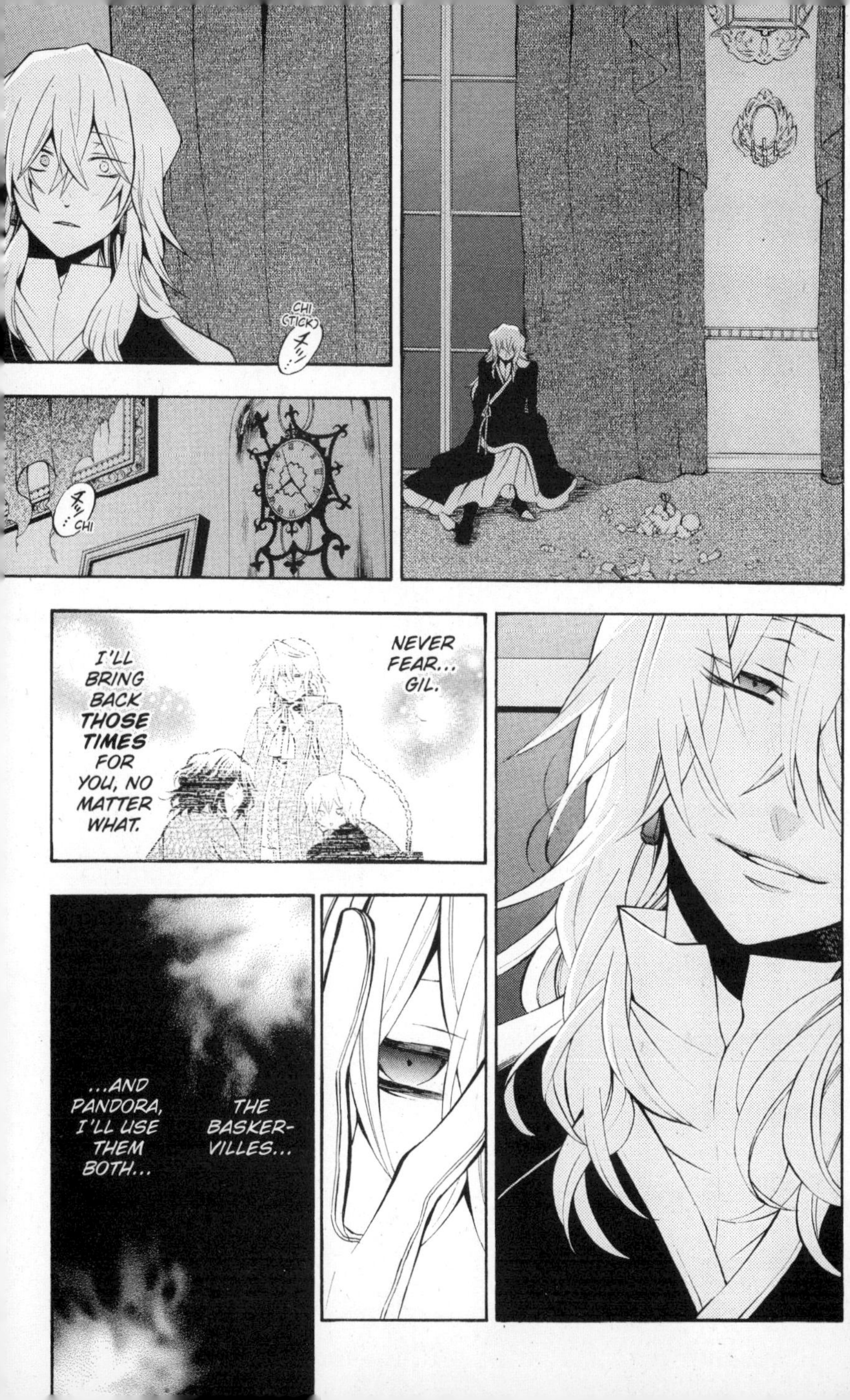
CHI (TICK)
CHI
NEVER FEAR... GIL.
I'LL BRING BACK THOSE TIMES FOR YOU, NO MATTER WHAT.
THE BASKER-VILLES...
...AND PANDORA, I'LL USE THEM BOTH...

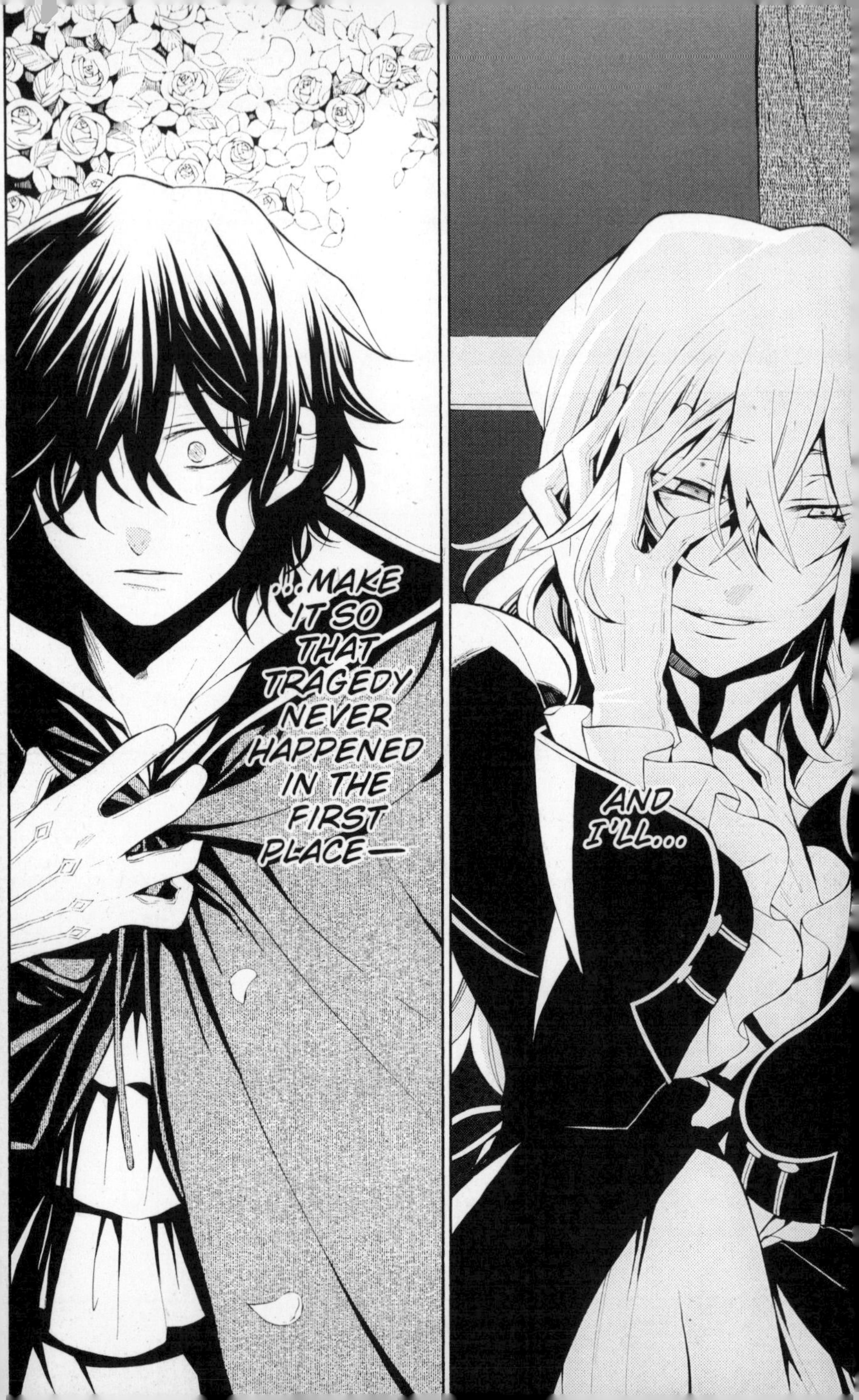
AND I'LL...
...MAKE IT SO THAT TRAGEDY NEVER HAPPENED IN THE FIRST PLACE—

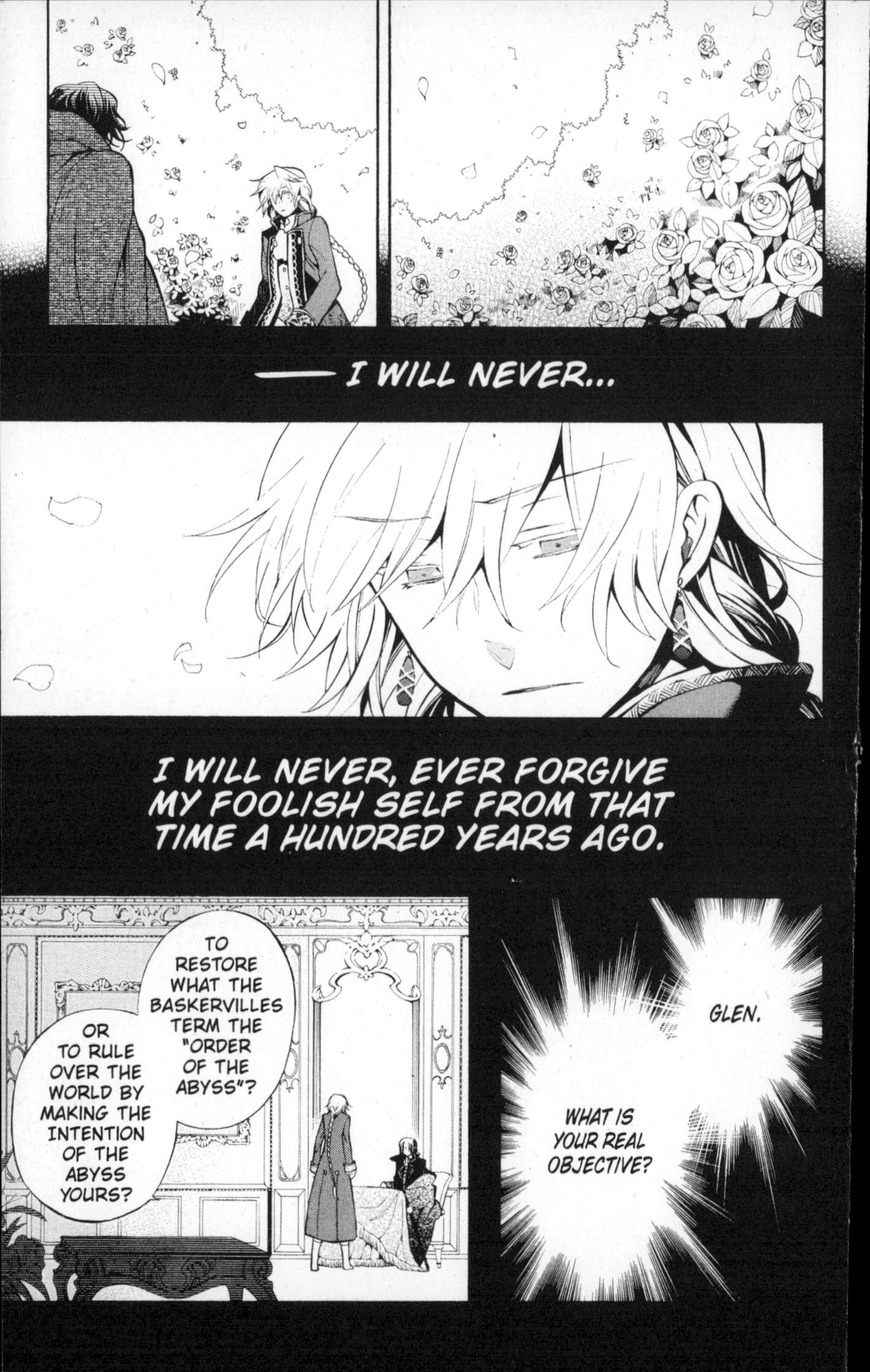
—I WILL NEVER...
I WILL NEVER, EVER FORGIVE MY FOOLISH SELF FROM THAT TIME A HUNDRED YEARS AGO.
GLEN.
WHAT IS YOUR REAL OBJECTIVE?
TO RESTORE WHAT THE BASKERVILLES TERM THE "ORDER OF THE ABYSS"?
OR TO RULE OVER THE WORLD BY MAKING THE INTENTION OF THE ABYSS YOURS?

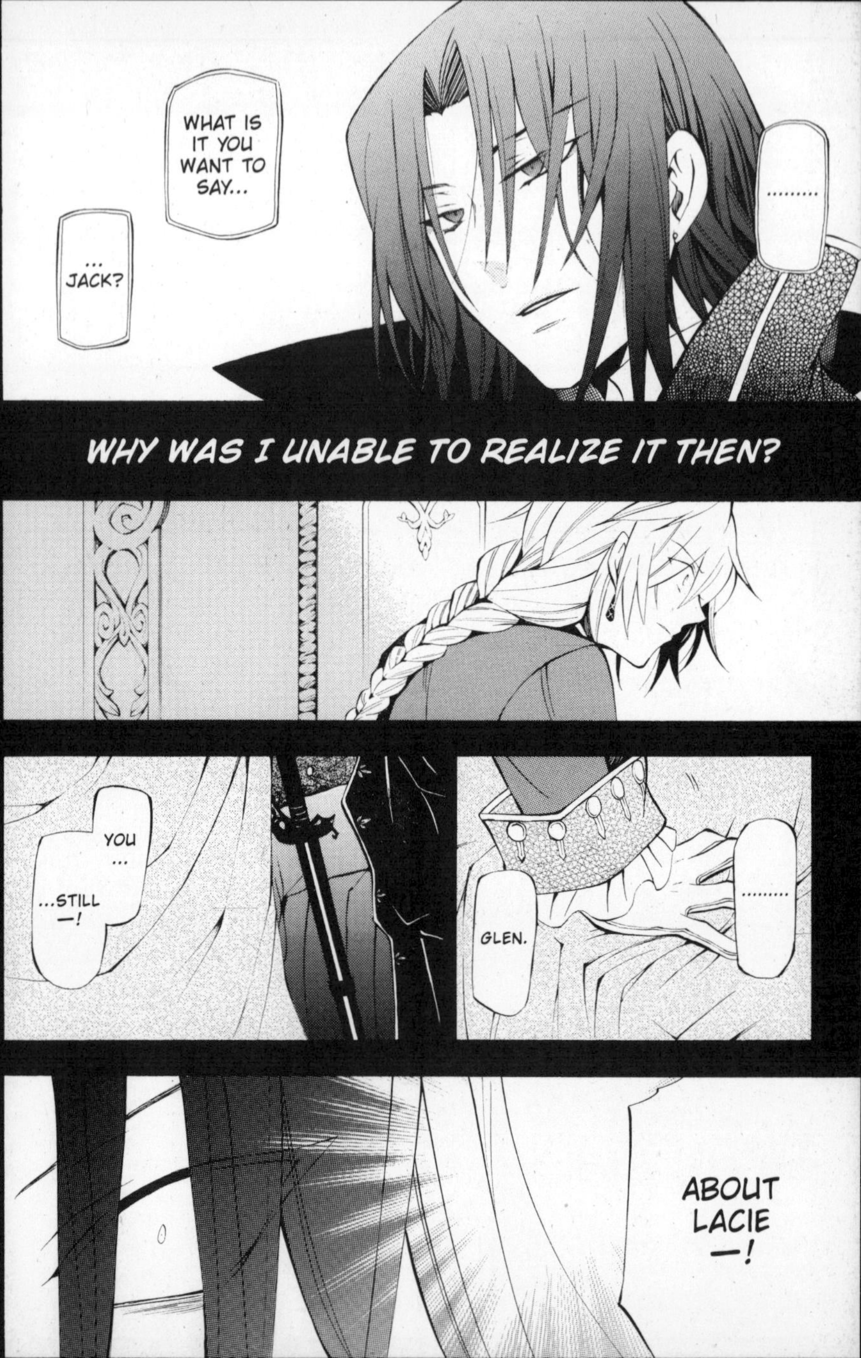
....
WHAT IS IT YOU WANT TO SAY...
...JACK?
WHY WAS I UNABLE TO REALIZE IT THEN?
....
GLEN.
YOU... ...STILL —!
ABOUT LACIE —!

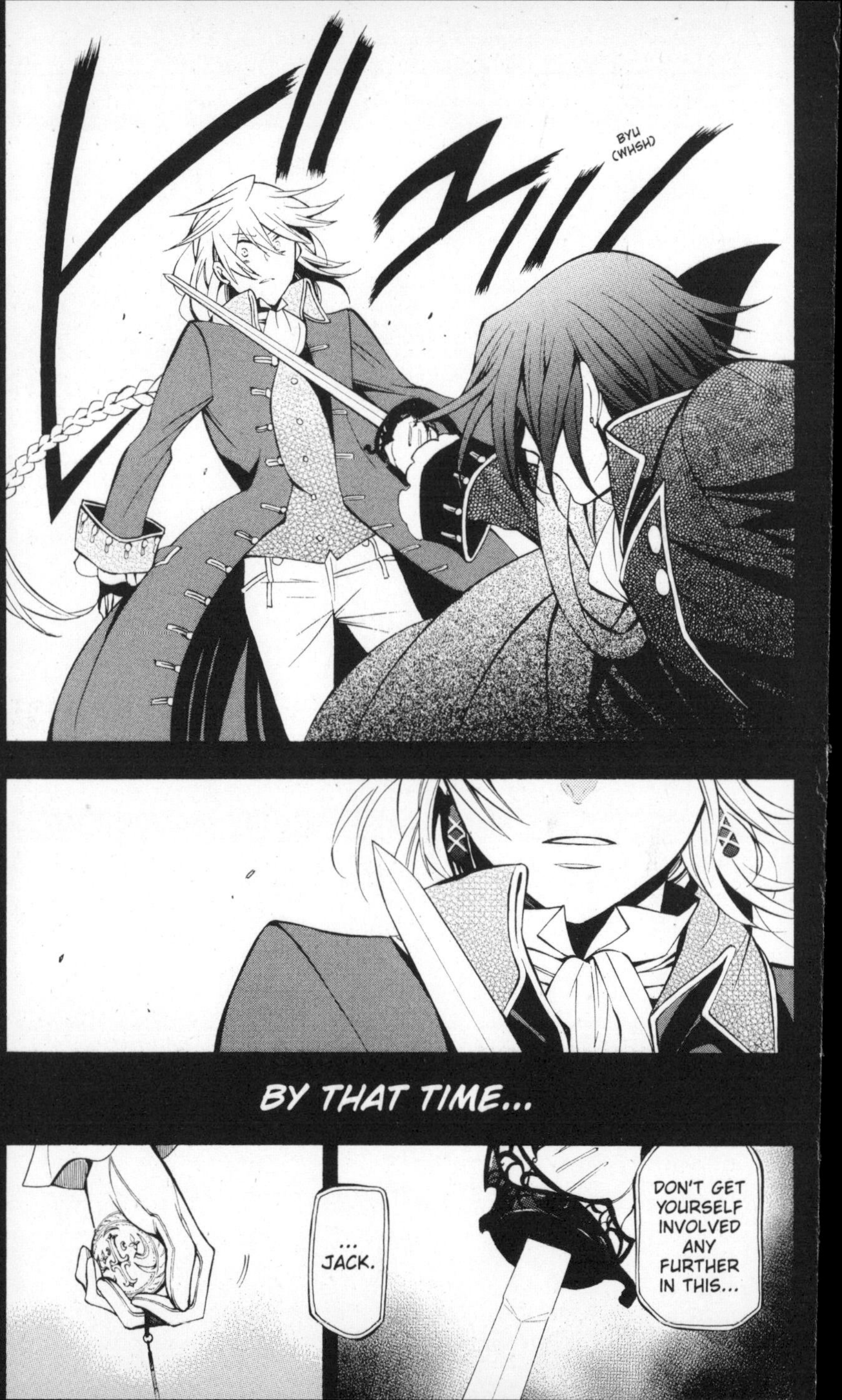
BYU (WHSH)
BY THAT TIME...
DON'T GET YOURSELF INVOLVED ANY FURTHER IN THIS...
...JACK.

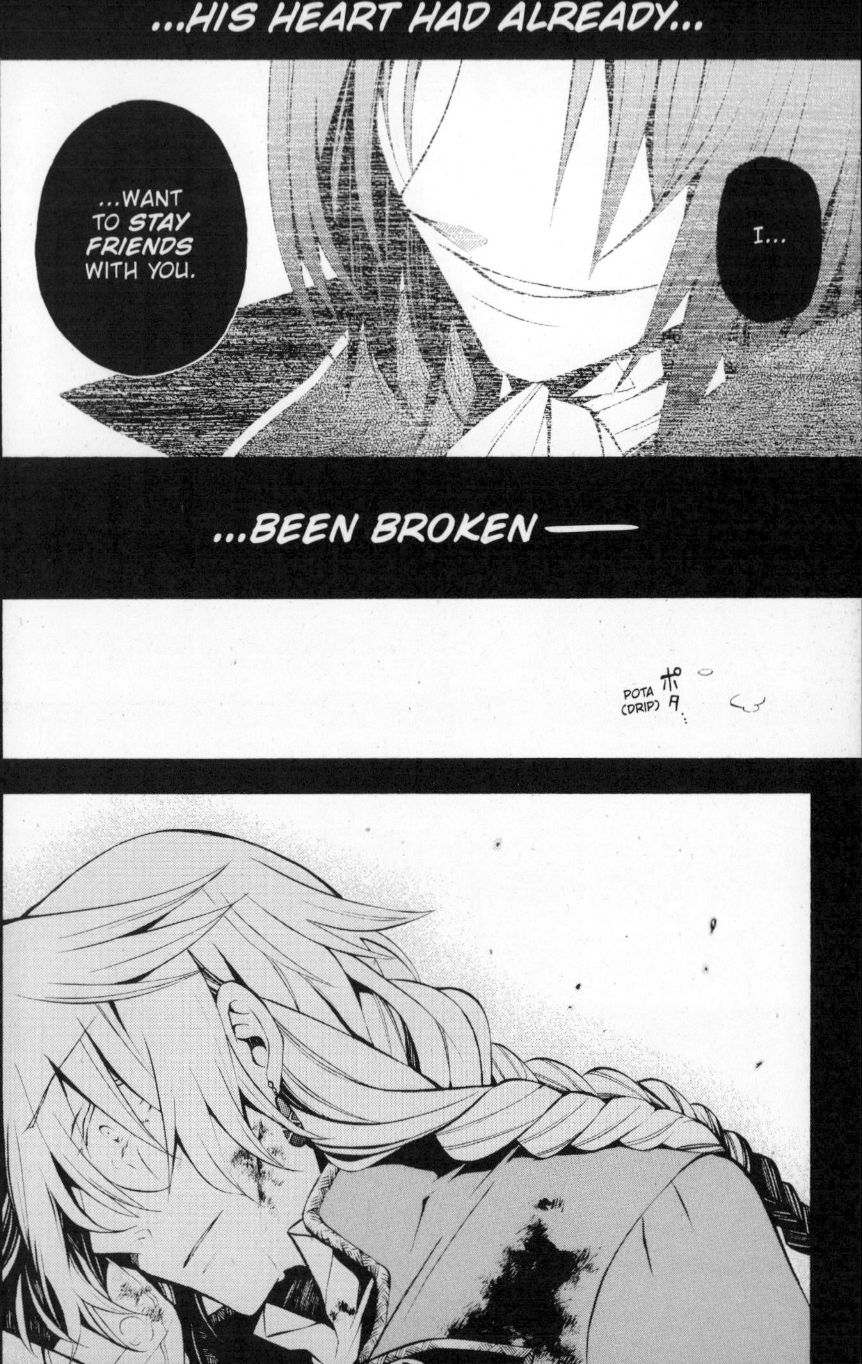
...HIS HEART HAD ALREADY...
I...
...WANT TO STAY FRIENDS WITH YOU.
...BEEN BROKEN——
ポタ...
POTA (DRIP)

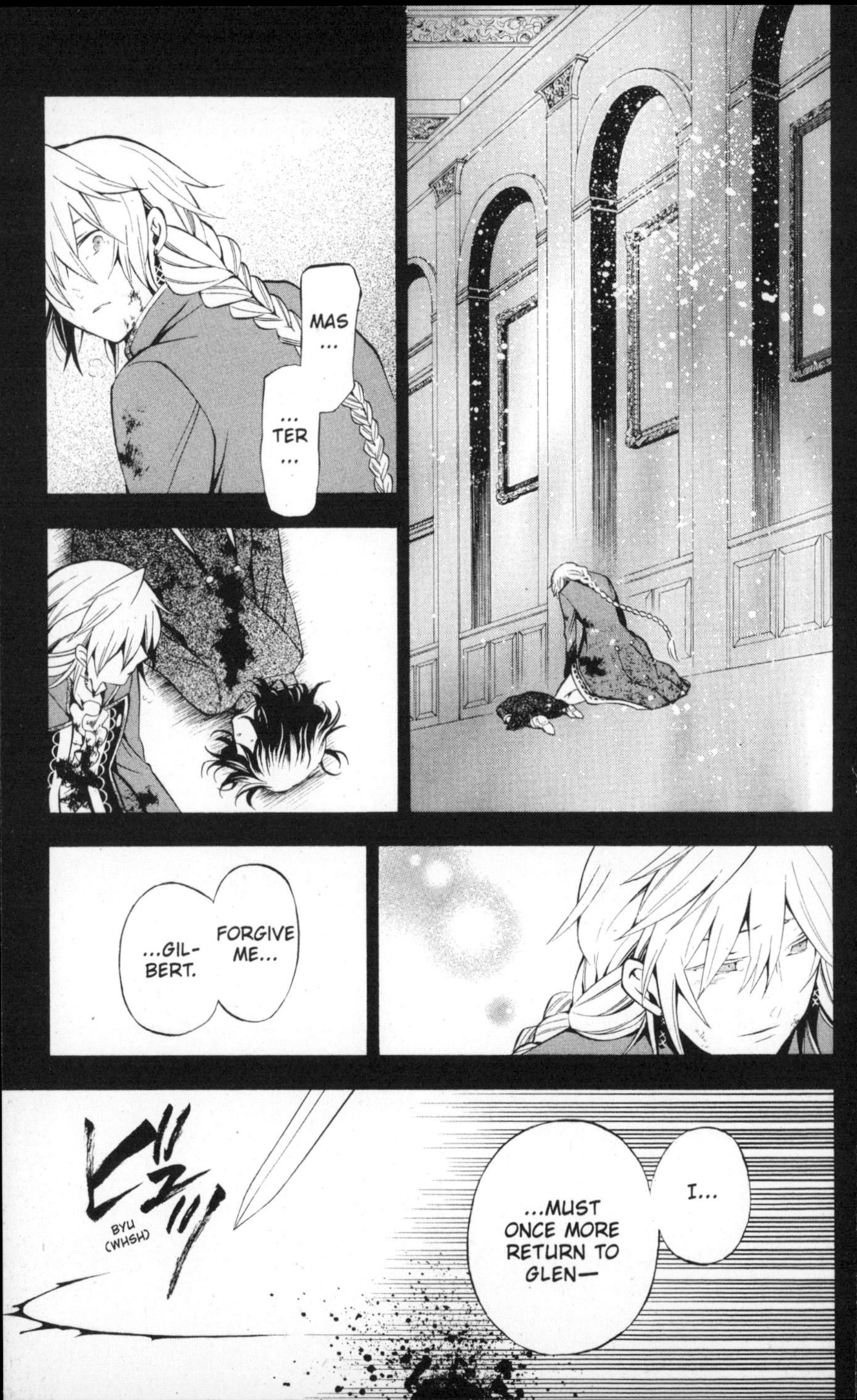
MAS...
...TER...
FORGIVE ME...
...GIL-BERT.
I...
...MUST ONCE MORE RETURN TO GLEN—
BYU (WHSH)

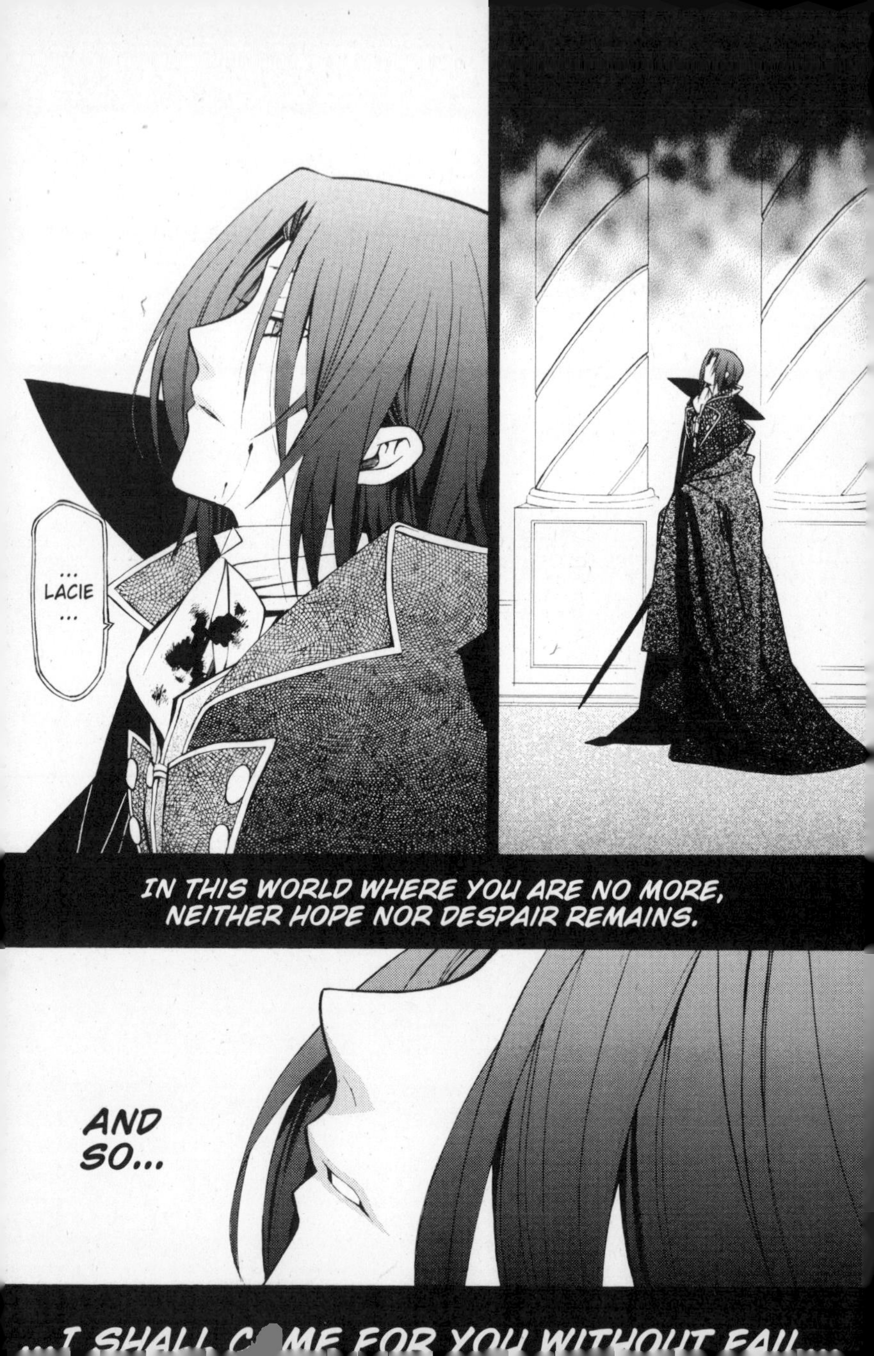
...LACIE...
IN THIS WORLD WHERE YOU ARE NO MORE, NEITHER HOPE NOR DESPAIR REMAINS.
AND SO...
...I SHALL COME FOR YOU WITHOUT FAIL...

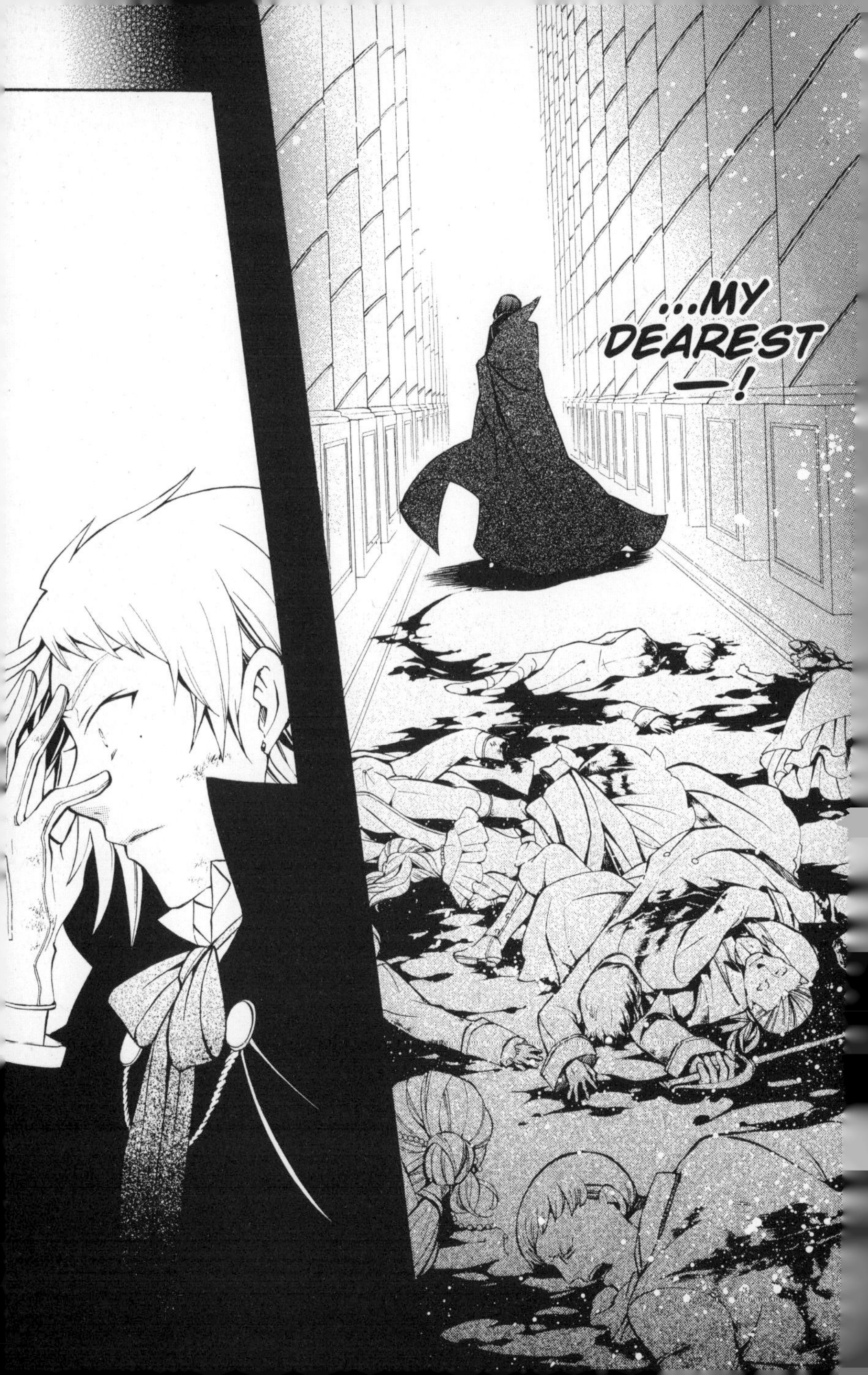
...MY DEAREST —!

ELLIOT!?

H''ɴ
ZA
(STEP)

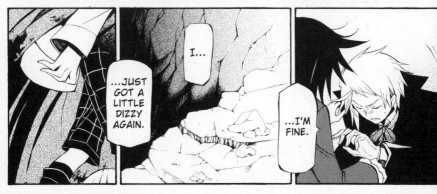

I...

...JUST GOT A LITTLE DIZZY AGAIN.

...I'M FINE.

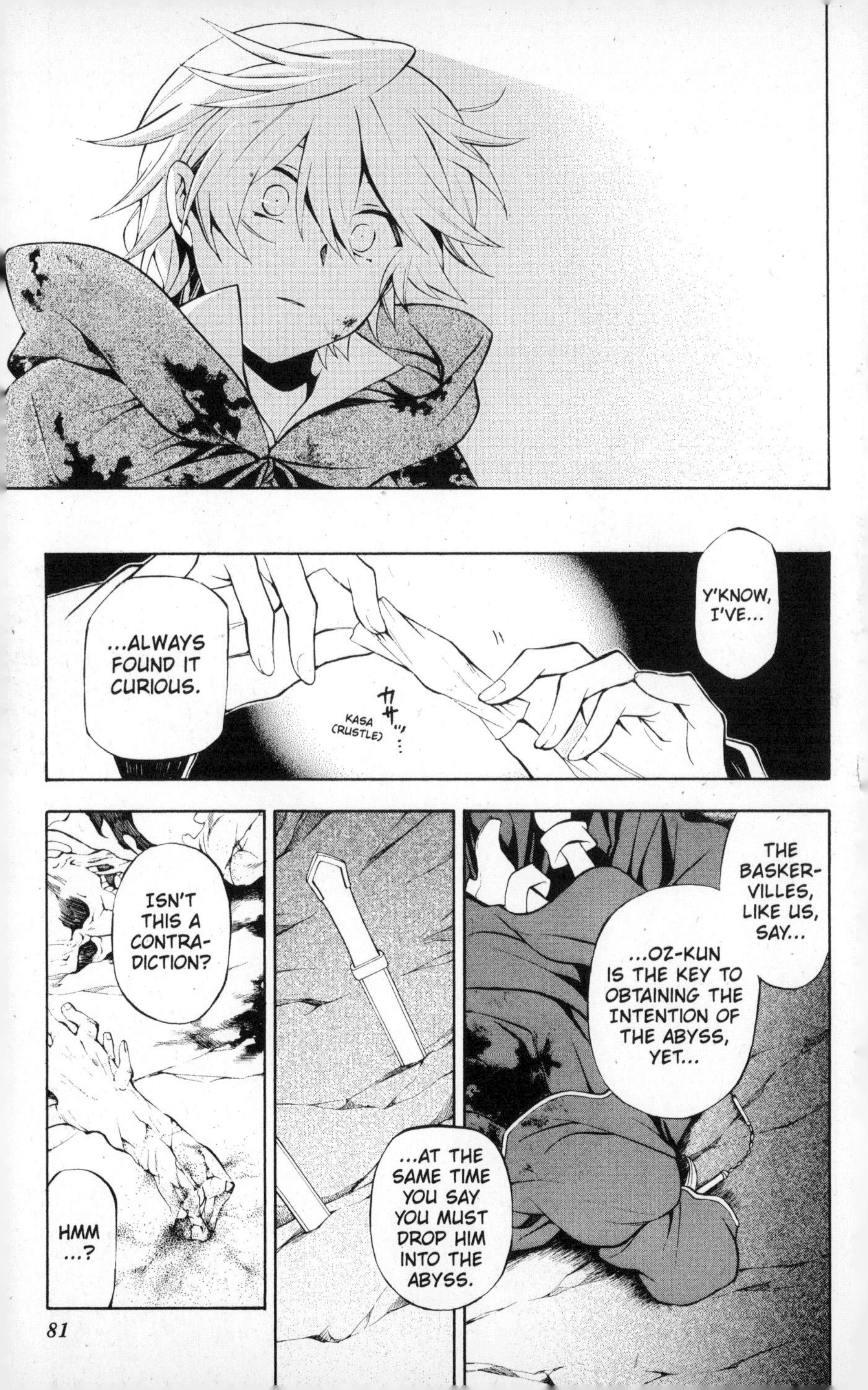
Y'KNOW, I'VE...
...ALWAYS FOUND IT CURIOUS.
KASA (RUSTLE)
THE BASKER-VILLES, LIKE US, SAY...
...OZ-KUN IS THE KEY TO OBTAINING THE INTENTION OF THE ABYSS, YET...
...AT THE SAME TIME YOU SAY YOU MUST DROP HIM INTO THE ABYSS.
ISN'T THIS A CONTRA-DICTION?
HMM ...?

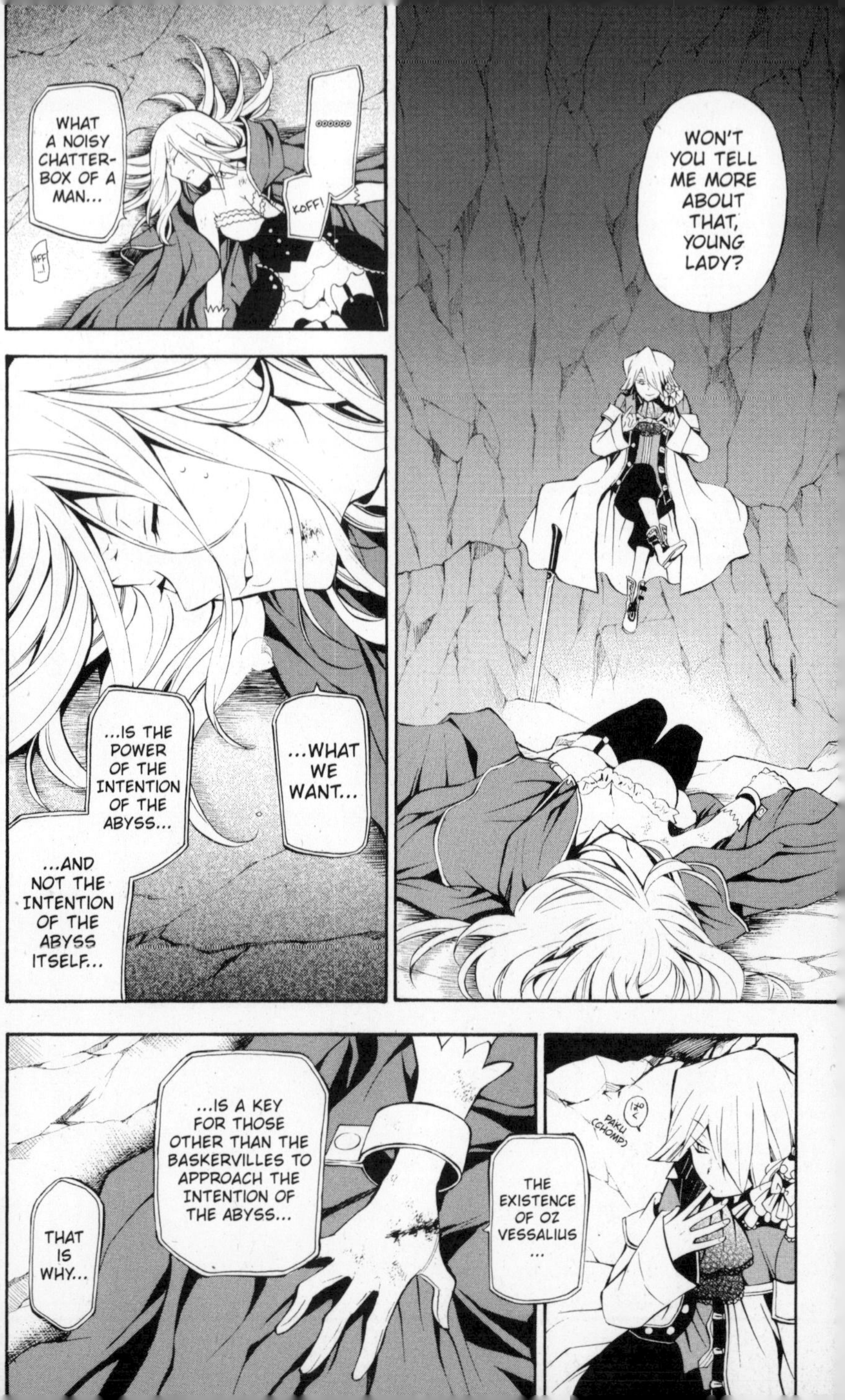
WON'T YOU TELL ME MORE ABOUT THAT, YOUNG LADY?
......
KOFF!
WHAT A NOISY CHATTER-BOX OF A MAN...
HFF...!
...WHAT WE WANT...
...IS THE POWER OF THE INTENTION OF THE ABYSS...
...AND NOT THE INTENTION OF THE ABYSS ITSELF...
PAKU (CHOMP)
THE EXISTENCE OF OZ VESSALIUS...
...IS A KEY FOR THOSE OTHER THAN THE BASKERVILLES TO APPROACH THE INTENTION OF THE ABYSS...
THAT IS WHY...

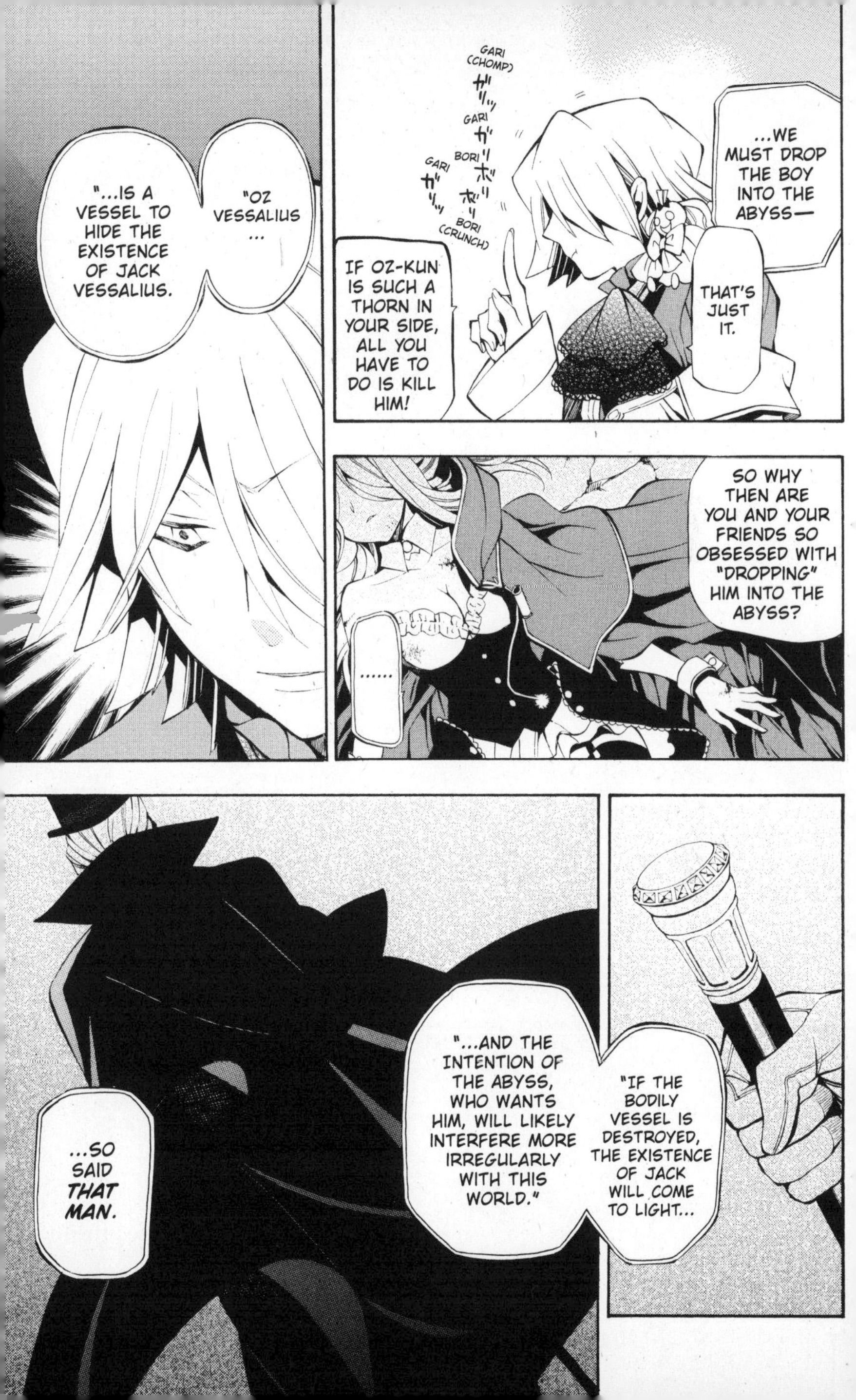

...WE MUST DROP THE BOY INTO THE ABYSS—
THAT'S JUST IT.
GARI (CHOMP)
GARI
BORI
GARI
BORI (CRUNCH)
IF OZ-KUN IS SUCH A THORN IN YOUR SIDE, ALL YOU HAVE TO DO IS KILL HIM!
SO WHY THEN ARE YOU AND YOUR FRIENDS SO OBSESSED WITH "DROPPING" HIM INTO THE ABYSS?
......
"OZ VESSALIUS ...
"...IS A VESSEL TO HIDE THE EXISTENCE OF JACK VESSALIUS.
"IF THE BODILY VESSEL IS DESTROYED, THE EXISTENCE OF JACK WILL COME TO LIGHT...
"...AND THE INTENTION OF THE ABYSS, WHO WANTS HIM, WILL LIKELY INTERFERE MORE IRREGULARLY WITH THIS WORLD."
...SO SAID *THAT MAN*.

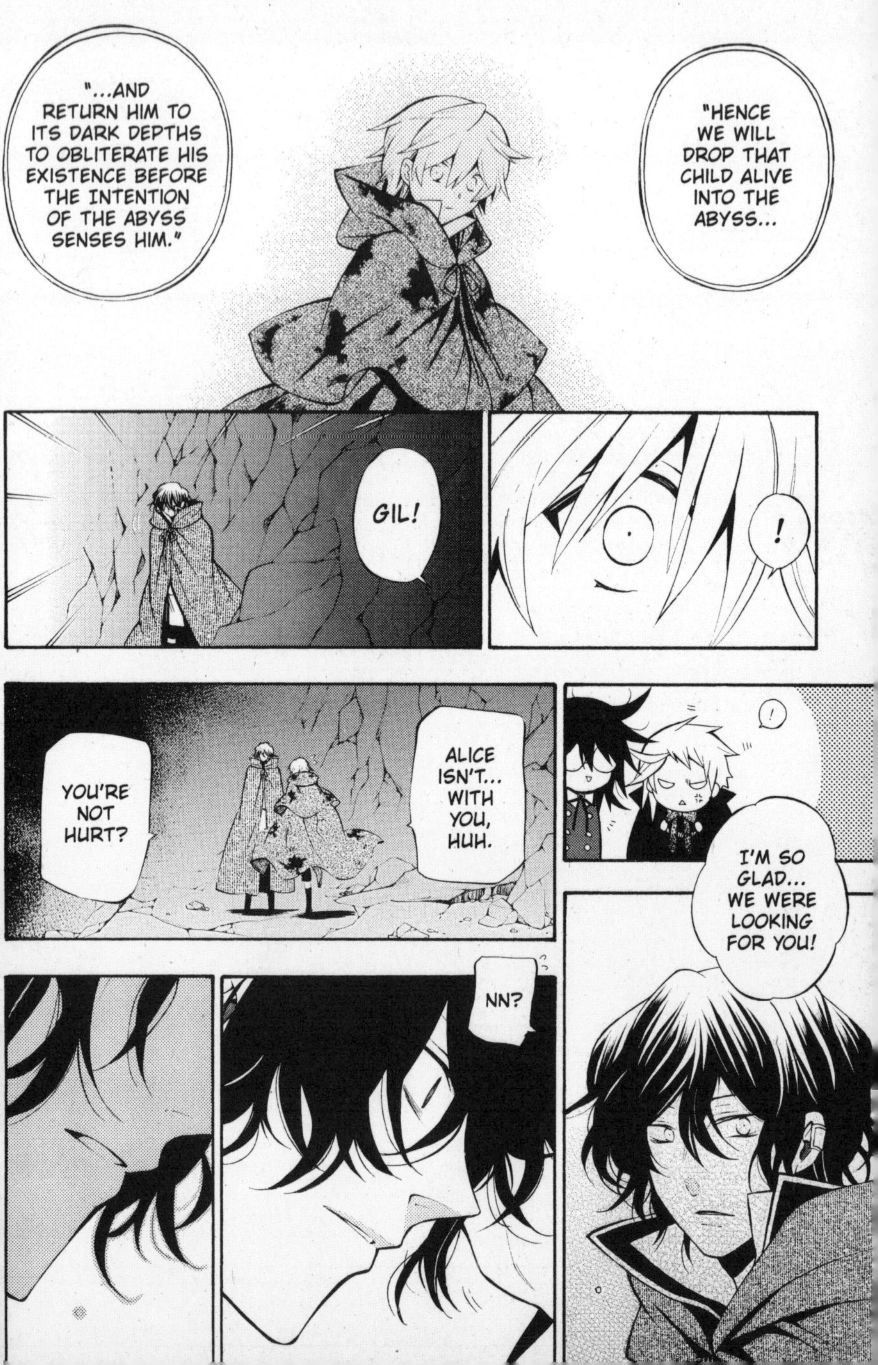
"HENCE WE WILL DROP THAT CHILD ALIVE INTO THE ABYSS...
"...AND RETURN HIM TO ITS DARK DEPTHS TO OBLITERATE HIS EXISTENCE BEFORE THE INTENTION OF THE ABYSS SENSES HIM."
!
GIL!
!
ALICE ISN'T... WITH YOU, HUH.
YOU'RE NOT HURT?
I'M SO GLAD... WE WERE LOOKING FOR YOU!
NN?

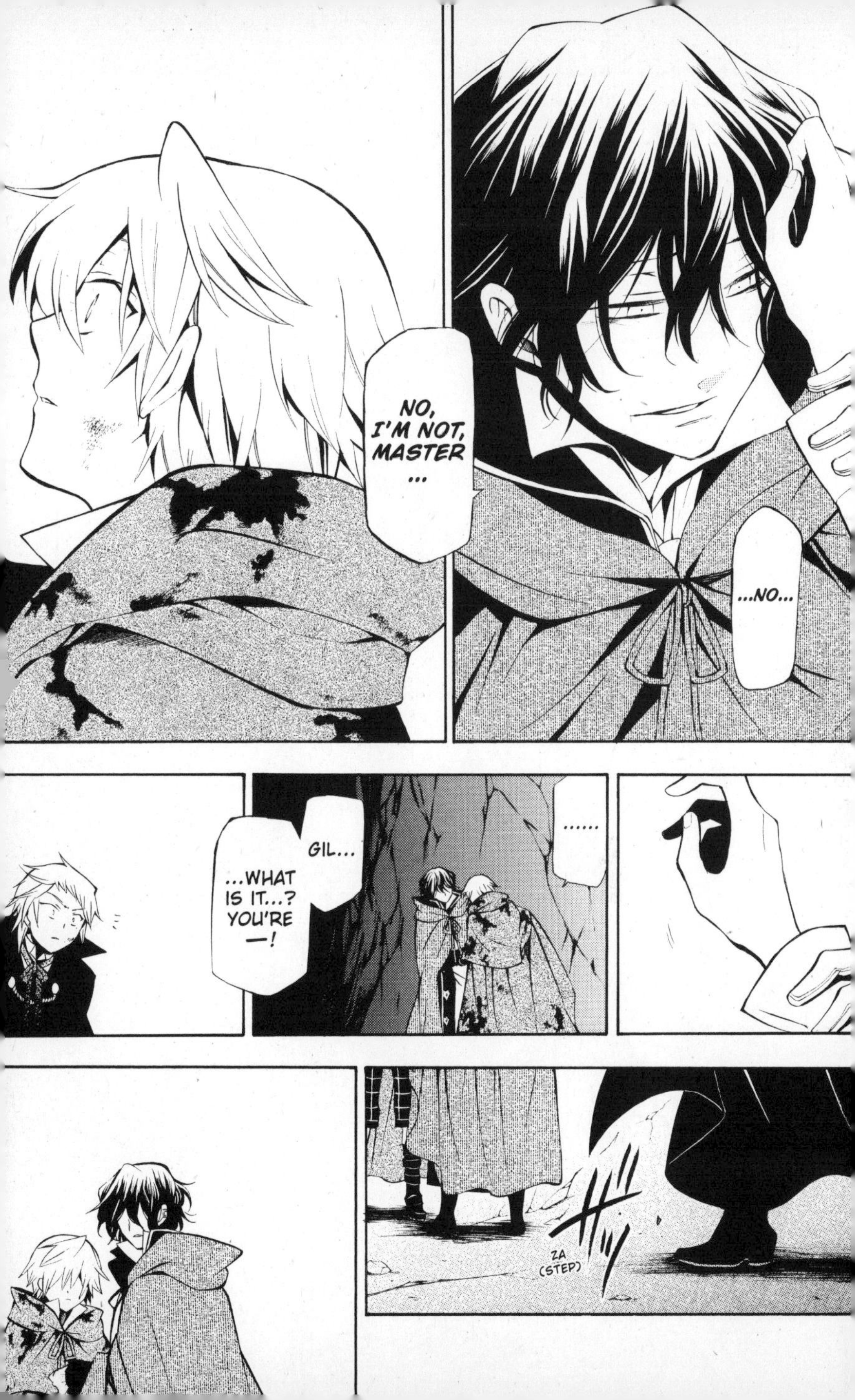
NO, I'M NOT, MASTER ...
...NO...
......
GIL...
...WHAT IS IT...? YOU'RE —!
ZA (STEP)

DOKUN
(BADUM)

86

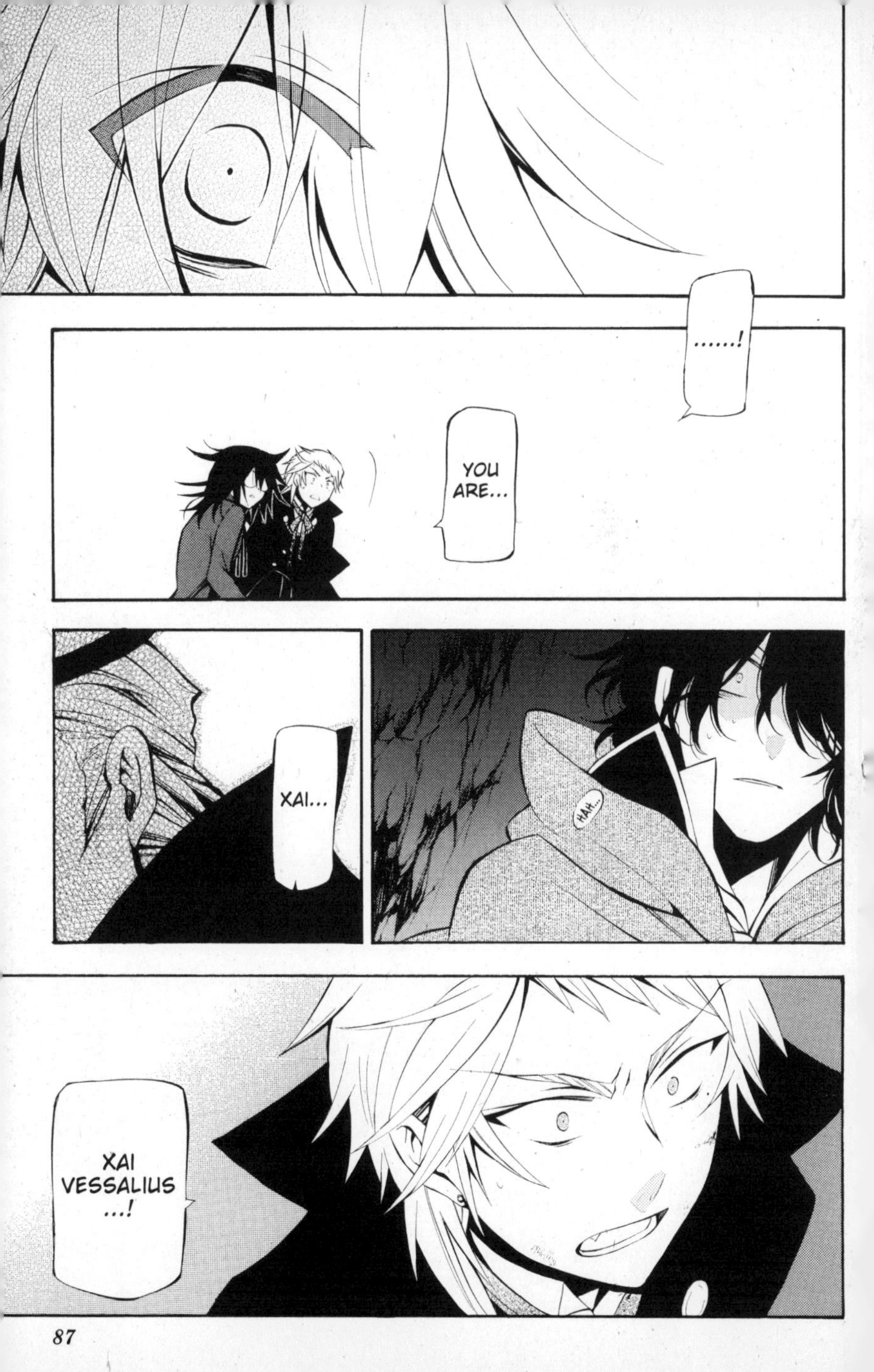
......!
YOU ARE...
HAH...
XAI...
XAI VESSALIUS ...!

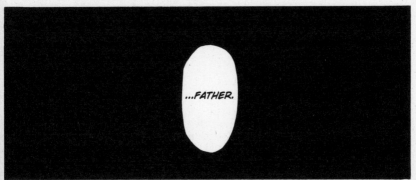

...FATHER.

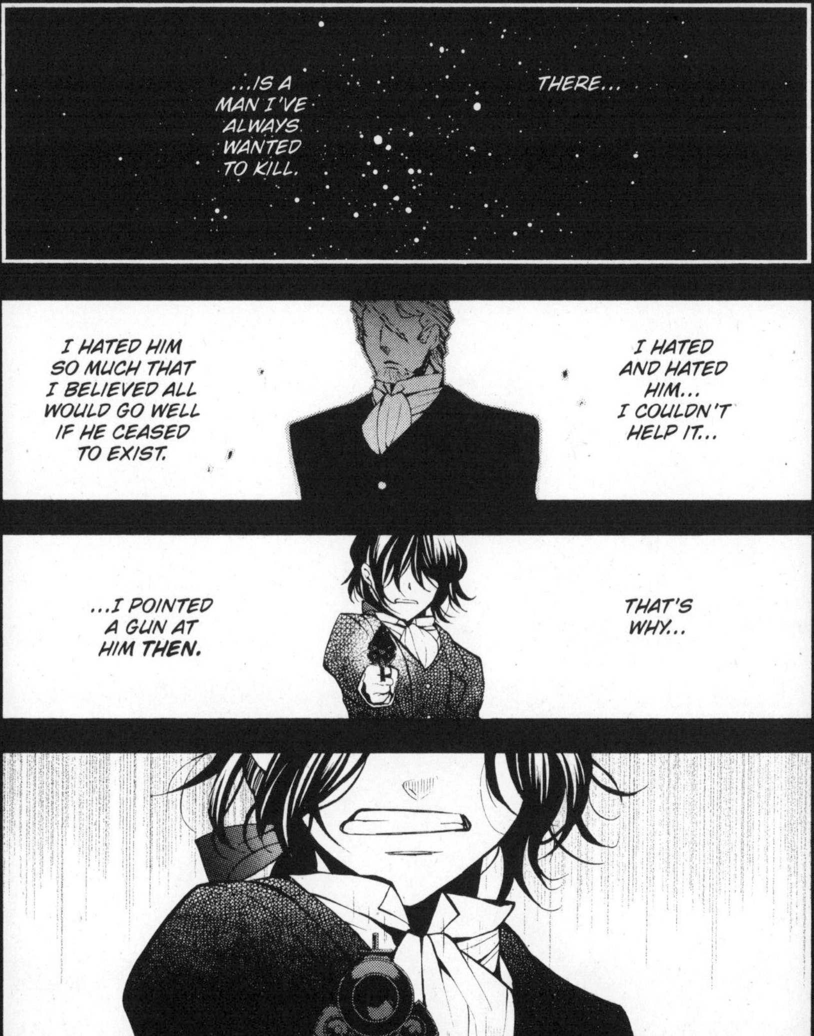
THERE...
...IS A MAN I'VE ALWAYS WANTED TO KILL.
I HATED AND HATED HIM... I COULDN'T HELP IT...
I HATED HIM SO MUCH THAT I BELIEVED ALL WOULD GO WELL IF HE CEASED TO EXIST.
THAT'S WHY...
...I POINTED A GUN AT HIM THEN.

Retrace:XL Blindness

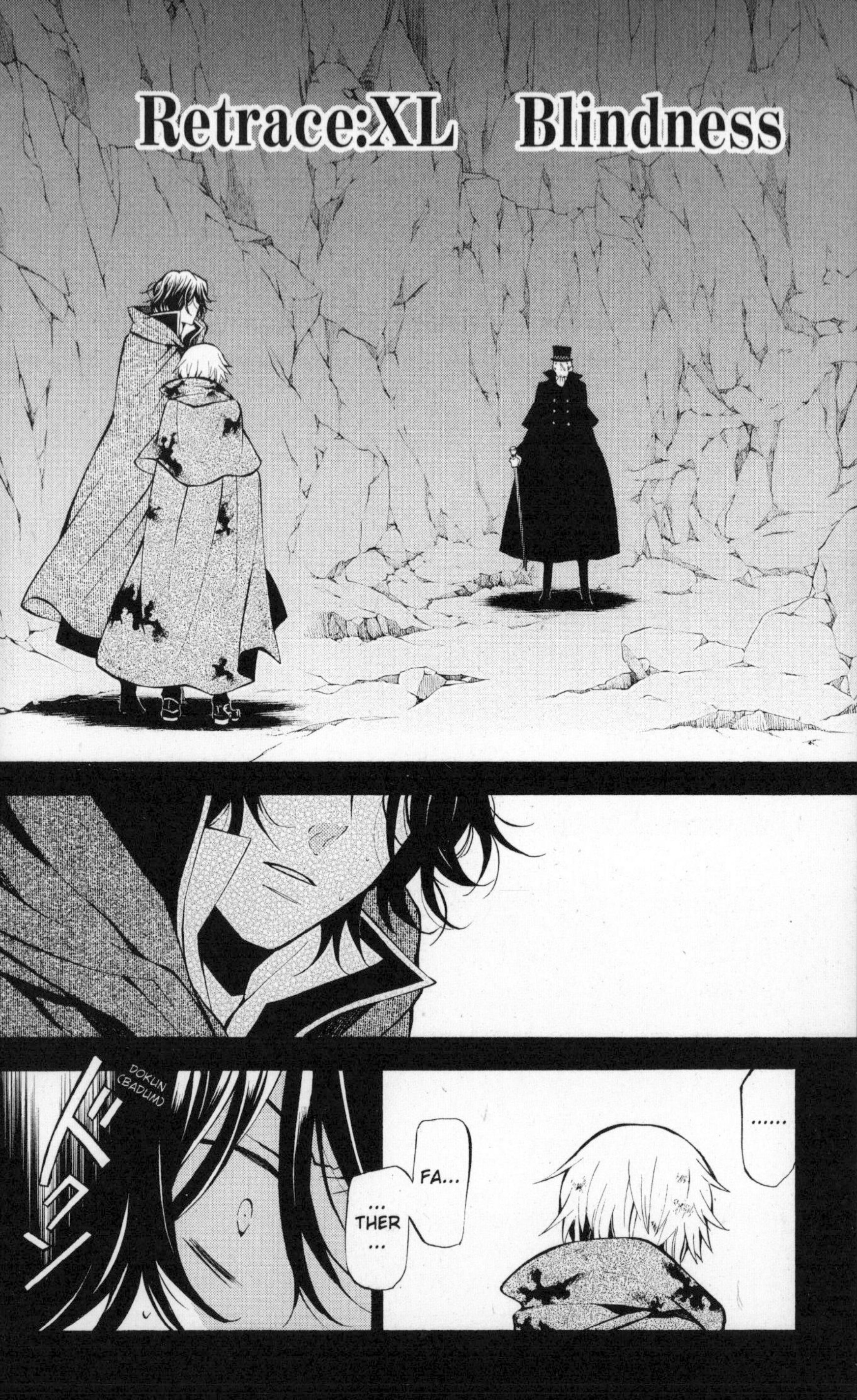
......
FA... ...THER...
DOKUN (BADUM)

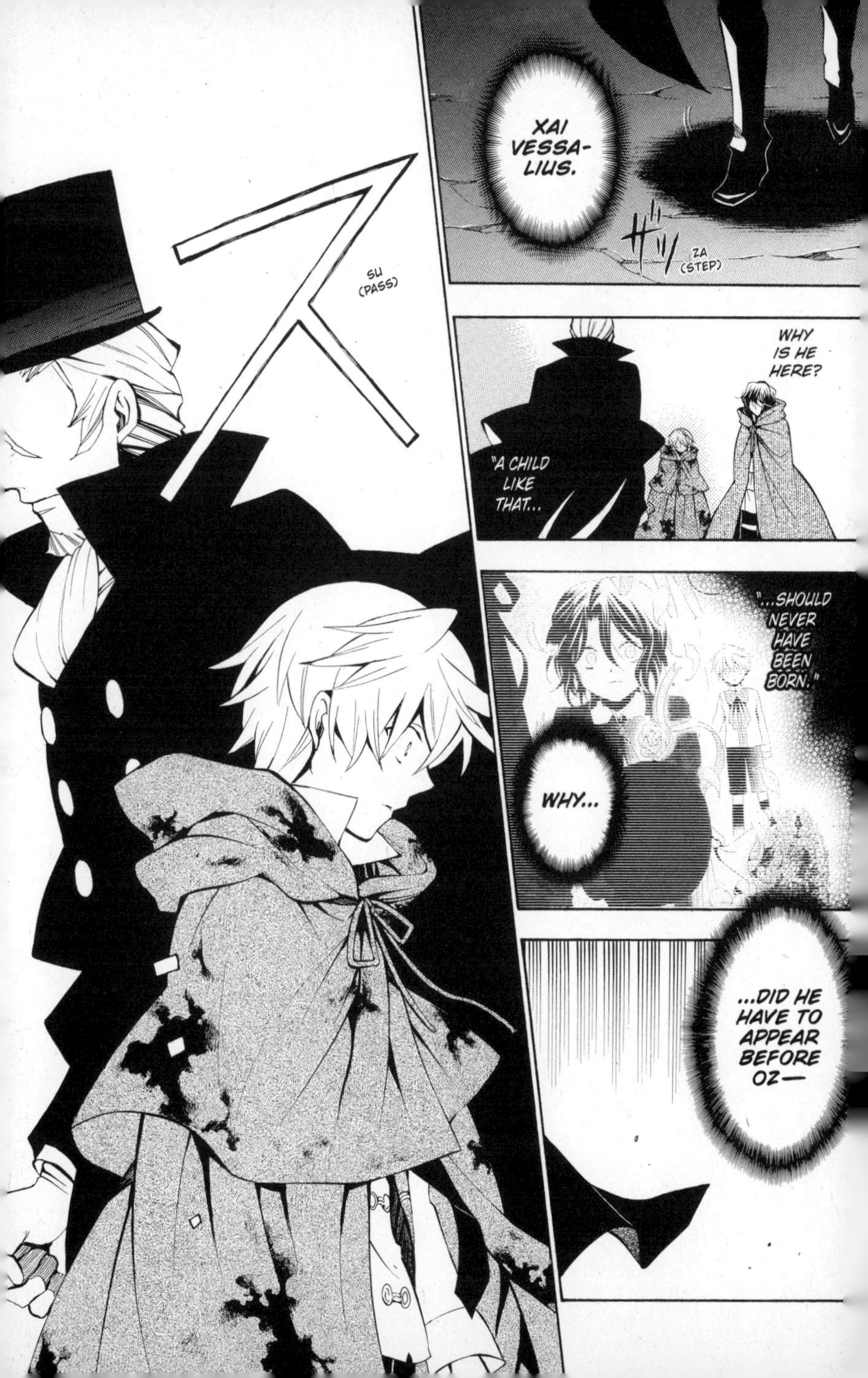
XAI VESSA-LIUS.
ZA (STEP)
WHY IS HE HERE?
"A CHILD LIKE THAT...
"...SHOULD NEVER HAVE BEEN BORN."
WHY...
...DID HE HAVE TO APPEAR BEFORE OZ—
SU (PASS)

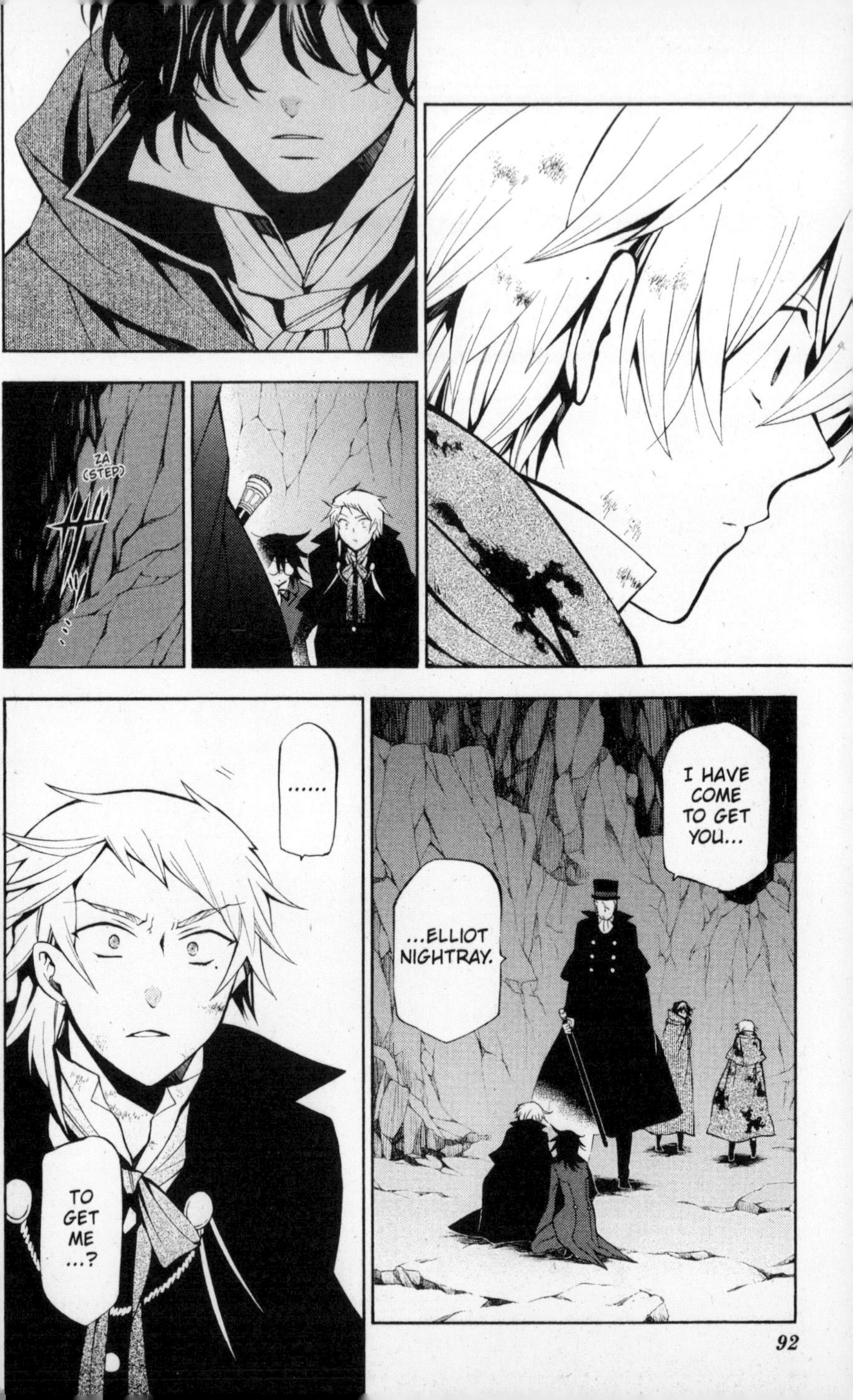
ZA (STEP)
I HAVE COME TO GET YOU...
...ELLIOT NIGHTRAY.
......
TO GET ME ...?

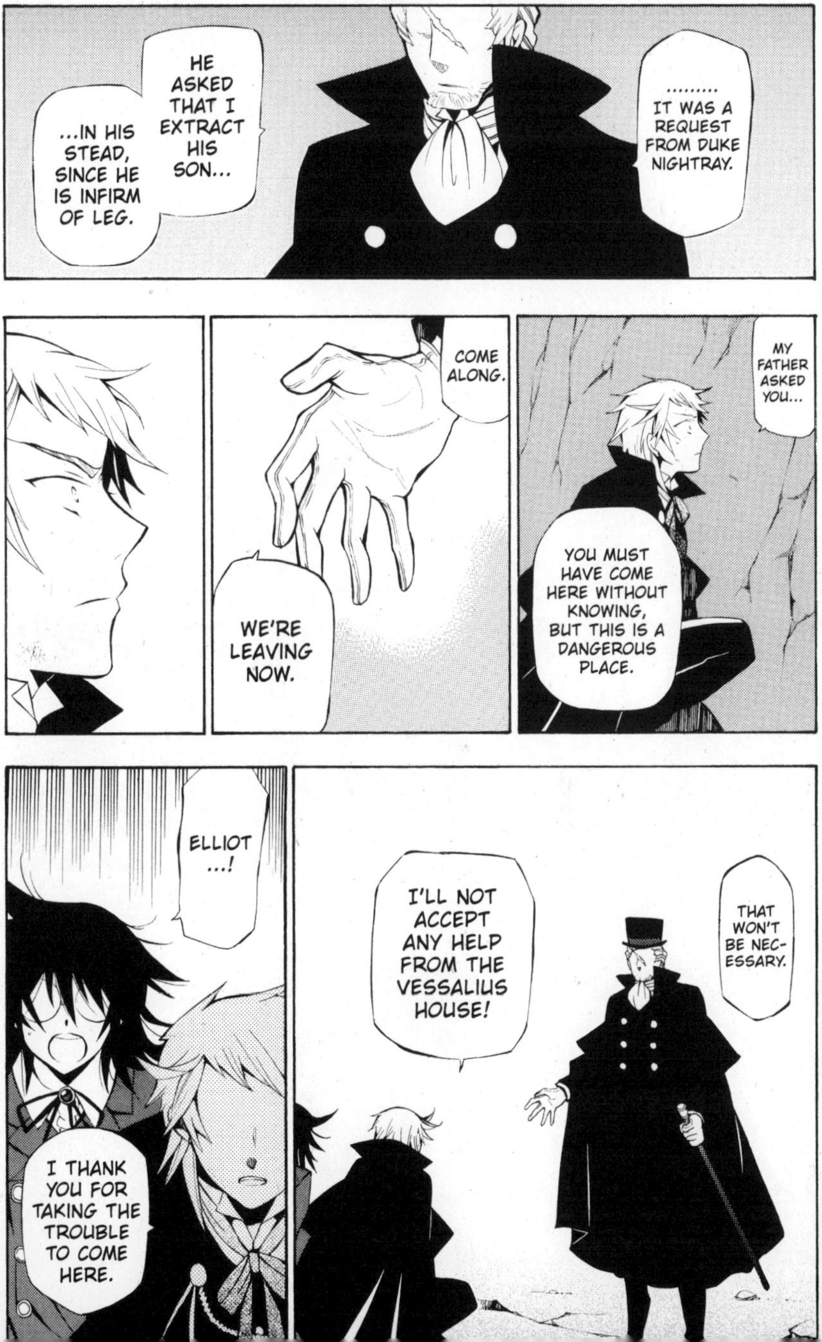
....
IT WAS A REQUEST FROM DUKE NIGHTRAY.
HE ASKED THAT I EXTRACT HIS SON...
...IN HIS STEAD, SINCE HE IS INFIRM OF LEG.
MY FATHER ASKED YOU...
YOU MUST HAVE COME HERE WITHOUT KNOWING, BUT THIS IS A DANGEROUS PLACE.
COME ALONG.
WE'RE LEAVING NOW.
THAT WON'T BE NEC-ESSARY.
I'LL NOT ACCEPT ANY HELP FROM THE VESSALIUS HOUSE!
ELLIOT ...!
I THANK YOU FOR TAKING THE TROUBLE TO COME HERE.

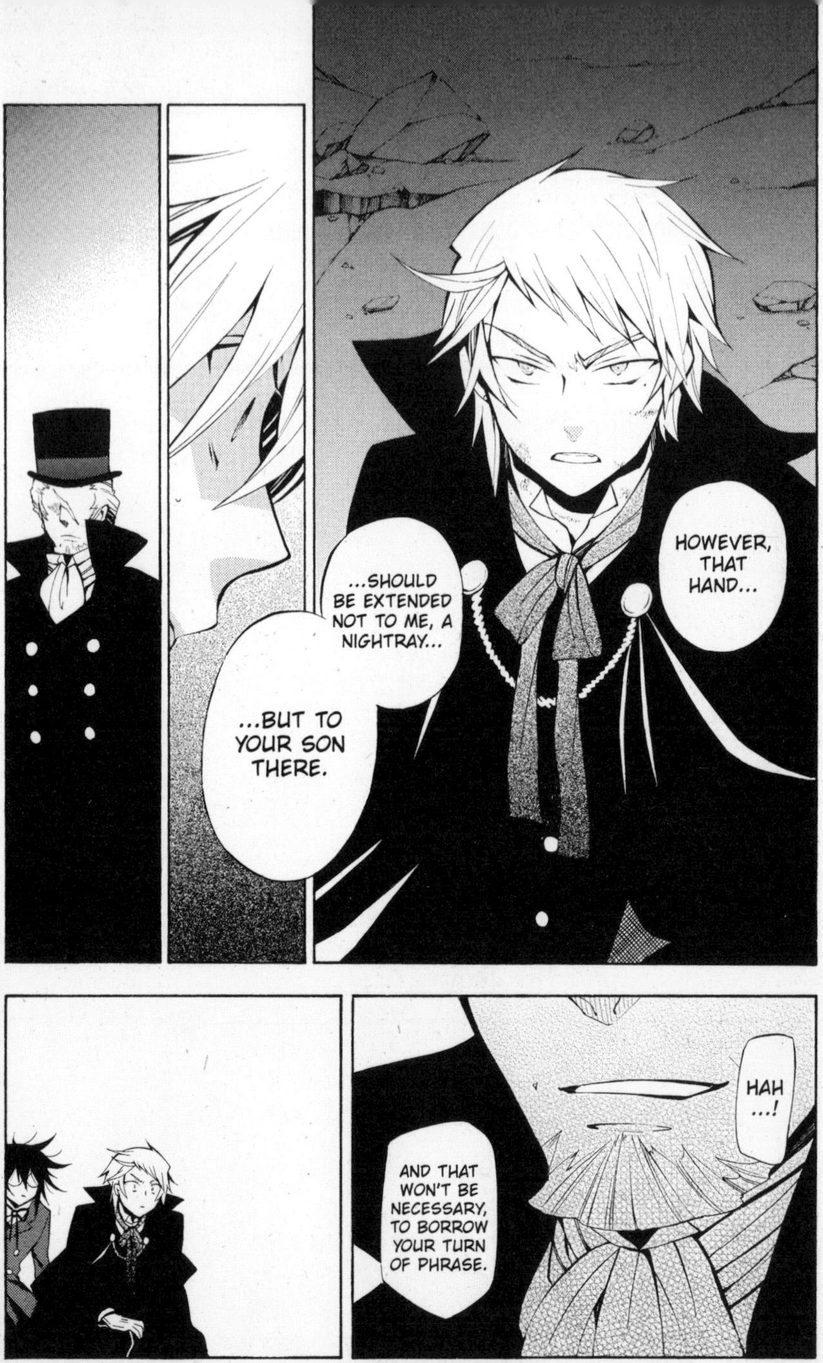
HOWEVER, THAT HAND...
...SHOULD BE EXTENDED NOT TO ME, A NIGHTRAY...
...BUT TO YOUR SON THERE.
HAH ...!
AND THAT WON'T BE NECESSARY, TO BORROW YOUR TURN OF PHRASE.

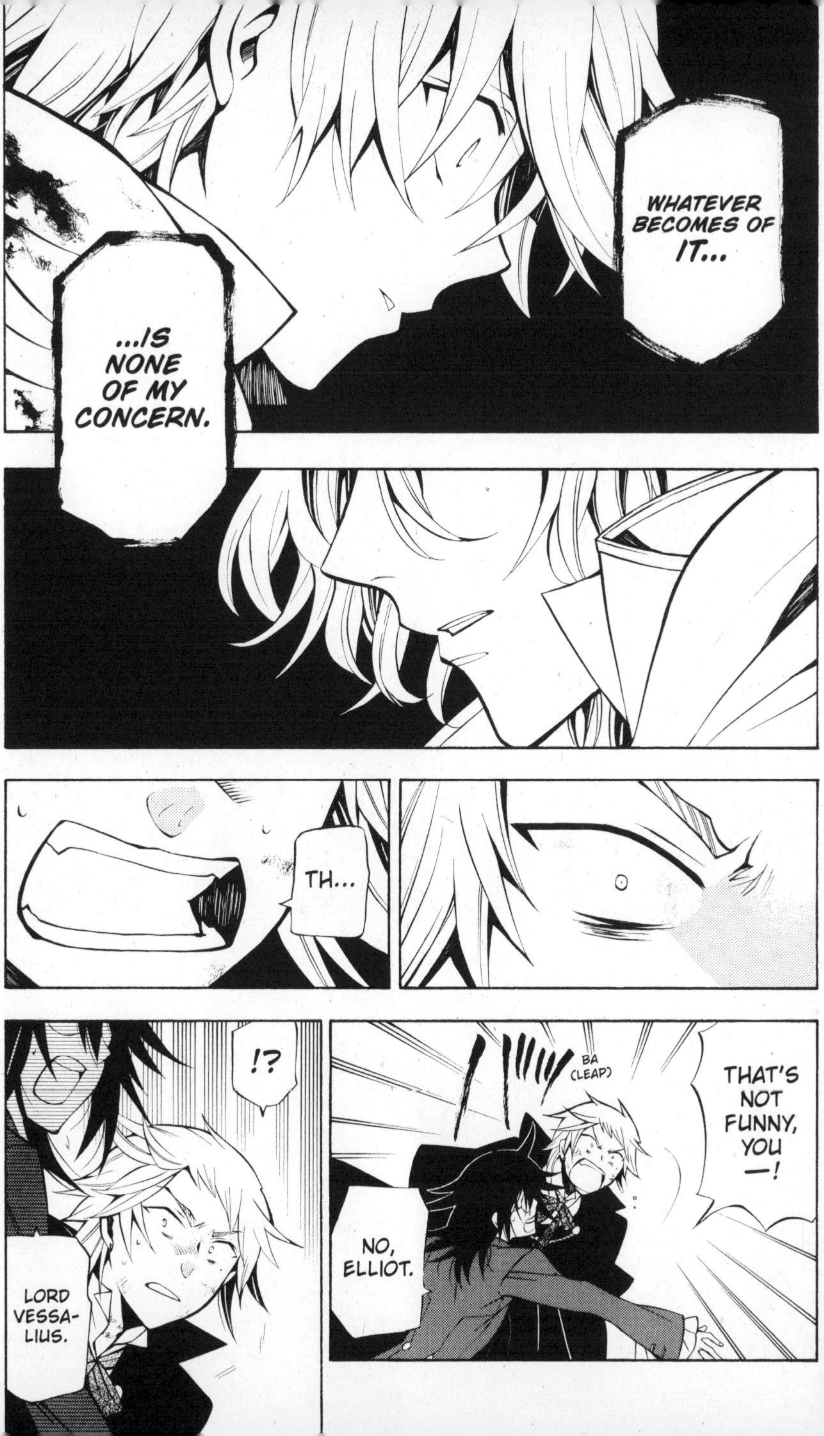
WHATEVER BECOMES OF IT...
...IS NONE OF MY CONCERN.
TH...
BA (LEAP)
THAT'S NOT FUNNY, YOU—!
NO, ELLIOT.
!?
LORD VESSALIUS.

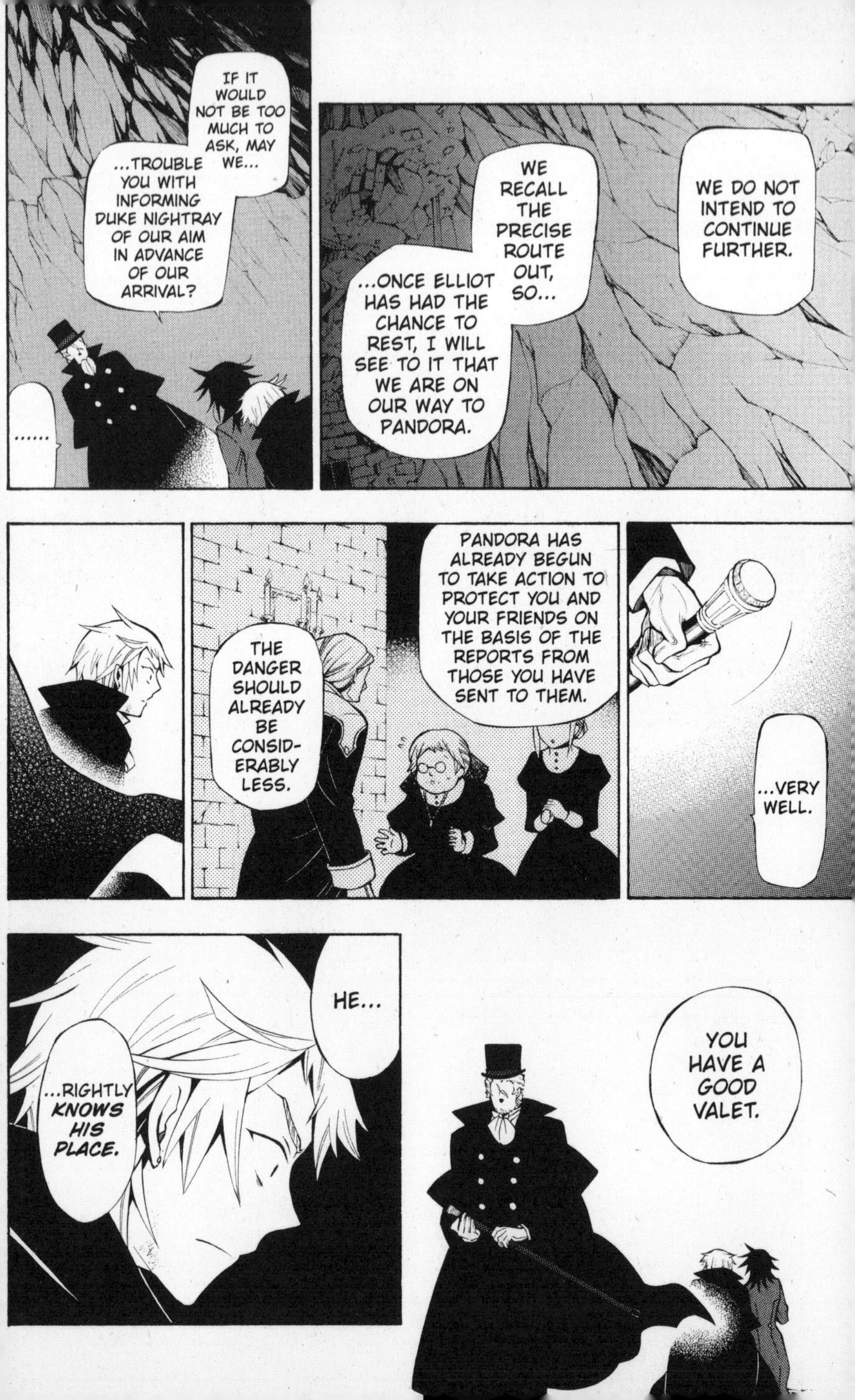
WE DO NOT INTEND TO CONTINUE FURTHER.
WE RECALL THE PRECISE ROUTE OUT, SO...
...ONCE ELLIOT HAS HAD THE CHANCE TO REST, I WILL SEE TO IT THAT WE ARE ON OUR WAY TO PANDORA.
IF IT WOULD NOT BE TOO MUCH TO ASK, MAY WE...
...TROUBLE YOU WITH INFORMING DUKE NIGHTRAY OF OUR AIM IN ADVANCE OF OUR ARRIVAL?
......
...VERY WELL.
PANDORA HAS ALREADY BEGUN TO TAKE ACTION TO PROTECT YOU AND YOUR FRIENDS ON THE BASIS OF THE REPORTS FROM THOSE YOU HAVE SENT TO THEM.
THE DANGER SHOULD ALREADY BE CONSIDERABLY LESS.
YOU HAVE A GOOD VALET.
HE...
...RIGHTLY KNOWS HIS PLACE.

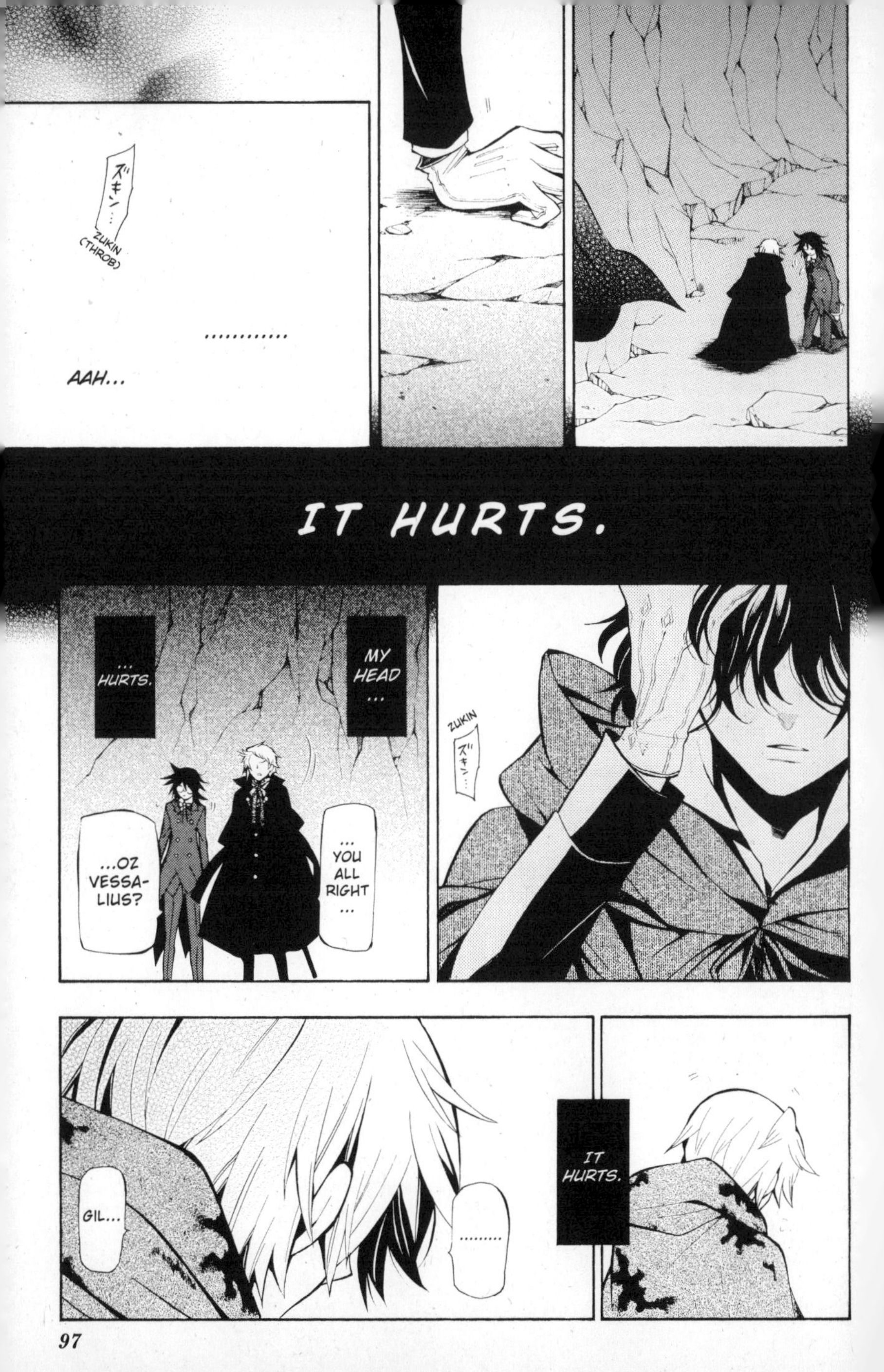

ズキン…
ZUKIN (THROB)
....
AAH...
IT HURTS.
ZUKIN
ズキン…
MY HEAD...
...HURTS.
...YOU ALL RIGHT...
...OZ VESSALIUS?
IT HURTS.
....
GIL...

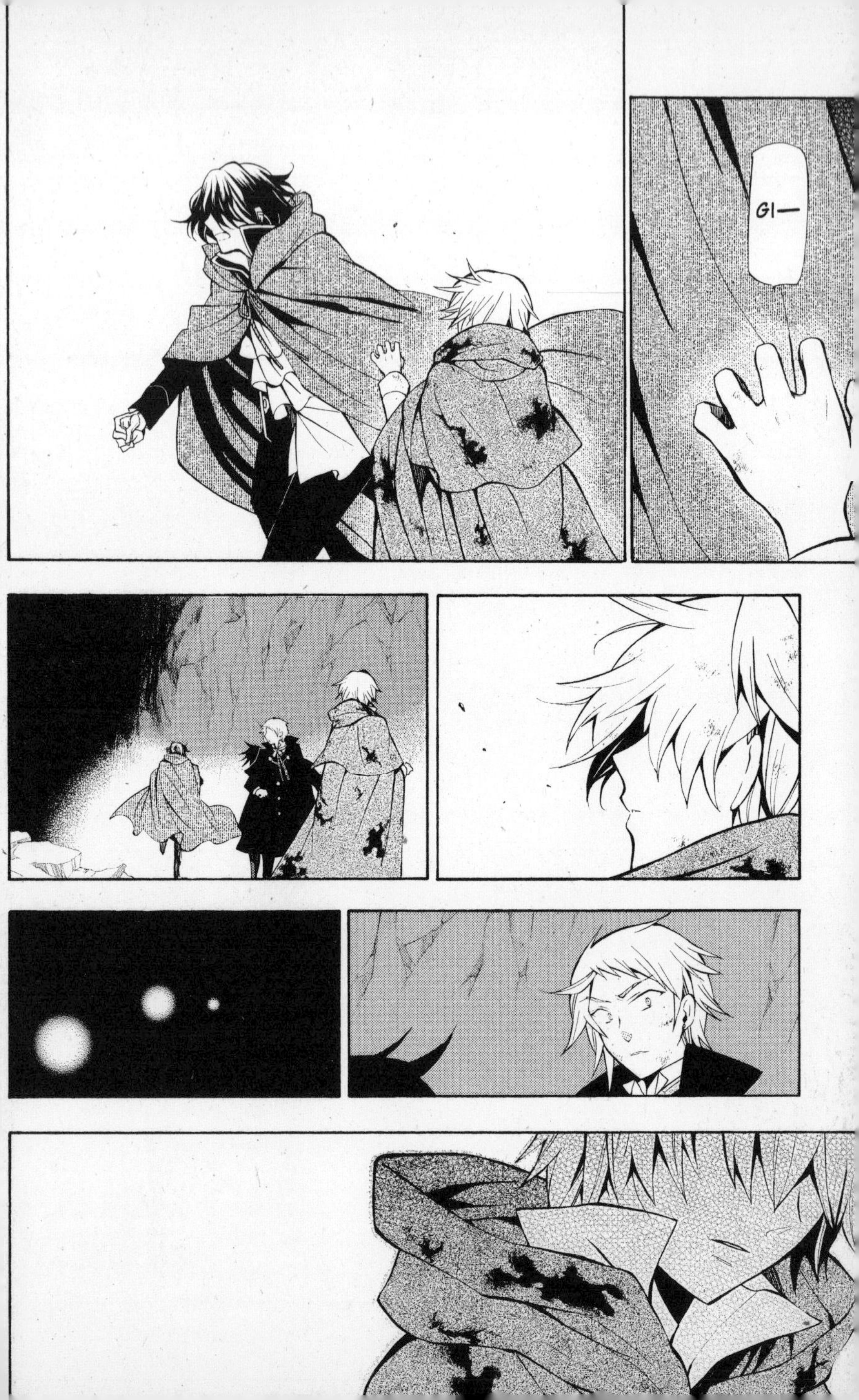
GI—

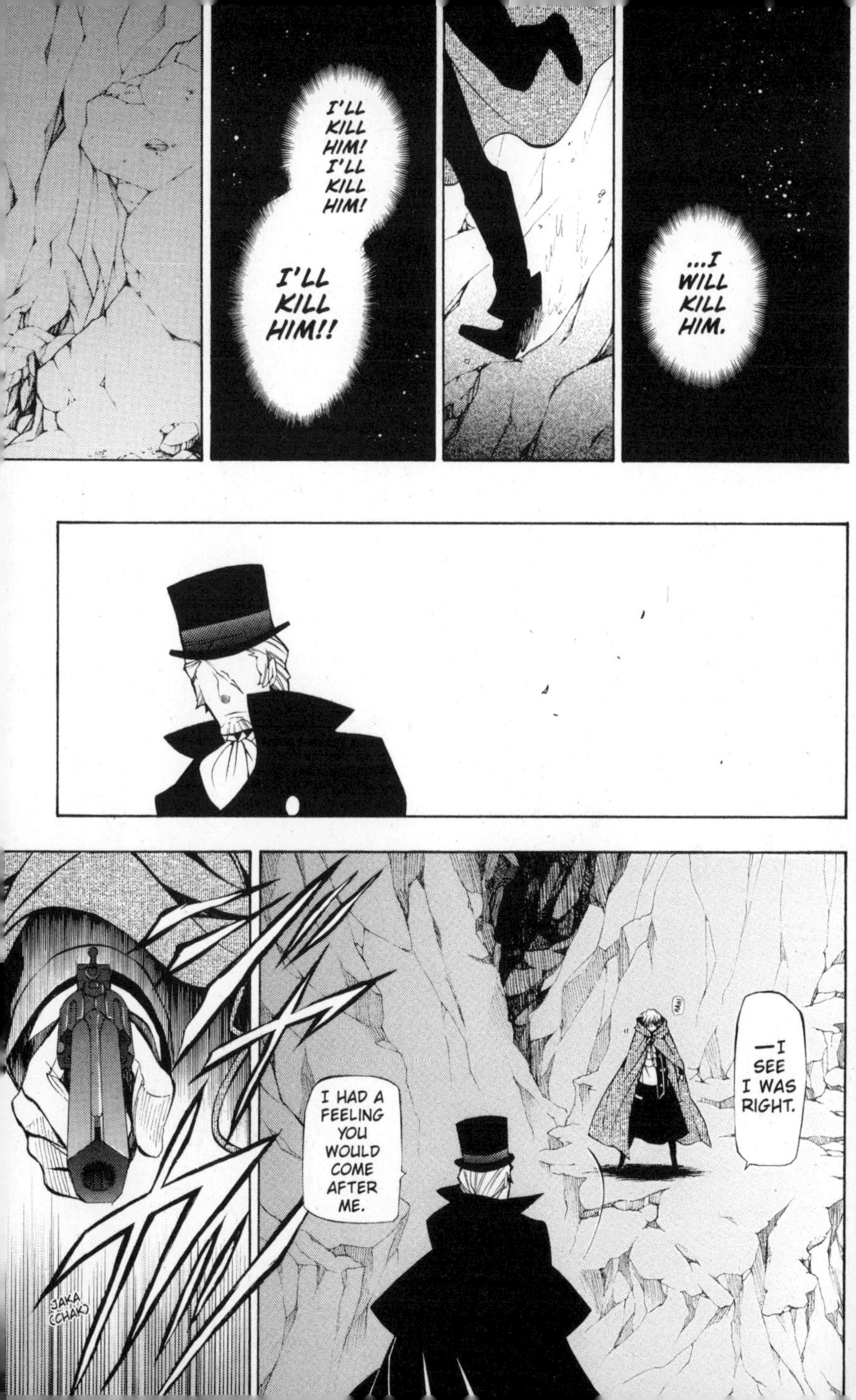
...I WILL KILL HIM.
I'LL KILL HIM! I'LL KILL HIM!
I'LL KILL HIM!!
HAH
—I SEE I WAS RIGHT.
I HAD A FEELING YOU WOULD COME AFTER ME.
JAKA (CHAK)

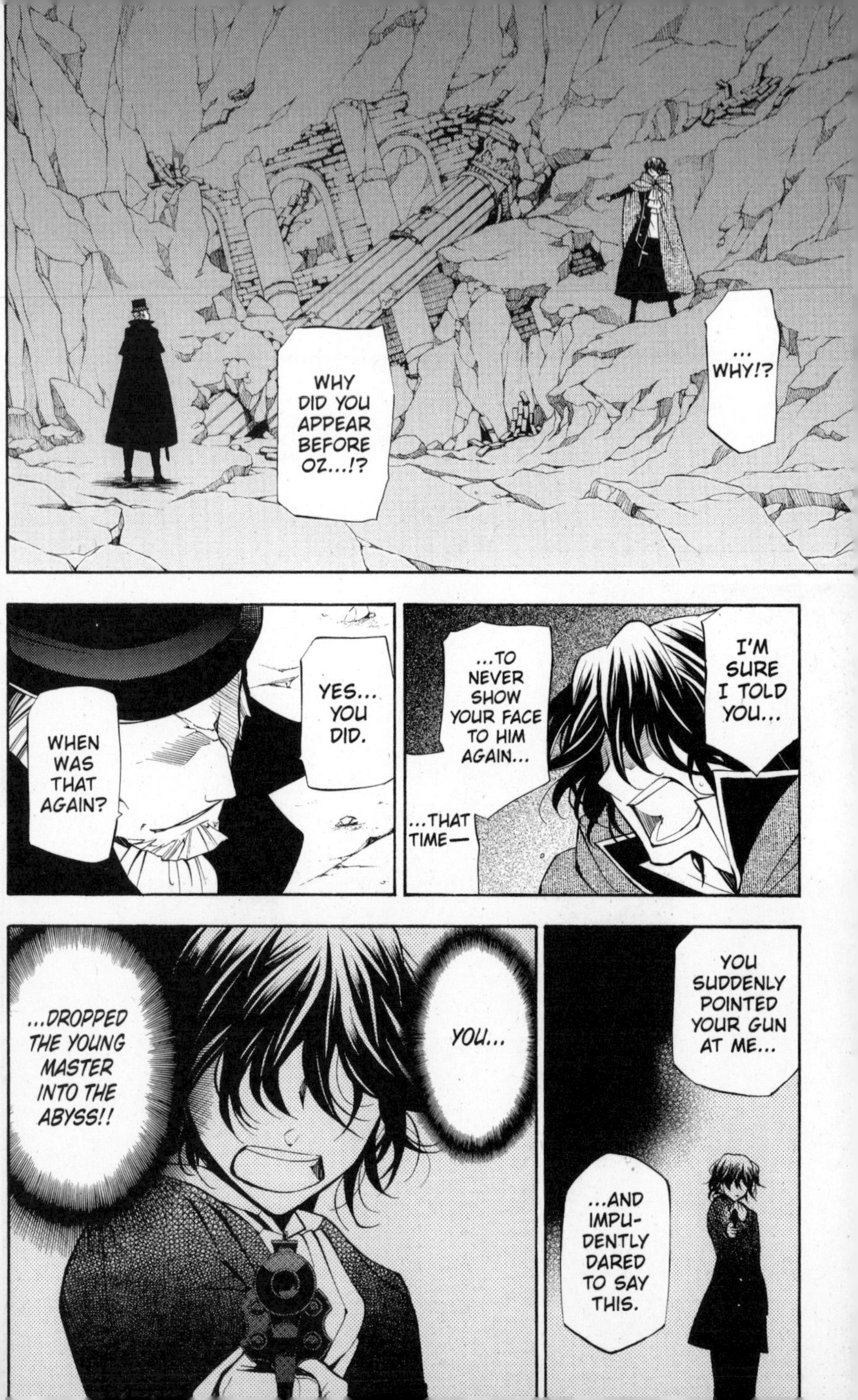
...WHY!?
WHY DID YOU APPEAR BEFORE OZ...!?
I'M SURE I TOLD YOU...
...TO NEVER SHOW YOUR FACE TO HIM AGAIN...
...THAT TIME—
YES... YOU DID.
WHEN WAS THAT AGAIN?
YOU SUDDENLY POINTED YOUR GUN AT ME...
...AND IMPUDENTLY DARED TO SAY THIS.
YOU...
...DROPPED THE YOUNG MASTER INTO THE ABYSS!!

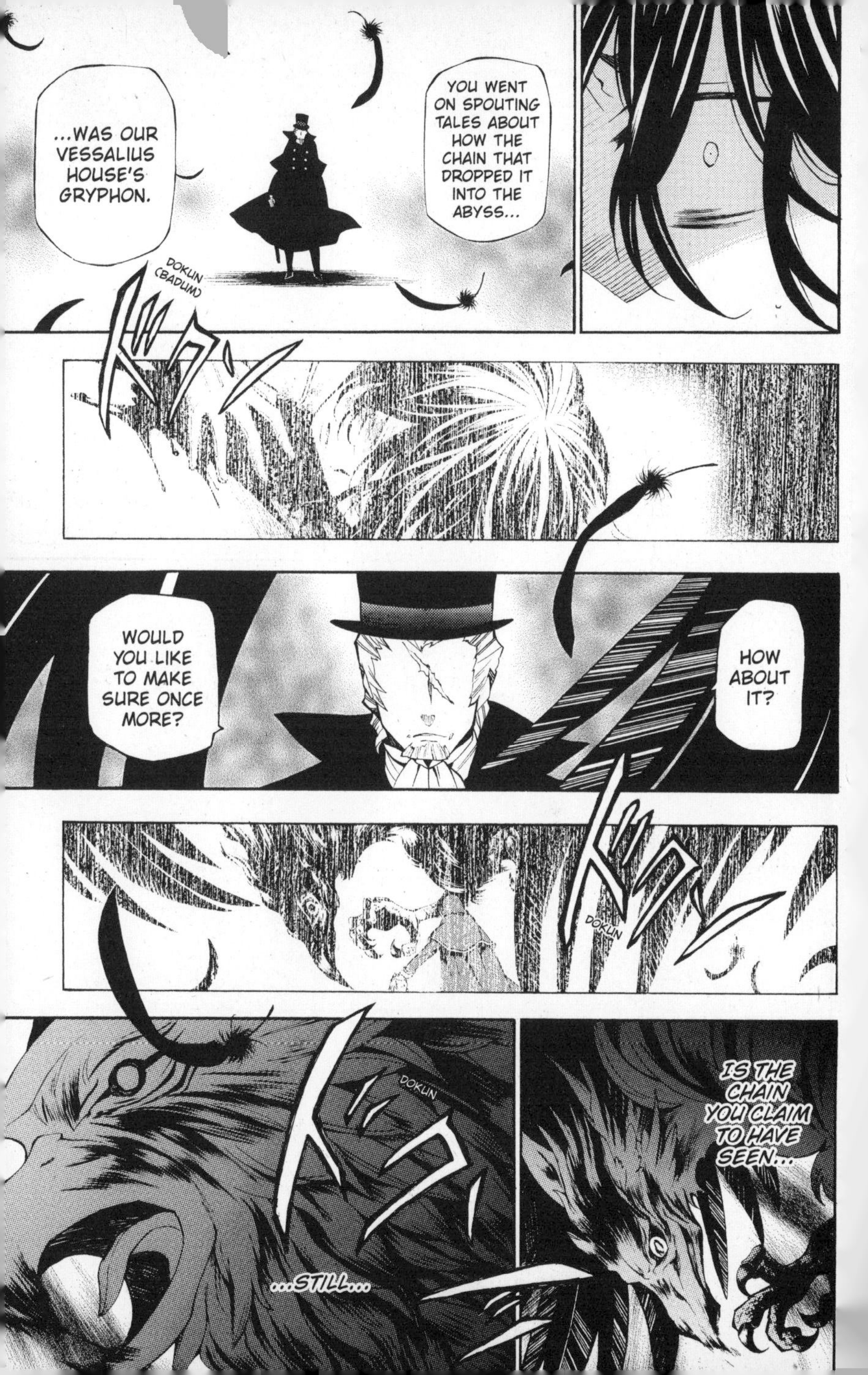
YOU WENT ON SPOUTING TALES ABOUT HOW THE CHAIN THAT DROPPED IT INTO THE ABYSS...
...WAS OUR VESSALIUS HOUSE'S GRYPHON.
DOKUN (BADUM)
HOW ABOUT IT?
WOULD YOU LIKE TO MAKE SURE ONCE MORE?
DOKUN
IS THE CHAIN YOU CLAIM TO HAVE SEEN...
DOKUN
...STILL...

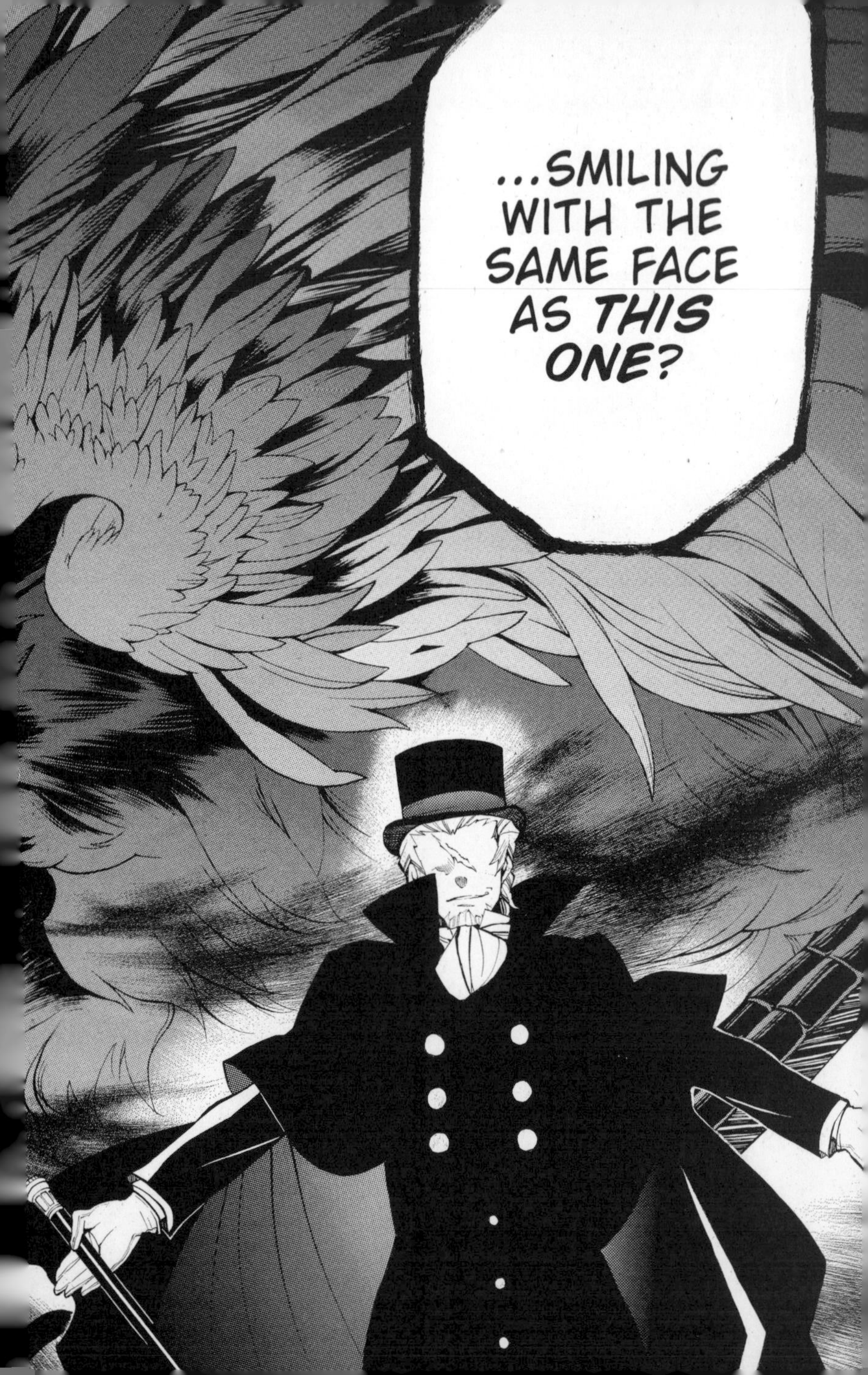
...SMILING WITH THE SAME FACE AS *THIS ONE*?

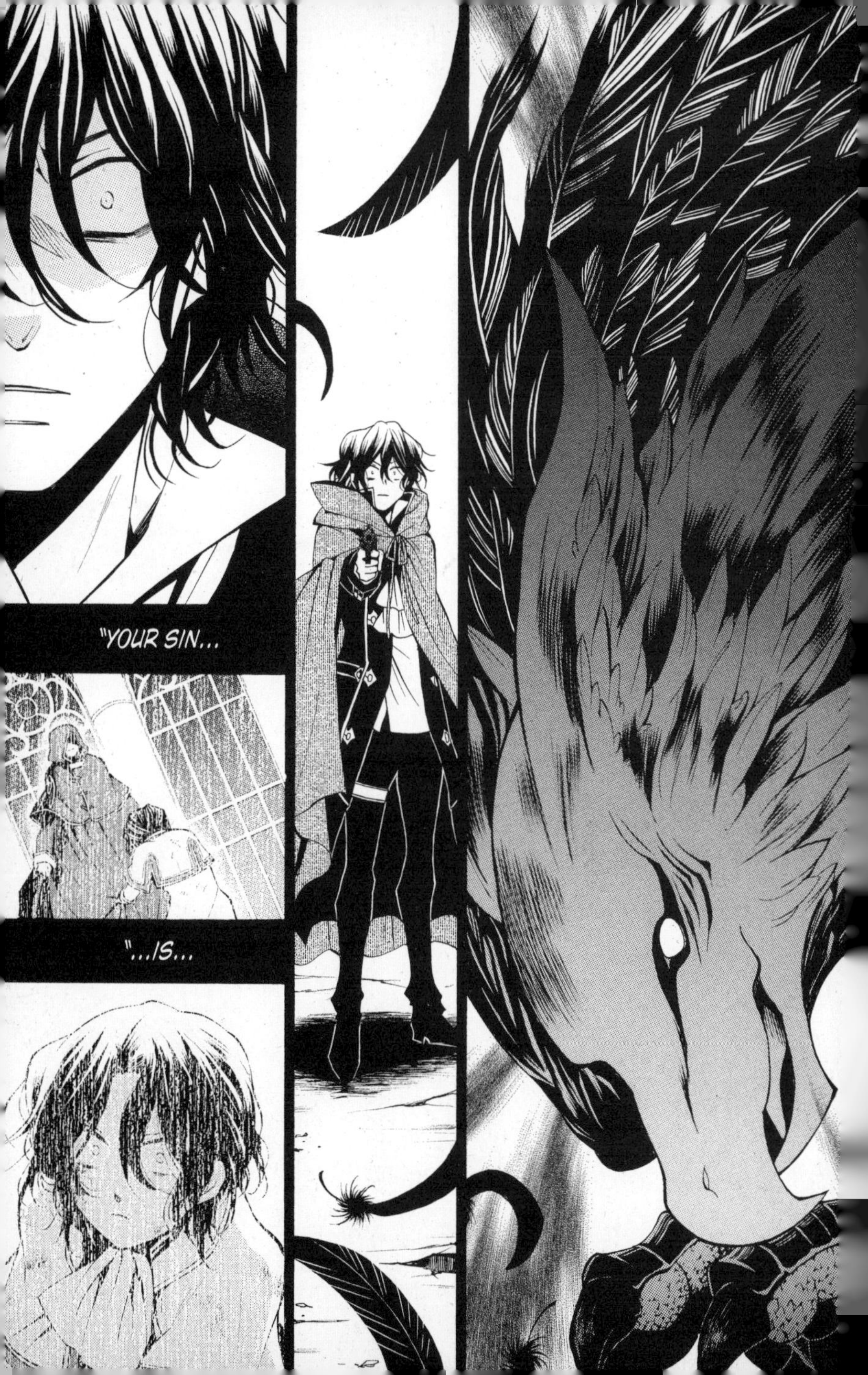
"YOUR SIN...
"...IS...

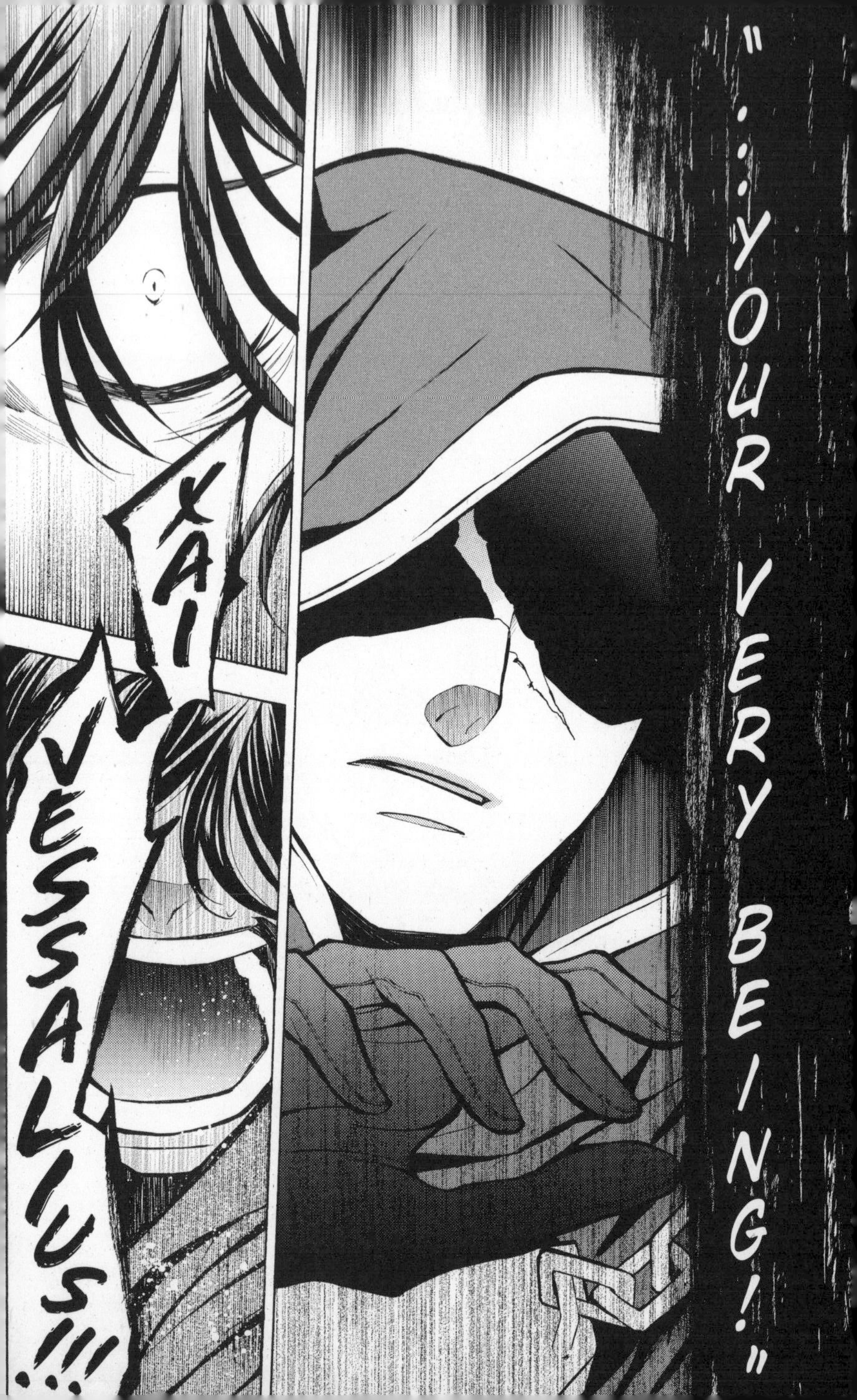
"...YOUR VERY BEING!"
XAI VESSALIUS!!!

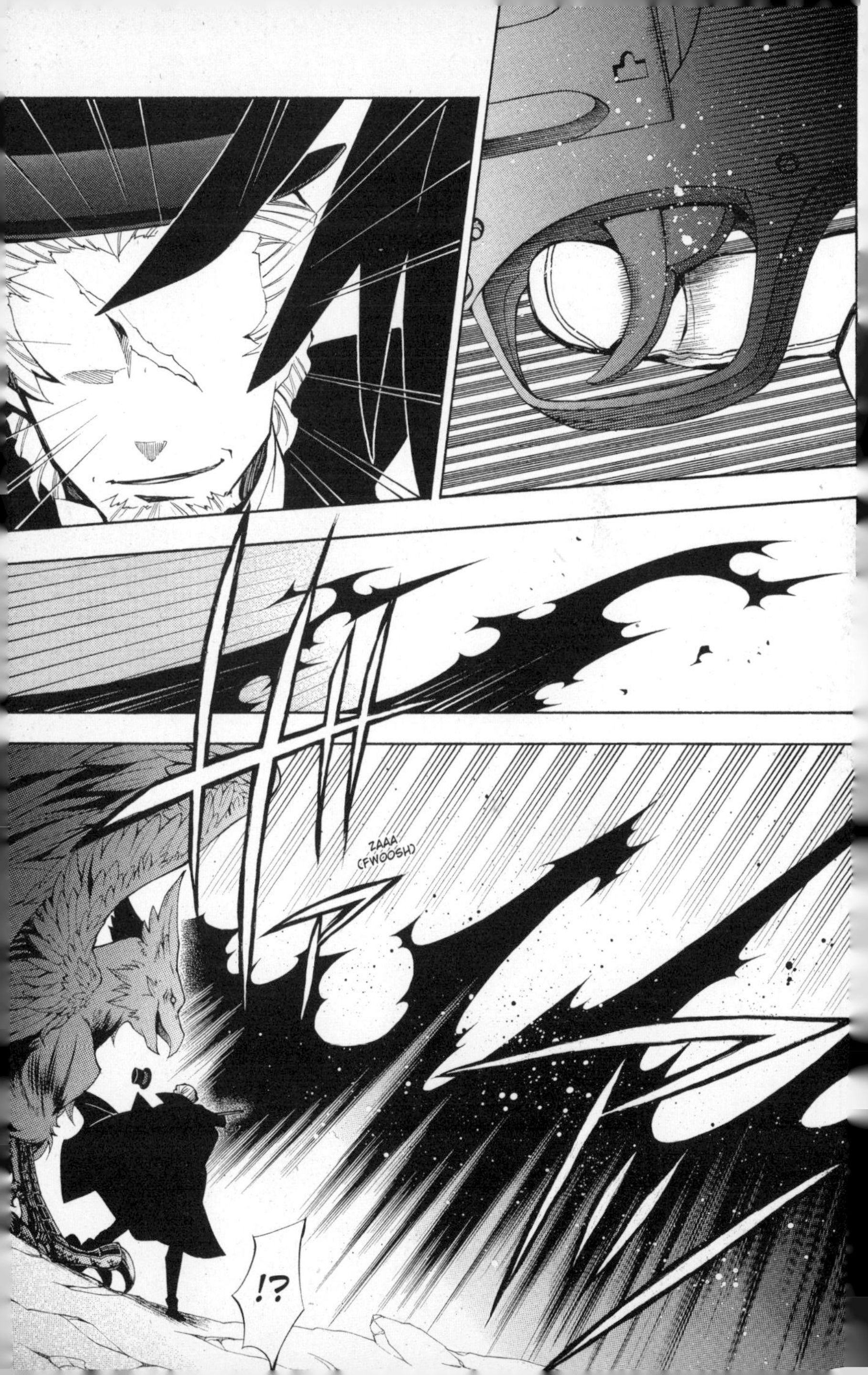
ZAAA
(FWOOSH)
!?

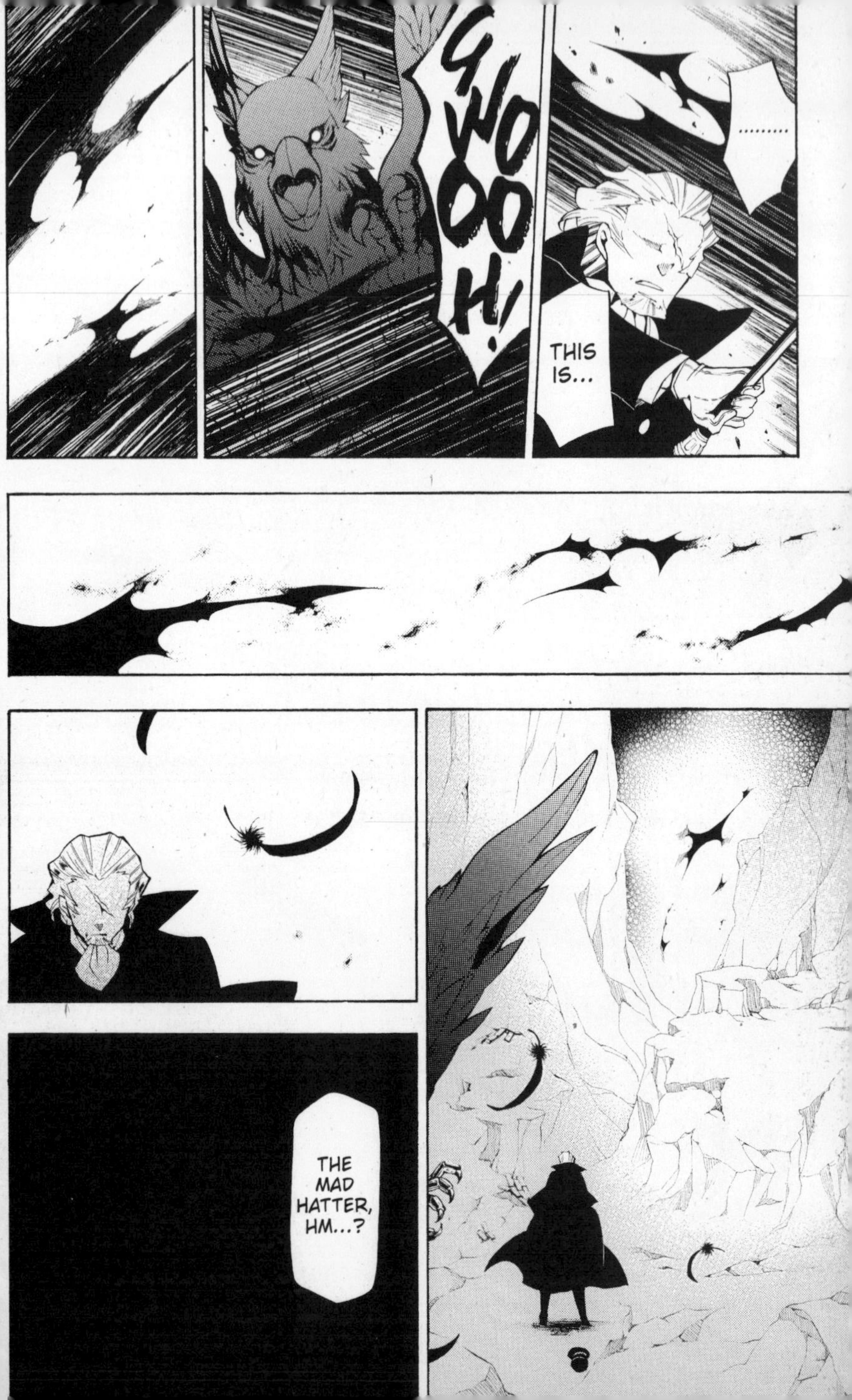
......
THIS IS...
GWOOOOH!
THE MAD HATTER, HM...?

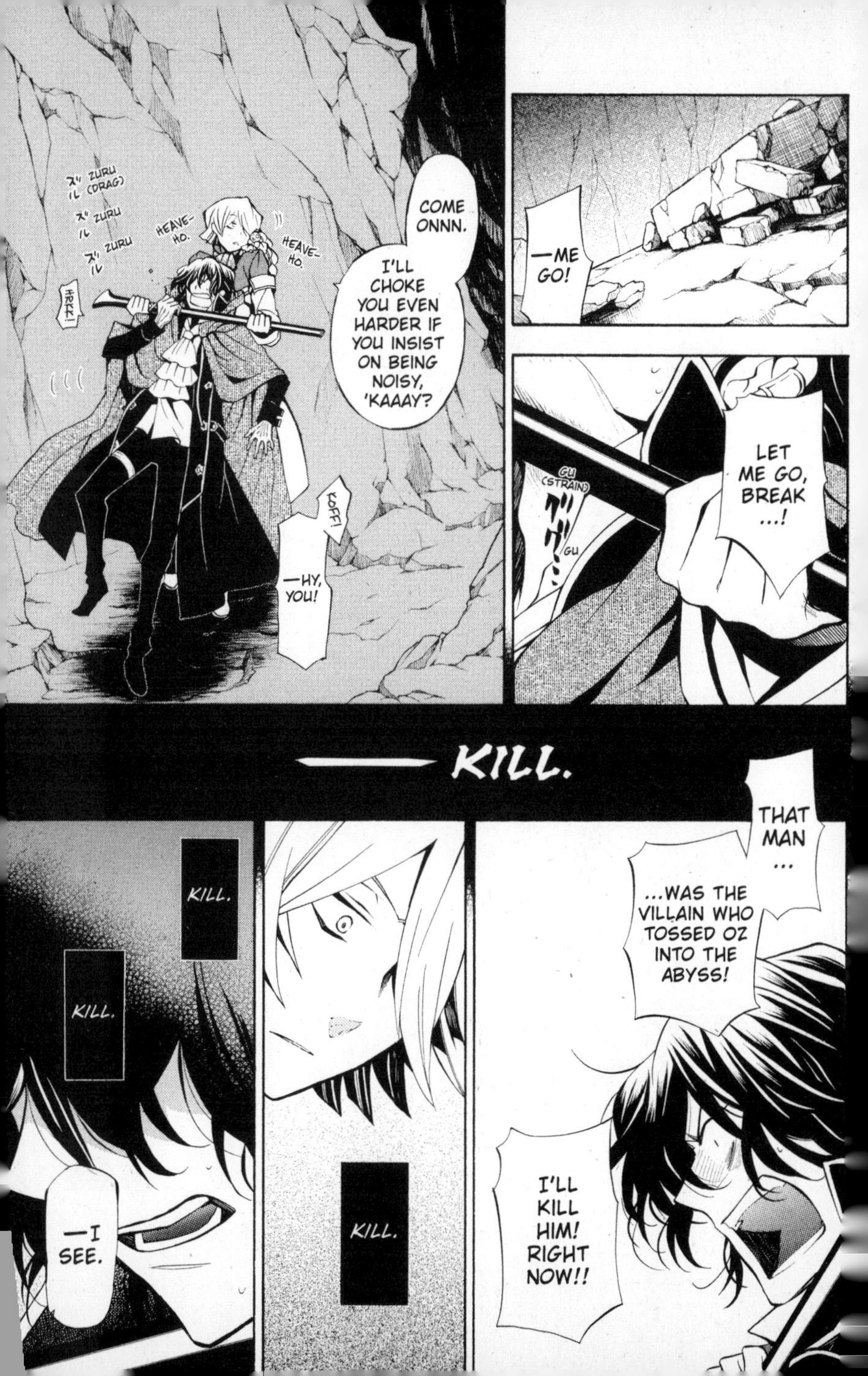
—ME GO!
LET ME GO, BREAK...!
GU (STRAIN)
GU
COME ONNN.
I'LL CHOKE YOU EVEN HARDER IF YOU INSIST ON BEING NOISY, 'KAAAY?
HEAVE-HO.
HEAVE-HO.
ZURU (DRAG)
ZURU
ZURU
HRRK!
KOFF!
—HY, YOU!
——KILL.
THAT MAN...
...WAS THE VILLAIN WHO TOSSED OZ INTO THE ABYSS!
I'LL KILL HIM! RIGHT NOW!!
KILL.
KILL.
KILL.
—I SEE.

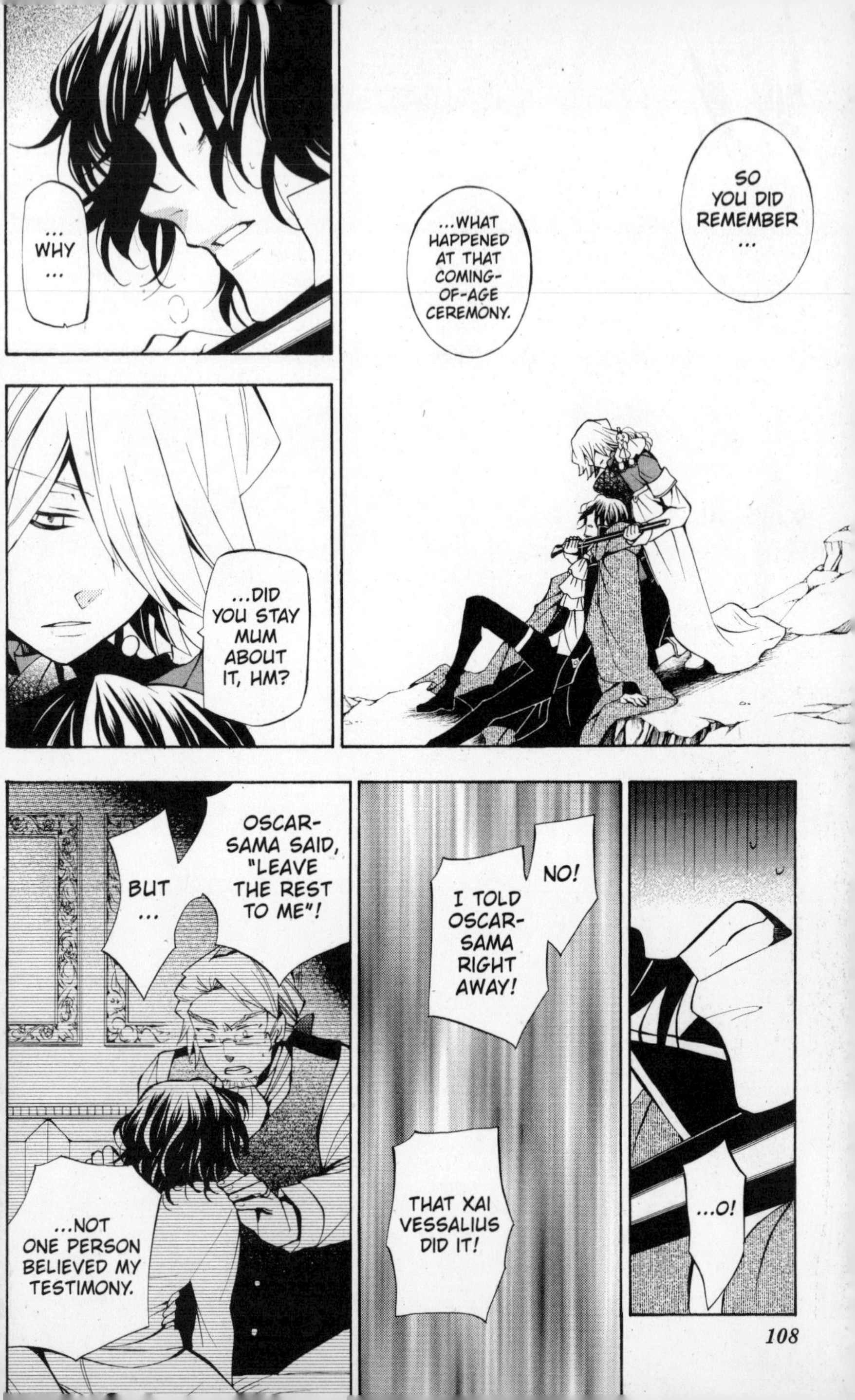
SO YOU DID REMEMBER ...
...WHAT HAPPENED AT THAT COMING-OF-AGE CEREMONY.
... WHY ...
...DID YOU STAY MUM ABOUT IT, HM?
...O!
NO!
I TOLD OSCAR-SAMA RIGHT AWAY!
THAT XAI VESSALIUS DID IT!
OSCAR-SAMA SAID, "LEAVE THE REST TO ME"!
BUT ...
...NOT ONE PERSON BELIEVED MY TESTIMONY.

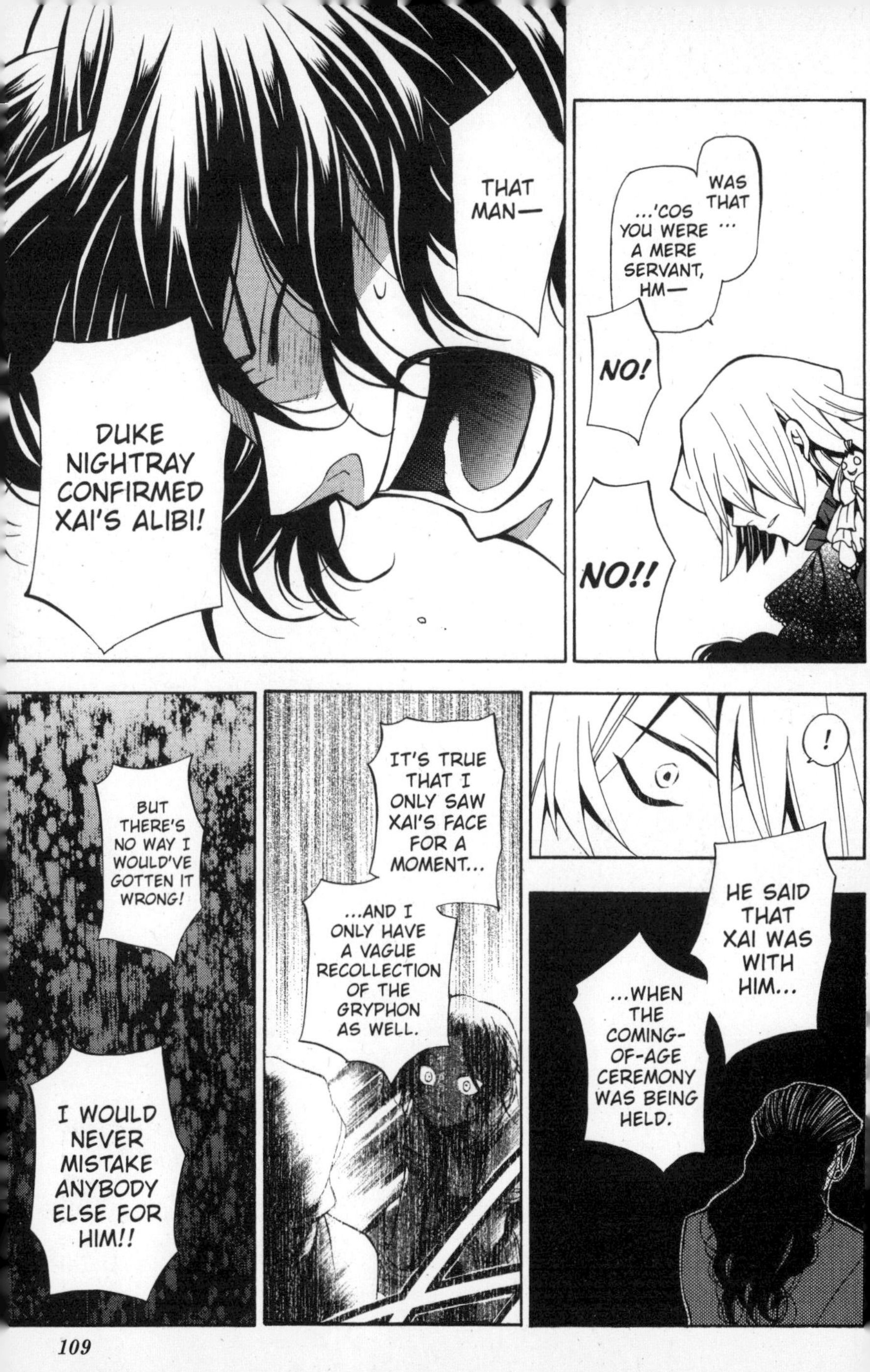
WAS THAT ...
...'COS YOU WERE A MERE SERVANT, HM—
NO!
NO!!
THAT MAN—
DUKE NIGHTRAY CONFIRMED XAI'S ALIBI!
!
HE SAID THAT XAI WAS WITH HIM...
...WHEN THE COMING-OF-AGE CEREMONY WAS BEING HELD.
IT'S TRUE THAT I ONLY SAW XAI'S FACE FOR A MOMENT...
...AND I ONLY HAVE A VAGUE RECOLLECTION OF THE GRYPHON AS WELL.
BUT THERE'S NO WAY I WOULD'VE GOTTEN IT WRONG!
I WOULD NEVER MISTAKE ANYBODY ELSE FOR HIM!!

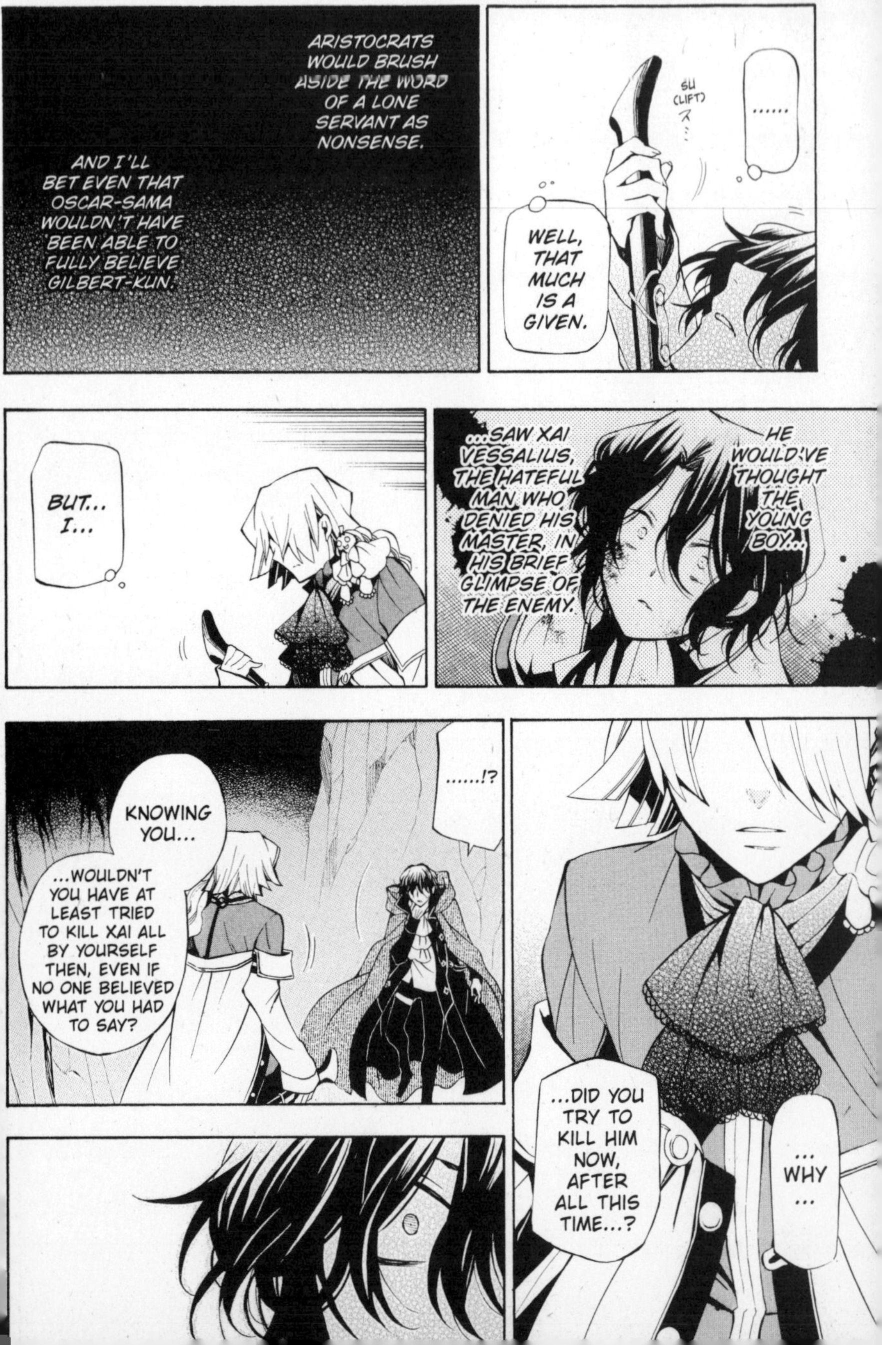
......
SU (LIFT)
WELL, THAT MUCH IS A GIVEN.
ARISTOCRATS WOULD BRUSH ASIDE THE WORD OF A LONE SERVANT AS NONSENSE.
AND I'LL BET EVEN THAT OSCAR-SAMA WOULDN'T HAVE BEEN ABLE TO FULLY BELIEVE GILBERT-KUN.
HE WOULD'VE THOUGHT THE YOUNG BOY...
...SAW XAI VESSALIUS, THE HATEFUL MAN WHO DENIED HIS MASTER, IN HIS BRIEF GLIMPSE OF THE ENEMY.
BUT... I...
...WHY...
...DID YOU TRY TO KILL HIM NOW, AFTER ALL THIS TIME...?
......!?
KNOWING YOU...
...WOULDN'T YOU HAVE AT LEAST TRIED TO KILL XAI ALL BY YOURSELF THEN, EVEN IF NO ONE BELIEVED WHAT YOU HAD TO SAY?

I DID TRY TO KILL HIM.

YOU'RE RIGHT.

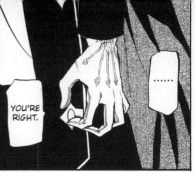

......

...AND WHY...

...WAS THAT?

...BUT...

...I COULD NOT DO IT.

...IS THE WORLD OZ WOULD RETURN TO.

BE-CAUSE-THIS...

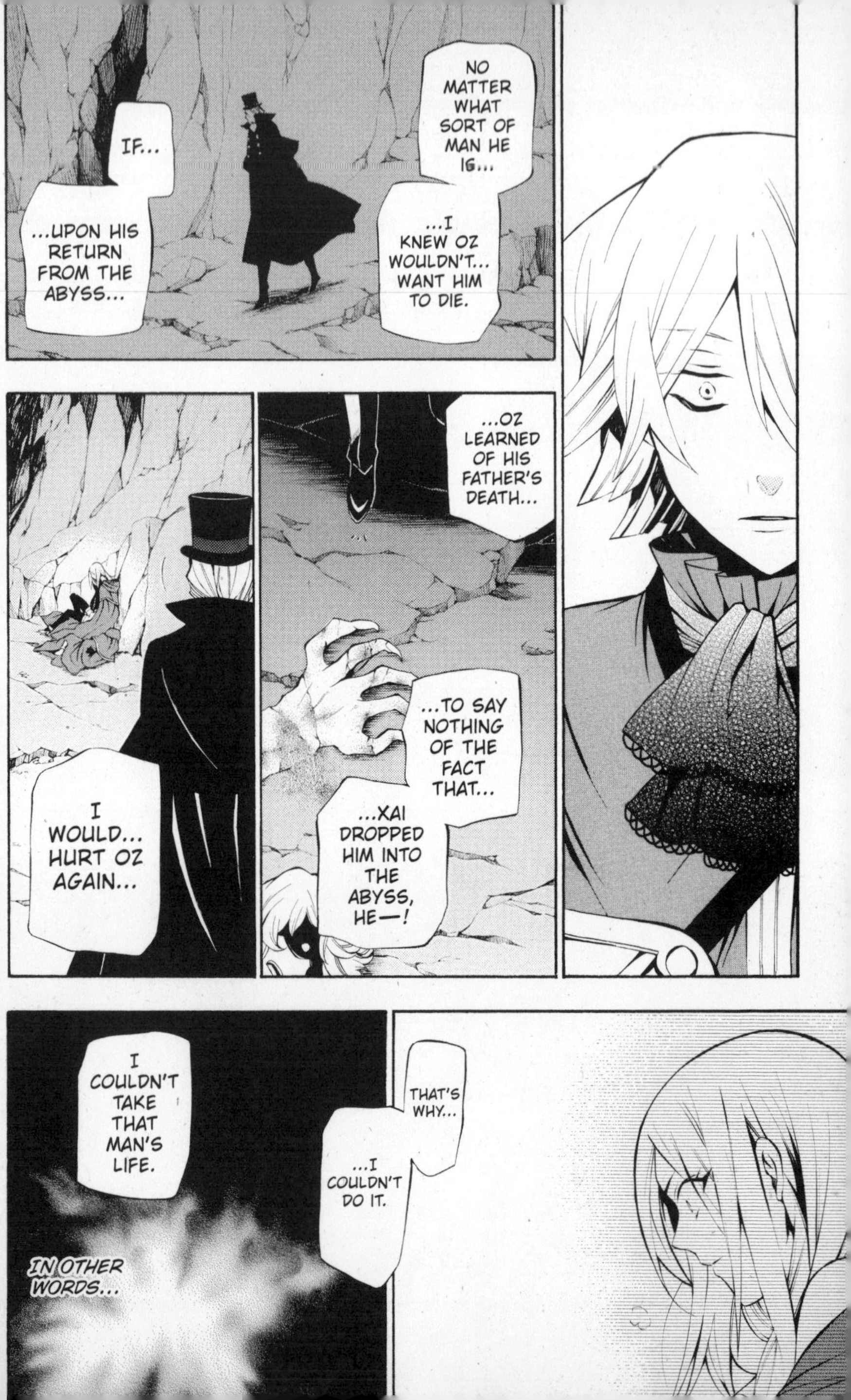
NO MATTER WHAT SORT OF MAN HE IS...
...I KNEW OZ WOULDN'T... WANT HIM TO DIE.
IF...
...UPON HIS RETURN FROM THE ABYSS...
...OZ LEARNED OF HIS FATHER'S DEATH...
...TO SAY NOTHING OF THE FACT THAT...
...XAI DROPPED HIM INTO THE ABYSS, HE—!
I WOULD... HURT OZ AGAIN...
THAT'S WHY...
...I COULDN'T DO IT.
I COULDN'T TAKE THAT MAN'S LIFE.
IN OTHER WORDS...

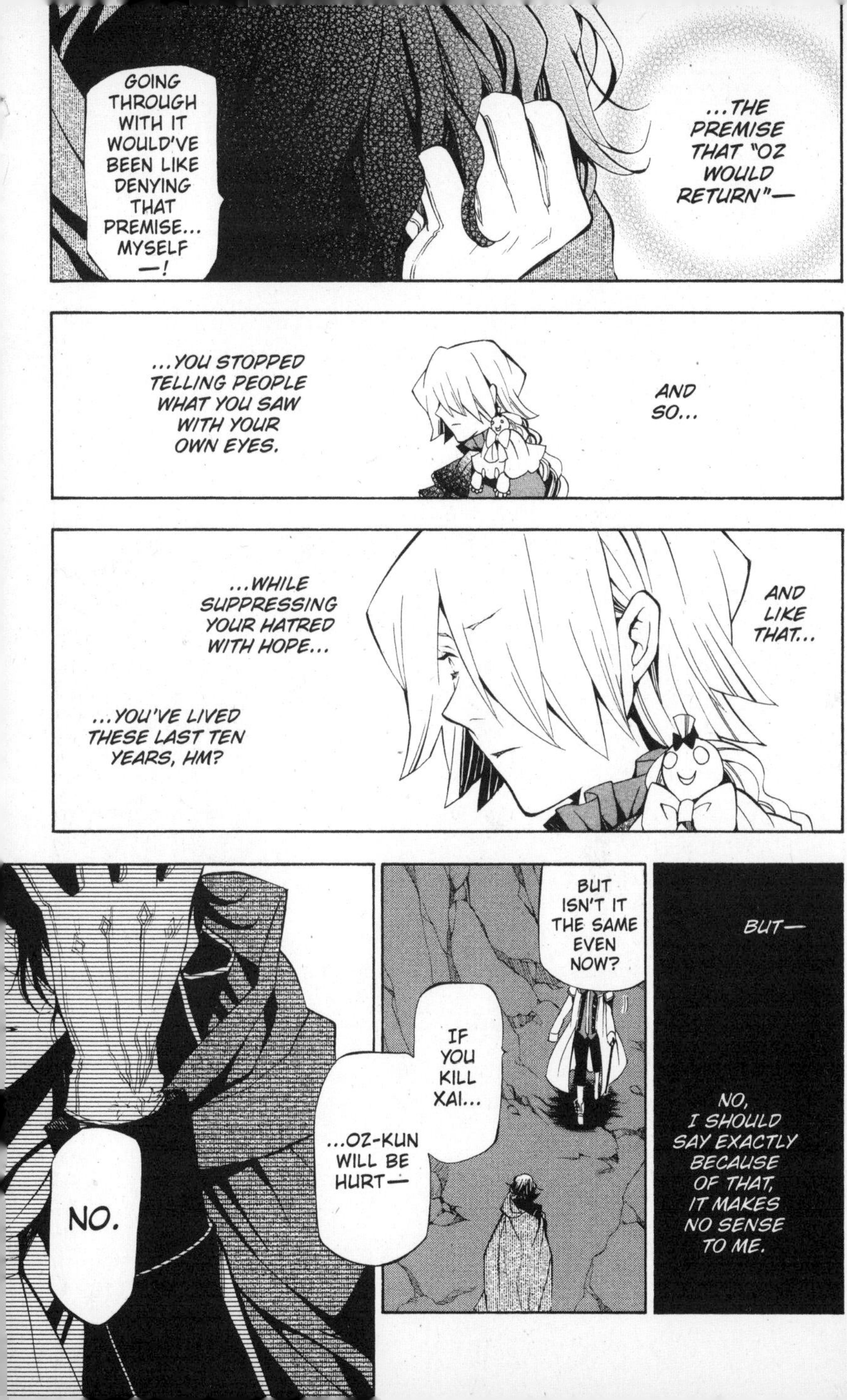
...THE PREMISE THAT "OZ WOULD RETURN"—
GOING THROUGH WITH IT WOULD'VE BEEN LIKE DENYING THAT PREMISE... MYSELF —!
AND SO...
...YOU STOPPED TELLING PEOPLE WHAT YOU SAW WITH YOUR OWN EYES.
AND LIKE THAT...
...WHILE SUPPRESSING YOUR HATRED WITH HOPE...
...YOU'VE LIVED THESE LAST TEN YEARS, HM?
BUT—
NO, I SHOULD SAY EXACTLY BECAUSE OF THAT, IT MAKES NO SENSE TO ME.
BUT ISN'T IT THE SAME EVEN NOW?
IF YOU KILL XAI...
...OZ-KUN WILL BE HURT—
NO.

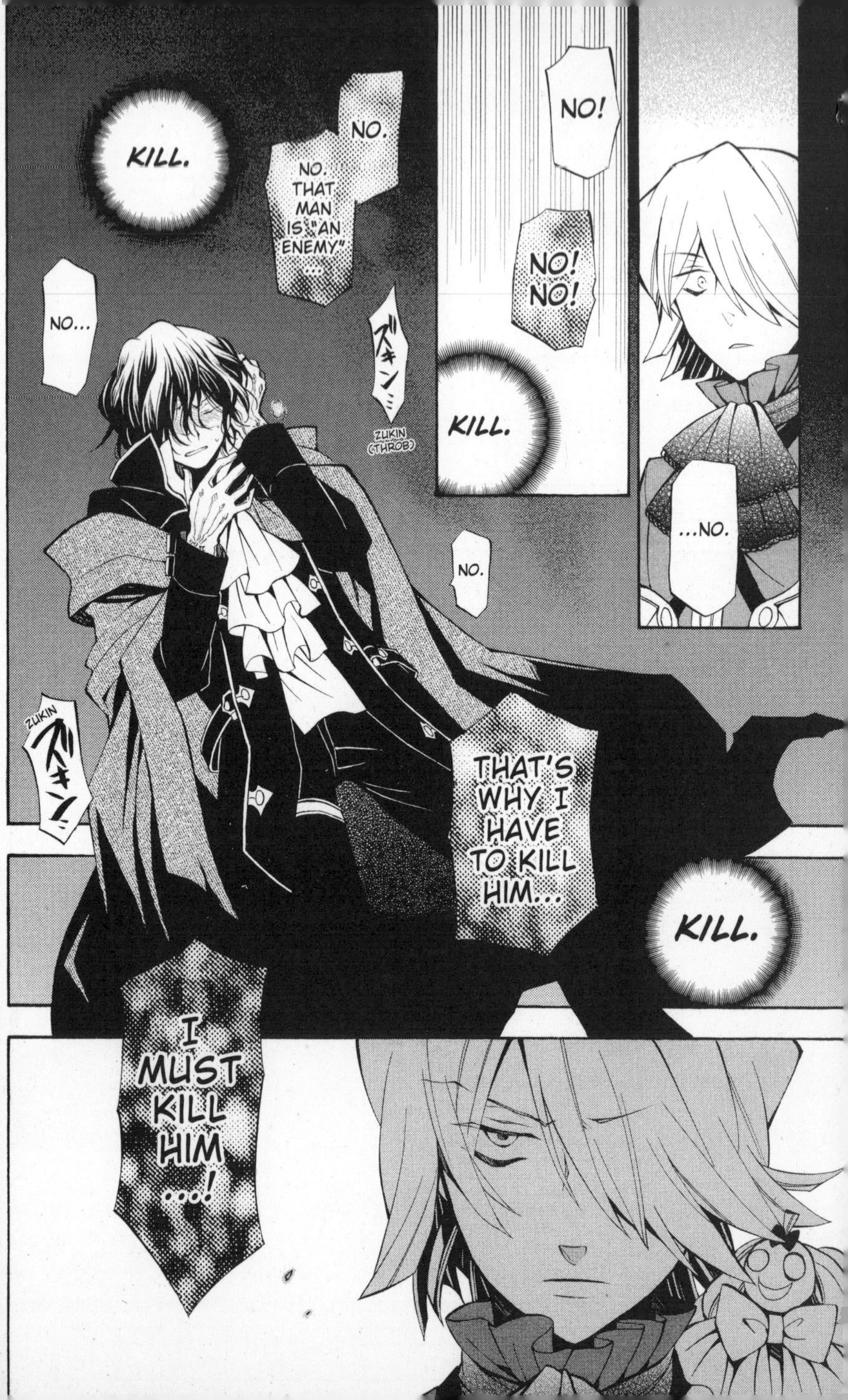
...NO.
NO!
NO! NO!
KILL.
NO.
NO. THAT MAN IS "AN ENEMY"...
KILL.
ZUKIN (THROB)
NO...
NO.
ZUKIN
THAT'S WHY I HAVE TO KILL HIM...
KILL.
I MUST KILL HIM...!

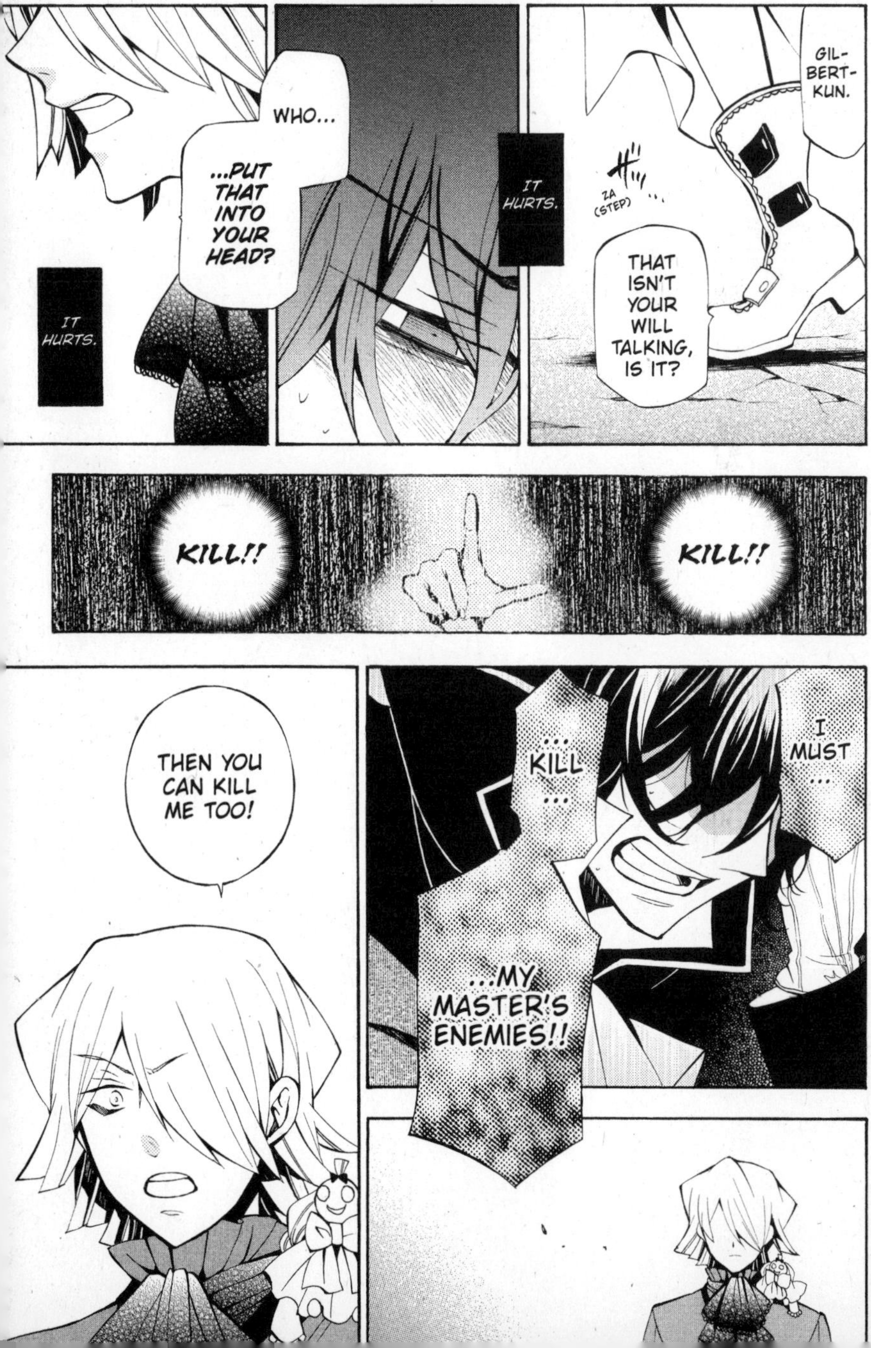
GIL-BERT-KUN.
ZA (STEP)
THAT ISN'T YOUR WILL TALKING, IS IT?
IT HURTS.
WHO...
...PUT THAT INTO YOUR HEAD?
IT HURTS.
KILL!!
KILL!!
I MUST...
...KILL...
...MY MASTER'S ENEMIES!!
THEN YOU CAN KILL ME TOO!

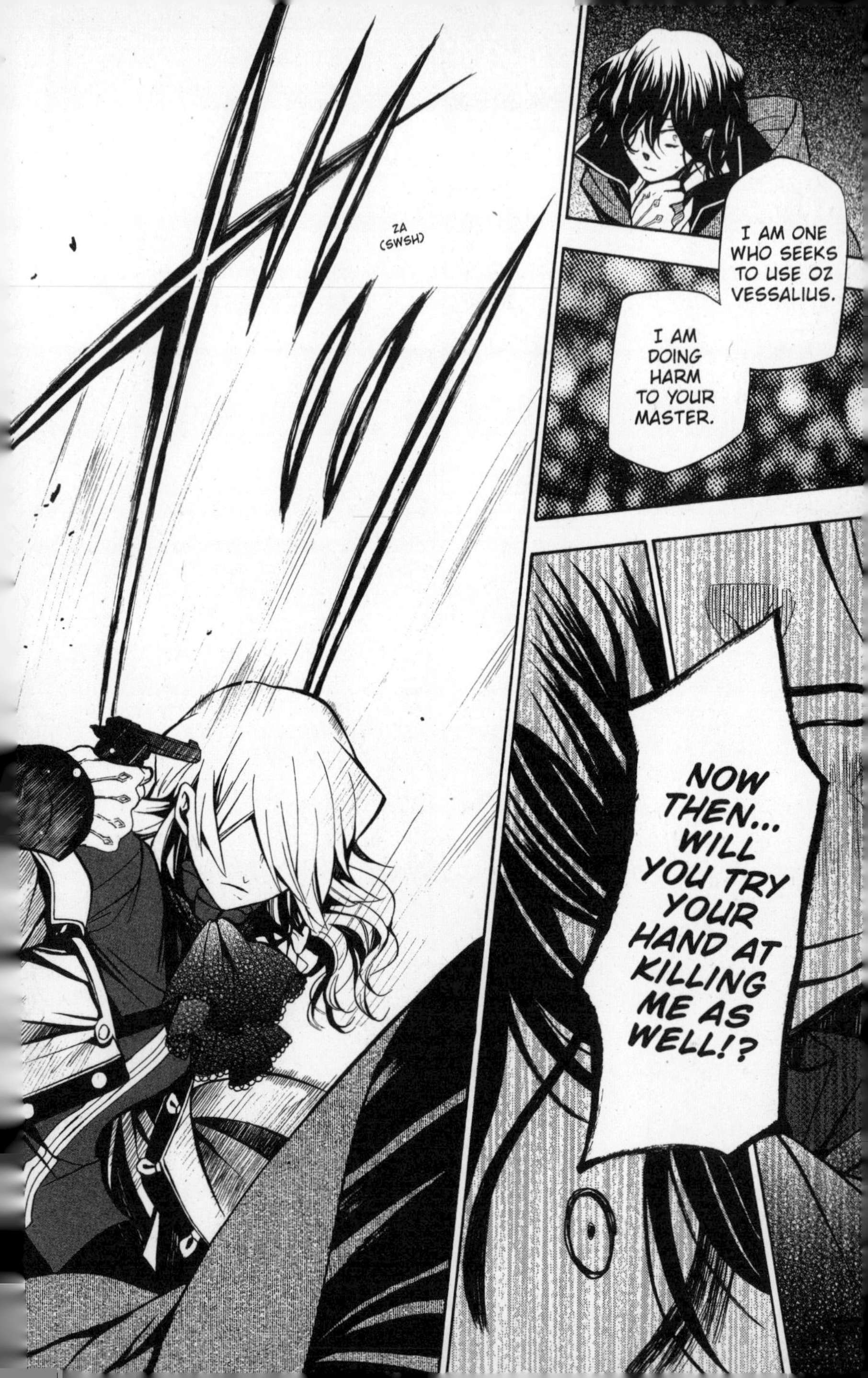
I AM ONE WHO SEEKS TO USE OZ VESSALIUS.
I AM DOING HARM TO YOUR MASTER.
NOW THEN... WILL YOU TRY YOUR HAND AT KILLING ME AS WELL!?
ZA (SWSH)

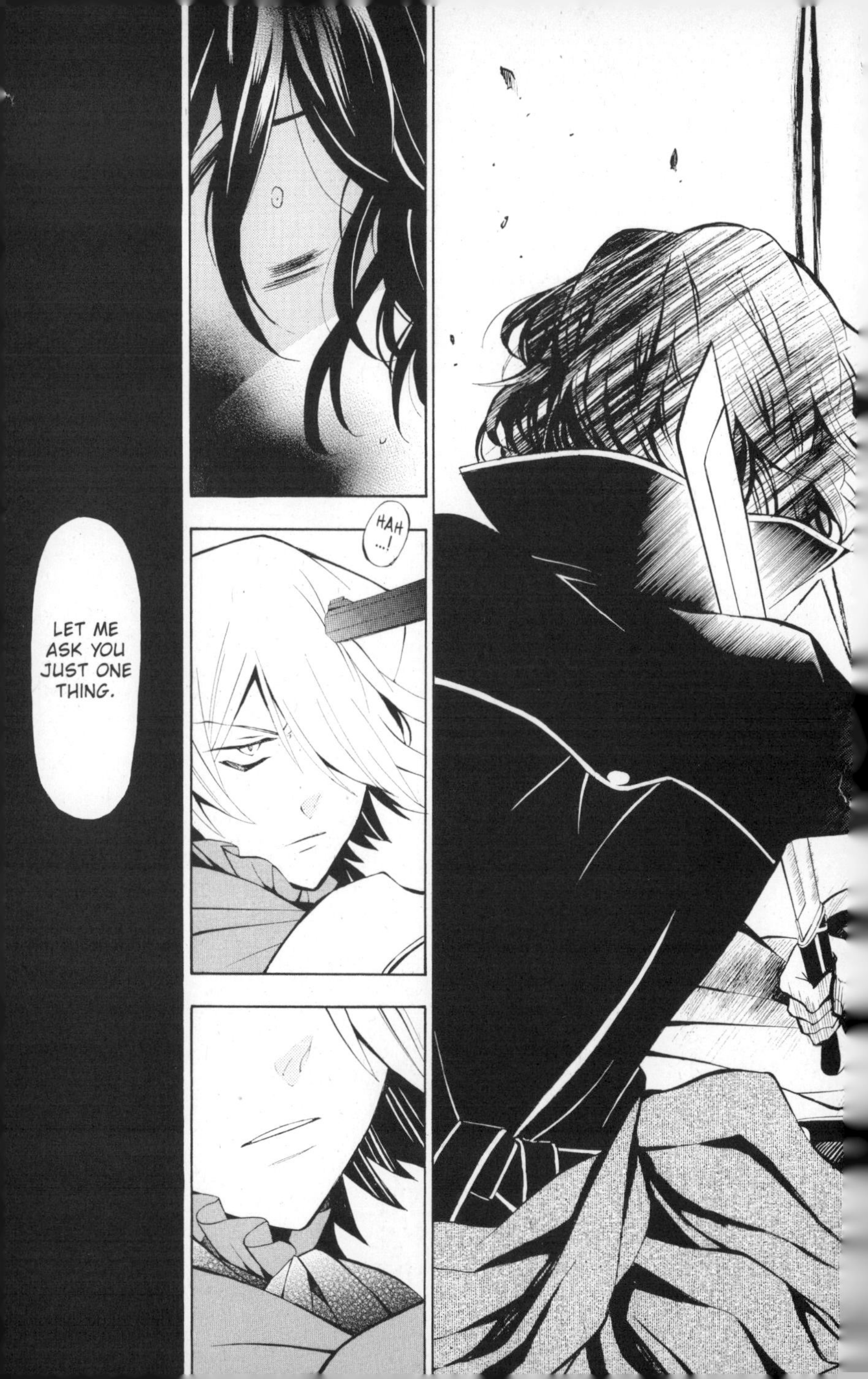
HAH ...!
LET ME ASK YOU JUST ONE THING.

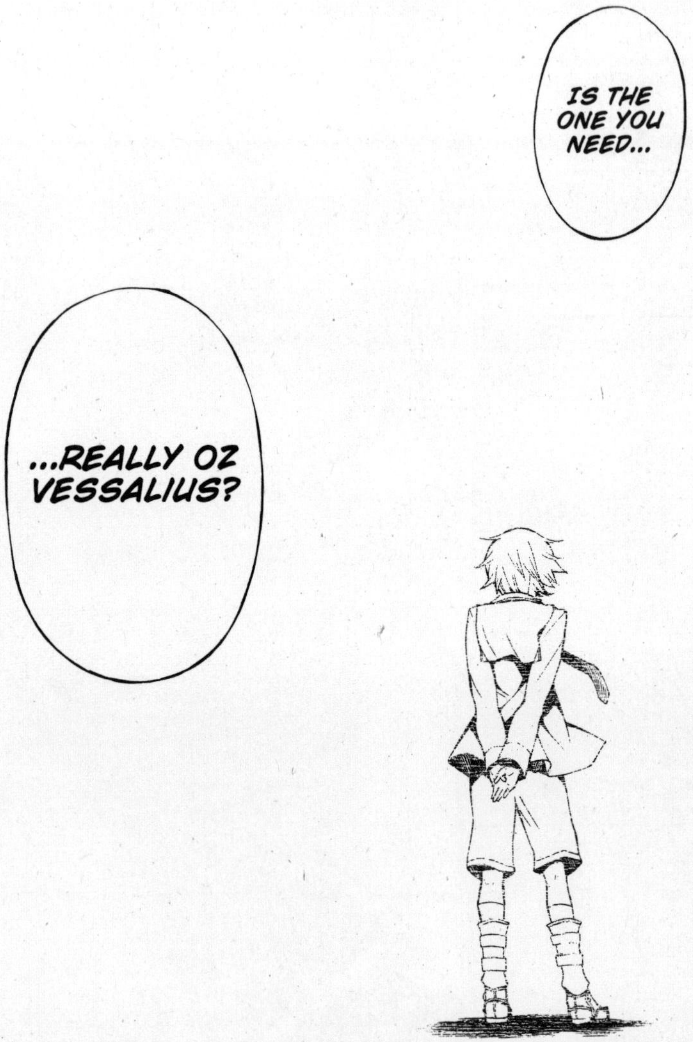
IS THE ONE YOU NEED...
...REALLY OZ VESSALIUS?

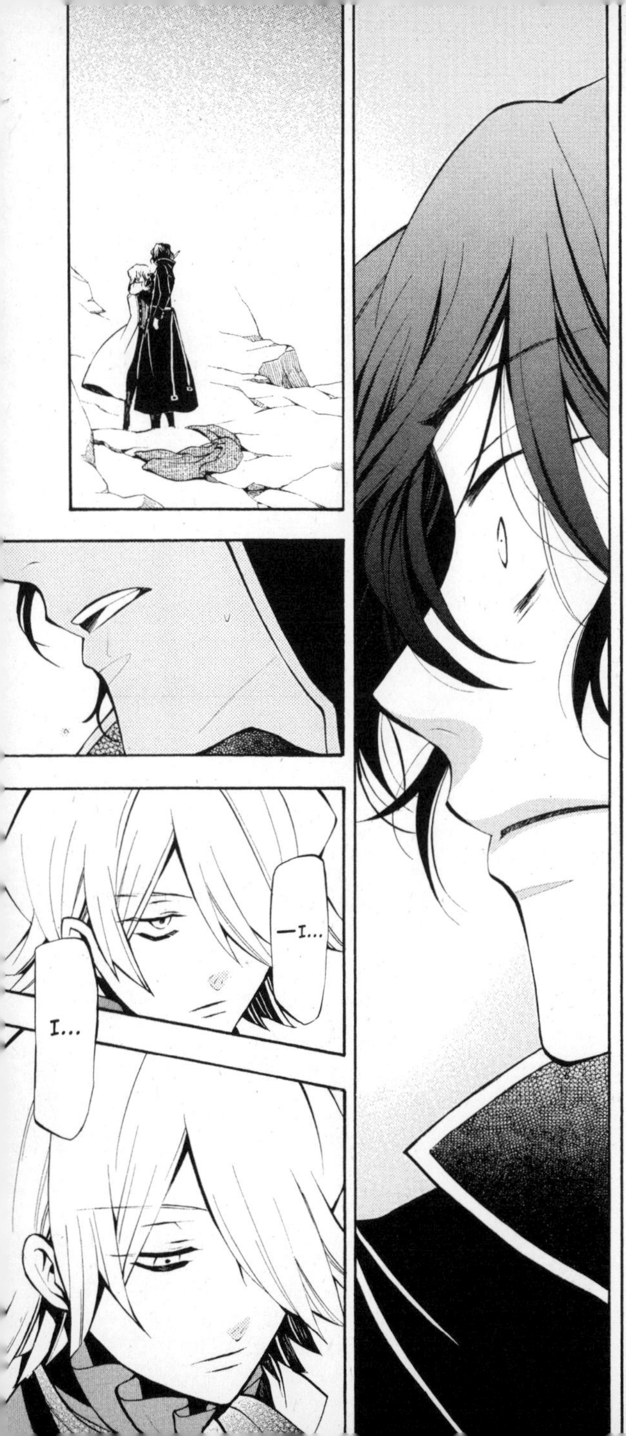
—I...
I...

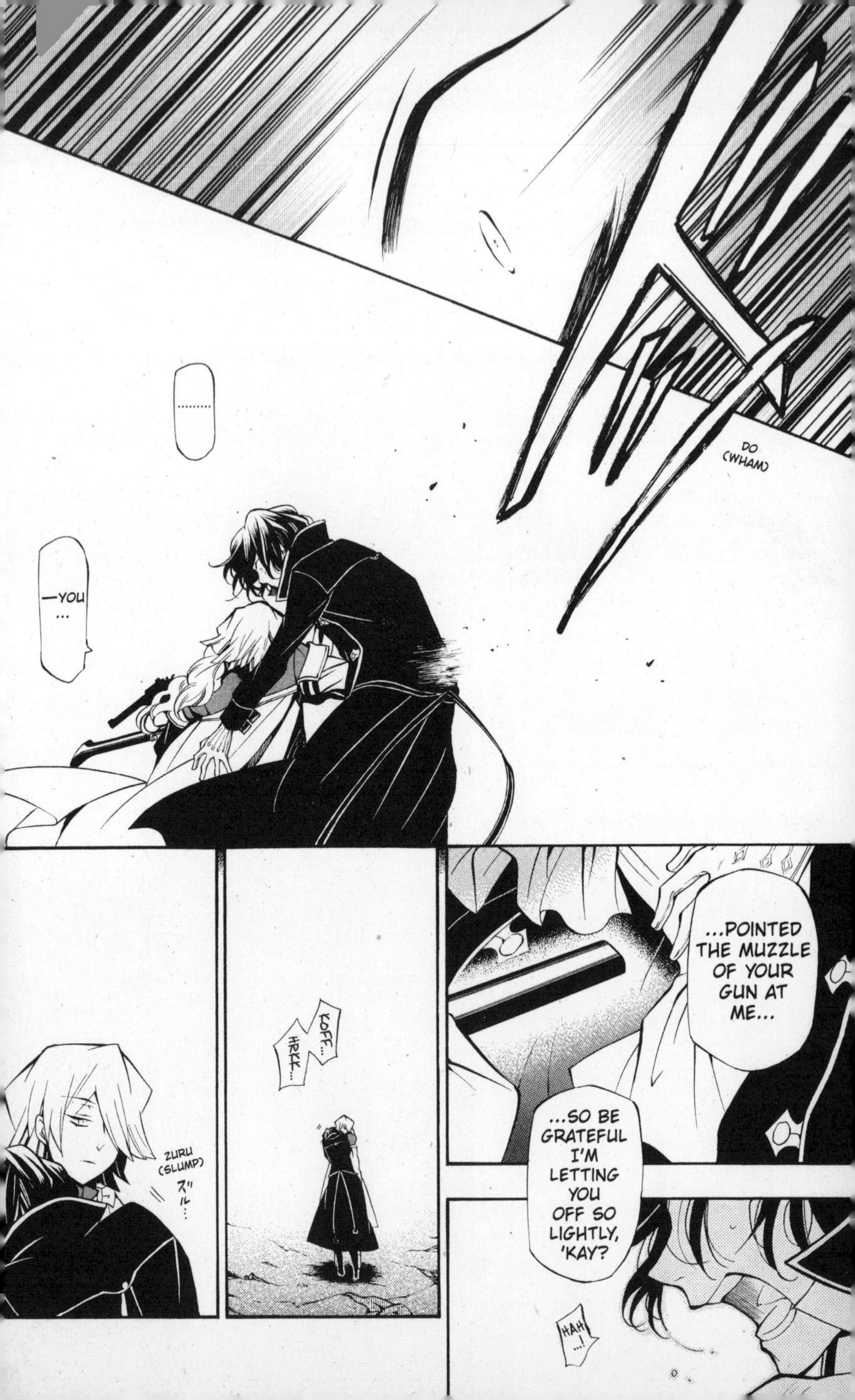
DO (WHAM)
....
—YOU ...
...POINTED THE MUZZLE OF YOUR GUN AT ME...
...SO BE GRATEFUL I'M LETTING YOU OFF SO LIGHTLY, 'KAY?
HAH ...!
KOFF... HRKK...
ZURU (SLUMP)
ズル…

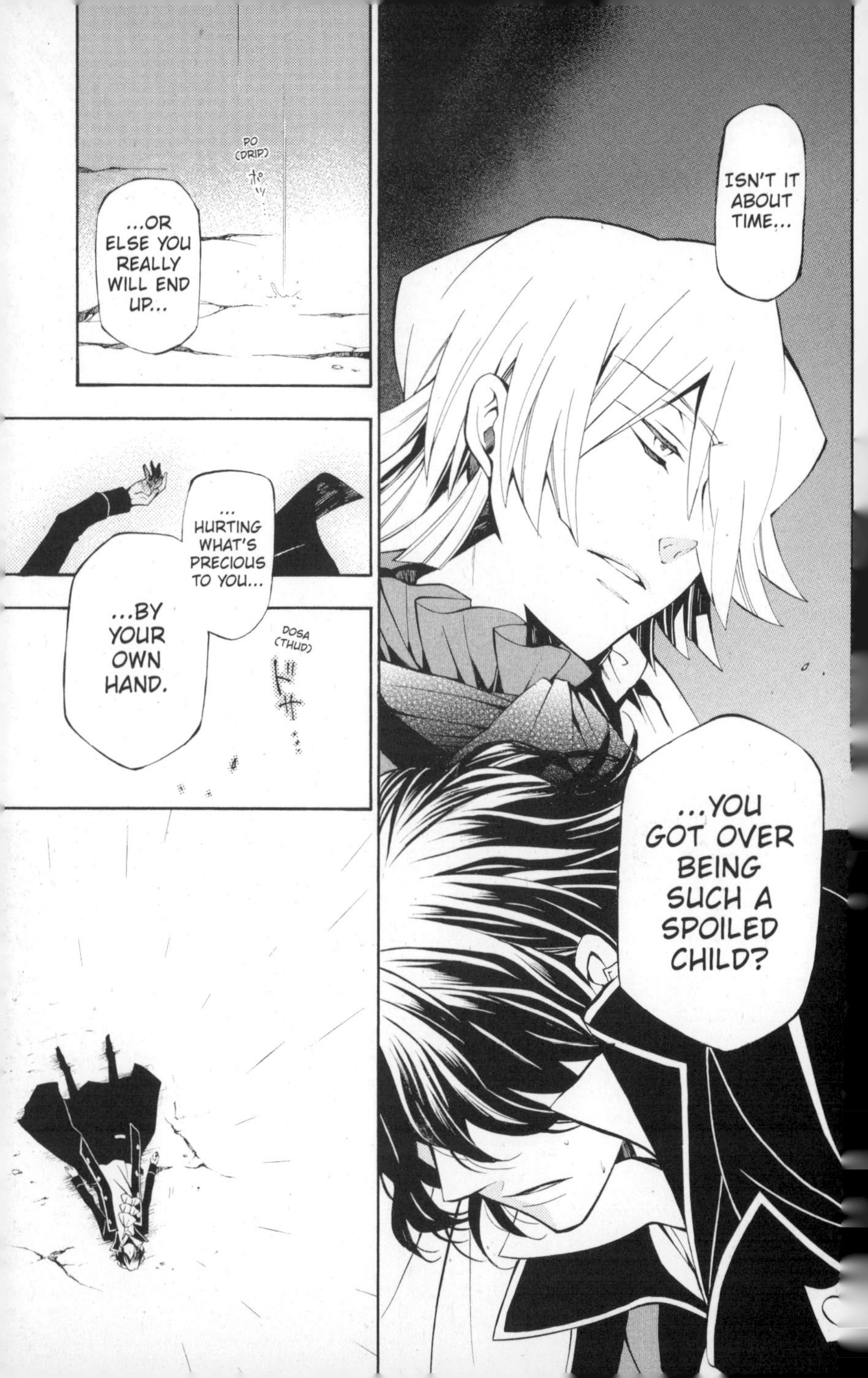
ISN'T IT ABOUT TIME...
...YOU GOT OVER BEING SUCH A SPOILED CHILD?
PO (DRIP)
...OR ELSE YOU REALLY WILL END UP...
...HURTING WHAT'S PRECIOUS TO YOU...
...BY YOUR OWN HAND.
DOSA (THUD)

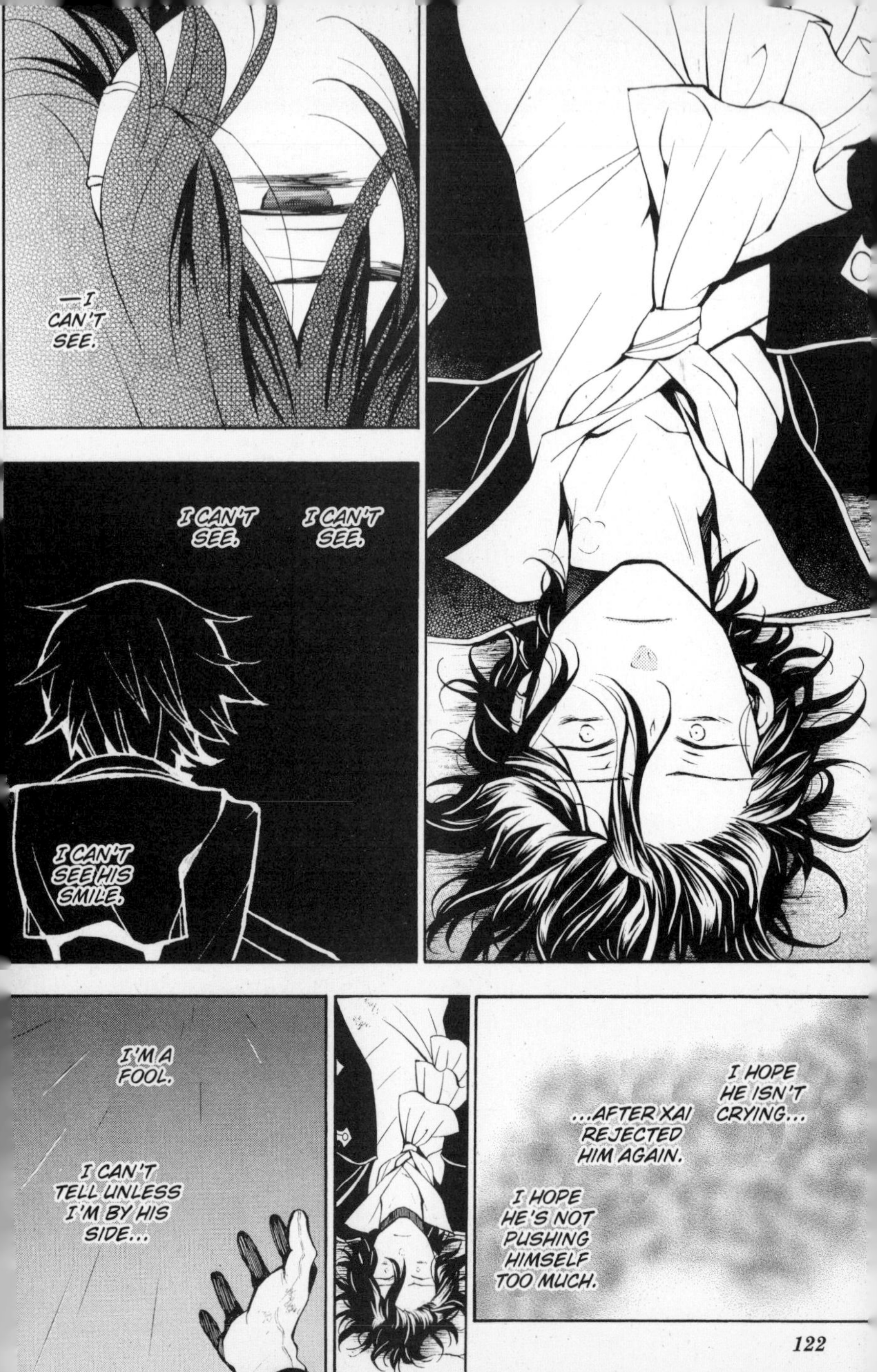
—I CAN'T SEE.
I CAN'T SEE.
I CAN'T SEE.
I CAN'T SEE HIS SMILE.
I HOPE HE ISN'T CRYING...
...AFTER XAI REJECTED HIM AGAIN.
I HOPE HE'S NOT PUSHING HIMSELF TOO MUCH.
I'M A FOOL.
I CAN'T TELL UNLESS I'M BY HIS SIDE...

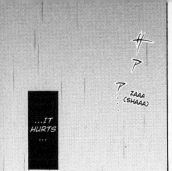

...IT
HURTS
...

AAH
...

ZAAA
(SHAAA)

IT
HURTS.

IT
HURTS.

IT
HURTS.

IT
HURTS.

MY
LEFT
HAND
...

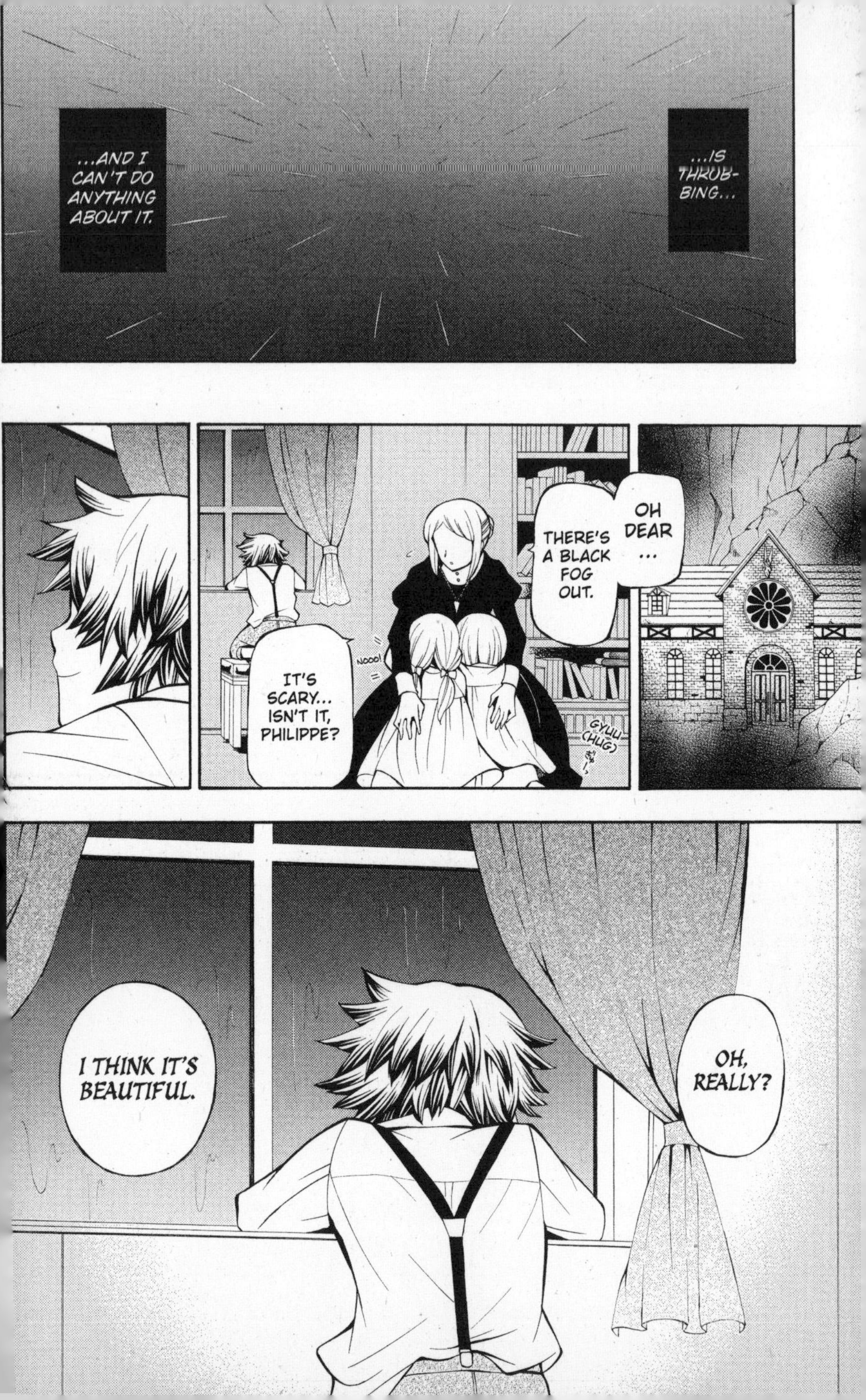
...IS THRUB-BING...
...AND I CAN'T DO ANYTHING ABOUT IT.
OH DEAR ...
THERE'S A BLACK FOG OUT.
NOOO!
IT'S SCARY... ISN'T IT, PHILIPPE?
GYUU (HUG)
OH, REALLY?
I THINK IT'S BEAUTIFUL.

Retrace:XLI Where am I?

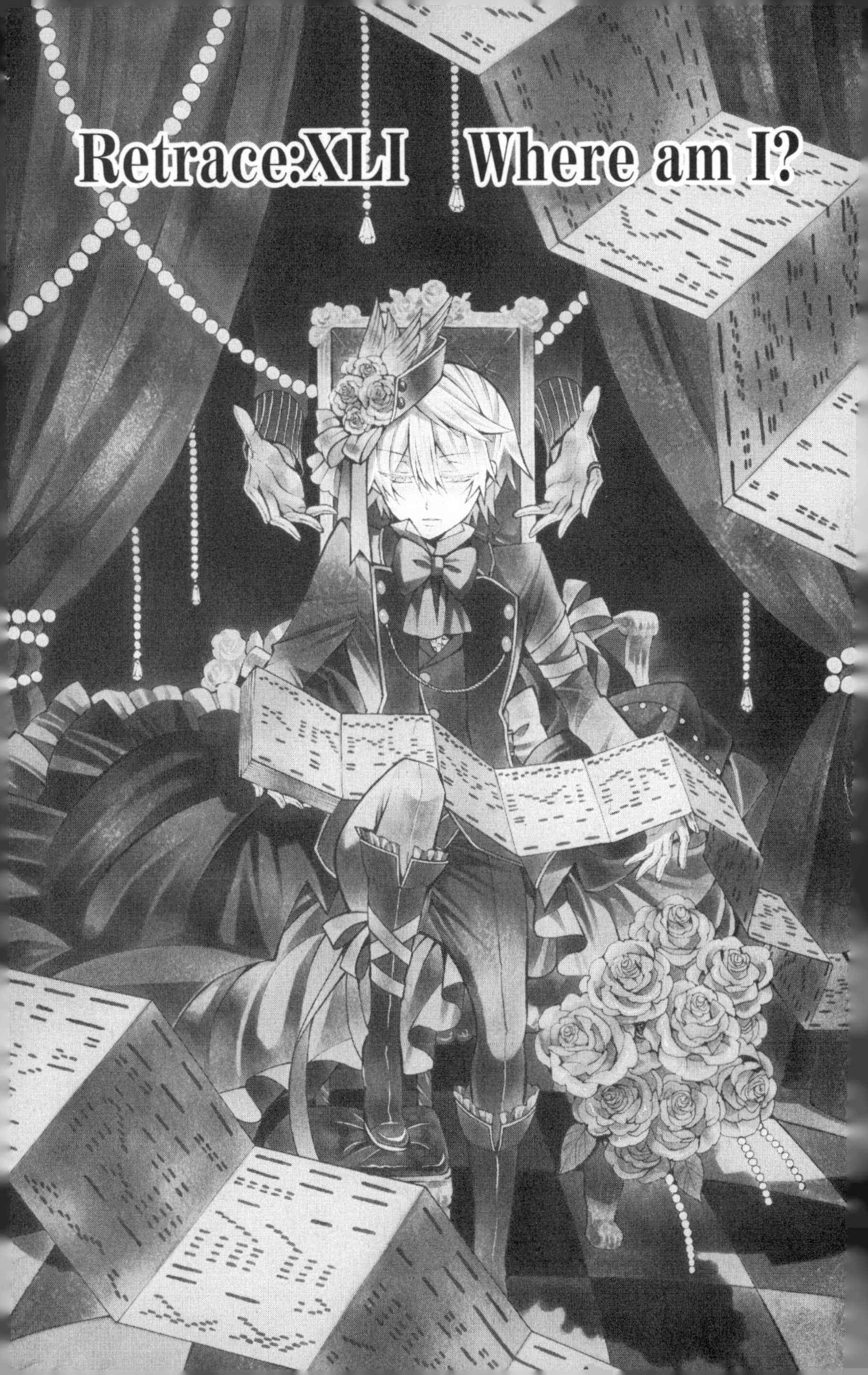

WHEN I WAS WORKING ON MY SCRIPT, I COULDN'T HELP VISUALIZING THIS SCENE LIKE SO.

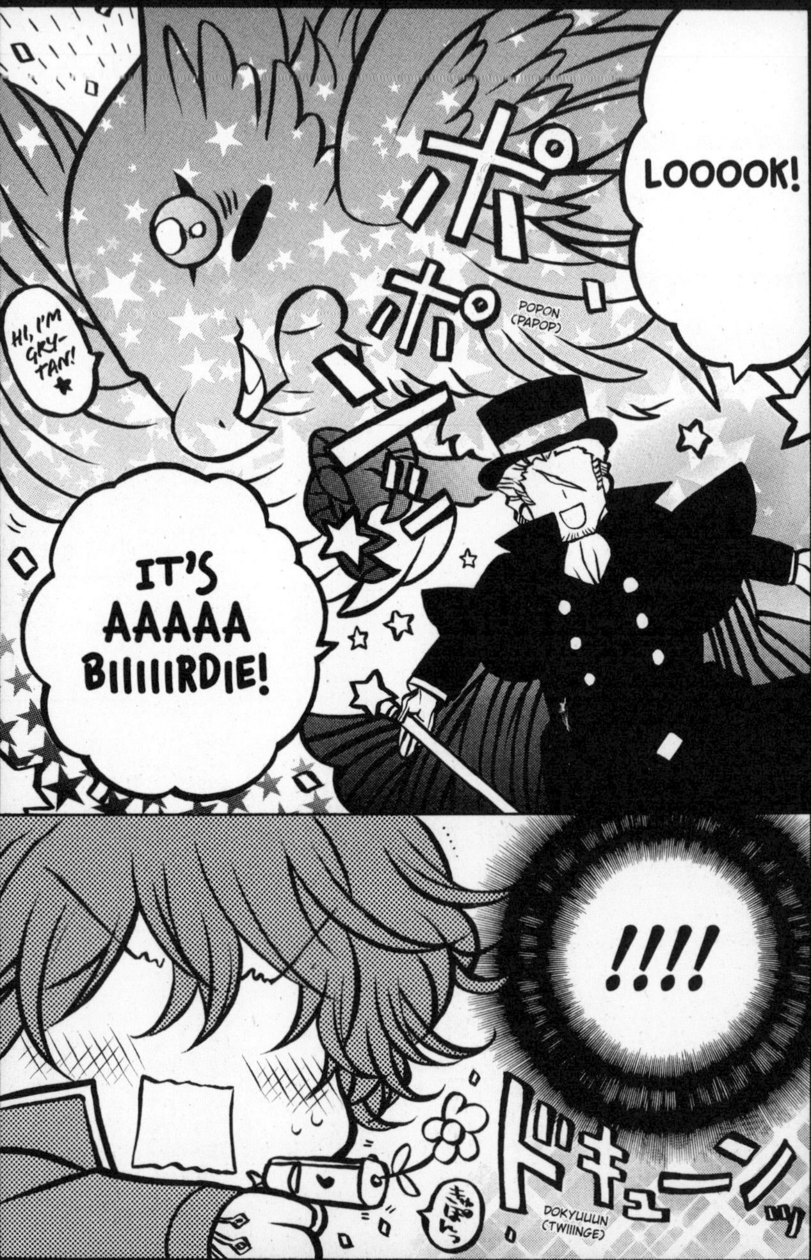
LOOOOK!
POPON (PAPOP)
HI, I'M GRY-TAN! ★
IT'S AAAAA BIIIIIRDIE!
!!!!
DOKYUUUN (TWIIINGE)

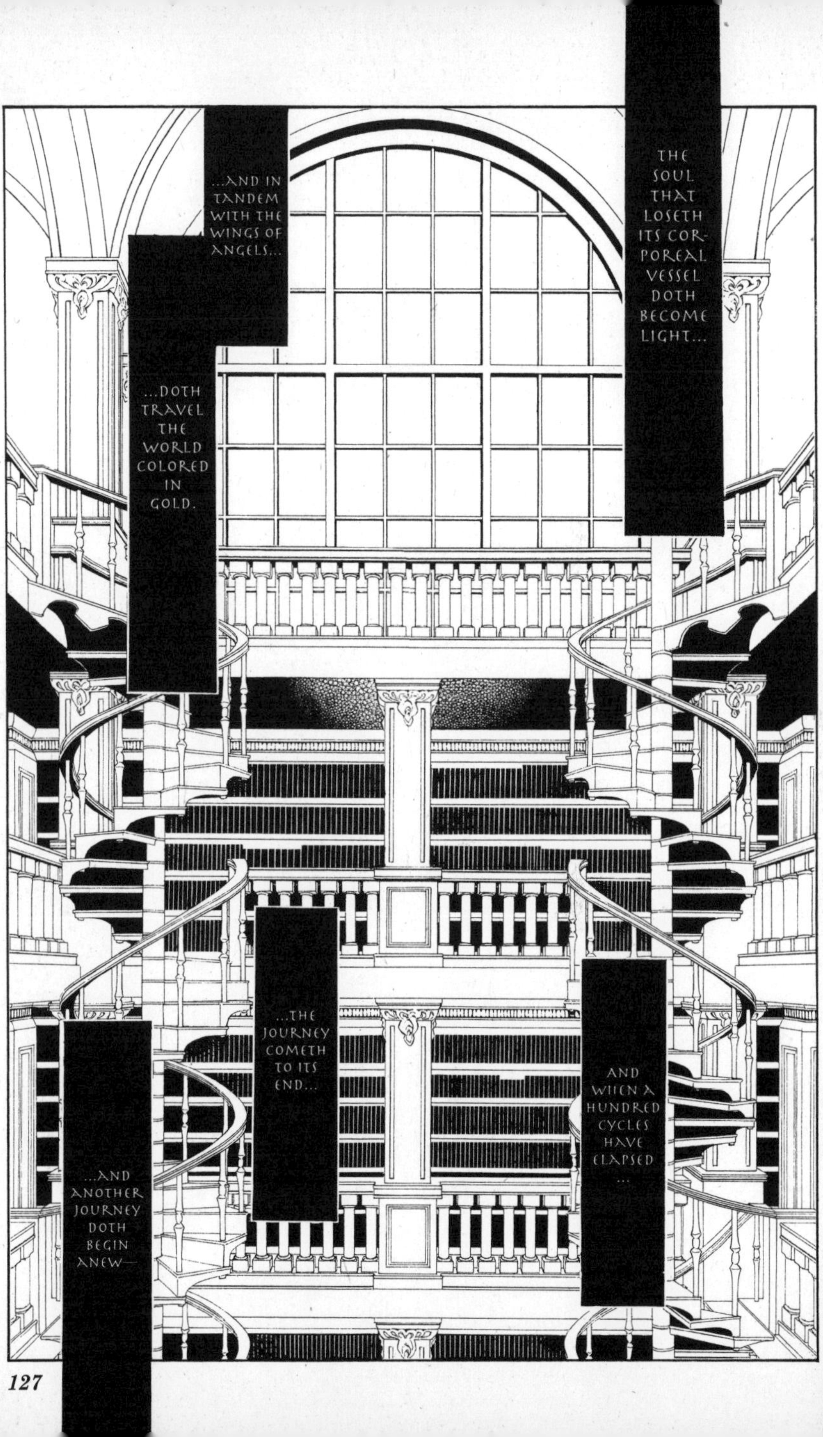
THE SOUL THAT LOSETH ITS CORPOREAL VESSEL DOTH BECOME LIGHT...
...AND IN TANDEM WITH THE WINGS OF ANGELS...
...DOTH TRAVEL THE WORLD COLORED IN GOLD.
AND WHEN A HUNDRED CYCLES HAVE ELAPSED...
...THE JOURNEY COMETH TO ITS END...
...AND ANOTHER JOURNEY DOTH BEGIN ANEW—

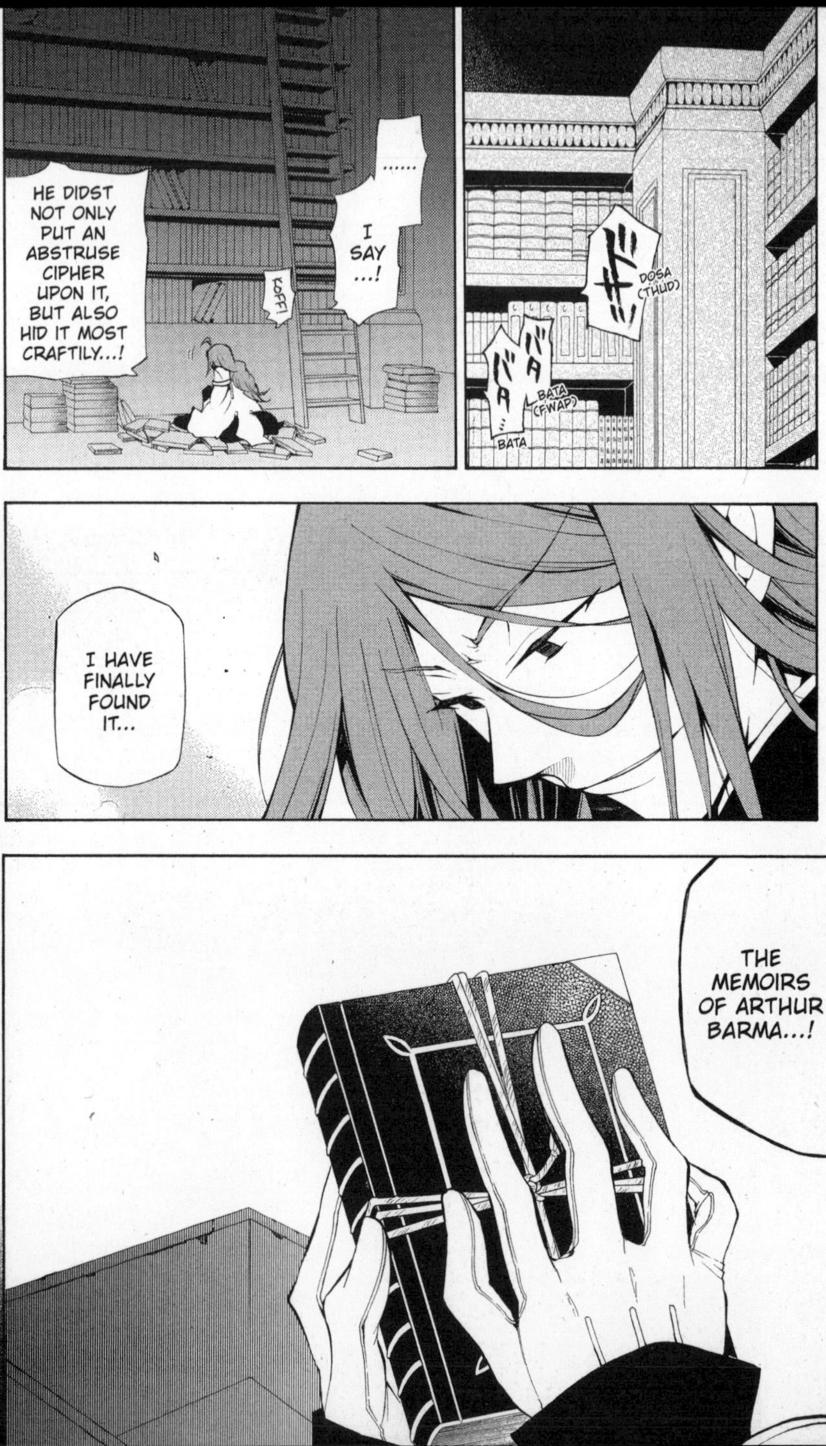
DOSA (THUD)
BATA (F'WAP)
BATA
......
I SAY ...!
KOFF!
HE DIDST NOT ONLY PUT AN ABSTRUSE CIPHER UPON IT, BUT ALSO HID IT MOST CRAFTILY...!
I HAVE FINALLY FOUND IT...
THE MEMOIRS OF ARTHUR BARMA...!

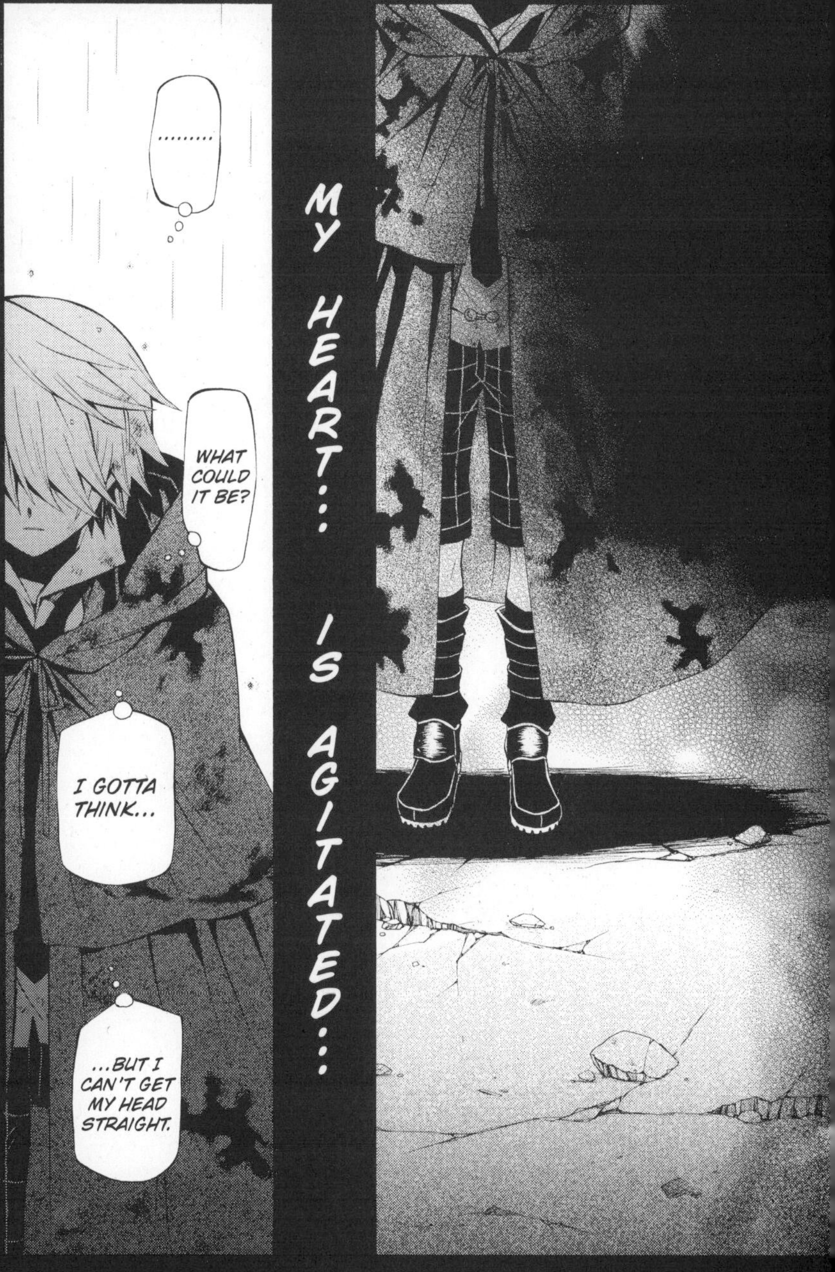
MY HEART... IS AGITATED...
....
WHAT COULD IT BE?
I GOTTA THINK...
...BUT I CAN'T GET MY HEAD STRAIGHT.

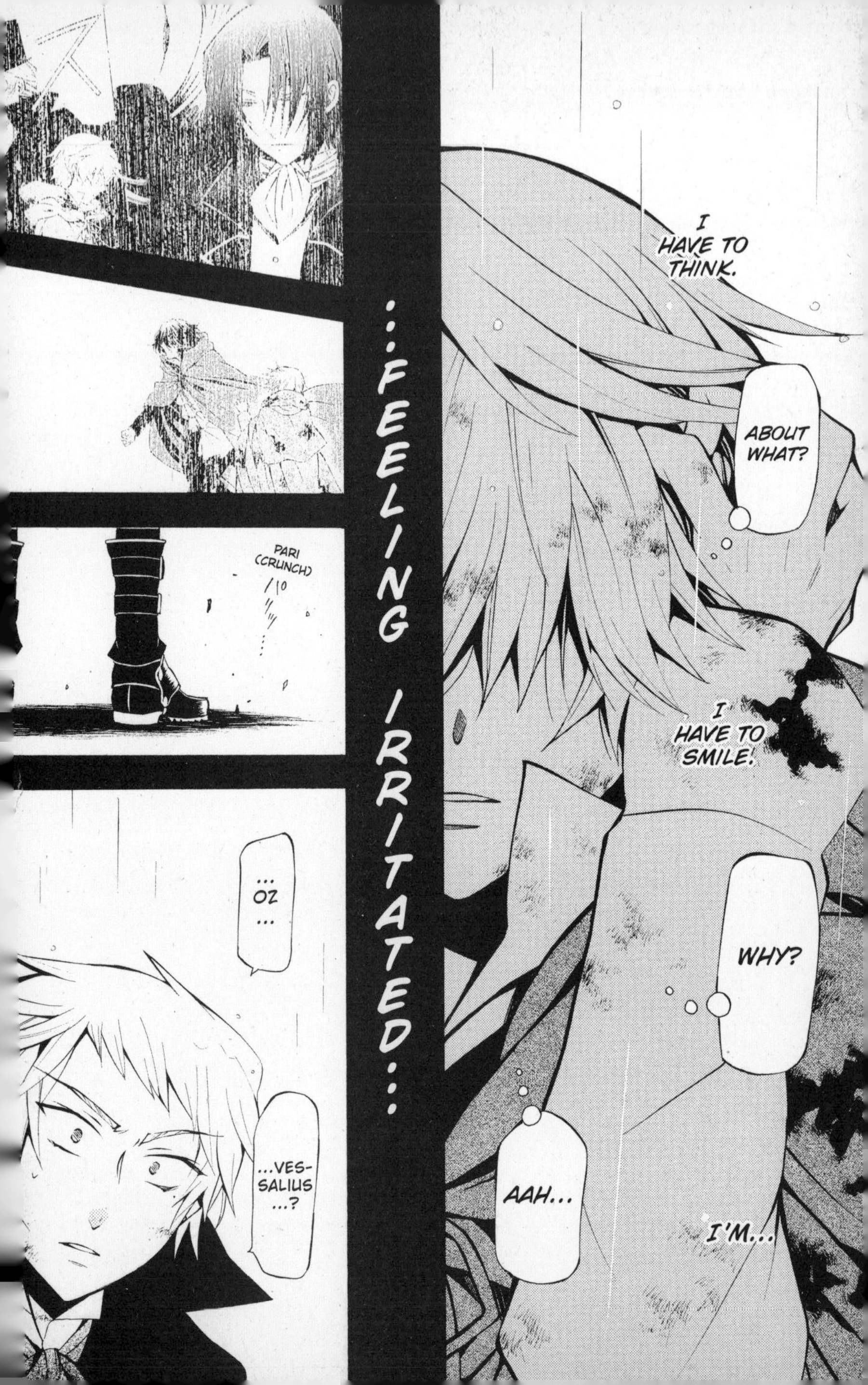
I HAVE TO THINK.
ABOUT WHAT?
I HAVE TO SMILE.
WHY?
AAH...
I'M...
...FEELING IRRITATED...
PARI (CRUNCH)
...OZ...
...VES-SALIUS...?

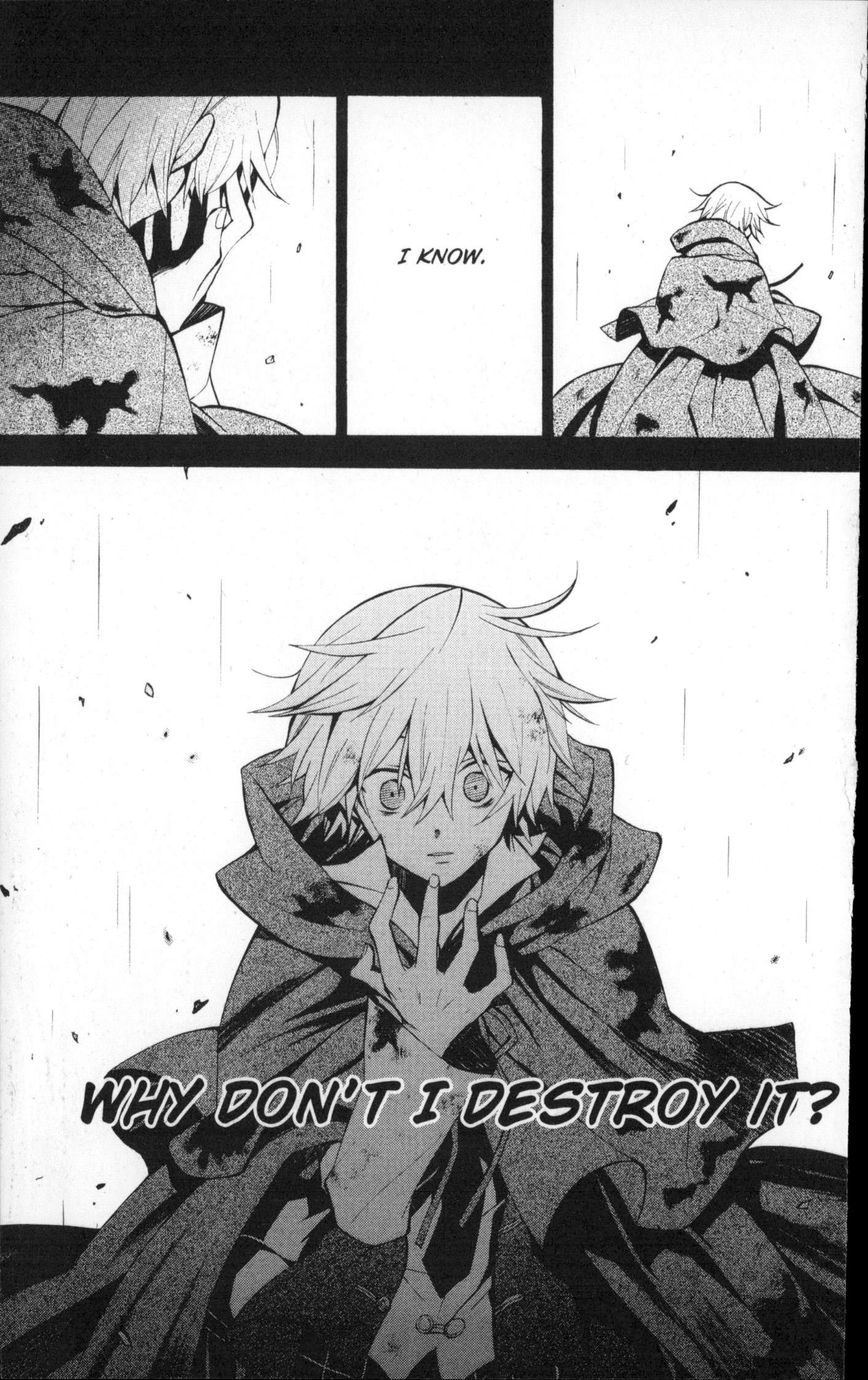
I KNOW.
WHY DON'T I DESTROY IT?

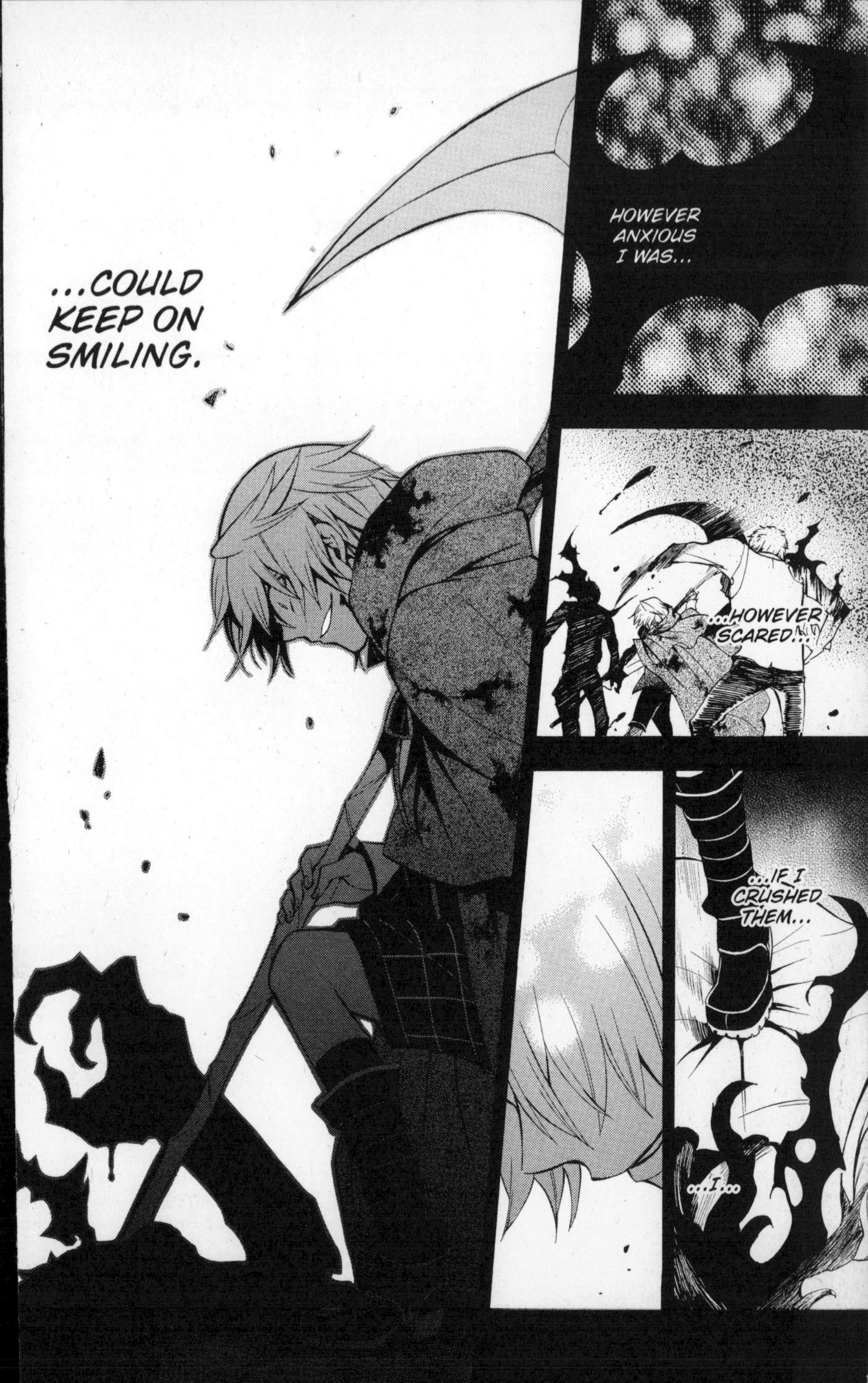
HOWEVER ANXIOUS I WAS...
...HOWEVER SCARED...
...IF I CRUSHED THEM...
...I...
...COULD KEEP ON SMILING.

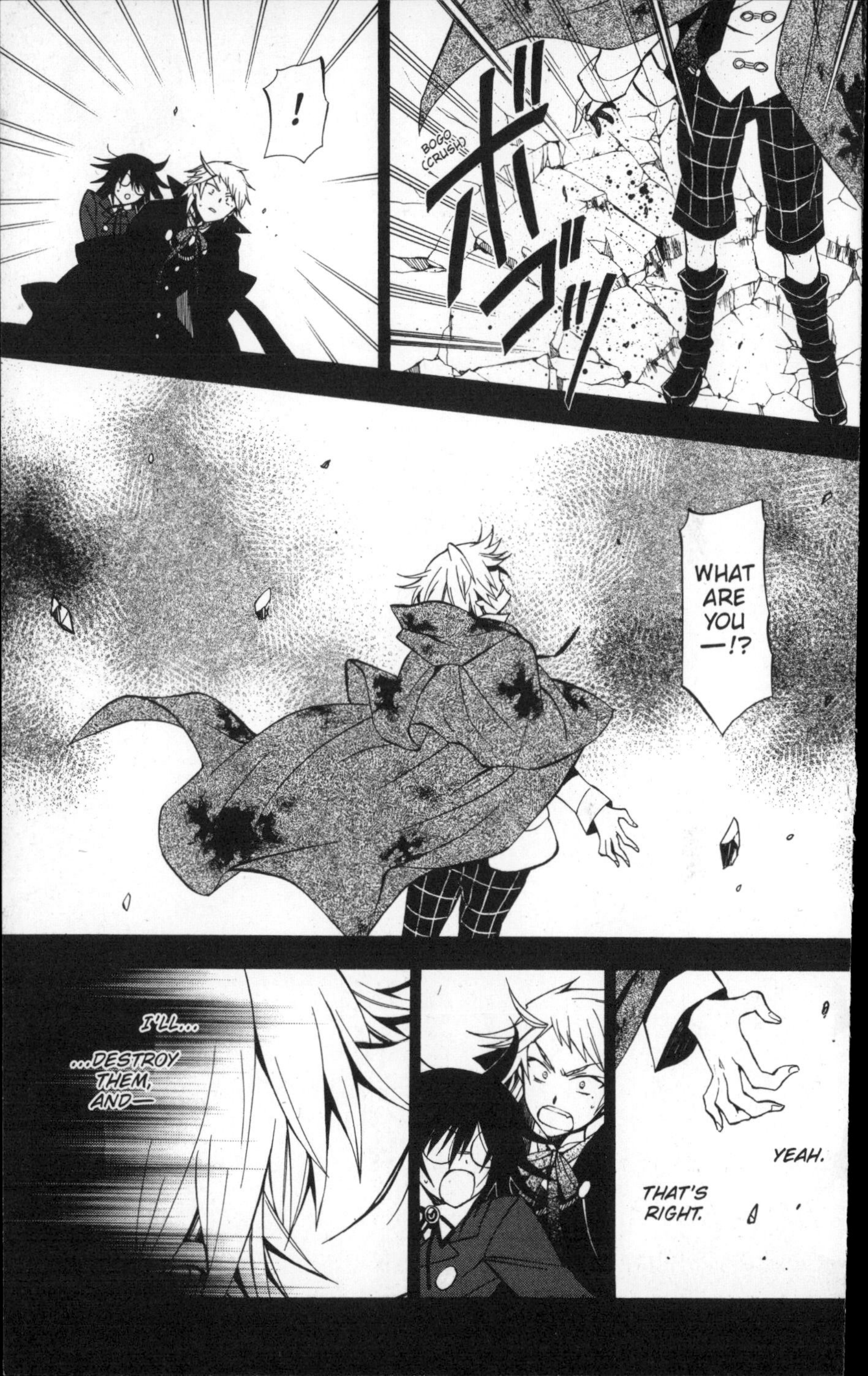
BOGO (CRUSH)
!
WHAT ARE YOU—!?
YEAH.
THAT'S RIGHT.
I'LL...
...DESTROY THEM, AND—

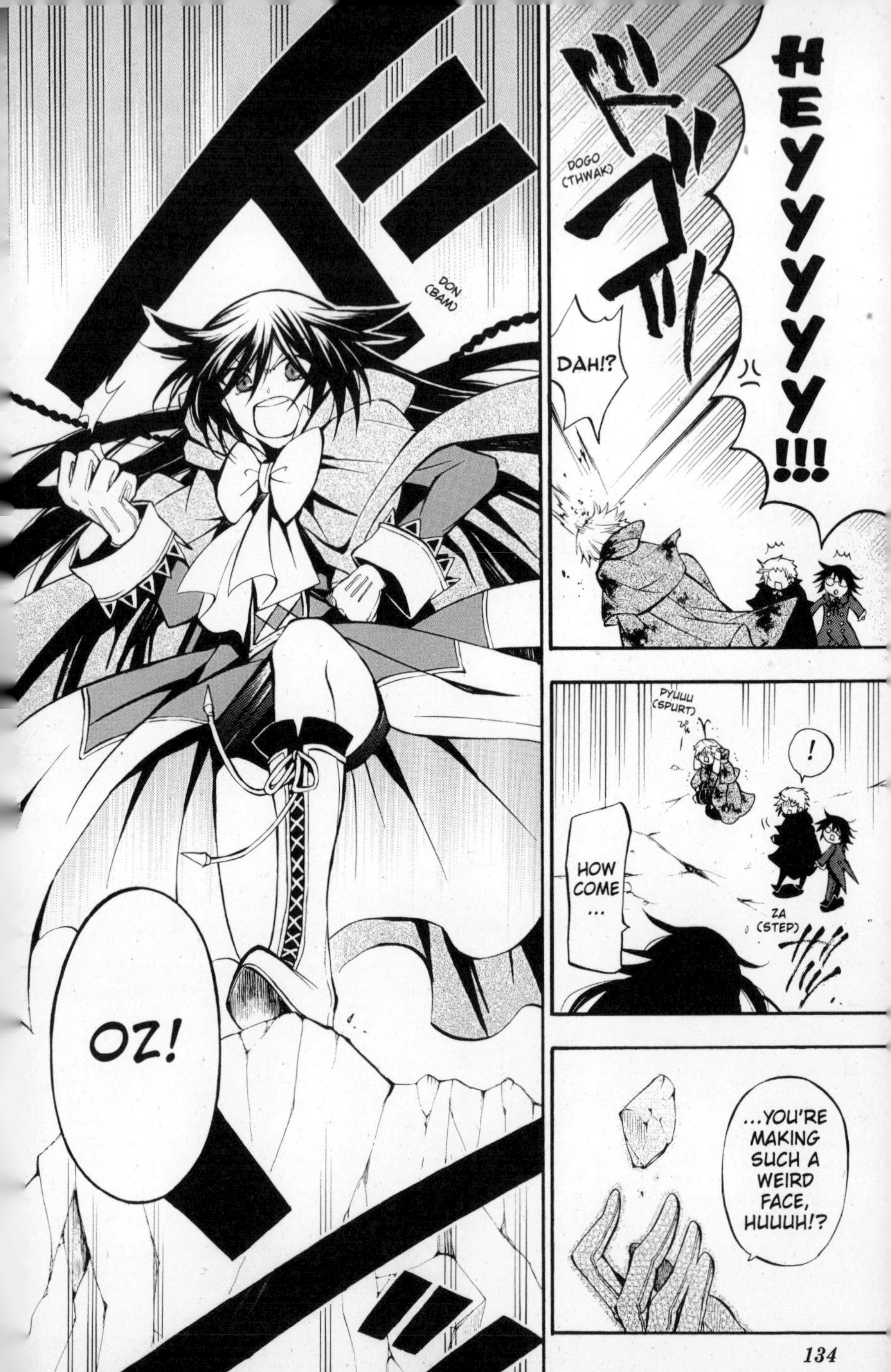
HEYYYYY!!!
DOGO (THWAK)
DAH!?
PYUUU (SPURT)
!
HOW COME...
ZA (STEP)
...YOU'RE MAKING SUCH A WEIRD FACE, HUUUH!?
DON (BAM)
OZ!

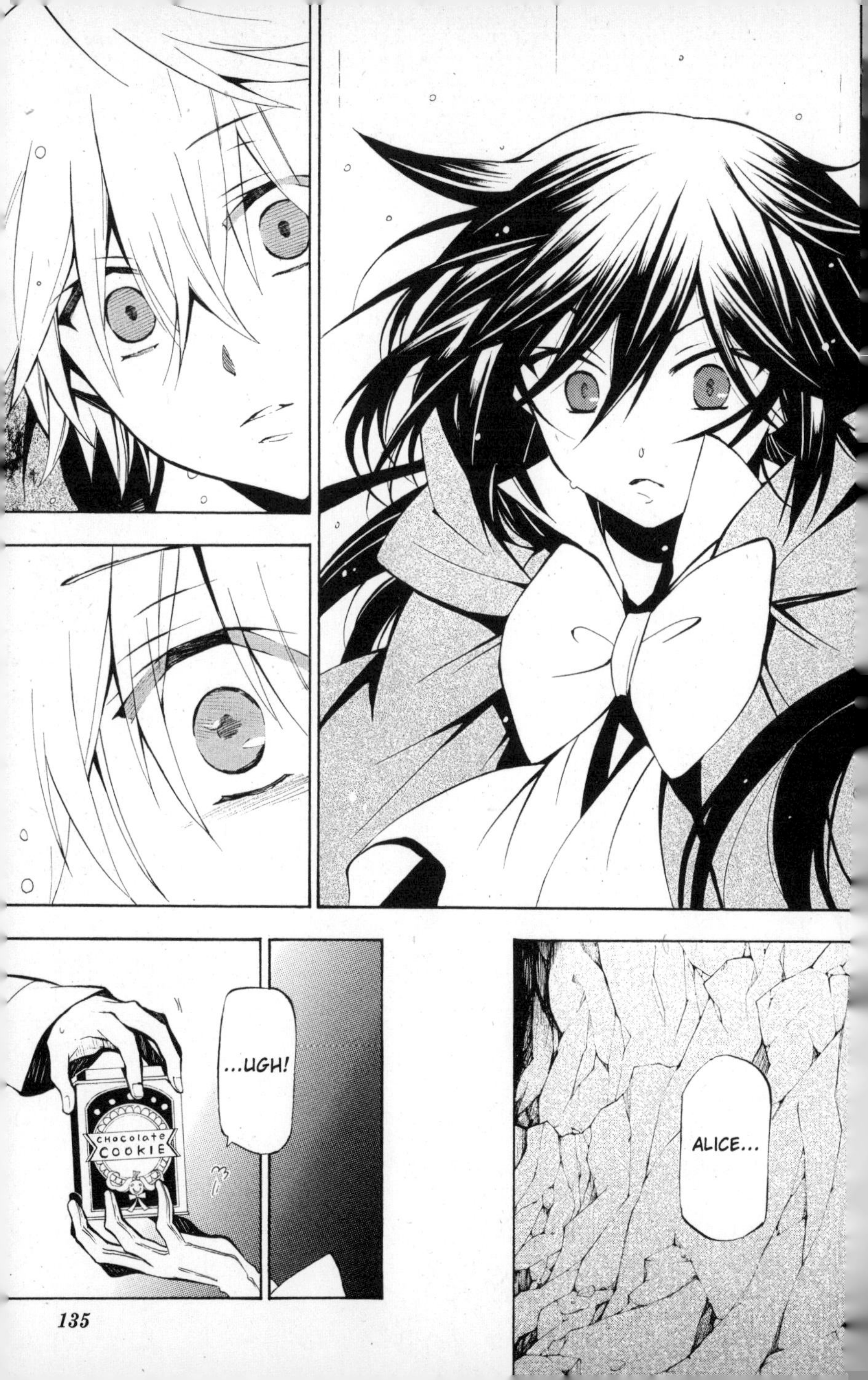
ALICE...
...UGH!
CHOCOLATE
COOKIE

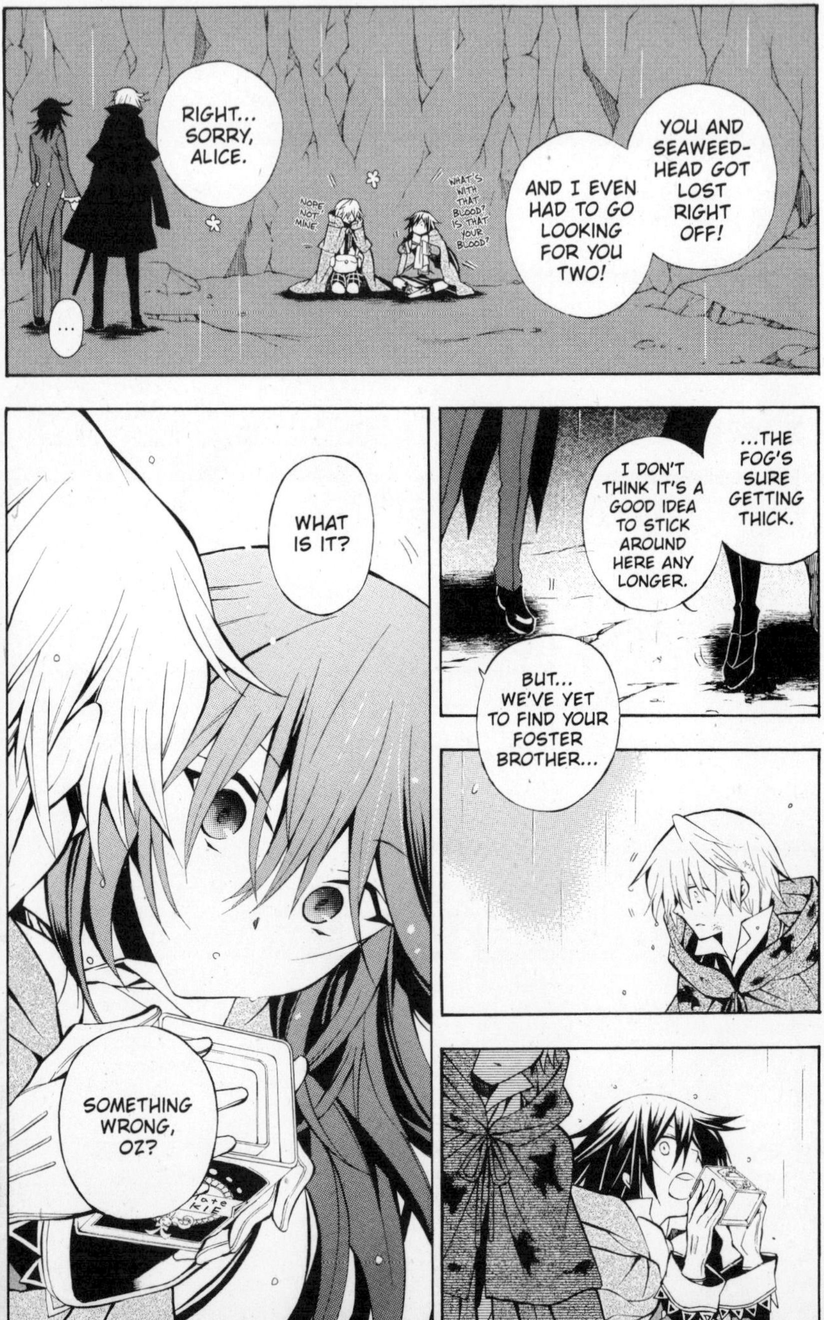
YOU AND SEAWEED-HEAD GOT LOST RIGHT OFF!
AND I EVEN HAD TO GO LOOKING FOR YOU TWO!
WHAT'S WITH THAT BLOOD? IS THAT YOUR BLOOD?
NOPE, NOT MINE.
RIGHT... SORRY, ALICE.
...
...THE FOG'S SURE GETTING THICK.
I DON'T THINK IT'S A GOOD IDEA TO STICK AROUND HERE ANY LONGER.
BUT... WE'VE YET TO FIND YOUR FOSTER BROTHER...
WHAT IS IT?
SOMETHING WRONG, OZ?

IT'S
...

...
NOTH-
ING...

....

NO...

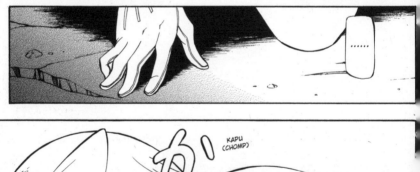

......

KAPU
(CHOMP)

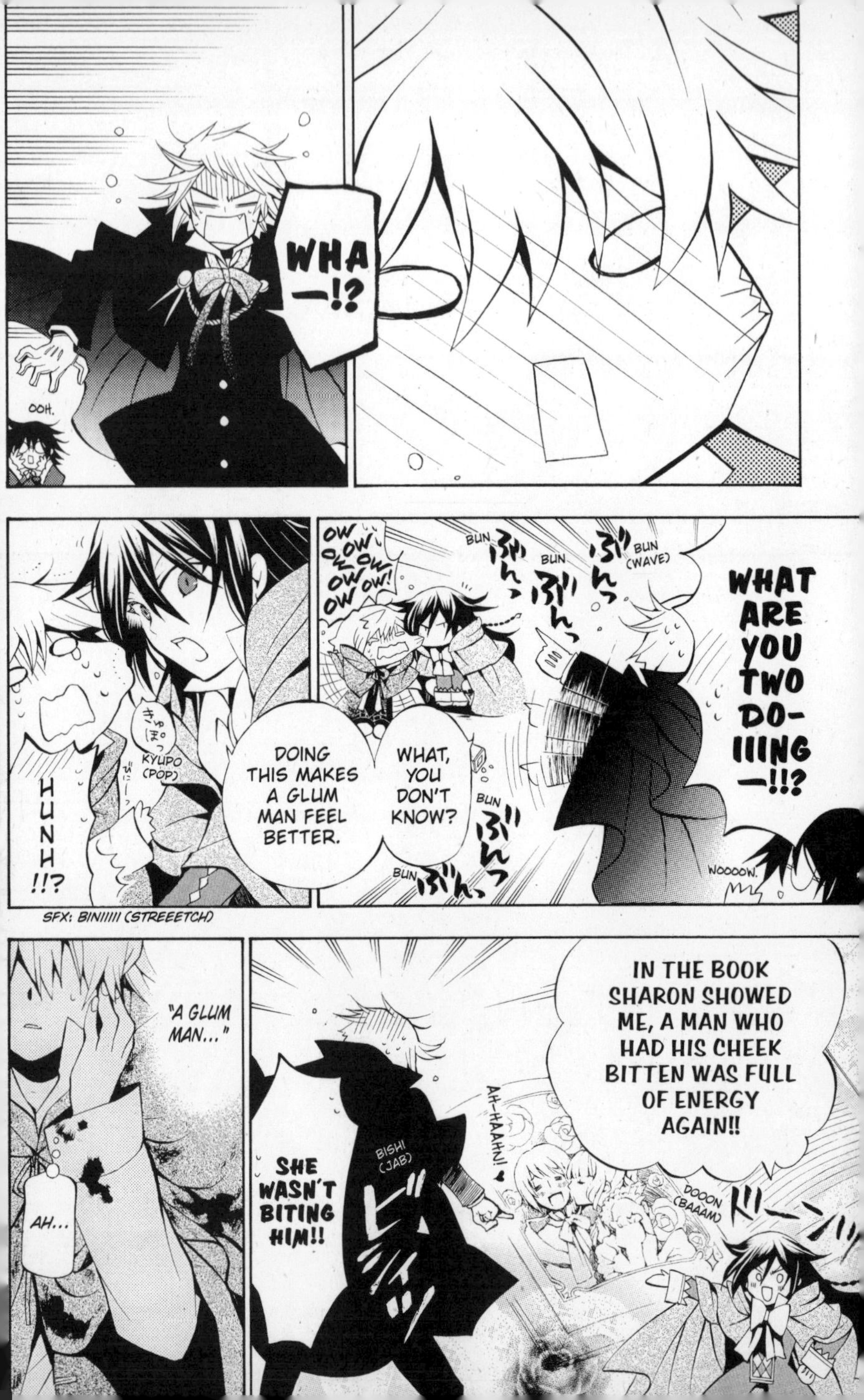
WHA—!?
OOH.
WHAT ARE YOU TWO DO-IIING—!!?
BUN (WAVE)
BUN
BUN
OW OW OW OW OW OW!
WHAT, YOU DON'T KNOW?
BUN
BUN
WOOOOW.
DOING THIS MAKES A GLUM MAN FEEL BETTER.
KYUPO (POP)
HUNH!!?
SFX: BINIIIII (STREEETCH)
IN THE BOOK SHARON SHOWED ME, A MAN WHO HAD HIS CHEEK BITTEN WAS FULL OF ENERGY AGAIN!!
DOOON (BAAAM)
AH-HAAHN!
BISHI (JAB)
SHE WASN'T BITING HIM!!
"A GLUM MAN..."
AH...

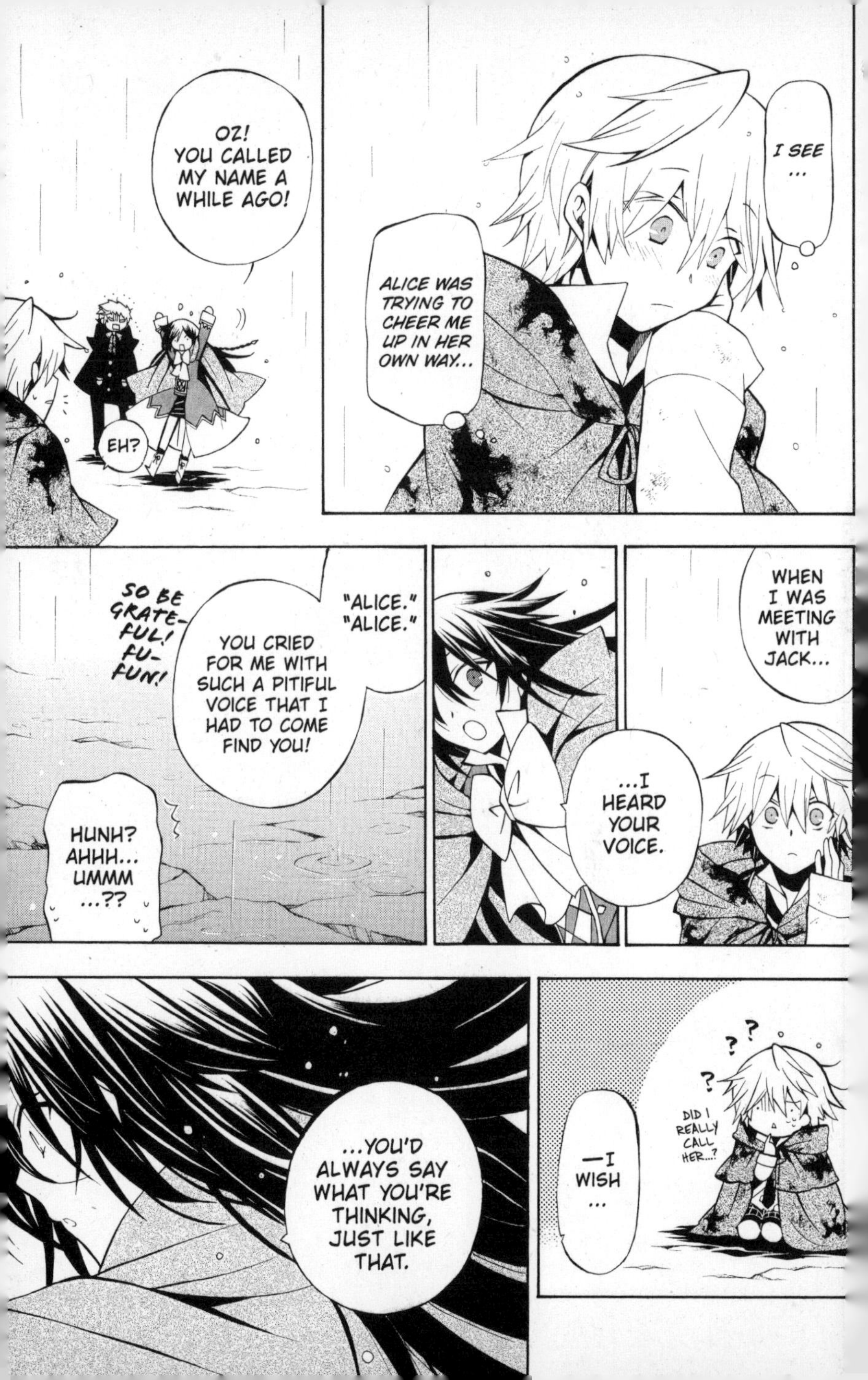
I SEE ...
ALICE WAS TRYING TO CHEER ME UP IN HER OWN WAY...
OZ! YOU CALLED MY NAME A WHILE AGO!
EH?
WHEN I WAS MEETING WITH JACK...
...I HEARD YOUR VOICE.
"ALICE." "ALICE." YOU CRIED FOR ME WITH SUCH A PITIFUL VOICE THAT I HAD TO COME FIND YOU!
SO BE GRATE-FUL! FU-FUN!
HUNH? AHHH... UMMM ...??
DID I REALLY CALL HER...?
—I WISH ...
...YOU'D ALWAYS SAY WHAT YOU'RE THINKING, JUST LIKE THAT.

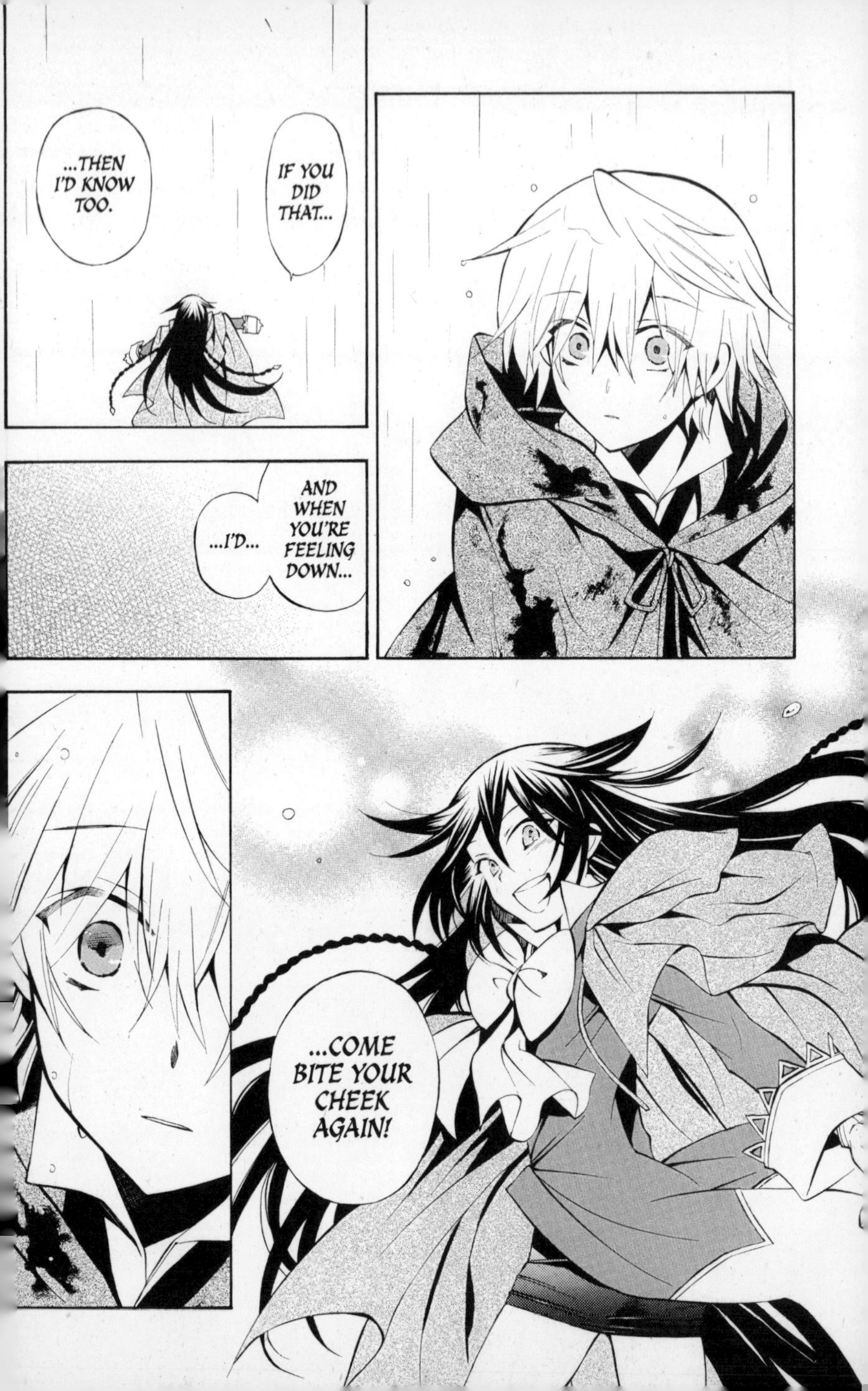
IF YOU DID THAT...
...THEN I'D KNOW TOO.
AND WHEN YOU'RE FEELING DOWN...
...I'D...
...COME BITE YOUR CHEEK AGAIN!

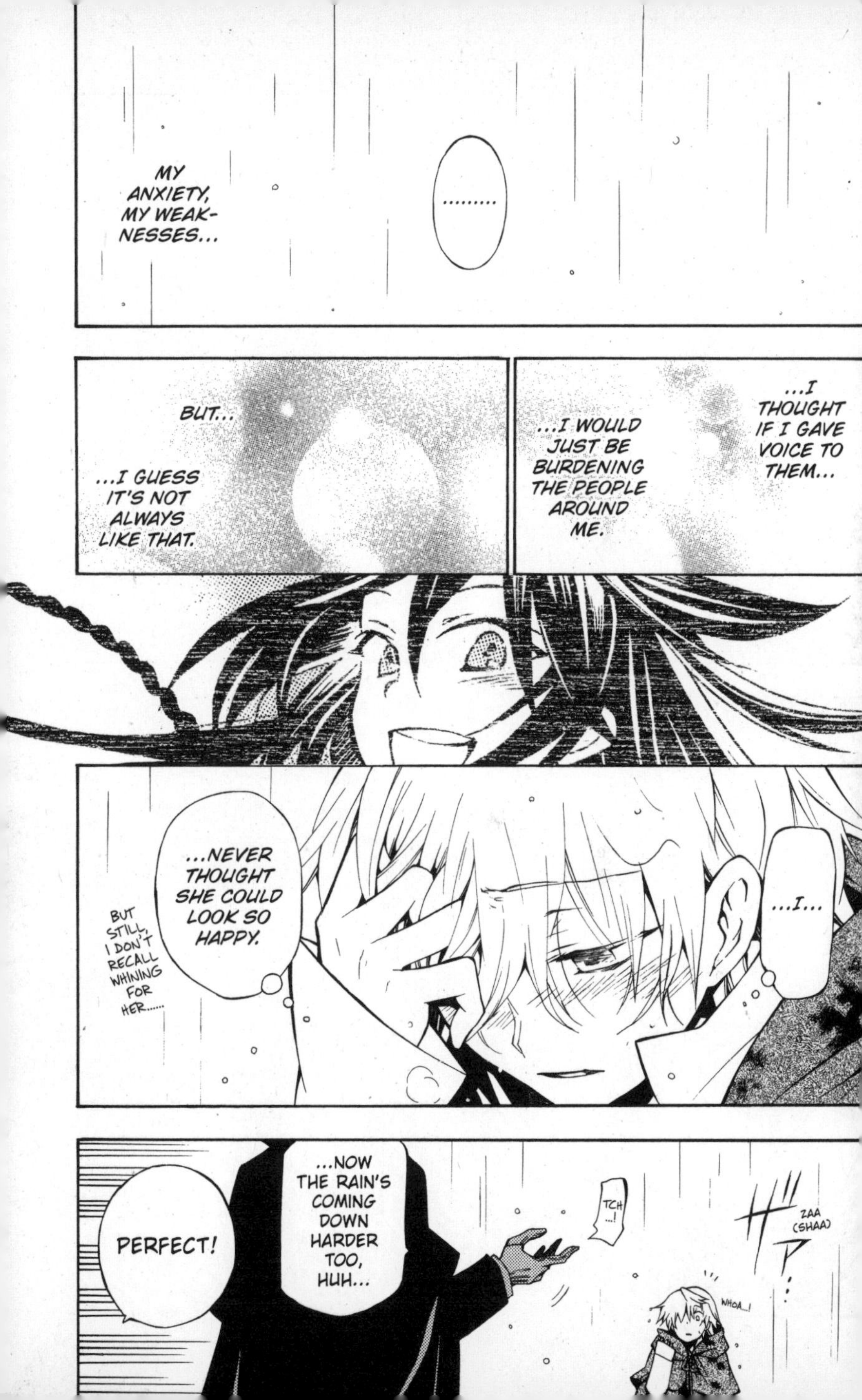
....
MY ANXIETY, MY WEAKNESSES...
...I THOUGHT IF I GAVE VOICE TO THEM...
...I WOULD JUST BE BURDENING THE PEOPLE AROUND ME.
BUT...
...I GUESS IT'S NOT ALWAYS LIKE THAT.
...I...
...NEVER THOUGHT SHE COULD LOOK SO HAPPY.
BUT STILL, I DON'T RECALL WHINING FOR HER......
ZAA (SHAA)
WHOA...!
TCH...!
...NOW THE RAIN'S COMING DOWN HARDER TOO, HUH...
PERFECT!

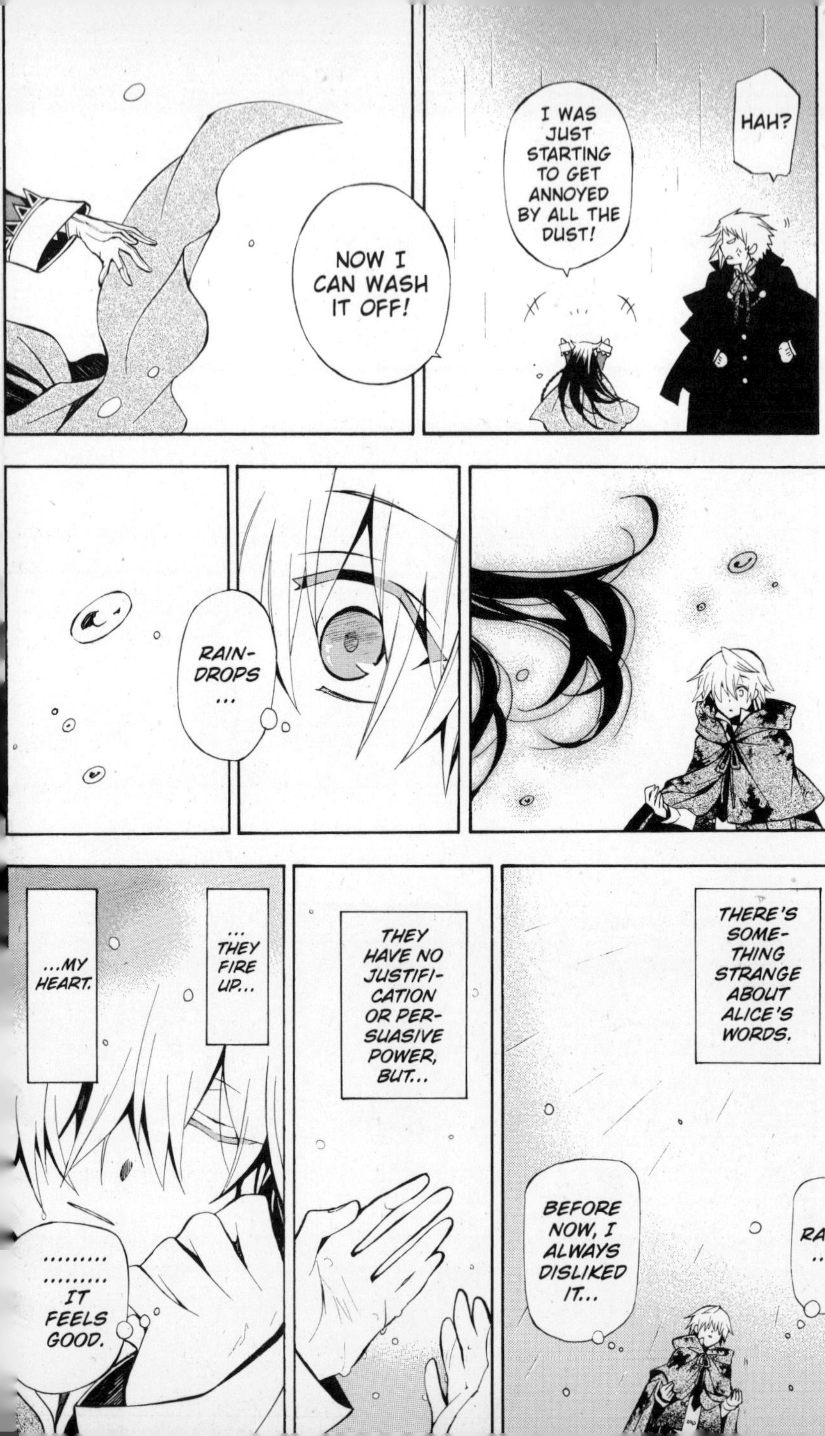
HAH?
I WAS JUST STARTING TO GET ANNOYED BY ALL THE DUST!
NOW I CAN WASH IT OFF!
RAIN-DROPS ...
THERE'S SOME-THING STRANGE ABOUT ALICE'S WORDS.
RAIN ...
BEFORE NOW, I ALWAYS DISLIKED IT...
THEY HAVE NO JUSTIFI-CATION OR PER-SUASIVE POWER, BUT...
... THEY FIRE UP...
...MY HEART.
.... IT FEELS GOOD.

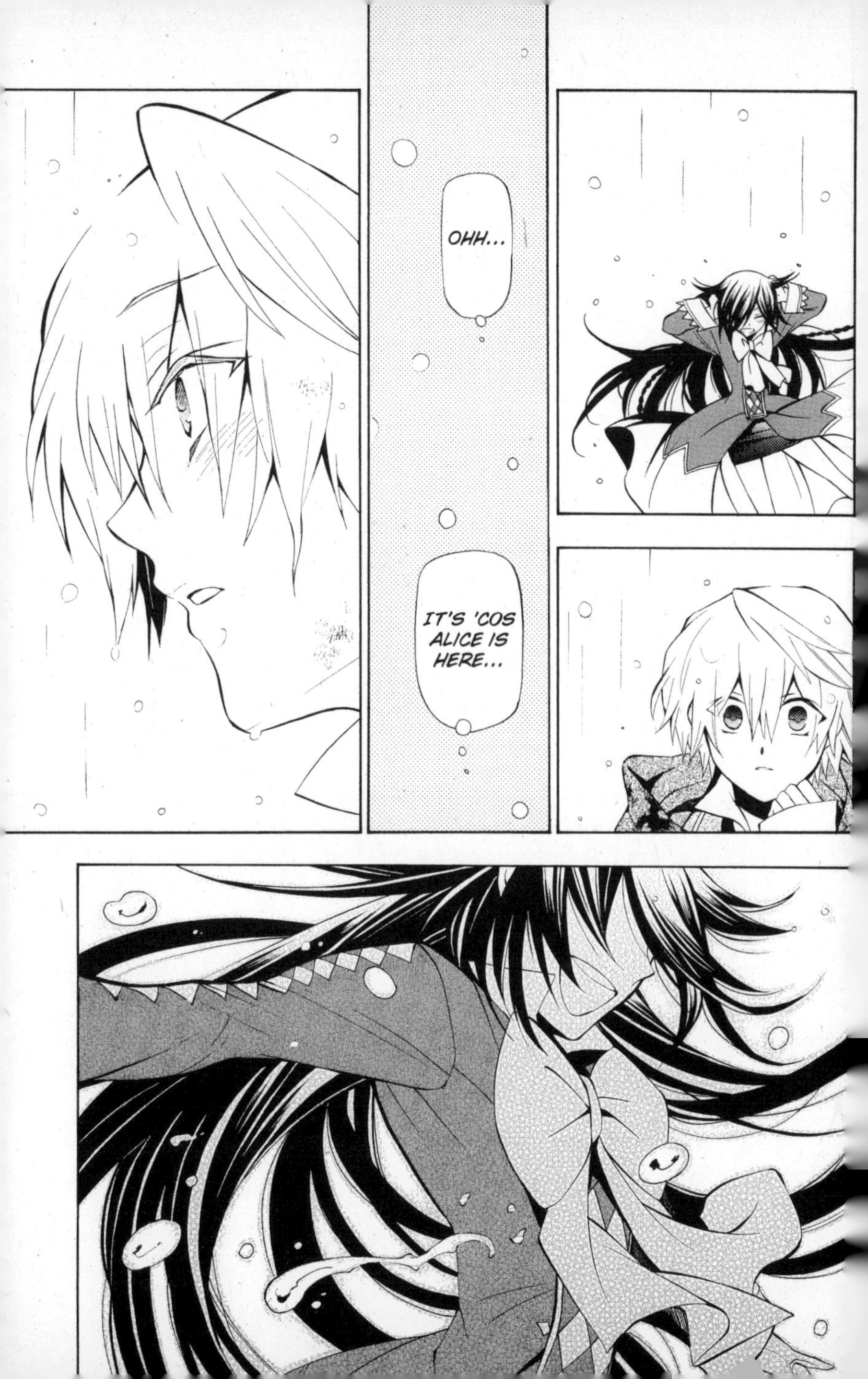
OHH...
IT'S 'COS ALICE IS HERE...

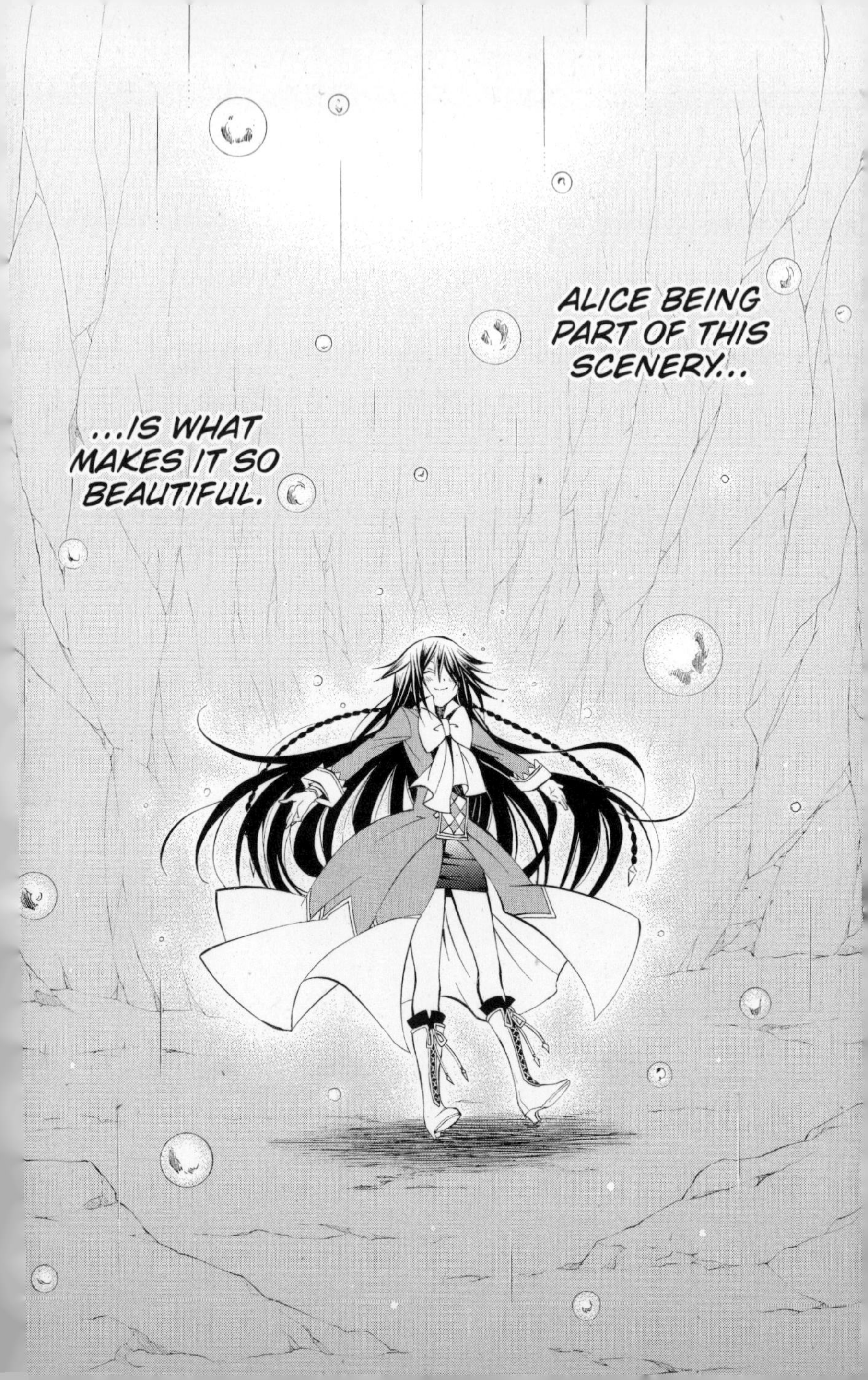
ALICE BEING PART OF THIS SCENERY...
...IS WHAT MAKES IT SO BEAUTIFUL.

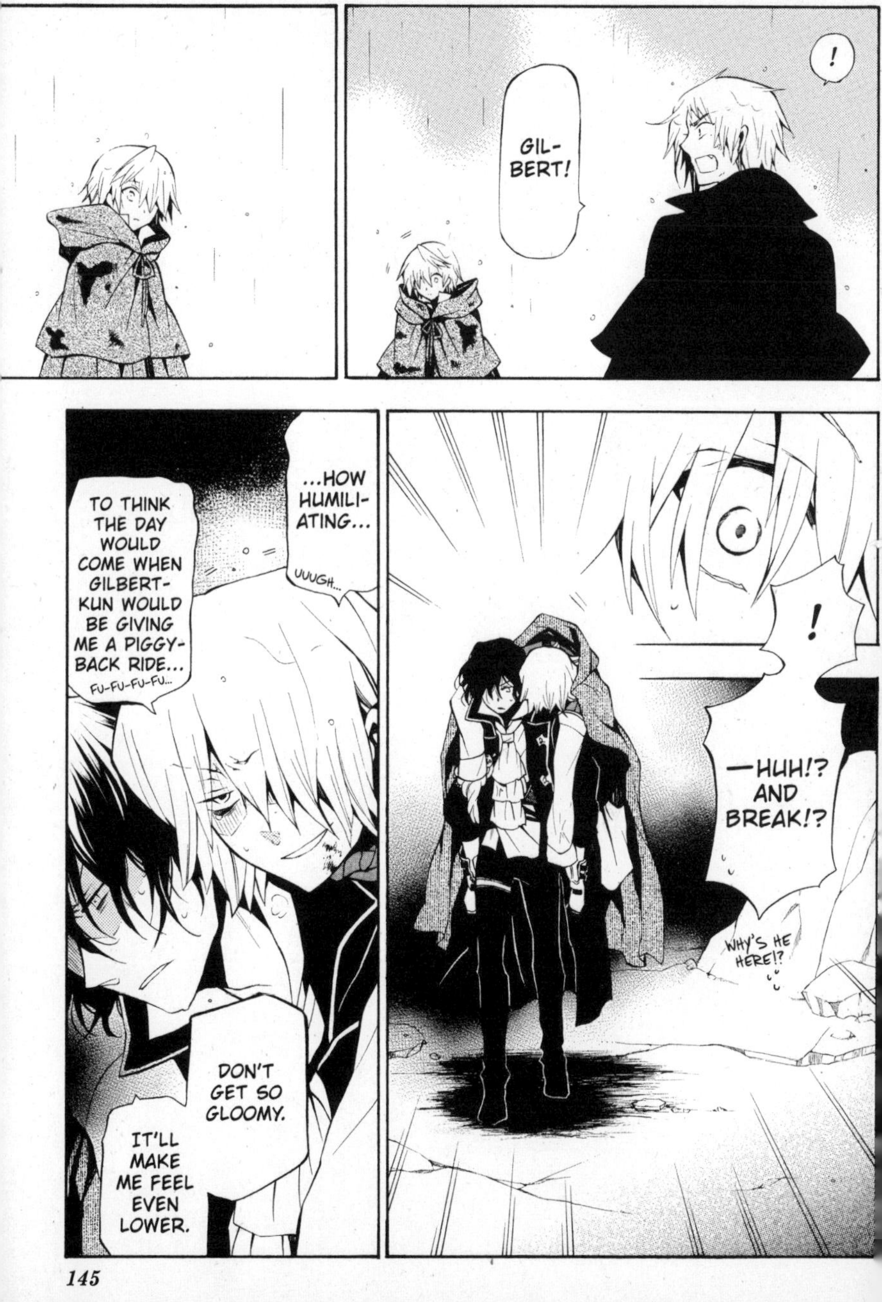
!
GIL-BERT!
!
—HUH!? AND BREAK!?
WHY'S HE HERE!?
...HOW HUMILI-ATING...
UUUGH...
TO THINK THE DAY WOULD COME WHEN GILBERT-KUN WOULD BE GIVING ME A PIGGY-BACK RIDE...
FU-FU-FU-FU...
DON'T GET SO GLOOMY.
IT'LL MAKE ME FEEL EVEN LOWER.

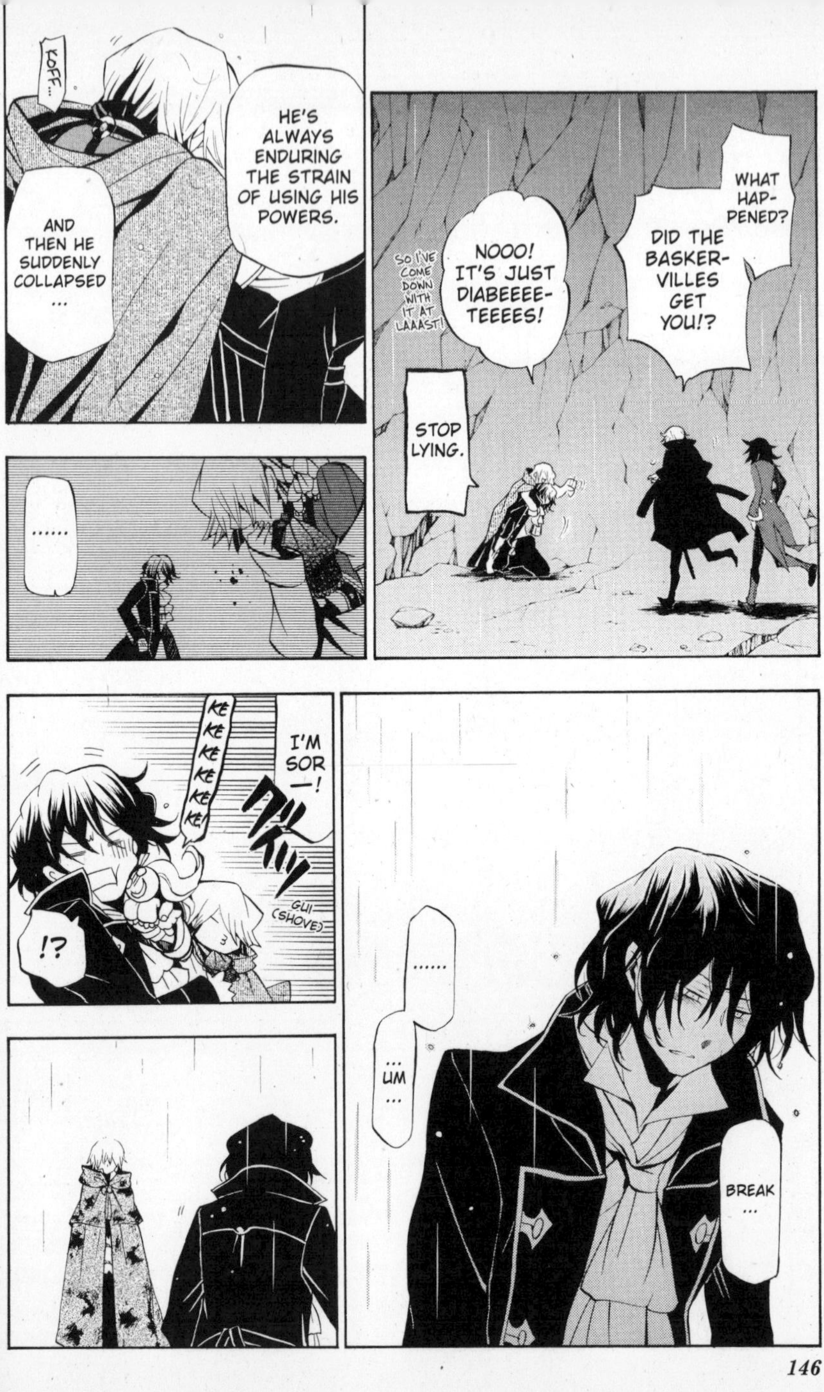
WHAT HAP-PENED?
DID THE BASKER-VILLES GET YOU!?
NOOO! IT'S JUST DIABEEEE-TEEEES!
SO I'VE COME DOWN WITH IT AT LAAAST!
STOP LYING.
KOFF...
HE'S ALWAYS ENDURING THE STRAIN OF USING HIS POWERS.
AND THEN HE SUDDENLY COLLAPSED...
......
......
...UM...
BREAK...
I'M SOR—!
KE KE KE KE KE KE!
GUI (SHOVE)
!?

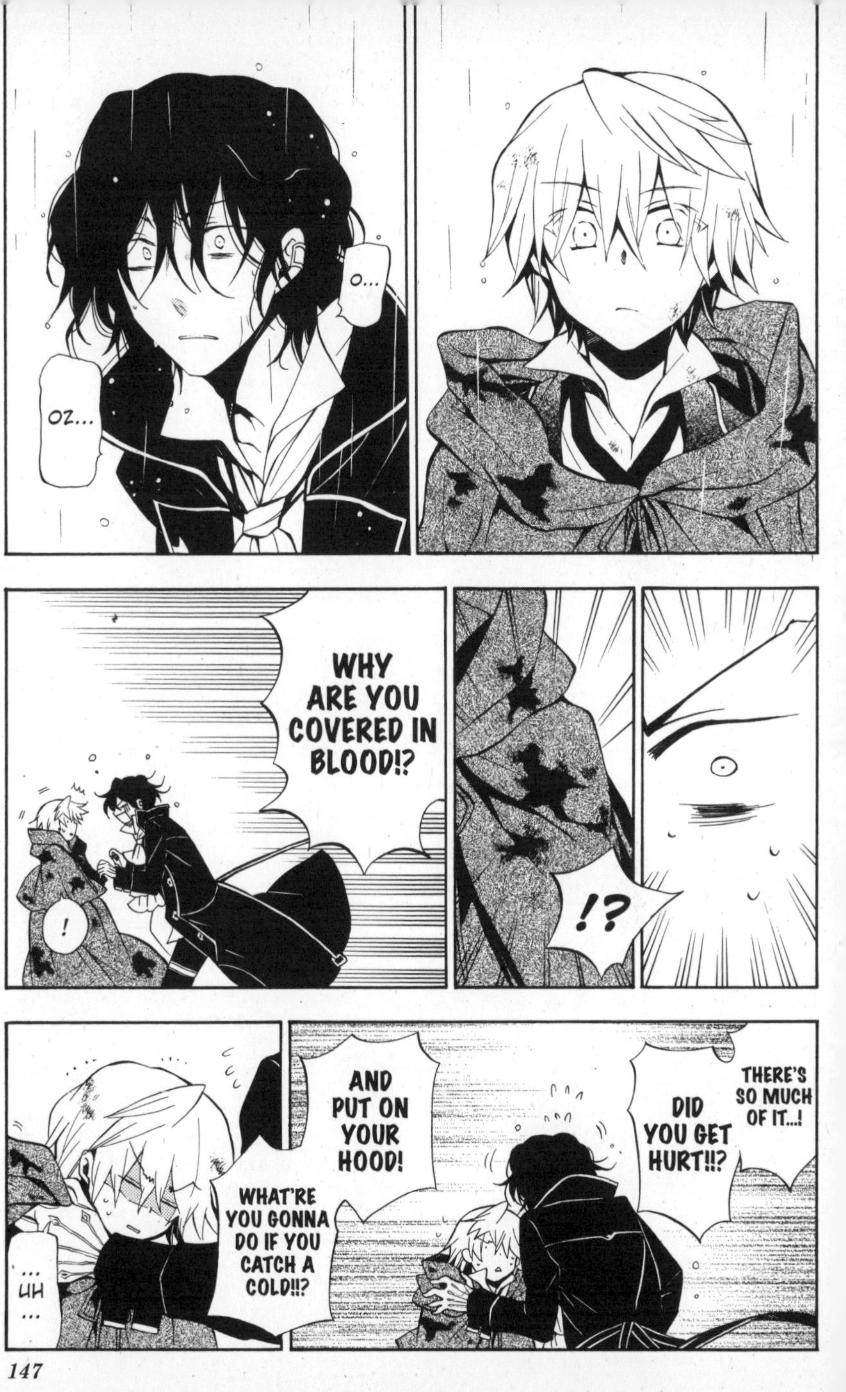
O...
OZ...
!?
WHY ARE YOU COVERED IN BLOOD!?
!
THERE'S SO MUCH OF IT...!
DID YOU GET HURT!!?
AND PUT ON YOUR HOOD!
WHAT'RE YOU GONNA DO IF YOU CATCH A COLD!!?
...UH...

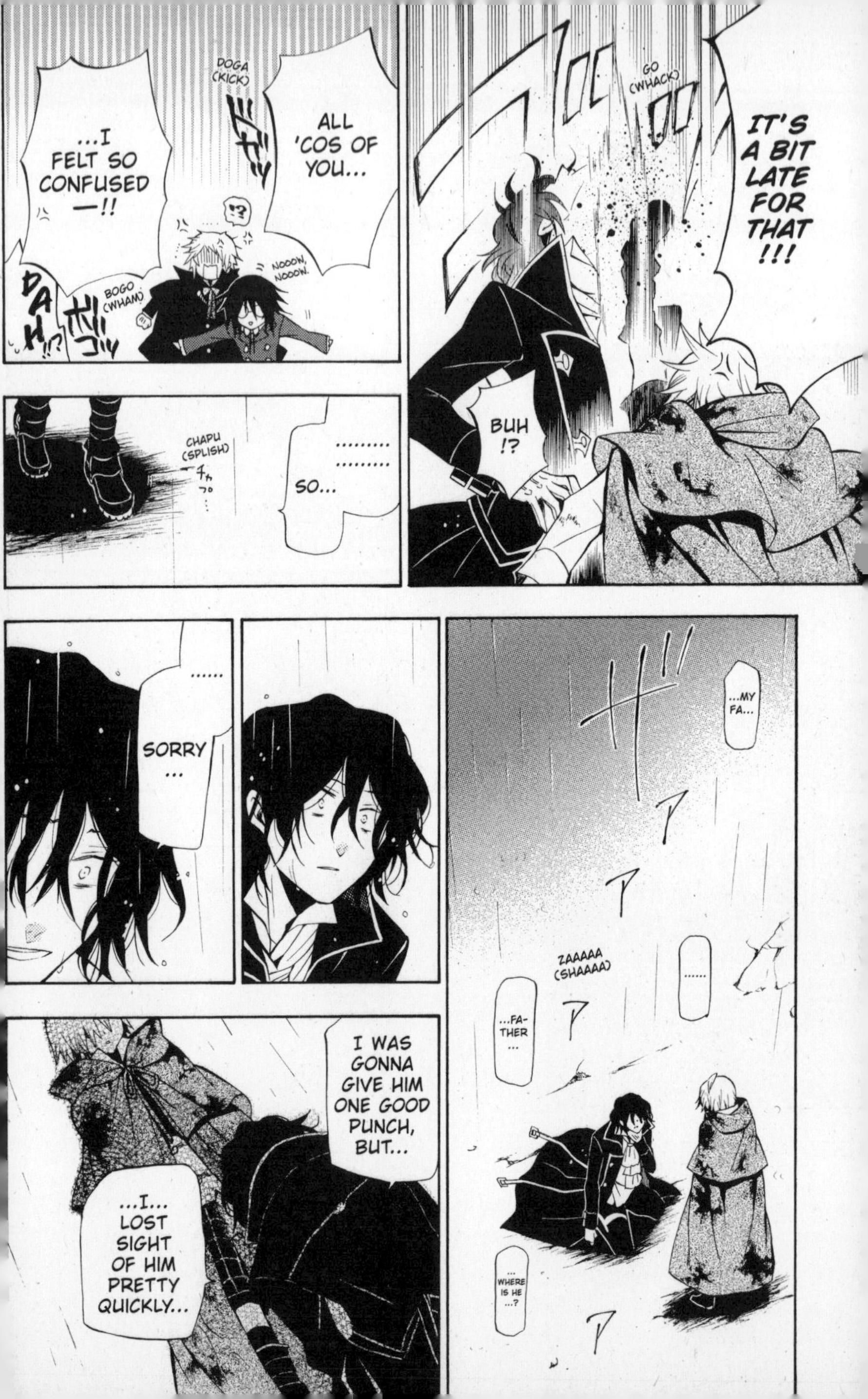
GO (WHACK)
IT'S A BIT LATE FOR THAT!!!
BUH!?
ALL 'COS OF YOU...
DOGA (KICK)
...I FELT SO CONFUSED—!!
!?
NOOOW, NOOOW.
BOGO (WHAM)
DAH!!?
....
....
SO...
CHAPU (SPLISH)
...MY FA...
......
ZAAAAA (SHAAAA)
...FA-THER...
...WHERE IS HE...?
......
SORRY...
I WAS GONNA GIVE HIM ONE GOOD PUNCH, BUT...
...I... LOST SIGHT OF HIM PRETTY QUICKLY...

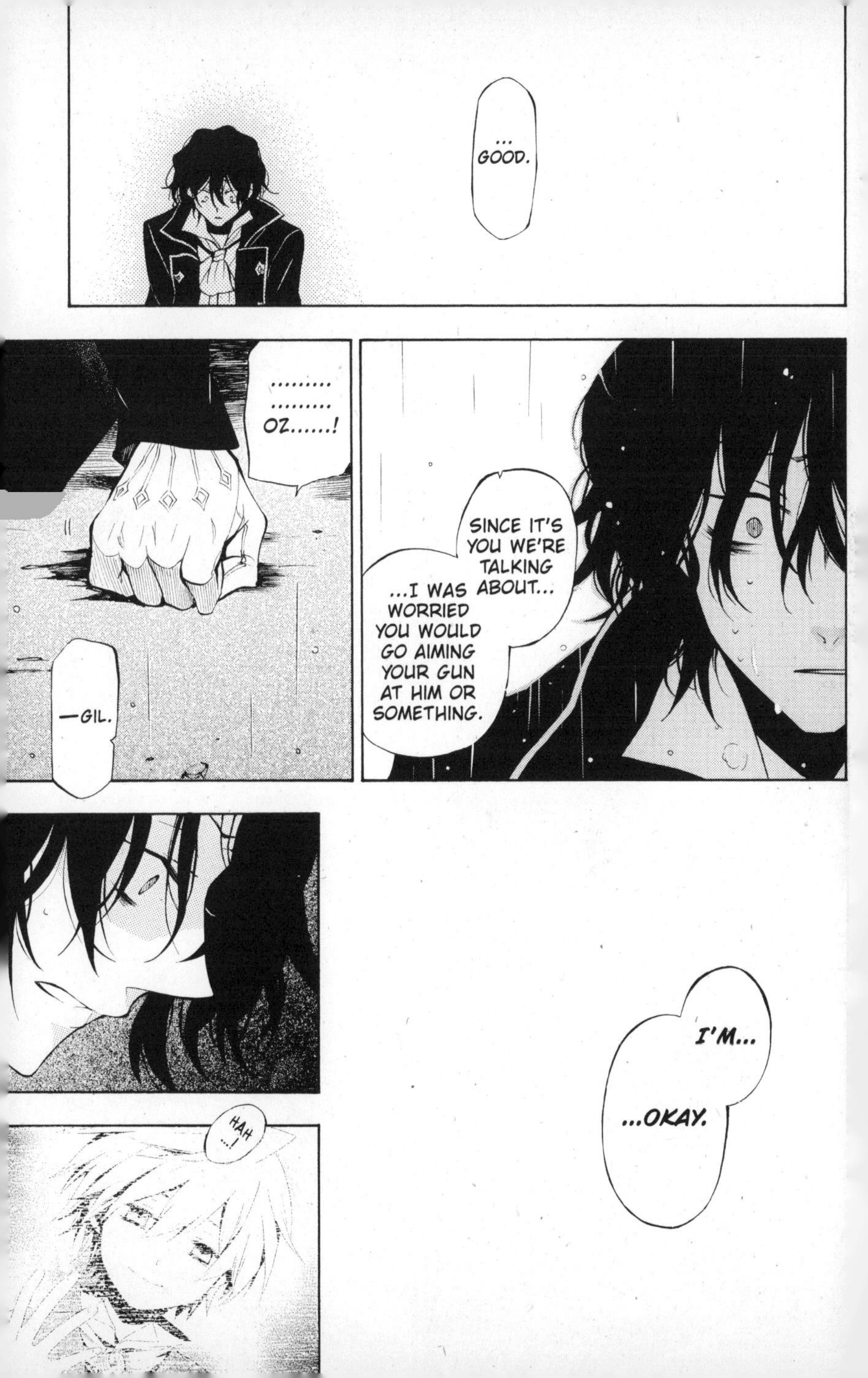

... GOOD.
SINCE IT'S YOU WE'RE TALKING ABOUT...
...I WAS WORRIED YOU WOULD GO AIMING YOUR GUN AT HIM OR SOMETHING.
.... OZ......!
—GIL.
I'M... ...OKAY.
HAH ...!

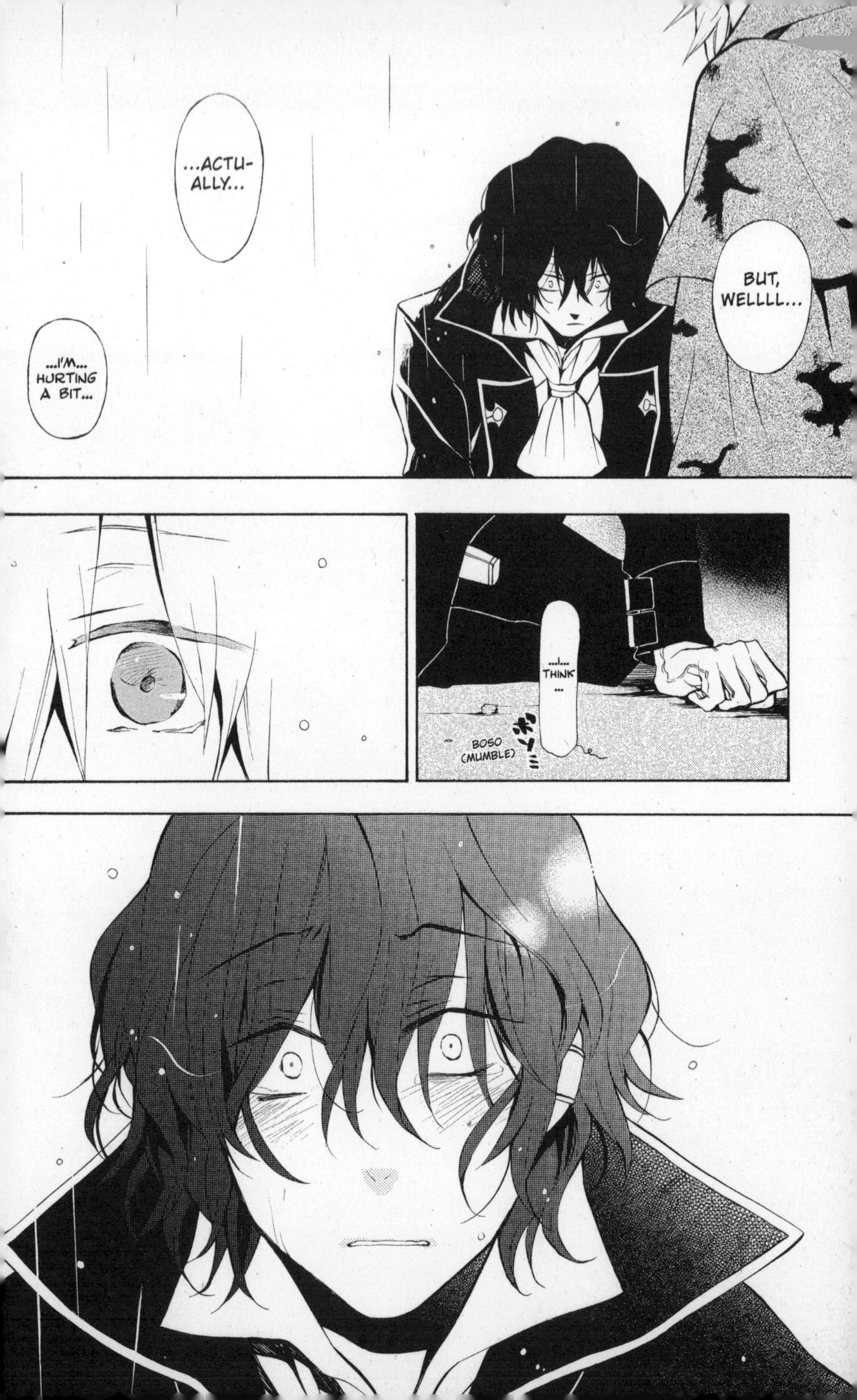
BUT, WELLLL...
...ACTU-ALLY...
...I'M... HURTING A BIT...
...I... THINK ...
BOSO (MUMBLE)

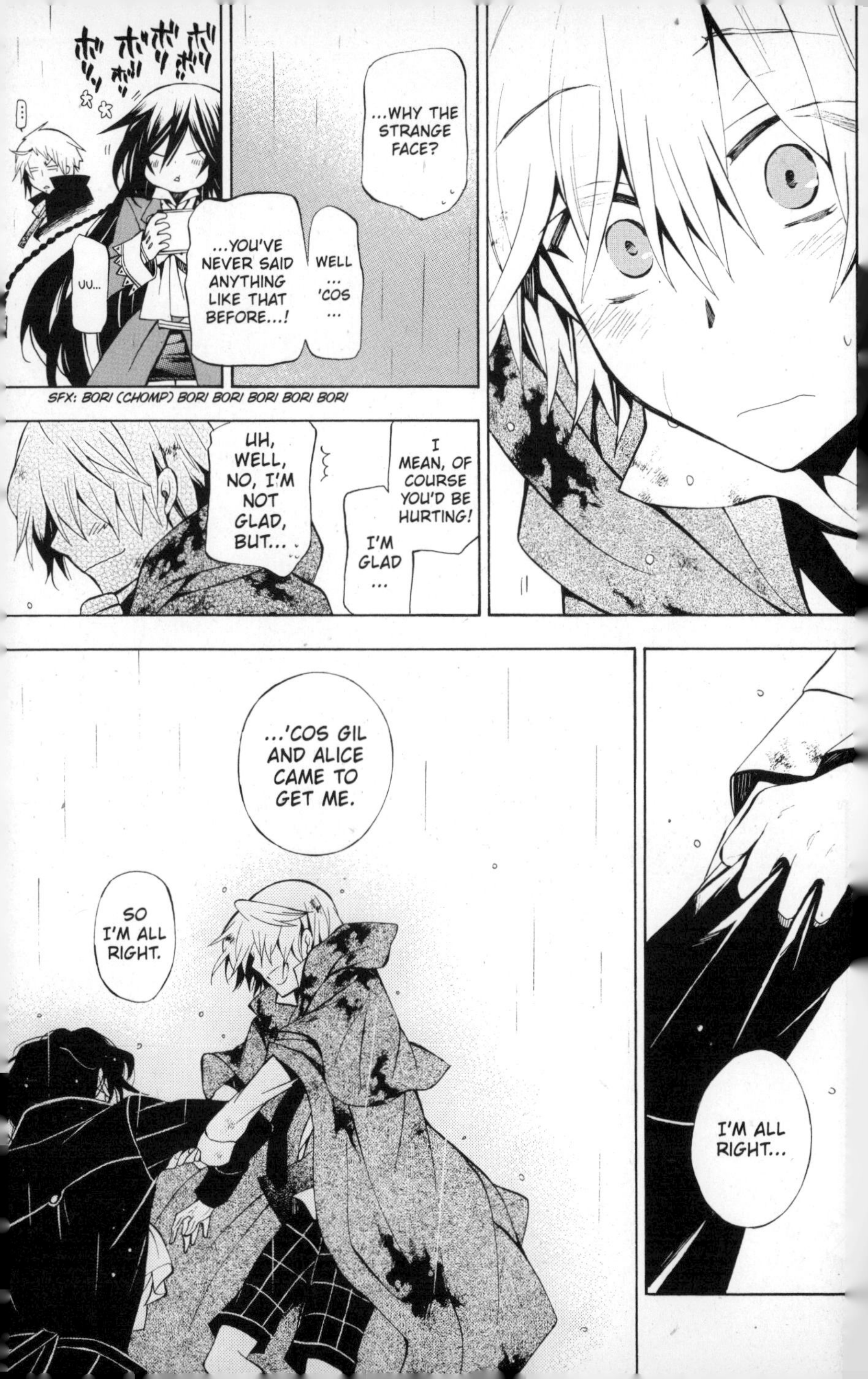
...WHY THE STRANGE FACE?
WELL ... 'COS ...
...YOU'VE NEVER SAID ANYTHING LIKE THAT BEFORE...!
...
UU...
SFX: BORI (CHOMP) BORI BORI BORI BORI BORI
I MEAN, OF COURSE YOU'D BE HURTING!
I'M GLAD ...
UH, WELL, NO, I'M NOT GLAD, BUT...
I'M ALL RIGHT...
...'COS GIL AND ALICE CAME TO GET ME.
SO I'M ALL RIGHT.

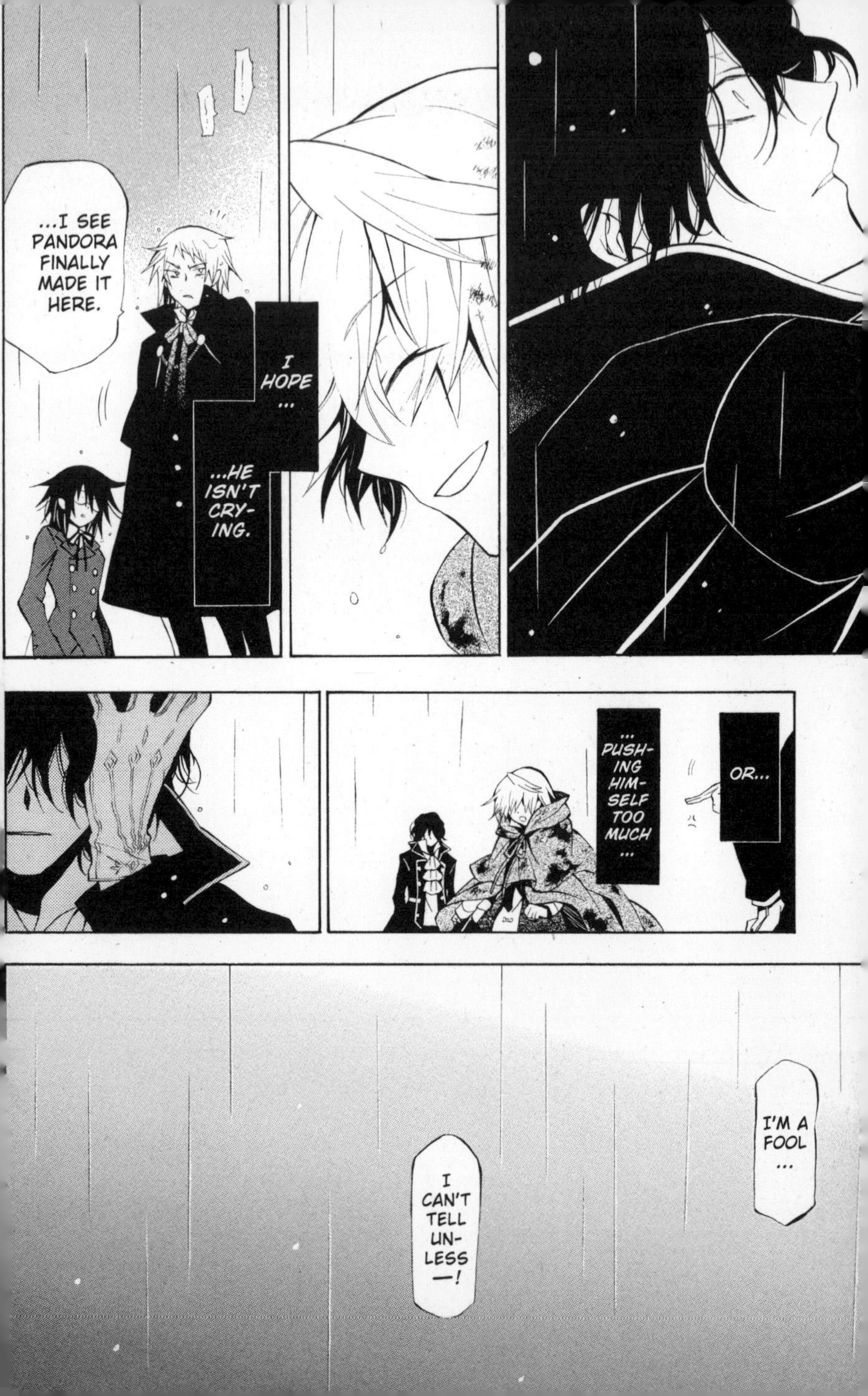
I HOPE...
...HE ISN'T CRYING.
...I SEE PANDORA FINALLY MADE IT HERE.
OR...
...PUSHING HIMSELF TOO MUCH...
I'M A FOOL...
I CAN'T TELL UNLESS—!

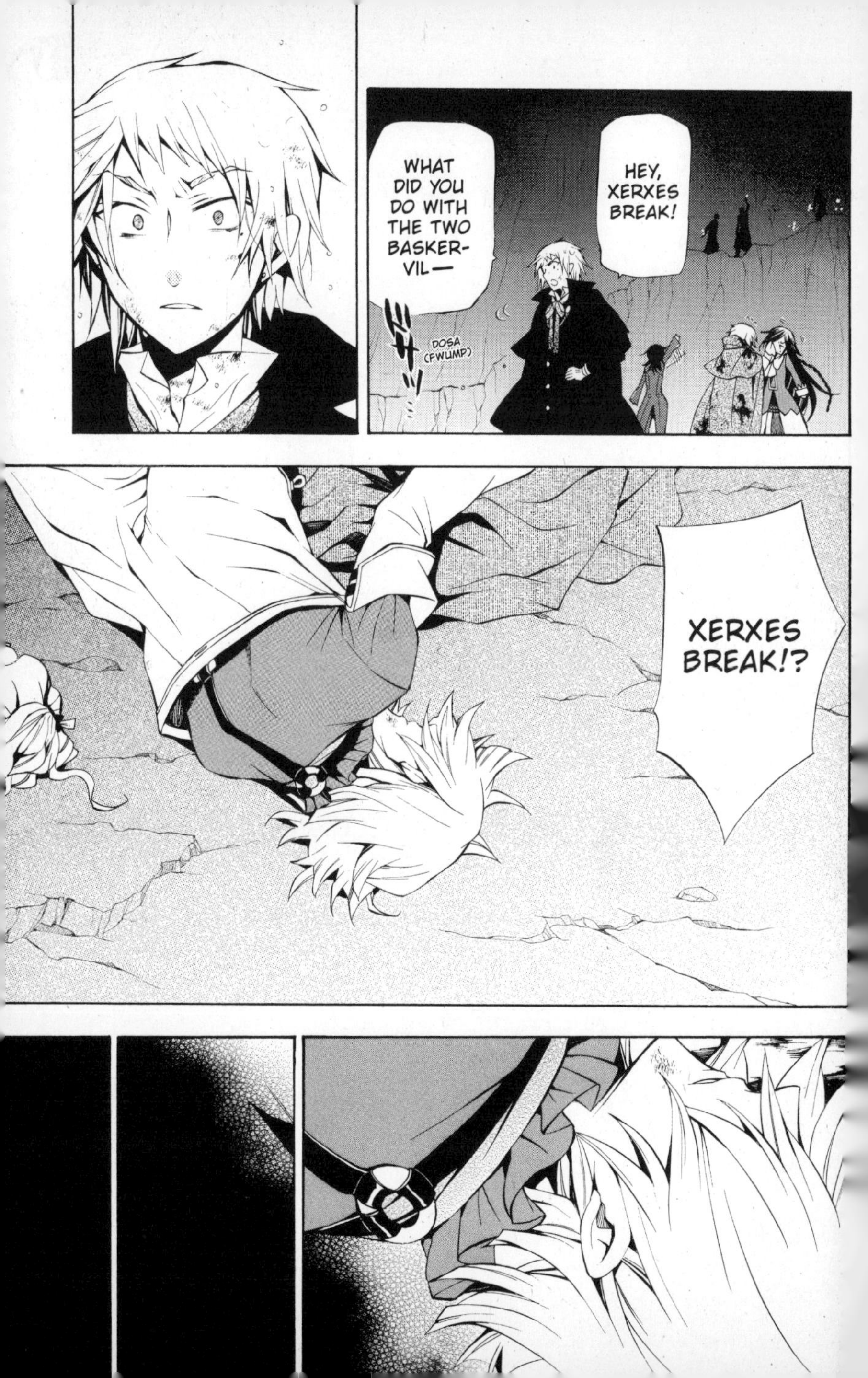
HEY, XERXES BREAK!
WHAT DID YOU DO WITH THE TWO BASKER-VIL—
DOSA (FWUMP)
XERXES BREAK!?

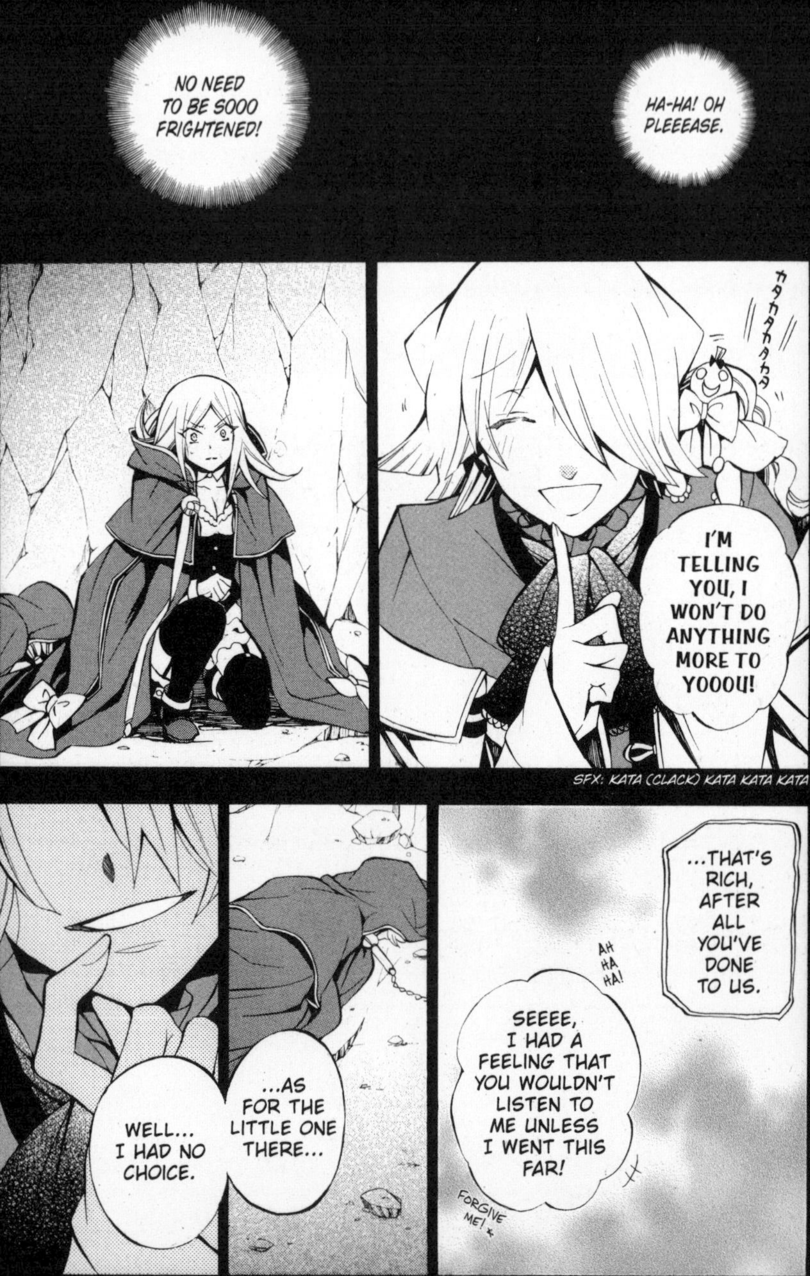
HA-HA! OH PLEEEASE.
NO NEED TO BE SOOO FRIGHTENED!
カタカタカタカタ
I'M TELLING YOU, I WON'T DO ANYTHING MORE TO YOOOU!
SFX: KATA (CLACK) KATA KATA KATA
...THAT'S RICH, AFTER ALL YOU'VE DONE TO US.
AH HA HA!
SEEEE, I HAD A FEELING THAT YOU WOULDN'T LISTEN TO ME UNLESS I WENT THIS FAR!
FORGIVE ME!
...AS FOR THE LITTLE ONE THERE...
WELL... I HAD NO CHOICE.

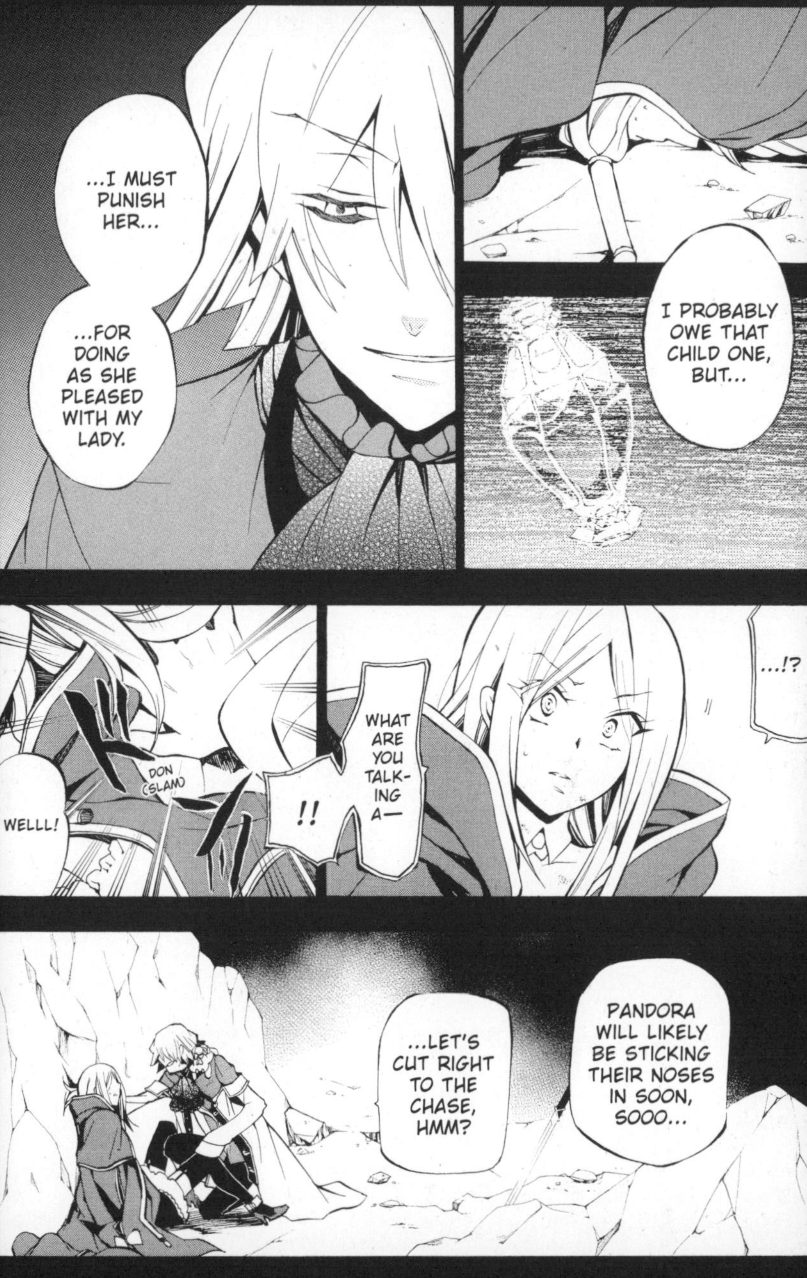
I PROBABLY OWE THAT CHILD ONE, BUT...
...I MUST PUNISH HER...
...FOR DOING AS SHE PLEASED WITH MY LADY.
...!?
WHAT ARE YOU TALKING A—
!!
DON (SLAM)
WELLL!
PANDORA WILL LIKELY BE STICKING THEIR NOSES IN SOON, SOOO...
...LET'S CUT RIGHT TO THE CHASE, HMM?

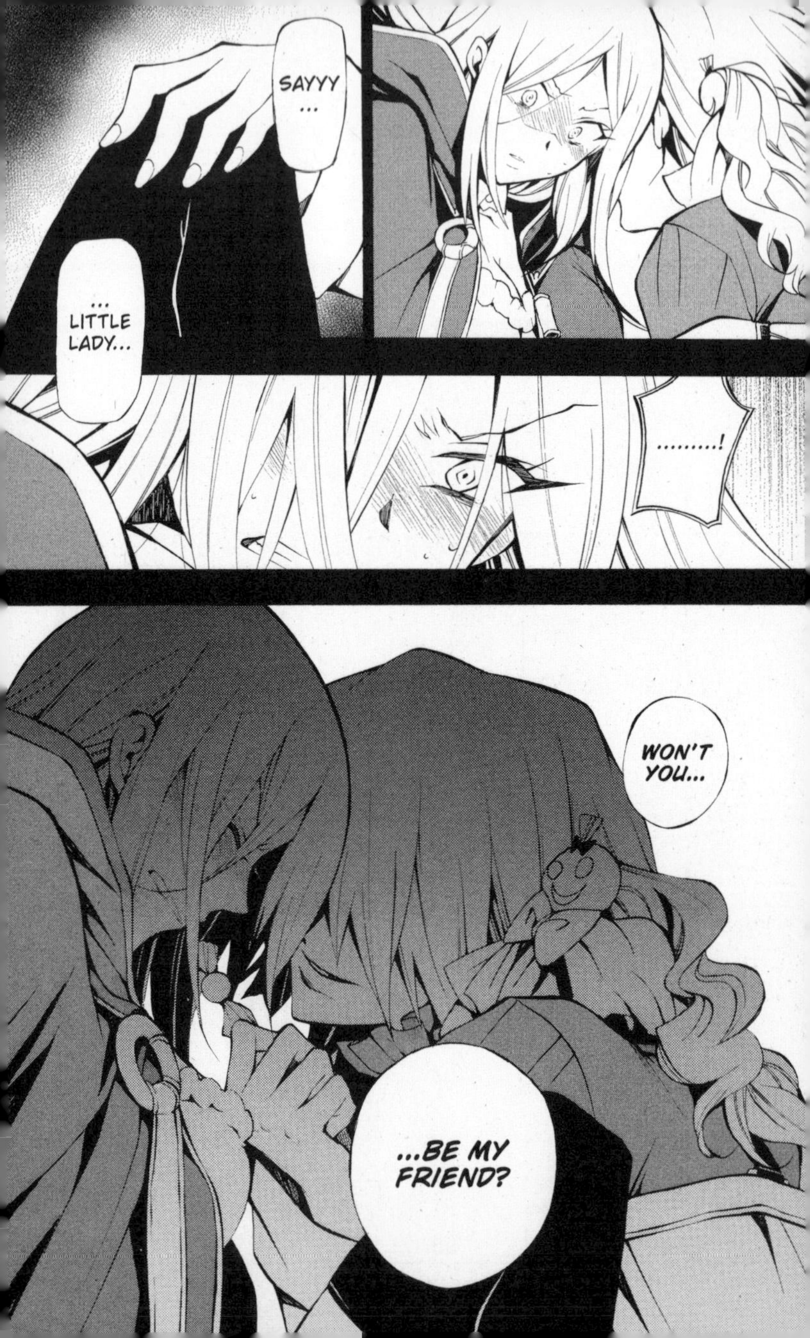
SAYYY ...
... LITTLE LADY...
.........!
WON'T YOU...
...BE MY FRIEND?

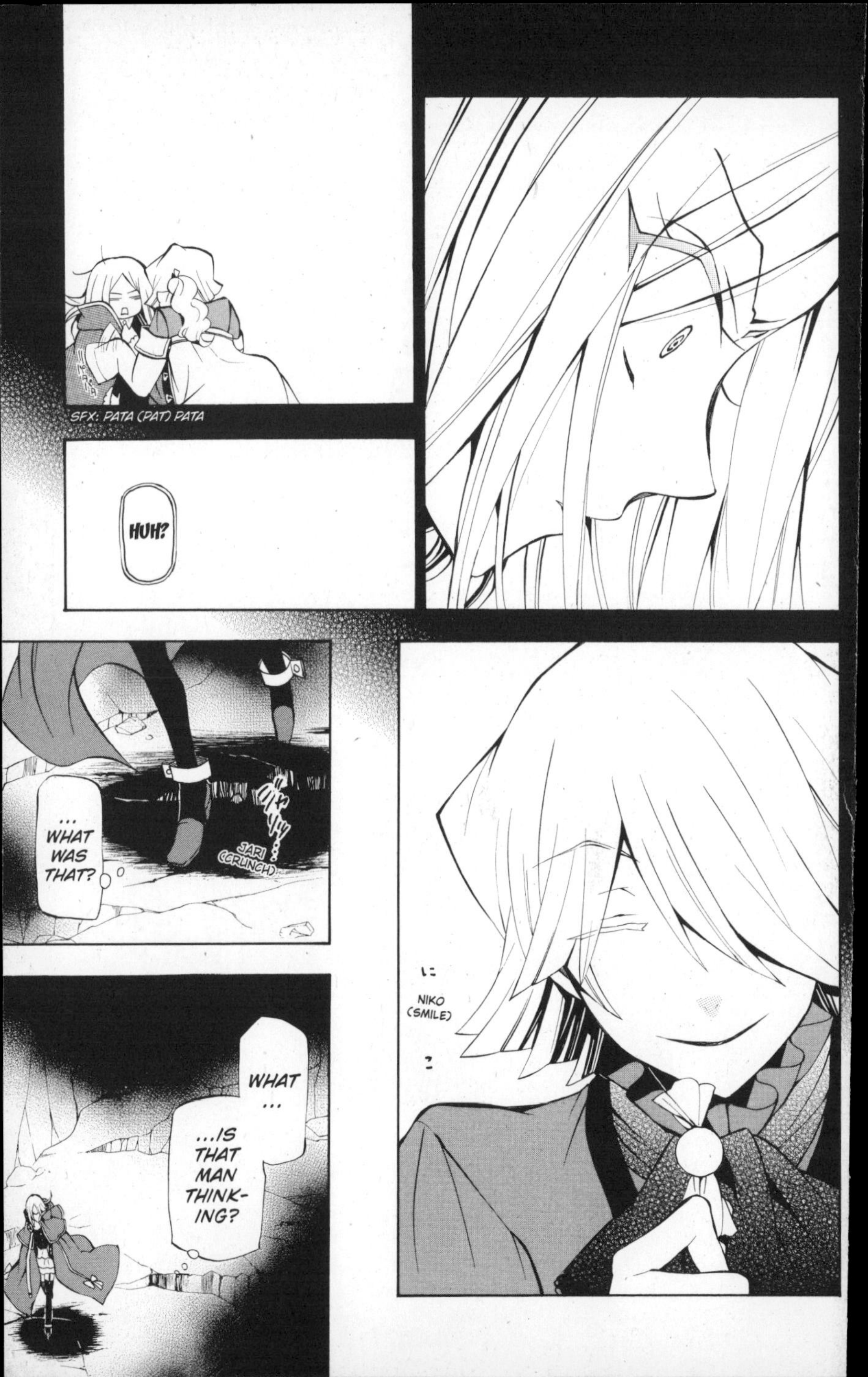
SFX: PATA (PAT) PATA
HUH?
NIKO (SMILE)
... WHAT WAS THAT?
JARI (CRUNCH)
WHAT ...
...IS THAT MAN THINKING?

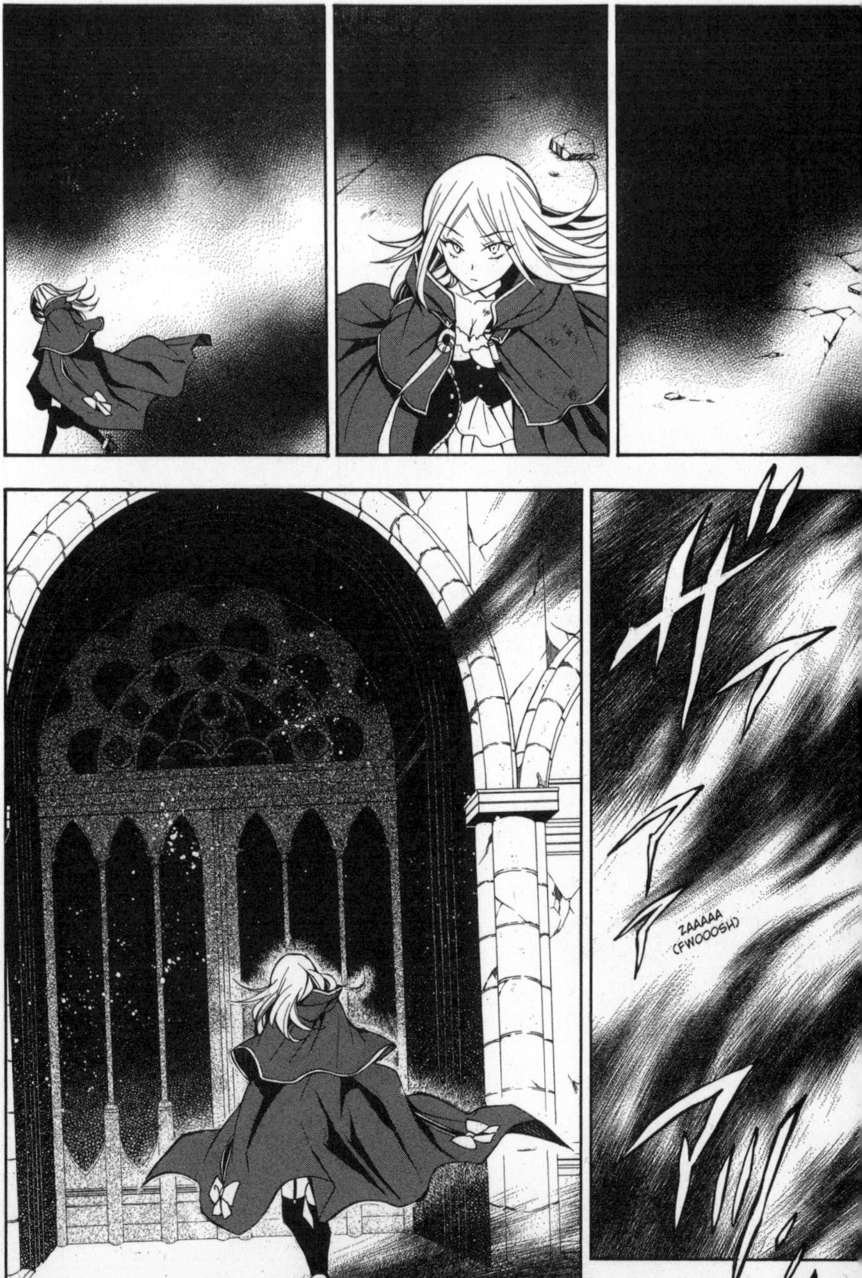
ZAAAAA
(FWOOOSH)

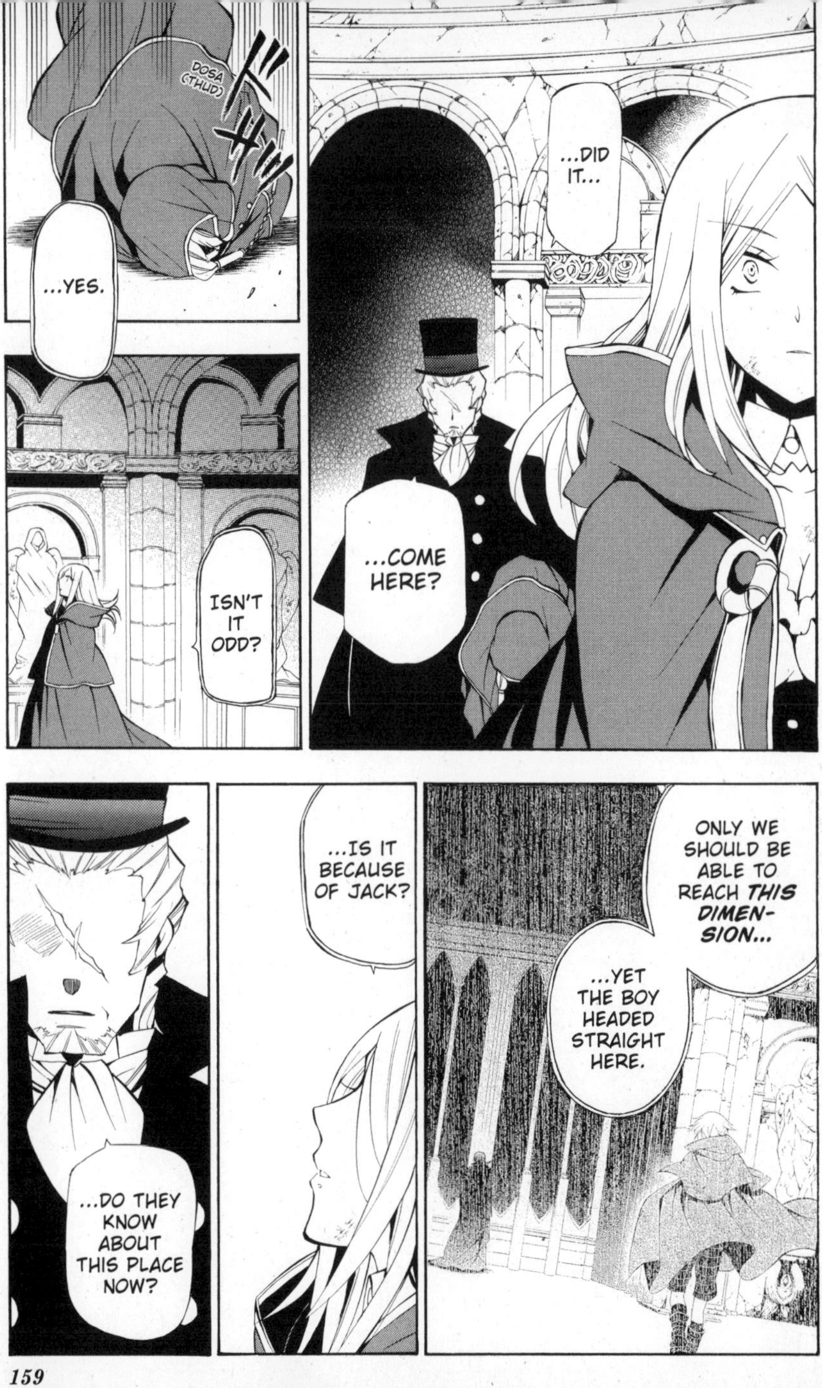
...DID IT...
...COME HERE?
DOSA (THUD)
...YES.
ISN'T IT ODD?
ONLY WE SHOULD BE ABLE TO REACH *THIS DIMENSION...*
...YET THE BOY HEADED STRAIGHT HERE.
...IS IT BECAUSE OF JACK?
...DO THEY KNOW ABOUT THIS PLACE NOW?

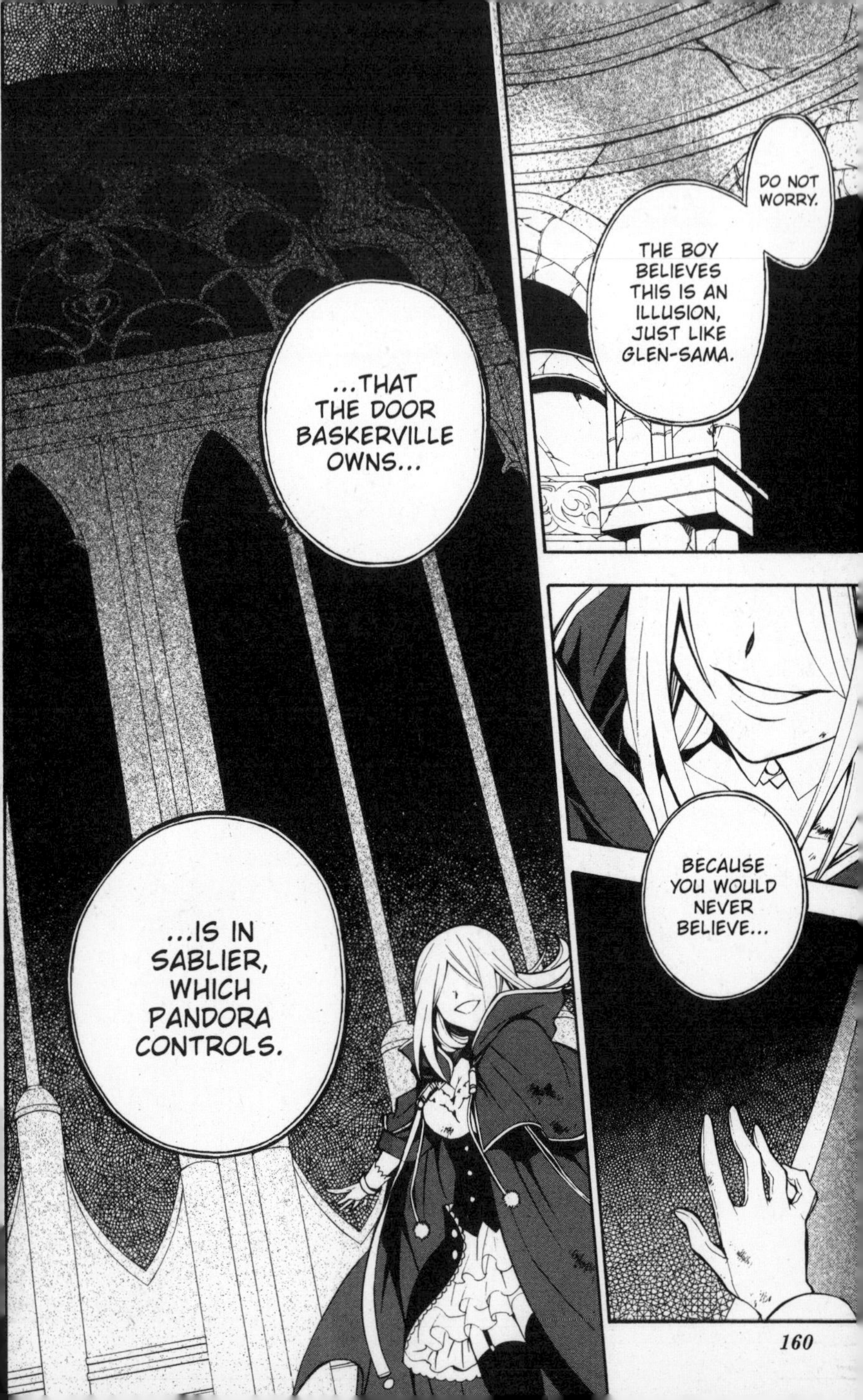
DO NOT WORRY.
THE BOY BELIEVES THIS IS AN ILLUSION, JUST LIKE GLEN-SAMA.
BECAUSE YOU WOULD NEVER BELIEVE...
...THAT THE DOOR BASKERVILLE OWNS...
...IS IN SABLIER, WHICH PANDORA CONTROLS.

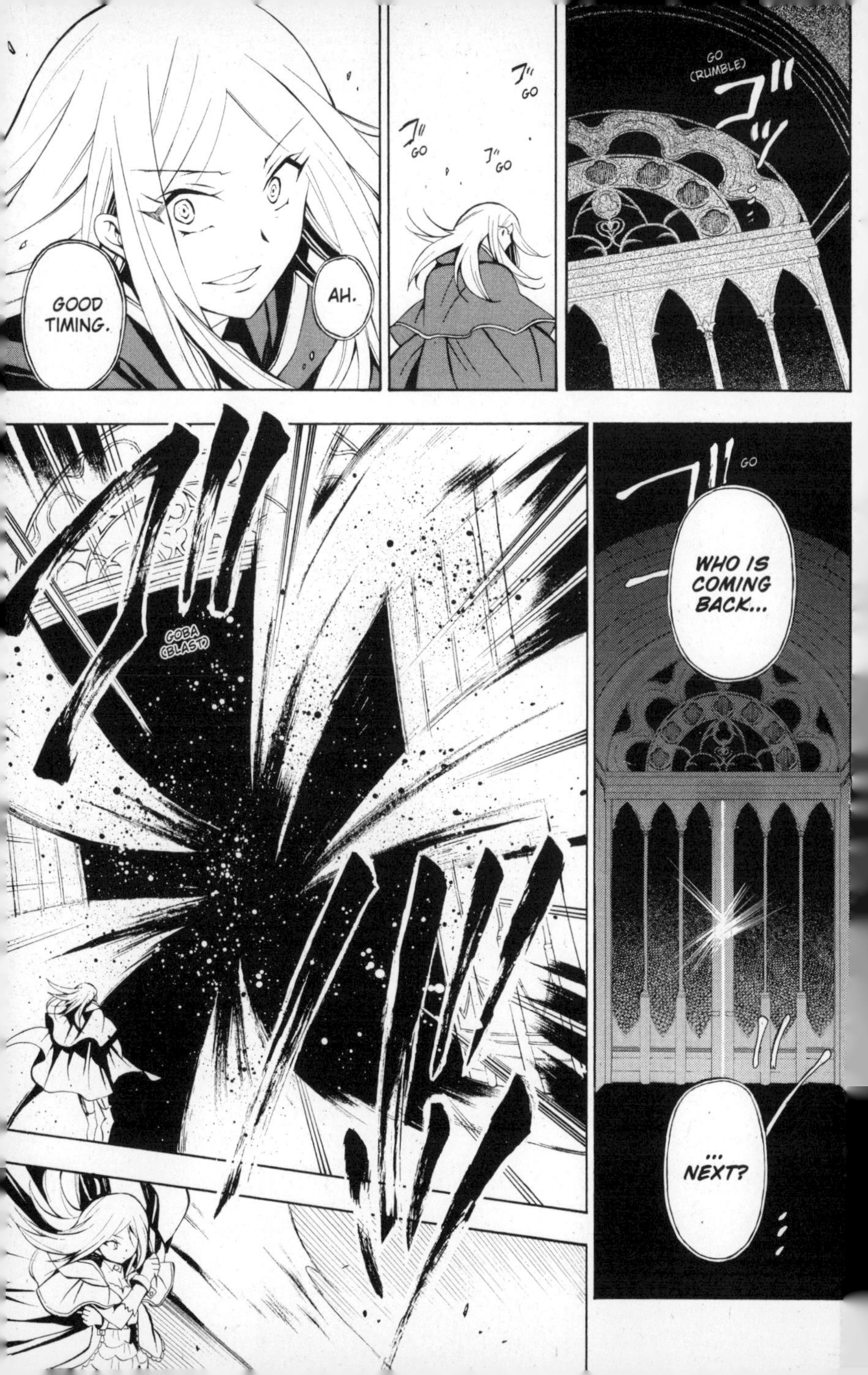
GO
(RUMBLE)
GO
GO
GO
AH.
GOOD TIMING.
GO
WHO IS COMING BACK...
... NEXT?
GOBA
(BLAST)

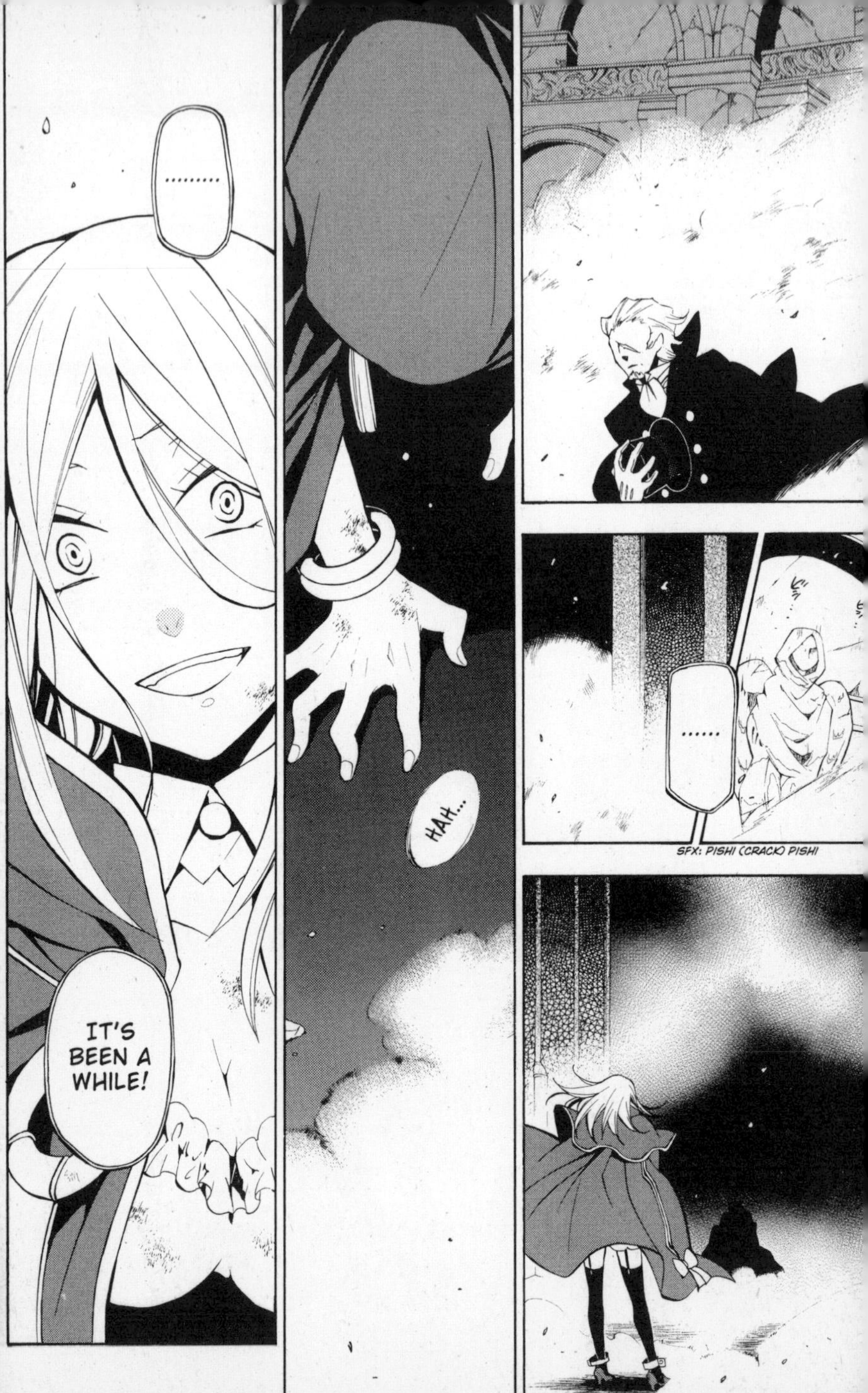
......
SFX: PISHI (CRACK) PISHI
HAH...
....
IT'S BEEN A WHILE!

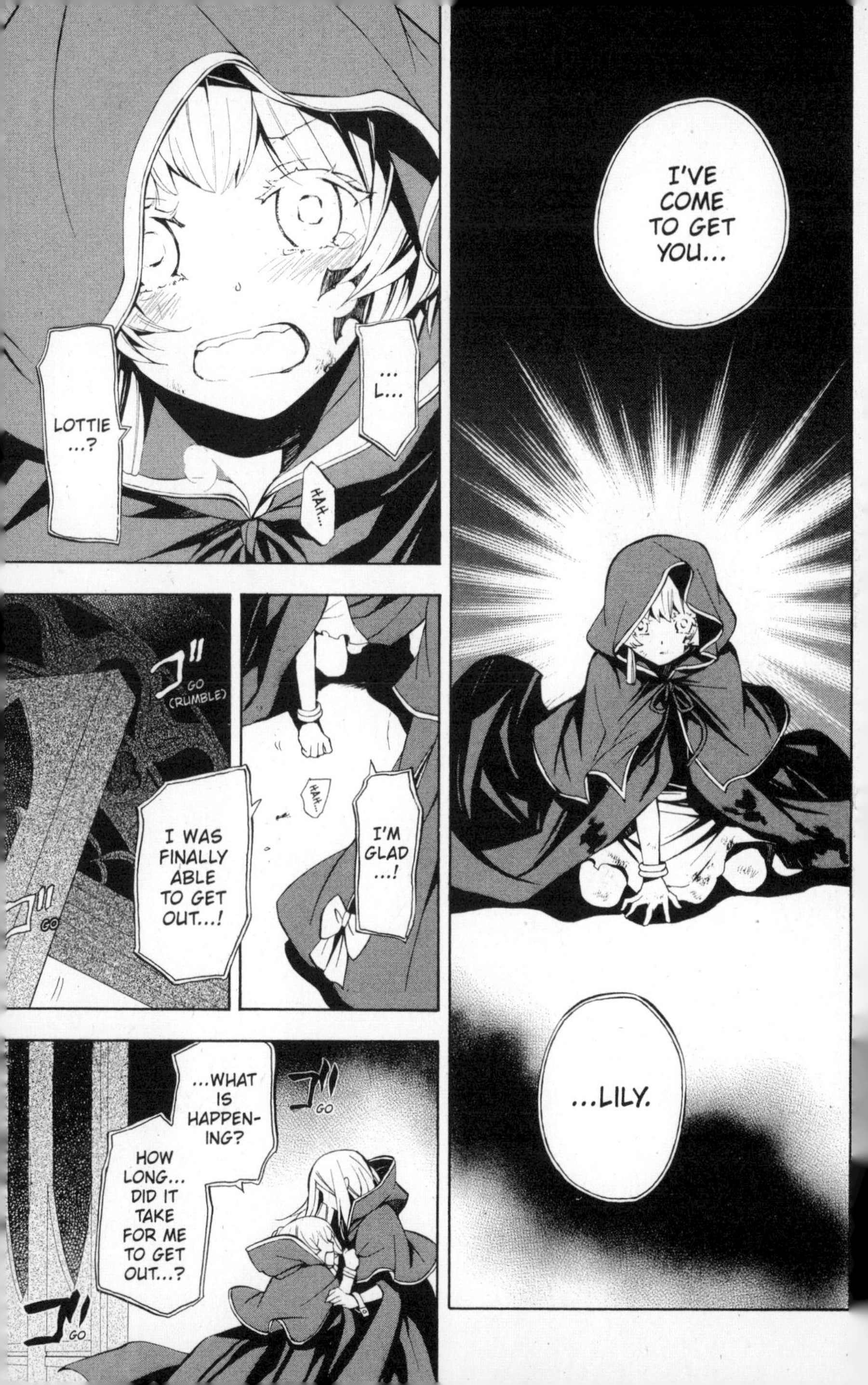
I'VE COME TO GET YOU...
...LILY.
...L...
HAH...
LOTTIE...?
HAH...
I'M GLAD...!
I WAS FINALLY ABLE TO GET OUT...!
GO (RUMBLE)
GO
GO
...WHAT IS HAPPENING?
HOW LONG... DID IT TAKE FOR ME TO GET OUT...?
GO

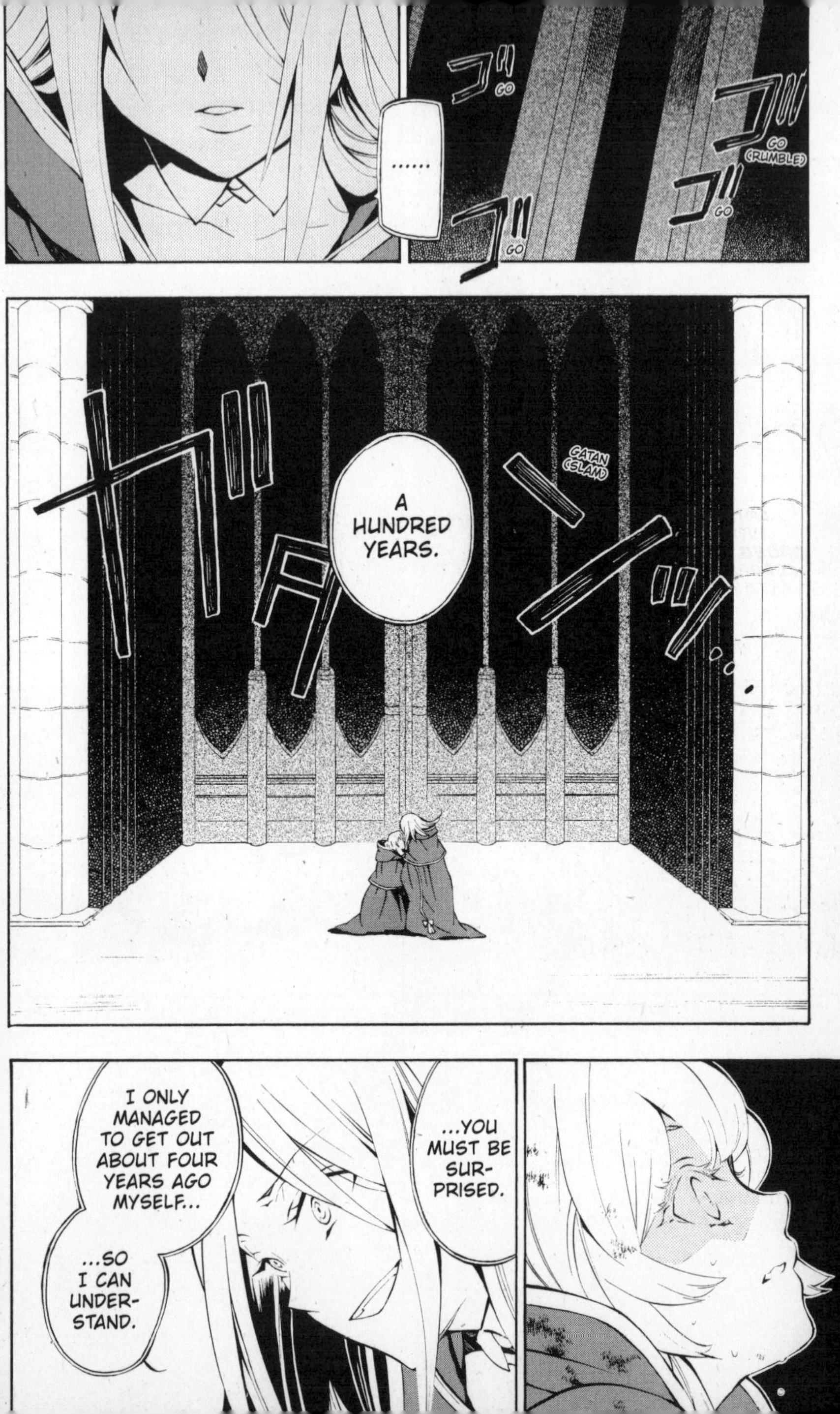
GO
GO (RUMBLE)
GO
GO
......
GATAN (SLAM)
A HUNDRED YEARS.
...YOU MUST BE SURPRISED.
I ONLY MANAGED TO GET OUT ABOUT FOUR YEARS AGO MYSELF...
...SO I CAN UNDERSTAND.

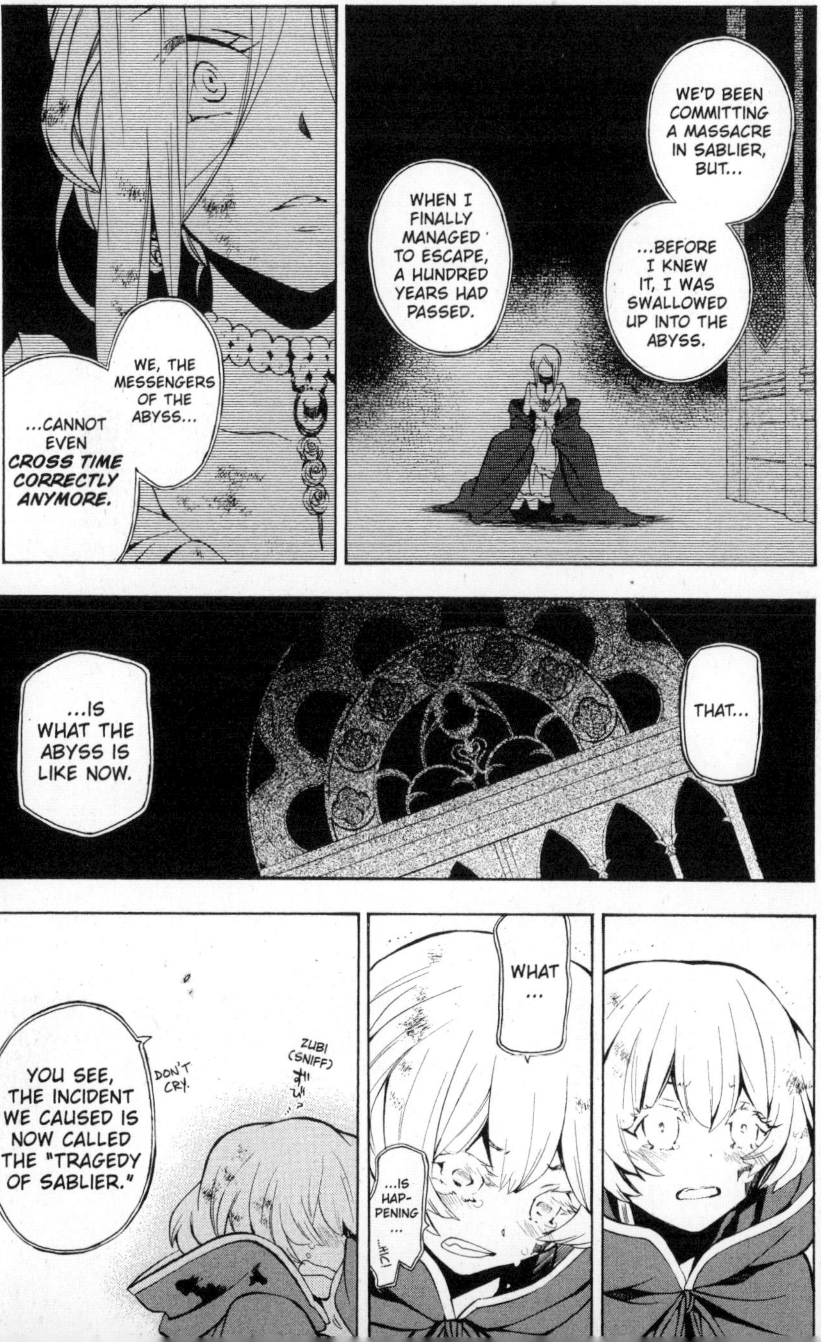
WE'D BEEN COMMITTING A MASSACRE IN SABLIER, BUT...
...BEFORE I KNEW IT, I WAS SWALLOWED UP INTO THE ABYSS.
WHEN I FINALLY MANAGED TO ESCAPE, A HUNDRED YEARS HAD PASSED.
WE, THE MESSENGERS OF THE ABYSS...
...CANNOT EVEN *CROSS TIME CORRECTLY ANYMORE.*
THAT...
...IS WHAT THE ABYSS IS LIKE NOW.
WHAT...
...IS HAPPENING...
...HIC!
ZUBI (SNIFF)
DON'T CRY.
YOU SEE, THE INCIDENT WE CAUSED IS NOW CALLED THE "TRAGEDY OF SABLIER."

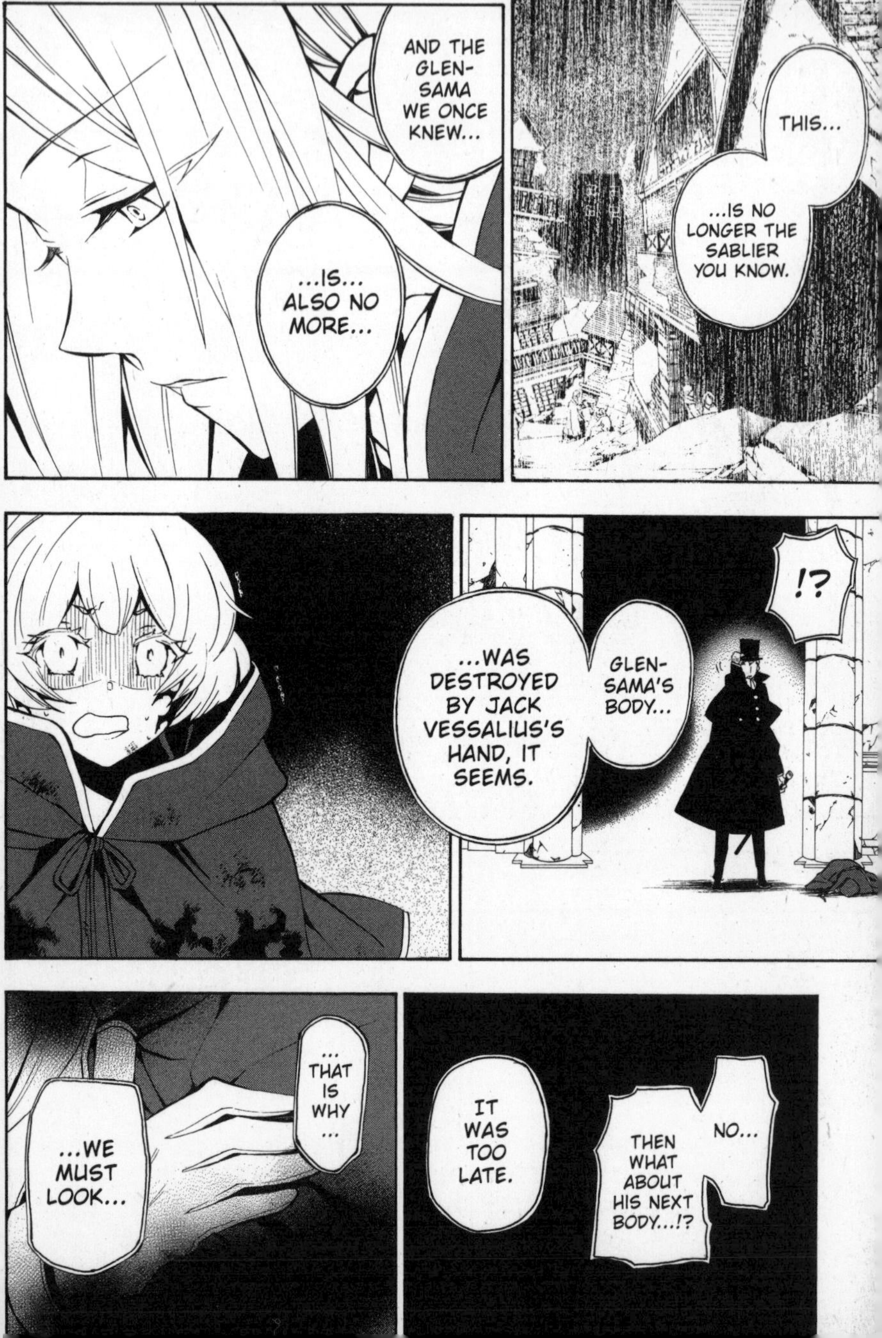
THIS...
...IS NO LONGER THE SABLIER YOU KNOW.
AND THE GLEN-SAMA WE ONCE KNEW...
...IS... ALSO NO MORE...
!?
GLEN-SAMA'S BODY...
...WAS DESTROYED BY JACK VESSALIUS'S HAND, IT SEEMS.
NO...
THEN WHAT ABOUT HIS NEXT BODY...!?
IT WAS TOO LATE.
...THAT IS WHY...
...WE MUST LOOK...

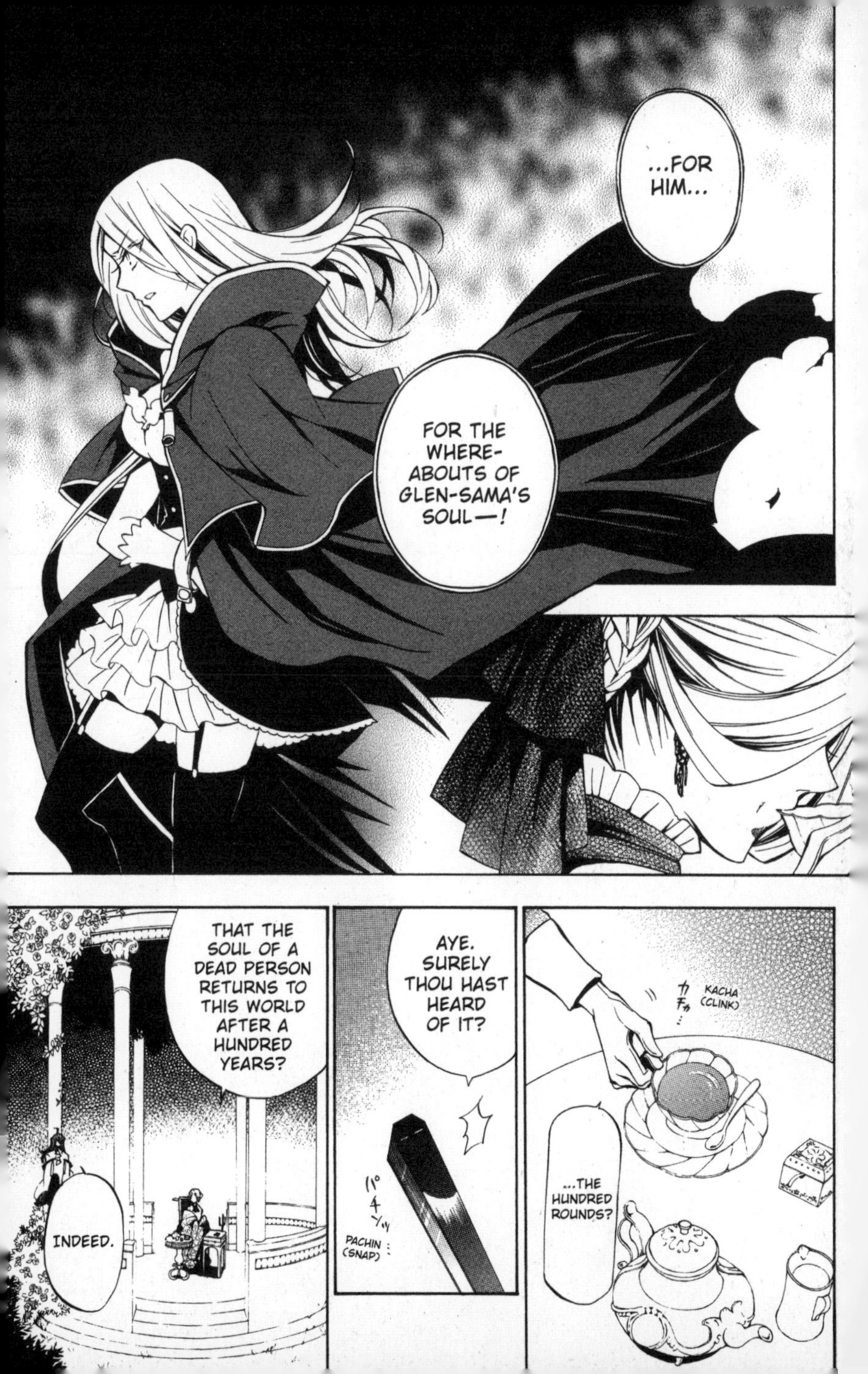
...FOR HIM...
FOR THE WHERE-ABOUTS OF GLEN-SAMA'S SOUL—!
KACHA (CLINK)
...THE HUNDRED ROUNDS?
AYE. SURELY THOU HAST HEARD OF IT?
PACHIN (SNAP)
THAT THE SOUL OF A DEAD PERSON RETURNS TO THIS WORLD AFTER A HUNDRED YEARS?
INDEED.

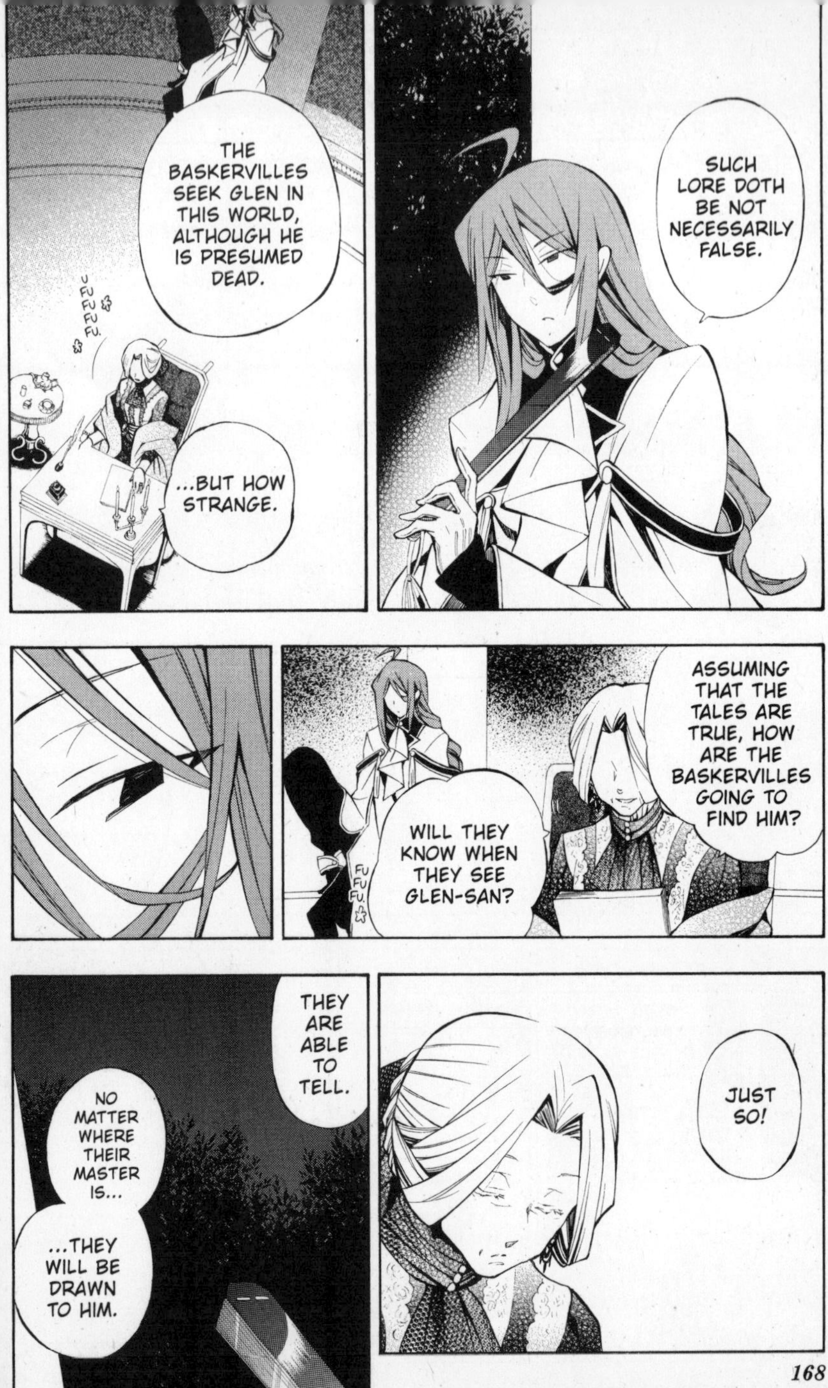
SUCH LORE DOTH BE NOT NECESSARILY FALSE.
THE BASKERVILLES SEEK GLEN IN THIS WORLD, ALTHOUGH HE IS PRESUMED DEAD.
U FU FU FU FU.
...BUT HOW STRANGE.
ASSUMING THAT THE TALES ARE TRUE, HOW ARE THE BASKERVILLES GOING TO FIND HIM?
WILL THEY KNOW WHEN THEY SEE GLEN-SAN?
FU FU FU.
JUST SO!
THEY ARE ABLE TO TELL.
NO MATTER WHERE THEIR MASTER IS...
...THEY WILL BE DRAWN TO HIM.

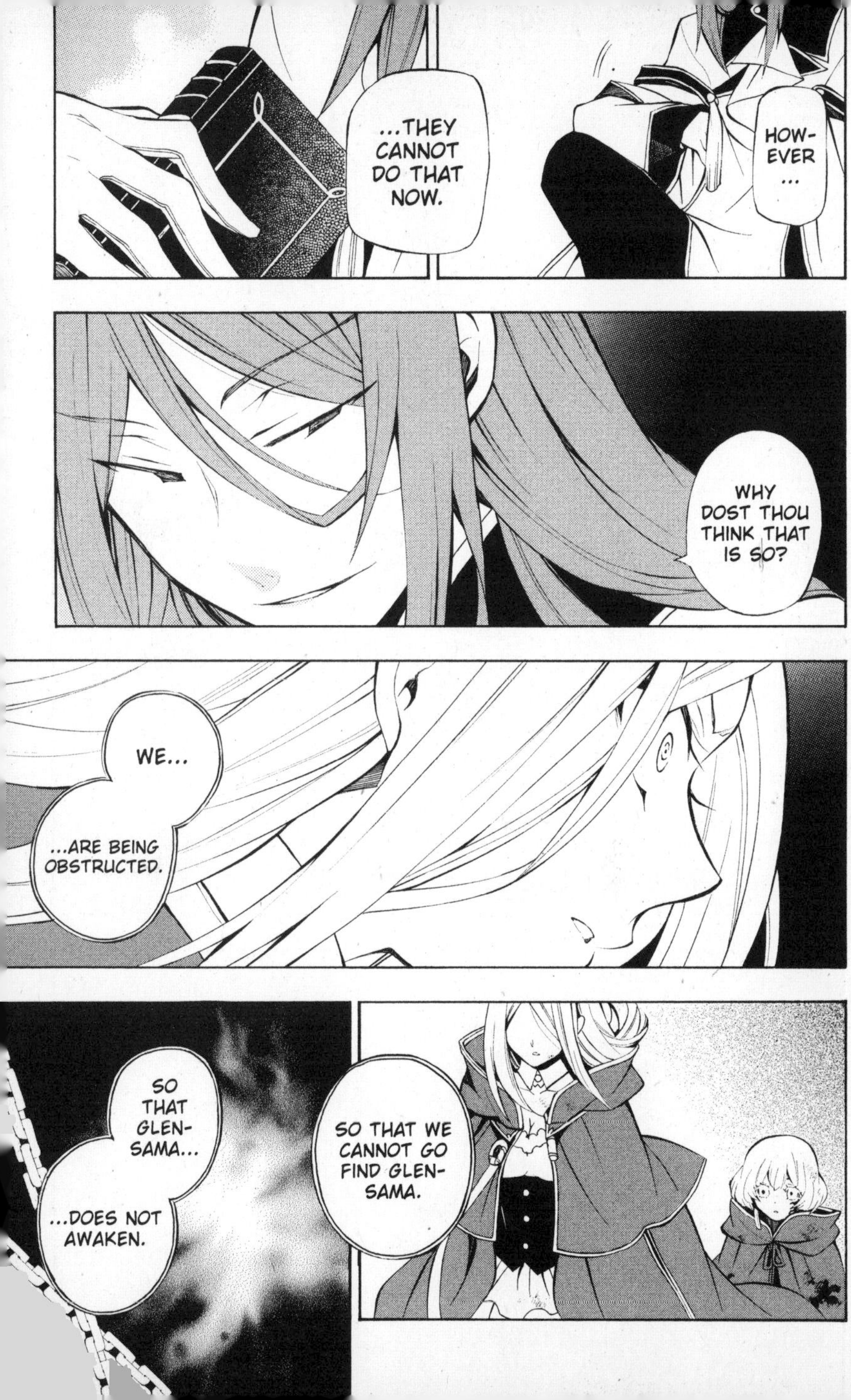
HOW-EVER...
...THEY CANNOT DO THAT NOW.
WHY DOST THOU THINK THAT IS SO?
WE...
...ARE BEING OBSTRUCTED.
SO THAT WE CANNOT GO FIND GLEN-SAMA.
SO THAT GLEN-SAMA...
...DOES NOT AWAKEN.

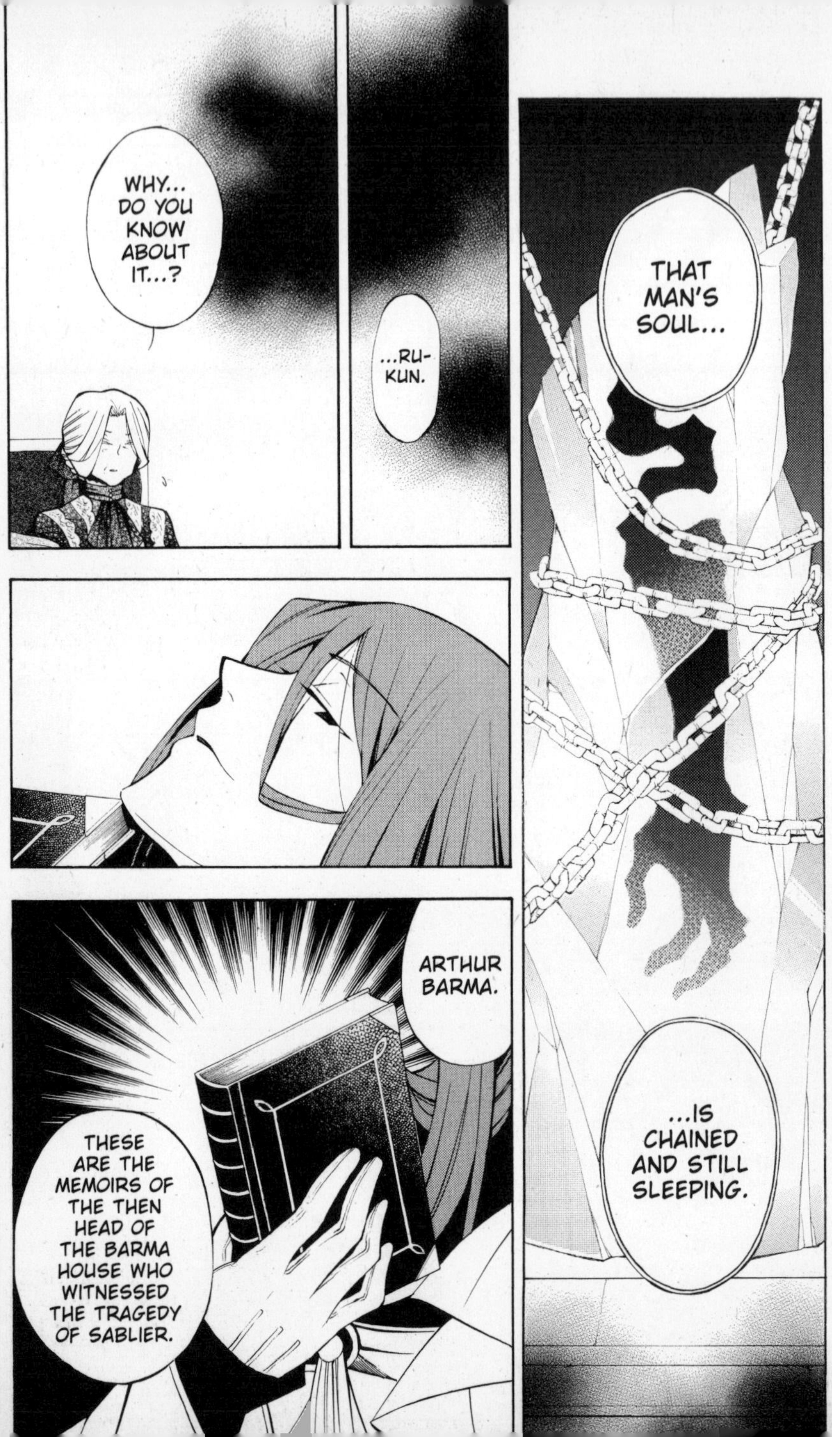
...RU-KUN.
WHY... DO YOU KNOW ABOUT IT...?
ARTHUR BARMA.
THESE ARE THE MEMOIRS OF THE THEN HEAD OF THE BARMA HOUSE WHO WITNESSED THE TRAGEDY OF SABLIER.
THAT MAN'S SOUL...
...IS CHAINED AND STILL SLEEPING.

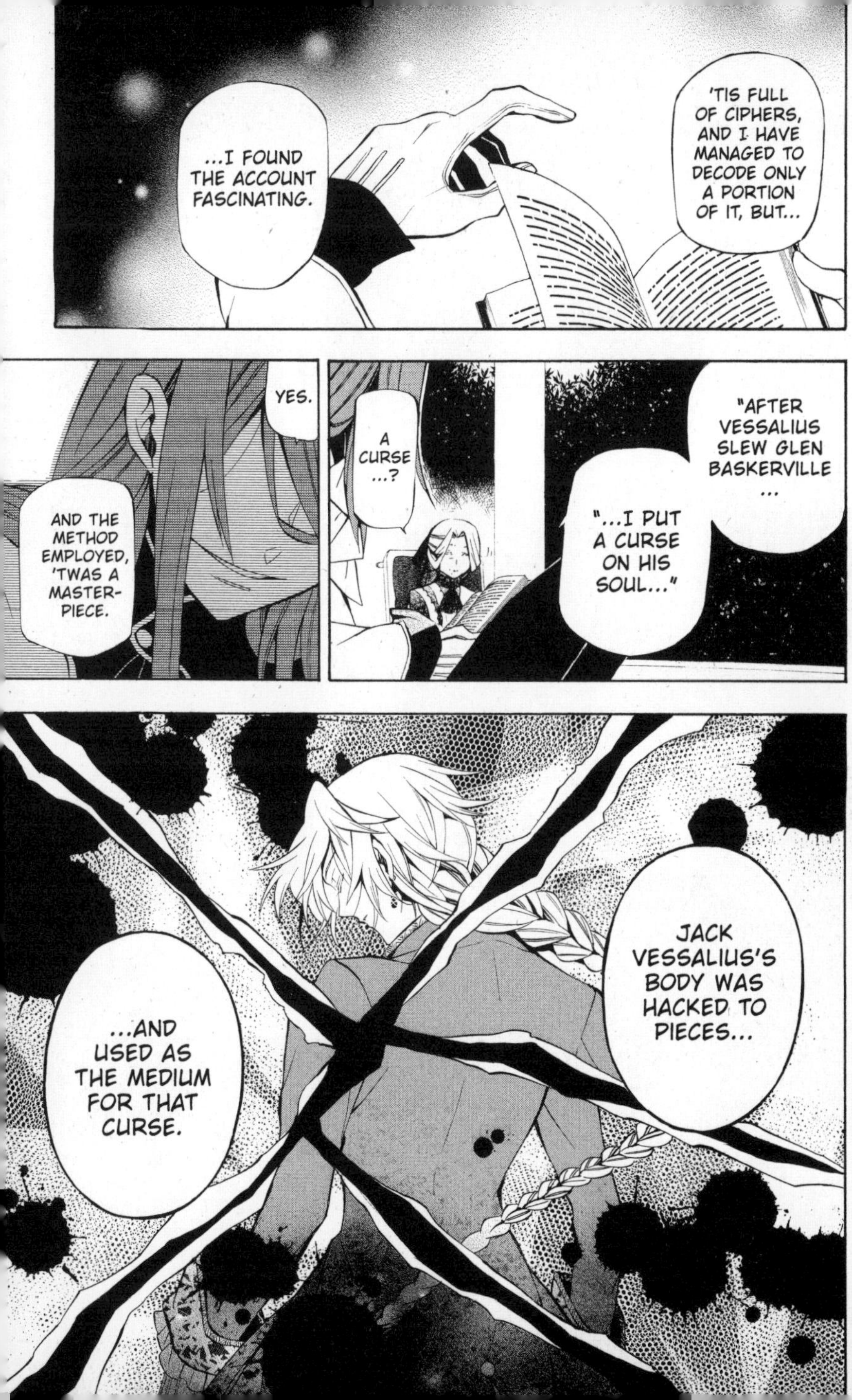
'TIS FULL OF CIPHERS, AND I HAVE MANAGED TO DECODE ONLY A PORTION OF IT, BUT...
...I FOUND THE ACCOUNT FASCINATING.
"AFTER VESSALIUS SLEW GLEN BASKERVILLE...
"...I PUT A CURSE ON HIS SOUL..."
A CURSE ...?
YES.
AND THE METHOD EMPLOYED, 'TWAS A MASTER-PIECE.
JACK VESSALIUS'S BODY WAS HACKED TO PIECES...
...AND USED AS THE MEDIUM FOR THAT CURSE.

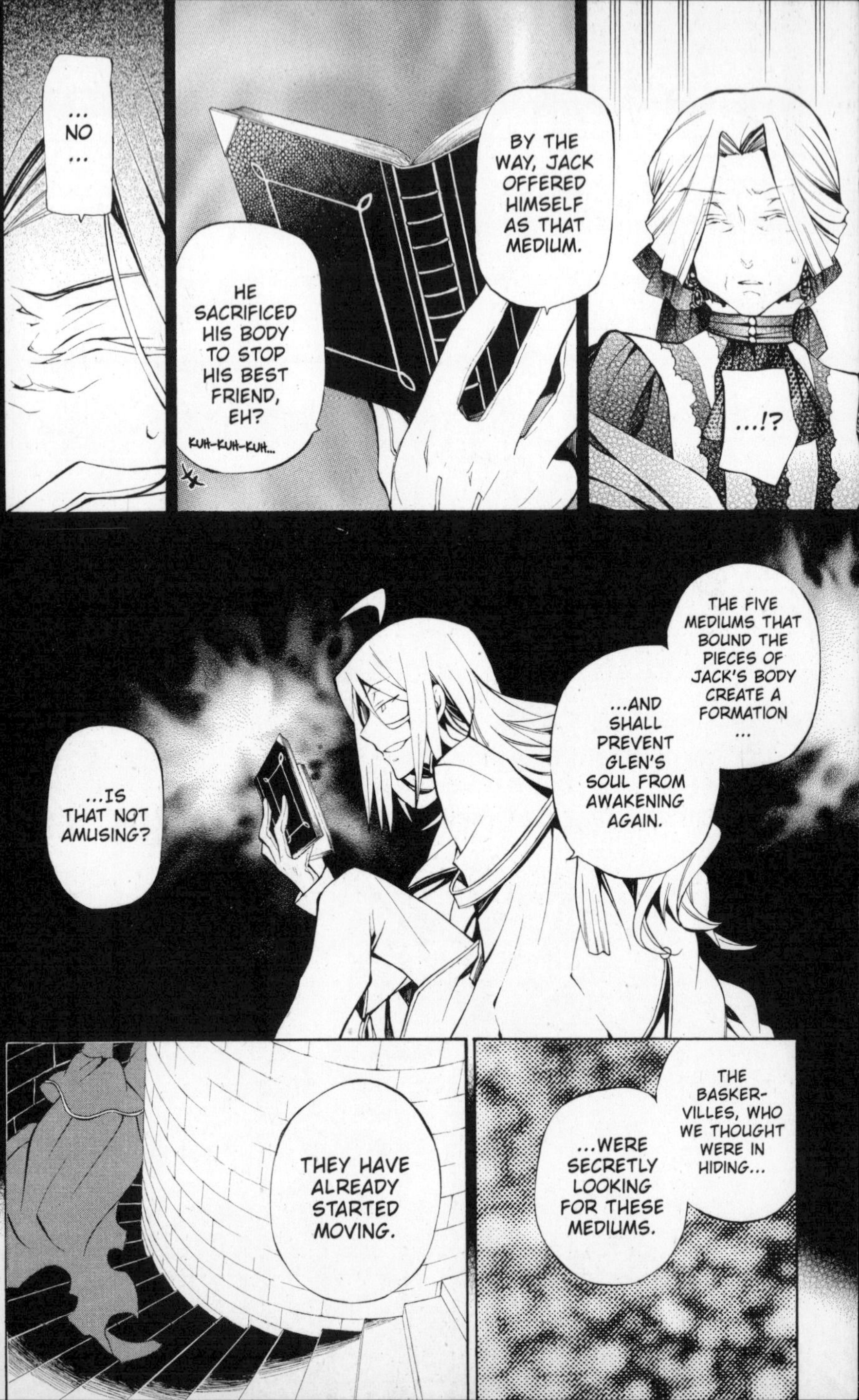
...!?
BY THE WAY, JACK OFFERED HIMSELF AS THAT MEDIUM.
HE SACRIFICED HIS BODY TO STOP HIS BEST FRIEND, EH?
KUH-KUH-KUH...
...NO...
THE FIVE MEDIUMS THAT BOUND THE PIECES OF JACK'S BODY CREATE A FORMATION...
...AND SHALL PREVENT GLEN'S SOUL FROM AWAKENING AGAIN.
...IS THAT NOT AMUSING?
THE BASKER-VILLES, WHO WE THOUGHT WERE IN HIDING...
...WERE SECRETLY LOOKING FOR THESE MEDIUMS.
THEY HAVE ALREADY STARTED MOVING.

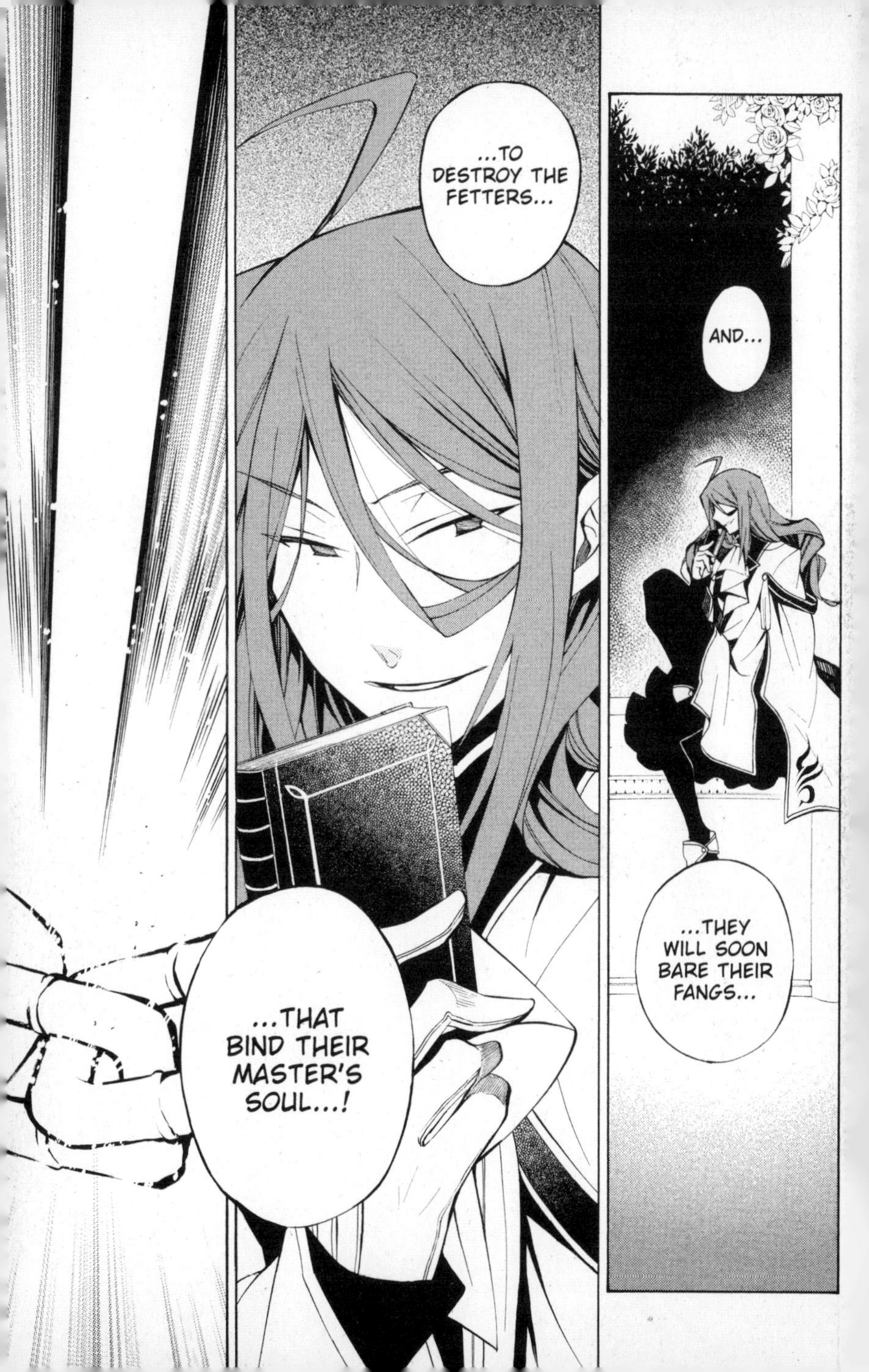
AND...
...THEY WILL SOON BARE THEIR FANGS...
...TO DESTROY THE FETTERS...
...THAT BIND THEIR MASTER'S SOUL...!

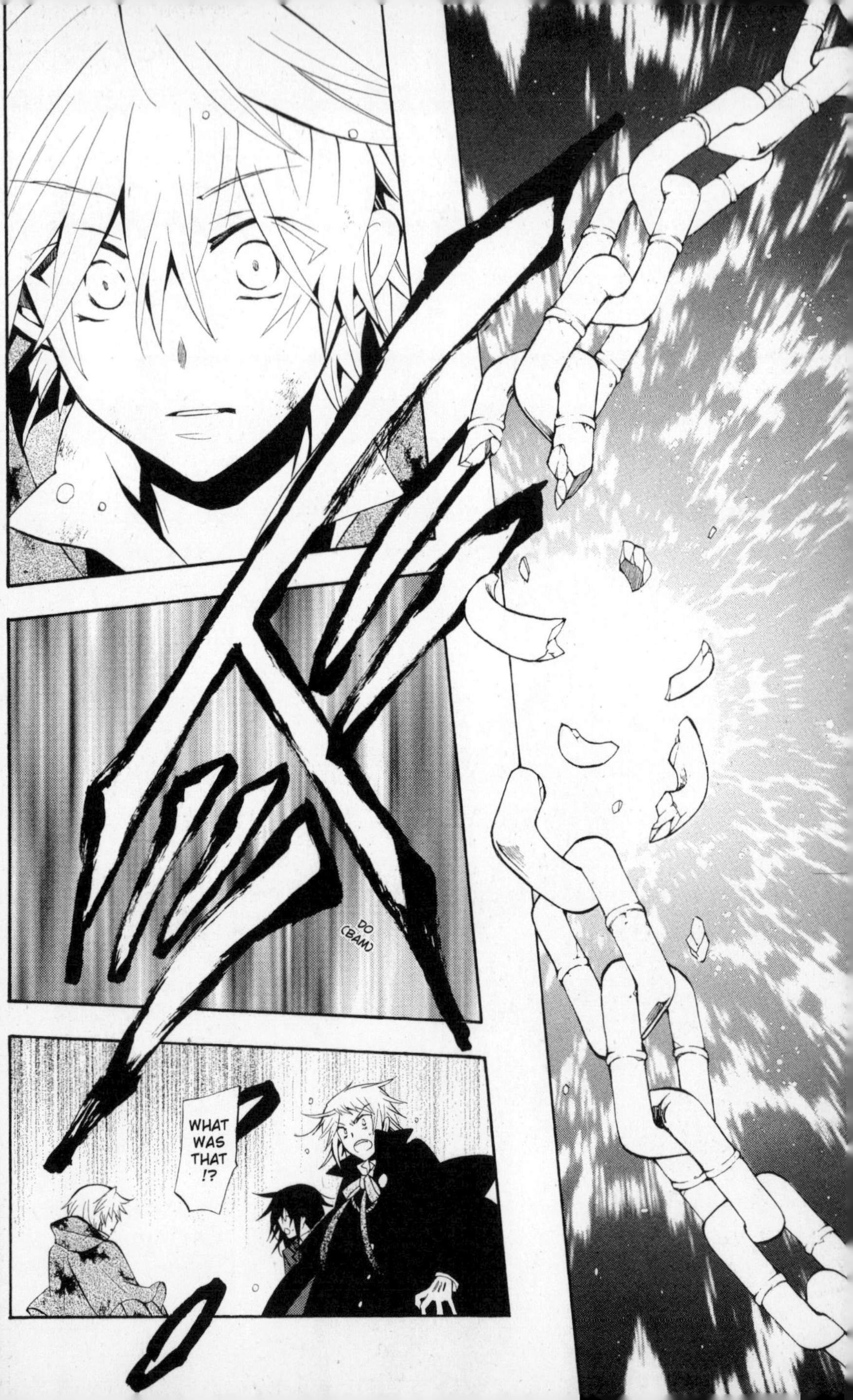
DO
(BAM)
WHAT WAS THAT !?

HOH...

AS WE SPEAK... EH?

PISHI

PISHI
(CRACKLE)

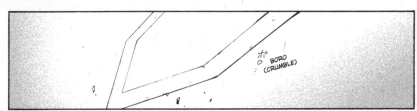

BORO
(CRUMBLE)

USING A DEAD MAN'S BODY AS A MEDIUM FOR A CURSE.

BARMA WAS MERCILESS.

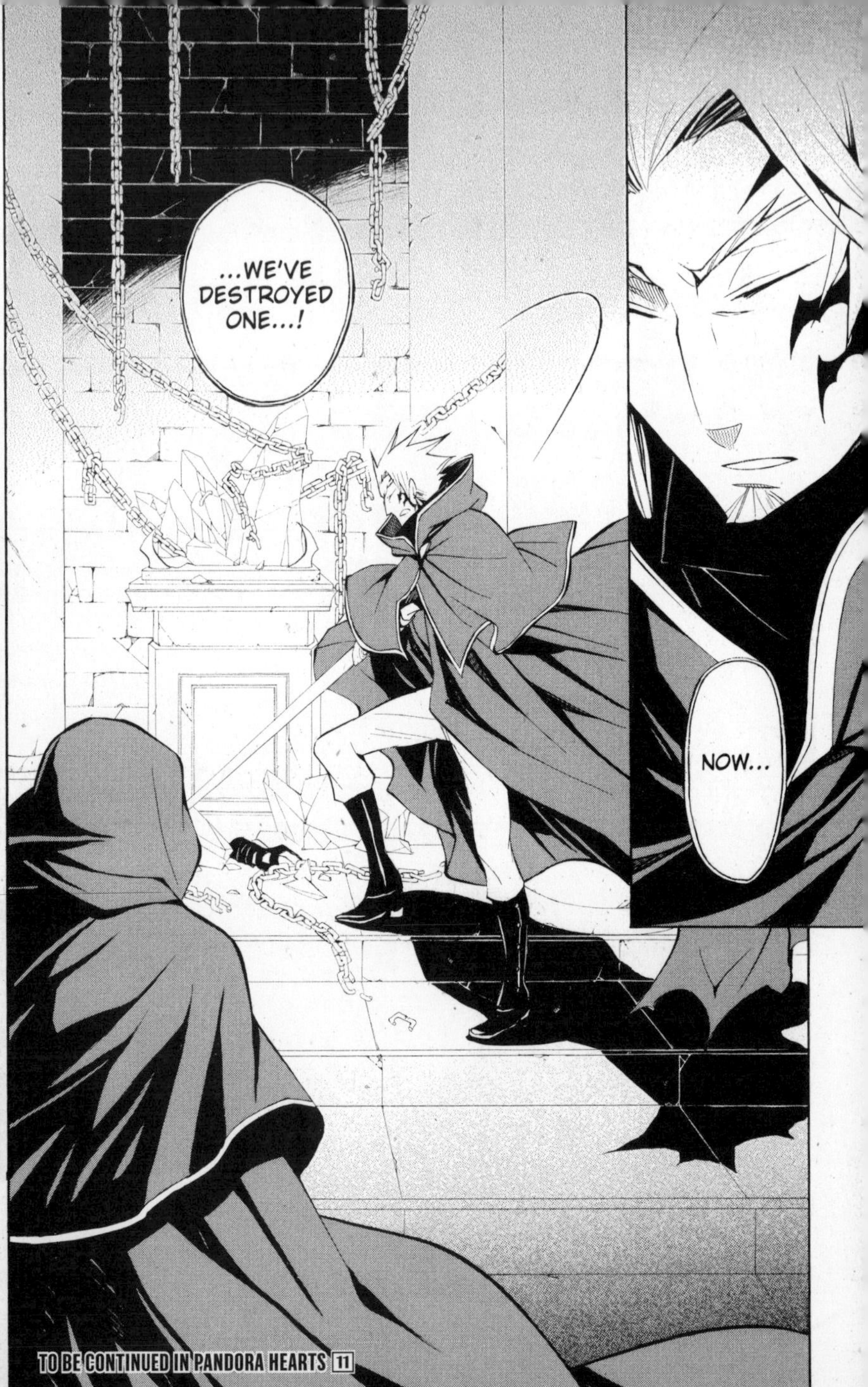
NOW...
...WE'VE DESTROYED ONE...!
TO BE CONTINUED IN PANDORA HEARTS 11

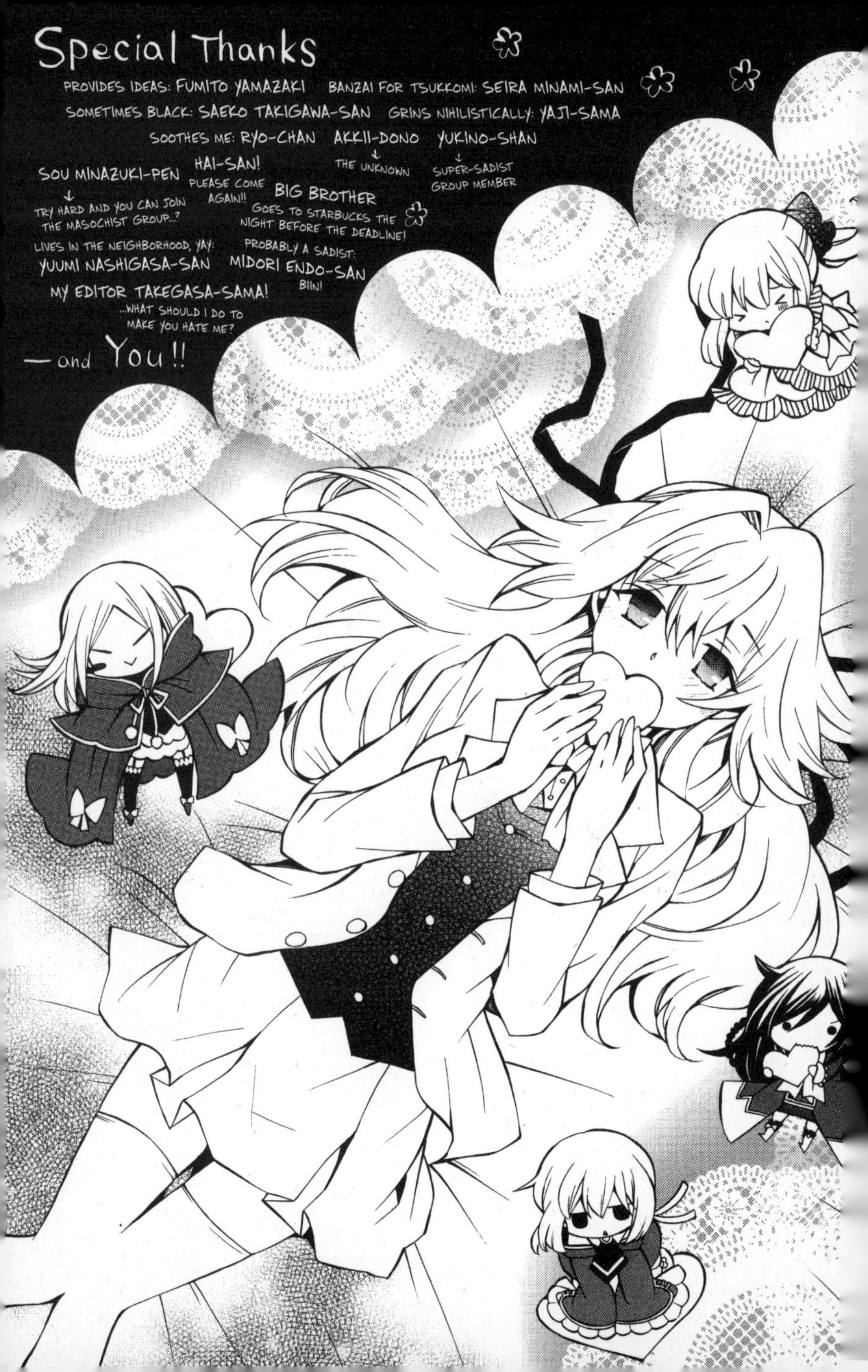
Special Thanks
PROVIDES IDEAS: FUMITO YAMAZAKI
BANZAI FOR TSUKKOMI: SEIRA MINAMI-SAN
SOMETIMES BLACK: SAEKO TAKIGAWA-SAN
GRINS NIHILISTICALLY: YAJI-SAMA
SOOTHES ME: RYO-CHAN
AKKII-DONO ↓ THE UNKNOWN
YUKINO-SHAN ↓ SUPER-SADIST GROUP MEMBER
SOU MINAZUKI-PEN ↓ TRY HARD AND YOU CAN JOIN THE MASOCHIST GROUP...?
HAI-SAN! PLEASE COME AGAIN!!
BIG BROTHER GOES TO STARBUCKS THE NIGHT BEFORE THE DEADLINE!
LIVES IN THE NEIGHBORHOOD, YAY: YUUMI NASHIGASA-SAN
PROBABLY A SADIST: MIDORI ENDO-SAN BIIN!
MY EDITOR TAKEGASA-SAMA! ...WHAT SHOULD I DO TO MAKE YOU HATE ME?
—and You!!

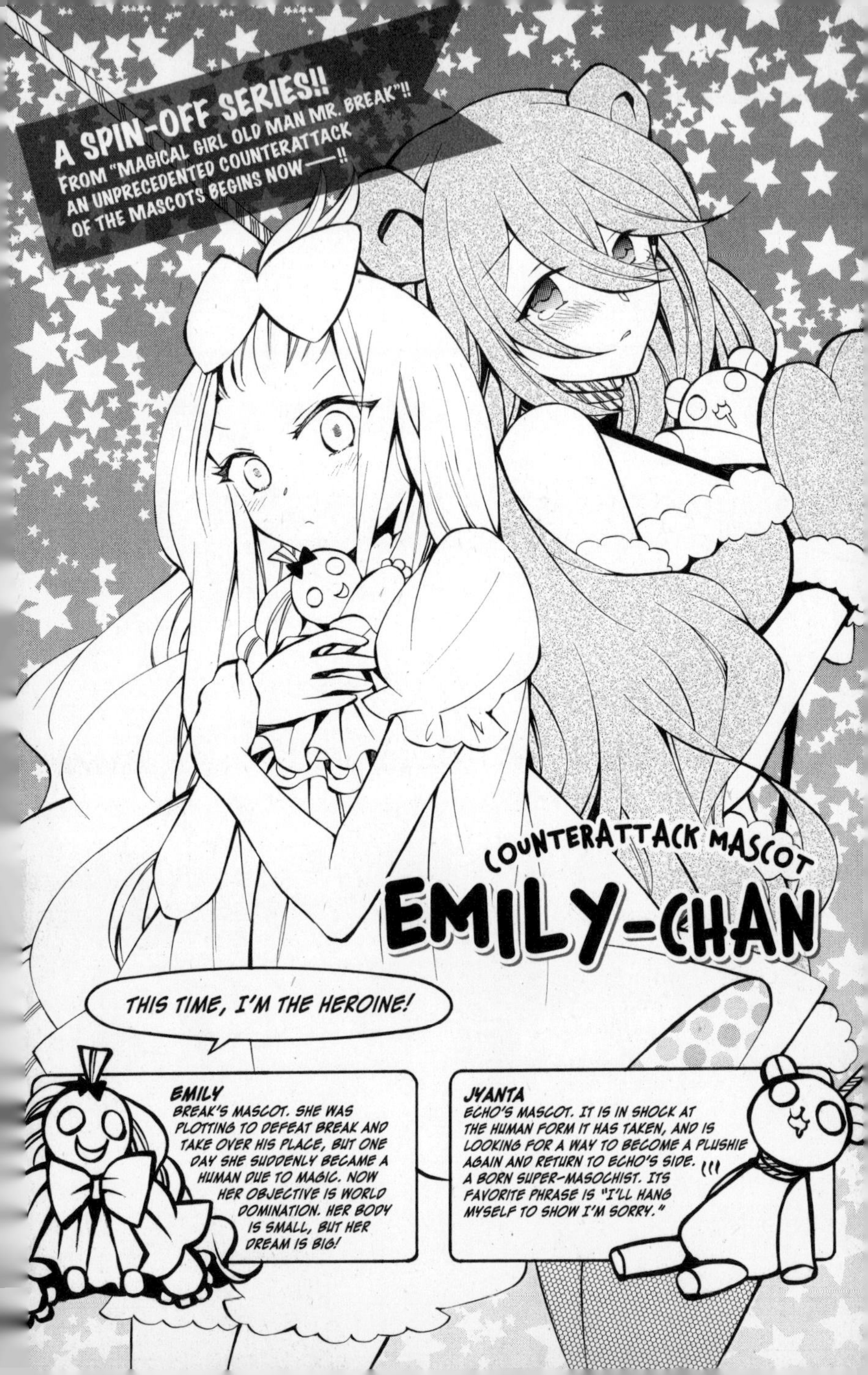
A SPIN-OFF SERIES!!
FROM "MAGICAL GIRL OLD MAN MR. BREAK"!! AN UNPRECEDENTED COUNTERATTACK OF THE MASCOTS BEGINS NOW——!!
COUNTERATTACK MASCOT
EMILY-CHAN
THIS TIME, I'M THE HEROINE!
EMILY
BREAK'S MASCOT. SHE WAS PLOTTING TO DEFEAT BREAK AND TAKE OVER HIS PLACE, BUT ONE DAY SHE SUDDENLY BECAME A HUMAN DUE TO MAGIC. NOW HER OBJECTIVE IS WORLD DOMINATION. HER BODY IS SMALL, BUT HER DREAM IS BIG!
JYANTA
ECHO'S MASCOT. IT IS IN SHOCK AT THE HUMAN FORM IT HAS TAKEN, AND IS LOOKING FOR A WAY TO BECOME A PLUSHIE AGAIN AND RETURN TO ECHO'S SIDE. A BORN SUPER-MASOCHIST. ITS FAVORITE PHRASE IS "I'LL HANG MYSELF TO SHOW I'M SORRY."

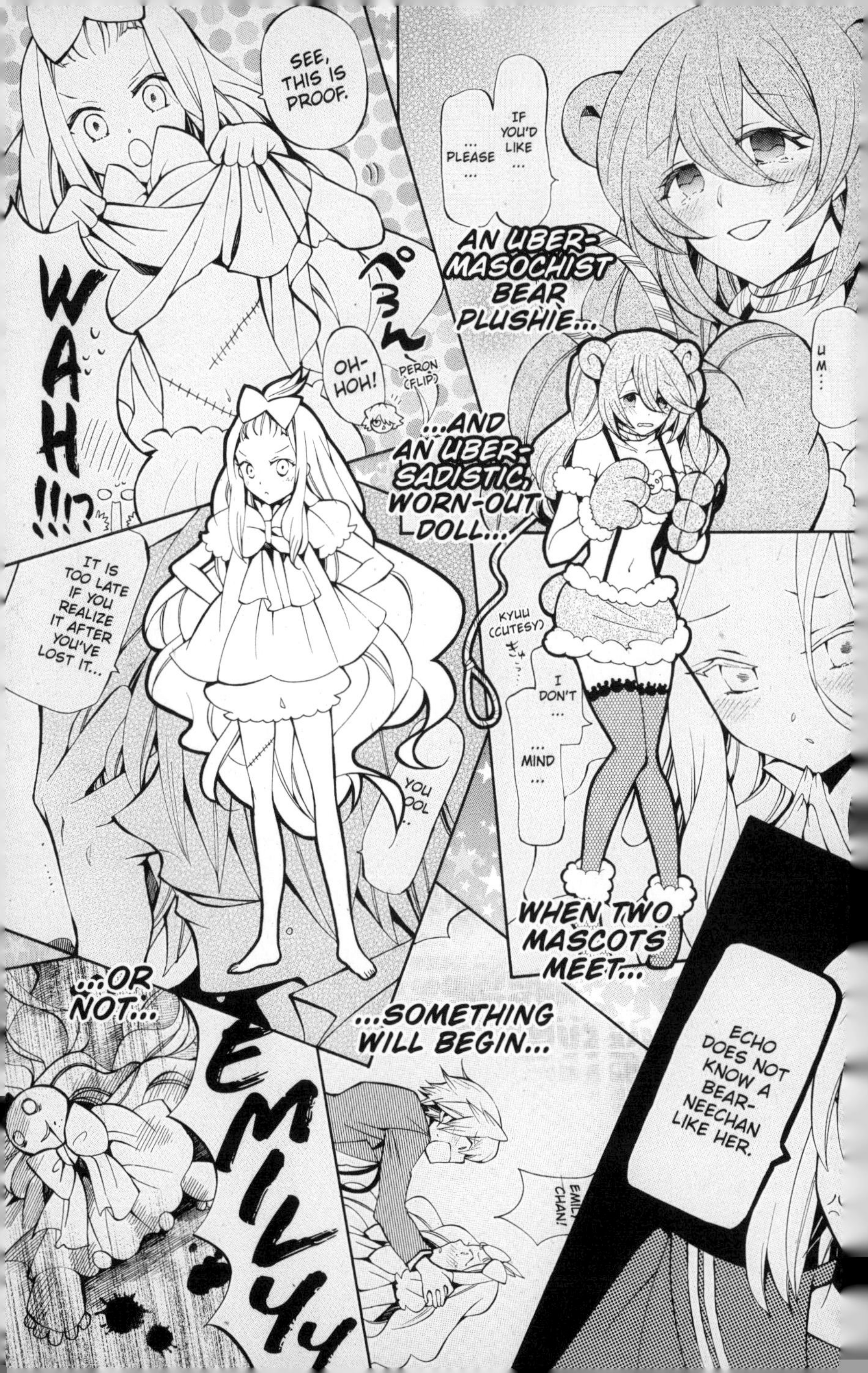
IF YOU'D LIKE ...
... PLEASE ...
UM ...
AN UBER-MASOCHIST BEAR PLUSHIE...
SEE, THIS IS PROOF.
PERON (FLIP)
OH-HOH!
WAH!!!?
...AND AN UBER-SADISTIC, WORN-OUT DOLL...
KYUU (CUTESY)
I DON'T ... ... MIND ...
WHEN TWO MASCOTS MEET...
IT IS TOO LATE IF YOU REALIZE IT AFTER YOU'VE LOST IT...
YOU OOL ..
...SOMETHING WILL BEGIN...
ECHO DOES NOT KNOW A BEAR-NEECHAN LIKE HER.
EMILY-CHAN!
EMILYYY
...OR NOT...

COMMON HONORIFICS

no honorific: Indicates familiarity or closeness; if used without permission or reason, addressing someone in this manner would constitute an insult.

-san: The Japanese equivalent of Mr./Mrs./Miss. If a situation calls for politeness, this is the fail-safe honorific.

-sama: Conveys great respect; may also indicate that the social status of the speaker is lower than that of the addressee.

-kun: Used most often when referring to boys (though it can be applied to girls as well), this indicates affection or familiarity. Occasionally used by older men among their peers, but it may also be used by anyone referring to a person of lower standing.

-chan: An affectionate honorific indicating familiarity used mostly in reference to girls; also used in reference to cute persons or animals of either gender.

-tan page 126

A cutesy version of the informal honorific *-chan*.

-neechan page 179

An informal honorific that means "big sister," but can also be used to refer to someone who is not necessarily related by blood but plays a big sister role to someone younger.

PandoraHearts

MOCHIZUKI'S MUSINGS

VOLUME 10

This summer, I took a long vacation and finally went to Great Britain! Edinburgh in the summertime...was simply wonderful!

I recently got married and thanks to my spouse's work, I'll be moving to London next year. Of course I do have my concerns, but my heart's full of hope right now!

...Both are my friends' stories. Any complaints?

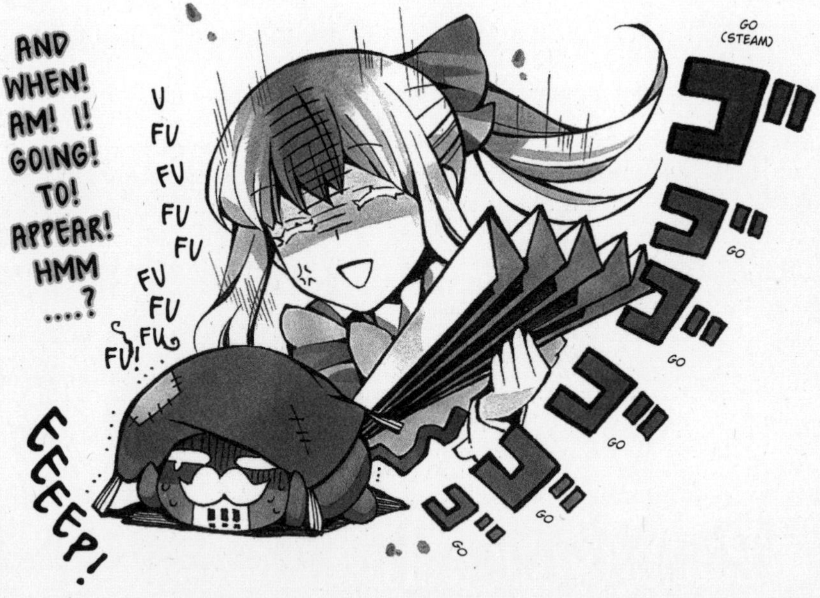
GO (STEAM)
ゴ
ゴ GO
ゴ GO
ゴ GO
ゴ GO
ゴ GO
ゴ GO
AND WHEN! AM! I! GOING! TO! APPEAR! HMM ....?
V FU FU FU FU FU FU FU FU!
EEEEP!

PandoraHearts

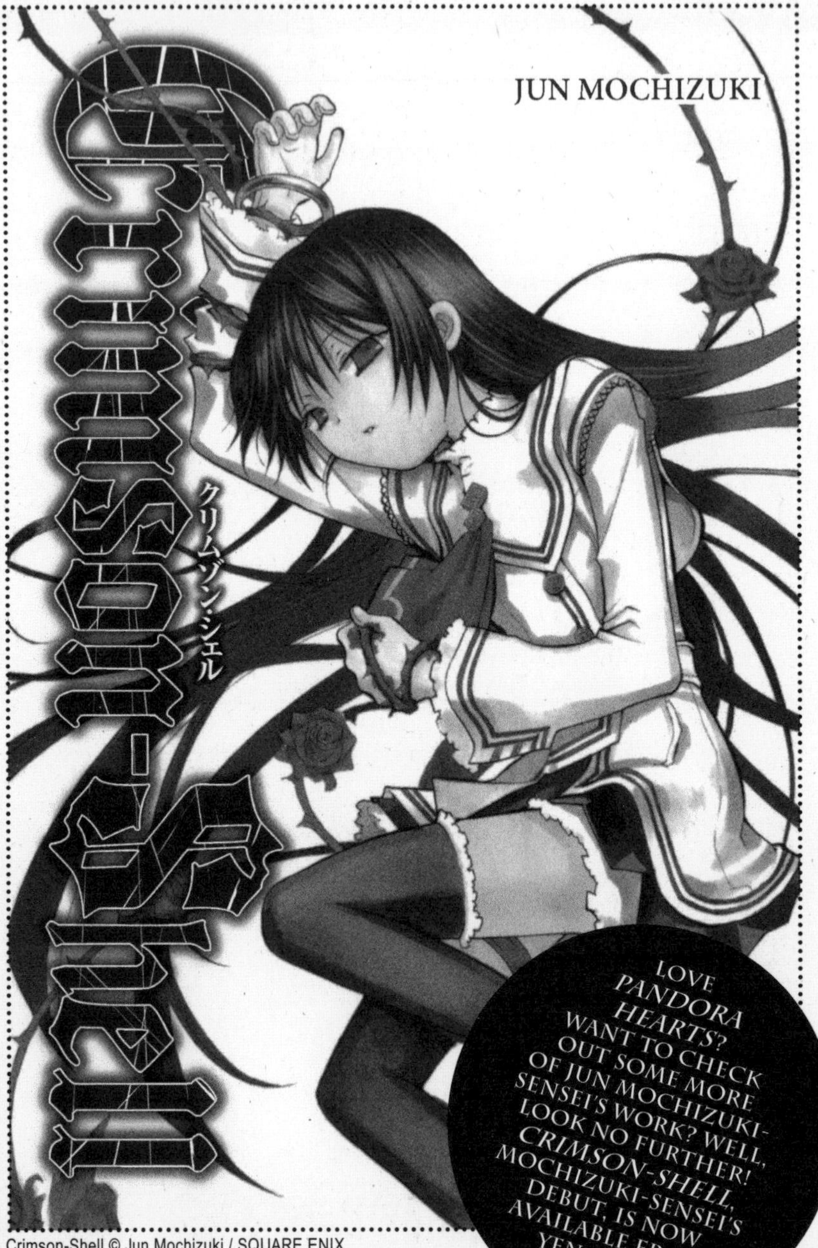
JUN MOCHIZUKI
Crimson-Shell
クリムゾン・シェル
LOVE *PANDORA HEARTS*? WANT TO CHECK OUT SOME MORE OF JUN MOCHIZUKI-SENSEI'S WORK? WELL, LOOK NO FURTHER! *CRIMSON-SHELL*, MOCHIZUKI-SENSEI'S DEBUT, IS NOW AVAILABLE FROM YEN PRESS!

PandoraHearts

The Phantomhive family has a butler who's almost too good to be true...

...or maybe he's just too good to be human.

Black Butler

YANA TOBOSO

VOLUMES 1-8 IN STORES NOW!

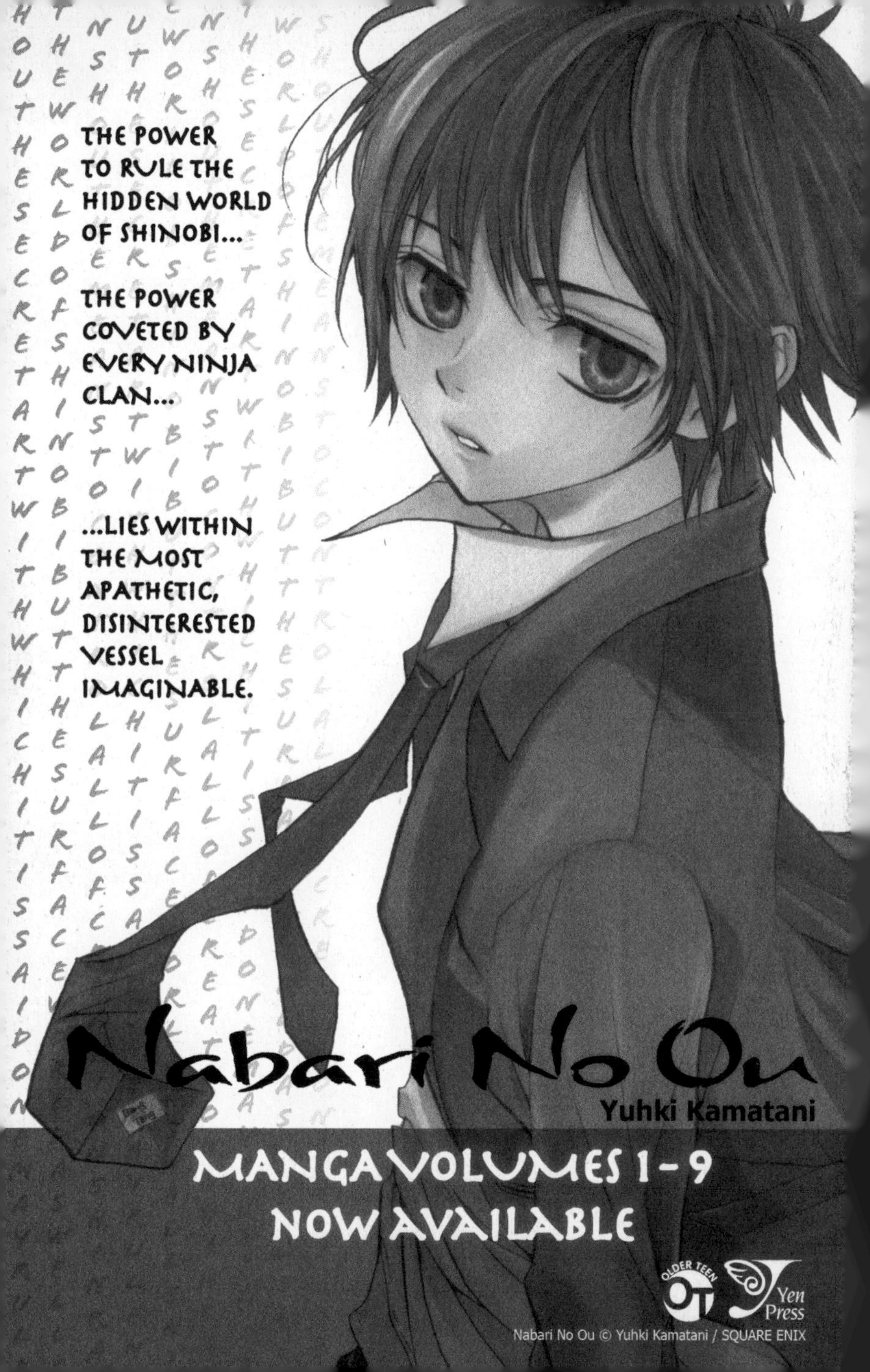
THE POWER TO RULE THE HIDDEN WORLD OF SHINOBI...
THE POWER COVETED BY EVERY NINJA CLAN...
...LIES WITHIN THE MOST APATHETIC, DISINTERESTED VESSEL IMAGINABLE.
Nabari No Ou
Yuhki Kamatani
MANGA VOLUMES 1-9
NOW AVAILABLE
OLDER TEEN
OT
Yen Press
Nabari No Ou © Yuhki Kamatani / SQUARE ENIX

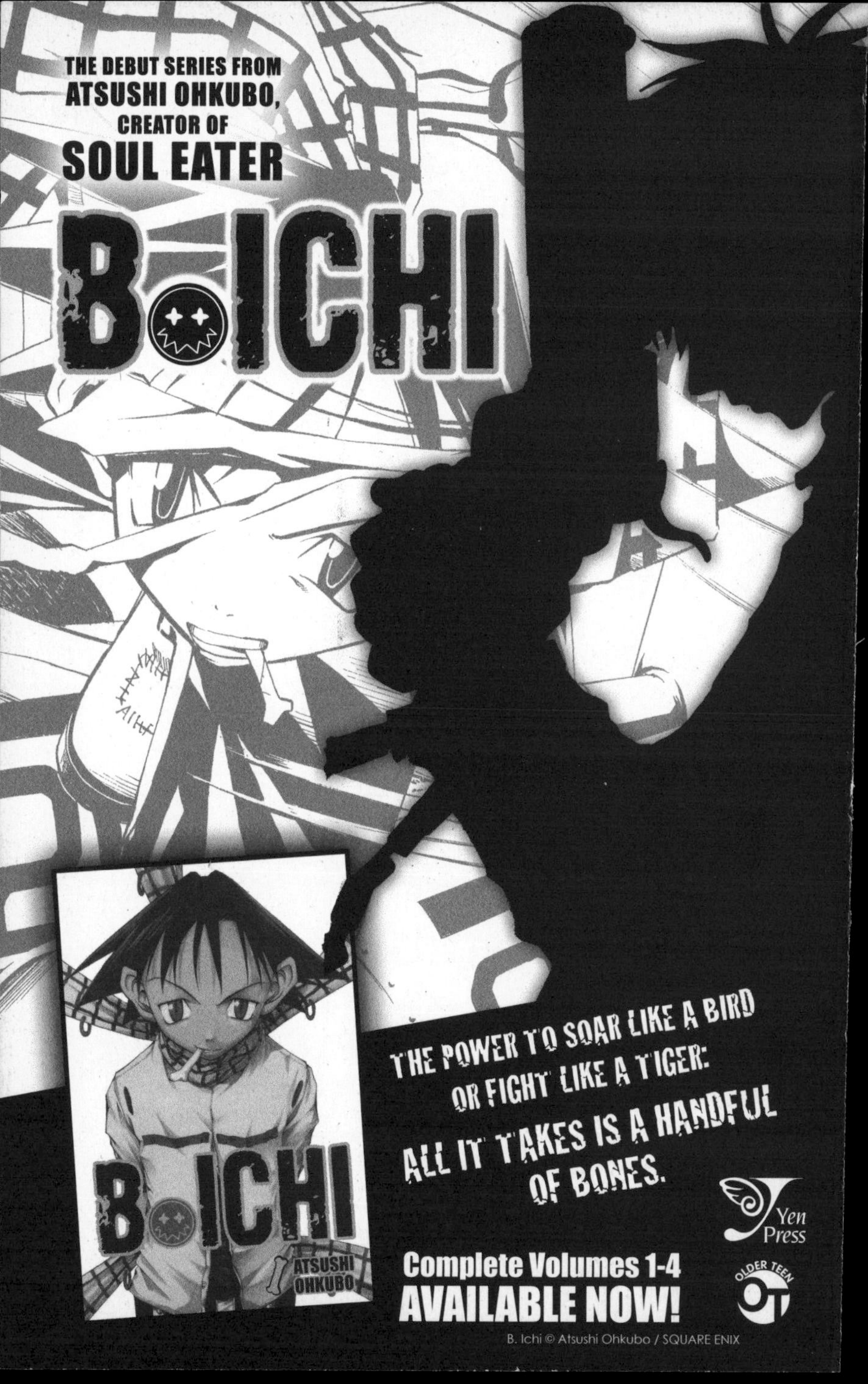
THE DEBUT SERIES FROM
ATSUSHI OHKUBO,
CREATOR OF
SOUL EATER
B. ICHI
B. ICHI
ATSUSHI OHKUBO
THE POWER TO SOAR LIKE A BIRD
OR FIGHT LIKE A TIGER:
ALL IT TAKES IS A HANDFUL
OF BONES.
Yen Press
Complete Volumes 1-4
AVAILABLE NOW!
OLDER TEEN
OT
B. Ichi © Atsushi Ohkubo / SQUARE ENIX

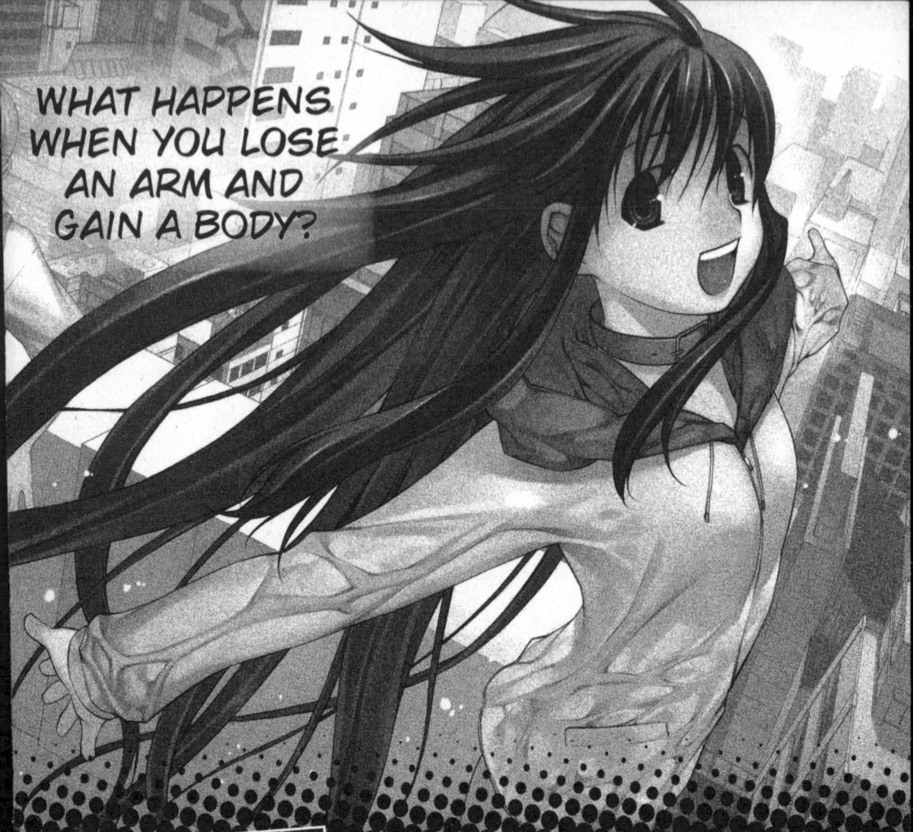
WHAT HAPPENS WHEN YOU LOSE AN ARM AND GAIN A BODY?

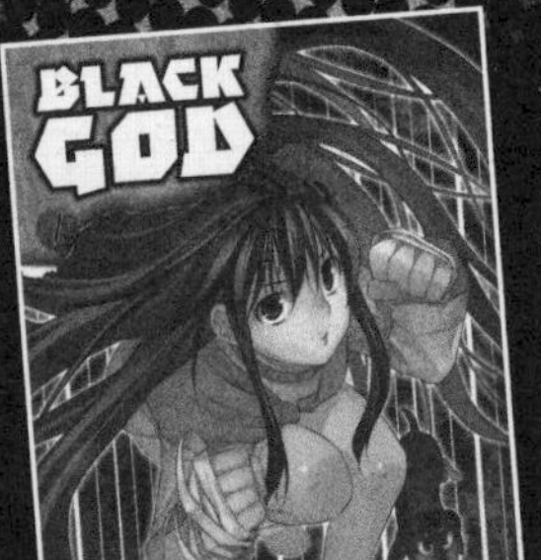
BLACK GOD
Story by Dall-Young Lim
Art by Sung-Woo Park

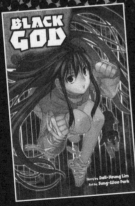

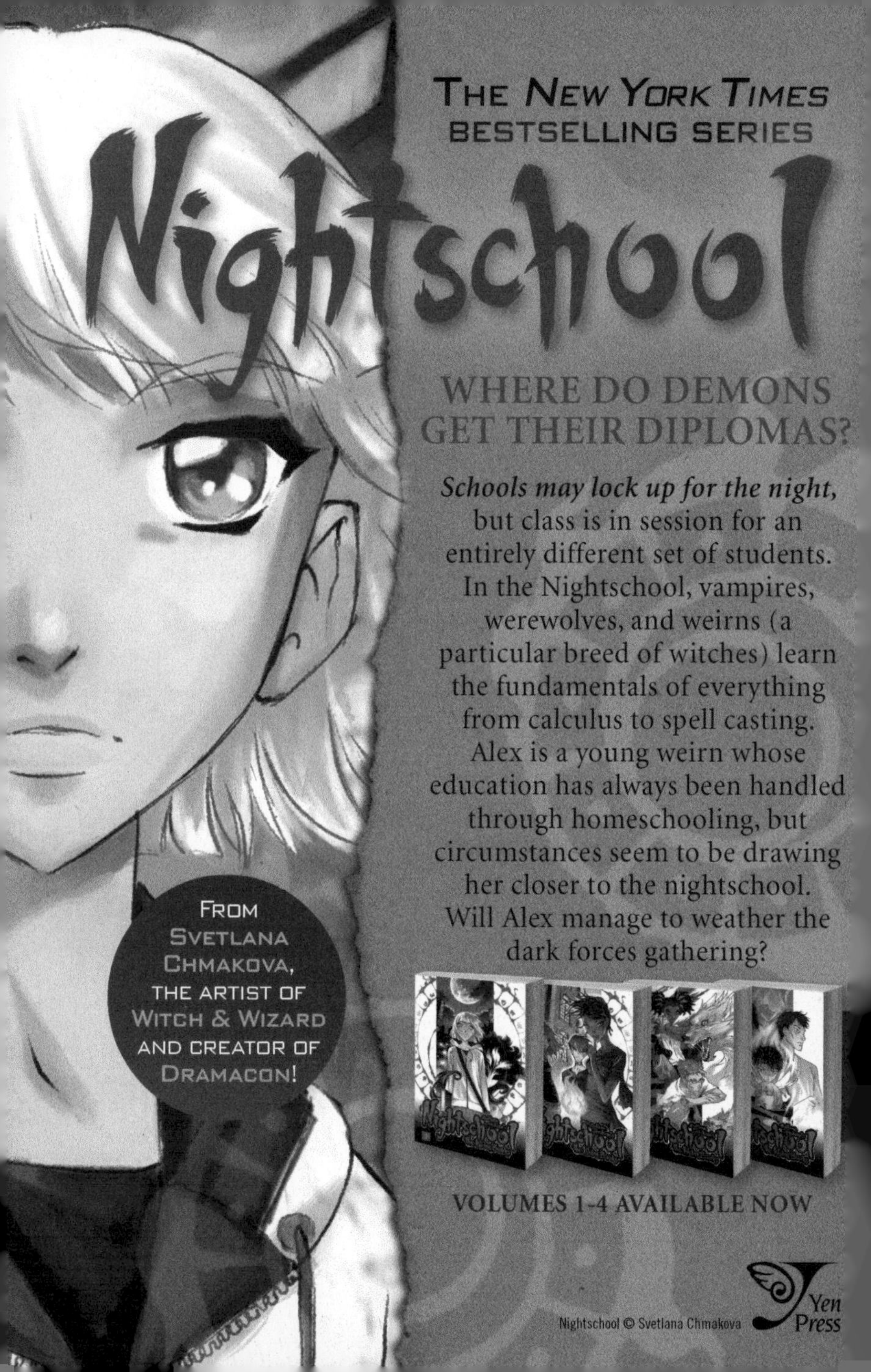
THE NEW YORK TIMES
BESTSELLING SERIES
Nightschool
WHERE DO DEMONS GET THEIR DIPLOMAS?
Schools may lock up for the night, but class is in session for an entirely different set of students. In the Nightschool, vampires, werewolves, and weirns (a particular breed of witches) learn the fundamentals of everything from calculus to spell casting. Alex is a young weirn whose education has always been handled through homeschooling, but circumstances seem to be drawing her closer to the nightschool. Will Alex manage to weather the dark forces gathering?
FROM SVETLANA CHMAKOVA, THE ARTIST OF WITCH & WIZARD AND CREATOR OF DRAMACON!
VOLUMES 1-4 AVAILABLE NOW
Nightschool © Svetlana Chmakova
Yen Press

PANDORA HEARTS ⑩

JUN MOCHIZUKI

Translation: Tomo Kimura • Lettering: Alexis Eckerman

PANDORA HEARTS Vol. 10 © 2009 Jun Mochizuki / SQUARE ENIX CO., LTD. All rights reserved. First published Japan in 2009 by SQUARE ENIX CO., LTD. English translation rights arranged with SQUARE ENIX CO., LTD. and Hachette Book Group through Tuttle-Mori Agency, Inc.

Translation © 2012 by SQUARE ENIX CO., LTD.

Yen Press
Hachette Book Group
237 Park Avenue, New York, NY 10017

www.HachetteBookGroup.com
www.YenPress.com

Yen Press is an imprint of Hachette Book Group, Inc. The Yen Press name and logo are trademarks of Hachette Book Group, Inc.

First Yen Press Edition: May 2012

ISBN: 978-0-316-19728-1

10 9 8 7 6 5 4 3

BVG

Printed in the United States of America